Kinship, Contract, Community, and State

STUDIES OF THE WEATHERHEAD EAST ASIAN INSTITUTE,
COLUMBIA UNIVERSITY

The Weatherhead East Asian Institute is
Columbia University's center for research,
publication, and teaching on modern East Asia.
The Studies of the Weatherhead East Asian Institute
were inaugurated in 1962 to bring to a wider public
the results of significant new research on
Japan, China, and Korea.

MYRON L. COHEN

Kinship, Contract, Community, and State

Anthropological Perspectives on China

STANFORD UNIVERSITY PRESS 2005

Stanford, California

Stanford University Press
Stanford, California
© 2005 by the Board of Trustees of the
Leland Stanford Junior University

Library of Congress Cataloging-in-Publication Data

Cohen, Myron L.
  Kinship, contract, community, and state : anthropological
perspectives on China / Myron L. Cohen.
      p. cm.
  Includes bibliographical references and index.
  ISBN 0-8047-5066-1 (cloth : alk. paper)—
  ISBN 0-8047-5067-X (pbk : alk. paper)
    1. Ethnology—China. 2. Kinship—China. 3. Patrilineal
kinship—China. 4. Family—China. 5. China—History.
6. China—Social life and customs. I. Title.
GN635.C6C64   2004
306'.0951 dc22   2004020533

Printed in the United States of America
Original Printing 2005
Last figure below indicates year of this printing:
14   13   12   11   10   09   08   07   06   05

Typeset at Stanford University Press in 10/13 Sabon

For HEIKE *and* SHOSHANA,
and in memory of AVIVA

Preface

This book brings together in modified form writings that originally appeared elsewhere. The versions first published have been changed to varying degrees to eliminate anachronisms, repetition, and a few errors. In modifying these essays, however, my main intent has been to bring them up to date, in some cases with respect to China's rapidly changing social and cultural scene, but also in light of more recent research. In regard to the material they use and the analyses they present, I have avoided making major changes in the text of any of these essays, confining myself as much as possible to incorporating new data into endnotes and references. I have made additions of substance to chapters 5 and 7, but these are presented as addenda to the main body of the text. I am grateful to the original publishers of the chapters in this book for their permission to let me use them here.

Chapter 1 first appeared as the "Introduction" in Arthur H. Smith's *Village Life in China*, published in 1970 by Little, Brown, and Co., Boston. Chapter 2 was originally published in *Dædalus* (vol. 120, no. 2, 1991), and chapter 3 in a later issue of the same journal (vol. 122, no. 2, 1993). They are reprinted by permission of *Dædalus*, Journal of the American Academy of Arts and Sciences. Chapter 4 was first published in *Études Chinoises*, vol. 17, nos. 1–2, 1998. Chapter 5 appeared in *The Chinese Family and Its Ritual Behavior*, edited by Hsieh Jih-chang and Chuang Ying-chang and published in 1985 by the Institute of Ethnology, Academia Sinica, in Nankang, Taipei (a second printing, with corrections, was published in 1992). Chapter 6 was in the *Journal of Asian Studies* (vol. 49, no. 3, 1990), and chapter 7 in the *Proceedings of the In-*

ternational Conference on Anthropology and the Museum, edited by Tsong-yuan Lin (Taipei: Taiwan Museum, 1995). Chapters 8 and 9 were included in earlier publications of the Stanford University Press: chapter 8 can be found in *Locating Capitalism in Time and Space: Global Restructuring, Politics, and Identity*, edited by David L. Nugent (2002); and chapter 9 in *Contract and Economic Culture in China*, edited by Madeleine Zelin, Jonathan Ocko, and Robert Gardella (2004).

Over the years many organizations have provided financial and logistical assistance for the research behind these chapters, and I want to express my gratitude to all of them. My stints of fieldwork in Taiwan and mainland China have been supported by fellowships or grants from the Social Science Research Council; the National Science Foundation; the Inter-University Program and Committee for Scientific and Scholarly Cooperation, Taipei; the Committee on Scholarly Communication with the People's Republic of China, National Program for Advanced Study and Research in China; the Henry Luce Foundation, United States–China Cooperative Research Program; the Joint Committee on Chinese Studies of the American Council of Learned Societies and the Social Science Research Council; and the Chiang Ching-kuo Foundation. Columbia University's East Asian Institute (now the Weatherhead East Asian Institute) has been a loyal and long-term source of research funding.

Formal affiliation as well as aid in facilitating field access and obtaining field data has been provided by the Institute of Ethnology of the Academia Sinica, Taipei; the National Program for Advanced Study and Research in China of the Committee on Scholarly Communication with the People's Republic of China, Washington, DC; the Institute of Sociology of the Chinese Academy of Social Sciences, Beijing; the Institute of Sociology of the Academy of Social Sciences in Hebei Province, in Sichuan Province, and in Shanghai Municipality; and the Hakka Research Center of Jiaying University in Meizhou Municipality, Guangdong Province. In particular I want to acknowledge the assistance and support given me by professors Li Yih-yuan and Chuang Ying-chang of the Institute of Ethnology, and by Professor Fang Xuejia of Jiaying University's Hakka Research Center. Robert Chung (Chung Fu-sung) of Meinong, Taiwan, has been a close friend and coworker since I first visited his home town to explore fieldwork opportunities there in 1964, and here I want to thank him for all he has done on my behalf. At Stanford University Press I am grateful to Muriel Bell, Carmen Borbón-Wu, John Feneron, Sharron Wood, and Linda Gregonis for all their help in bringing this book to print. I also want to express appreciation to the University Seminars at Columbia University for their help in publication. Material in this work was presented to the University Seminar on Modern China and the University Seminar on Traditional China.

Contents

Tables

Kinship, Contract, Community, and State

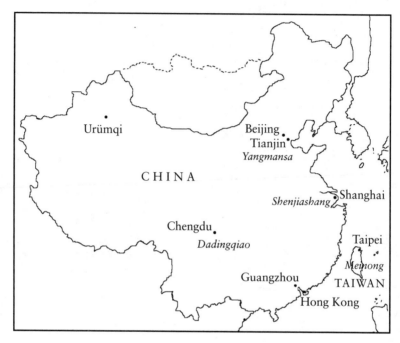

Location of field sites (in italics) mentioned in the text

Introduction

The essays in this volume, written and published over a period of more than thirty years, were selected for this book to provide an anthropological overview of major dimensions of Chinese culture and society. They reflect some of my research interests and research procedures, and their overriding theme is the relationship between late imperial and contemporary culture and society in China. By "late imperial," sometimes referred to as "late traditional," I mean the period of the Qing dynasty, usually dated from 1644 to 1911. Of course, culture continually changes in all human societies, and Chinese society during late imperial times was no exception. Yet major and unprecedented dislocations were set in motion starting with the mid-nineteenth-century assault on China by the Western powers, later joined by Japan. So by the time of the dynasty's fall important sectors of society had already begun to experience a process of change in response to these new outside forces, one that was to intensify throughout the twentieth century. Such changes continued through the 1912–49 era of the Republic of China. The establishment of the People's Republic in 1949 marked the expansion of major cultural change to the entire population, encompassing both the vast rural sectors and inland urban centers where, prior to Communist rule, dominant cultural patterns in areas such as family life and religion were still largely of late imperial derivation. With rapid change impacting all of China's population continuing to the present, it should be kept in mind that late imperial culture remains one of the constitutive major elements in the process of change itself.

For a recent example of the important role of late imperial culture in modern Chinese culture I refer to an encounter I experienced in December 2001, during a month-long trip to China and Taiwan. I was traveling in districts of Guangdong and Fujian provinces where, among the Han Chinese, the dominant local language is Hakka, one of several non-Mandarin but nevertheless Chinese languages spoken in the southeastern part of the country, unlike in most other parts of China, where as far as the Han Chinese are concerned the prevalent language is Mandarin.[1] In Fujian I visited a "common ancestral hall" (*gongci*) in Shibi Township, Ninghua County. Built in 1995, this large structure is situated in Shibi because this is the area proclaimed by countless Hakka genealogies of different surnames to be a key stopping point in the movement of their ancestors from north China to Fujian and then to Guangdong.[2] The temple contains exactly 152 ancestral tablets, each dedicated to the ancestors of a particular surname, with the entire assemblage thus held to represent the collective ancestry of the Hakka people as a whole. Likewise, on each side of the broad avenue leading to the main temple hall there are seventy-six stelae, on each of which is given the history of the origin of one surname. Framing the entrance to this avenue from the main road is an archway (*pailou*), across the top of which is engraved an inscription contributed by Yang Chengwu. Born in the area, he was a nationally prominent retired general in the People's Liberation Army before his death in 2004. With his calligraphy providing endorsement from the highest reaches of state power, other inscriptions are attributed to major Hong Kong and overseas Chinese donors. Twice a year major rituals of ancestor worship are carried out, attracting large groups from Hong Kong, Taiwan, and Overseas Chinese communities. Overall, Shibi Township, and Ninghua County as a whole, still give the appearance of relative poverty and underdevelopment, at least in comparison with nearby southeastern coastal regions centering on Guangzhou, Zhangzhou, Xiamen, and Quanzhou. As a center for the glorification of Hakka ethnic identity, and an attractor of Hakka attention and wealth, especially from Hong Kong, Taiwan, and overseas communities, Ninghua County's Shibi is in competition with the Hakka Museum and cultural center in the Changting county seat, next door, and with major institutions in Meixian, Guangdong. This latter area is better off economically than either Ninghua or Changting, but nevertheless it is far behind the regions centering on Guangzhou and Xiamen.[3]

Interpretation of the above ethnographic tidbit might involve issues of recent and current anthropological concern, such as ethnicity, globalization, and regional analysis, including a kind of reverse cultural flow such that "backward" or peripheral regions are feeding through their continuing mastery of "traditional" religious and other procedures into the growing demand for "tradition" precisely in the economically core areas. Shibi's Hakka "common ancestral hall" does not represent a straightforward continuation of late imperial ancestor worship, which had its own history of change, although with the revival of popular religion in many areas of China during recent decades some of the reconstructed ancestral halls do bear a much closer physical and functional resemblance to their late imperial predecessors. The Shibi temple is an ancestral hall built on the basis of constructed identities showing connections with late imperial culture but now mobilized to serve modern concerns. Although "Hakka" as a recognized social and linguistic category can certainly be traced back to early Qing if not before then, during the twentieth century there has been an emergence of the Hakka as a modern ethnic group within the larger category of Han Chinese ethnicity, giving rise to global Hakka associations and many other organizations focusing on and thereby elaborating common Hakka identity (Constable 1996; Lozada 2001). The Shibi temple plays a part in the development of this identity by providing it with an ancestry that can be worshiped. Late imperial ancestor worship did provide a context for the assertion of common ancestry on the basis of common surname, as in some of the larger urban ancestral halls, but by bringing together in one temple 152 surnames found among Hakka speakers, the Shibi temple transforms the worship of different ancestral lines into worship of common ethnic ancestry. In its use and transformation of late imperial cultural elements the Shibi temple exemplifies appeal to traditional verities in the context of modern projects of cultural construction, such projects being responses to and engagements with contemporary political, economic, and other forces. Similar developments in Japan have been labeled "traditionalism" by anthropologists doing research in that county (as in Bestor 1989), and the term can also be usefully employed in a Chinese context, precisely because such uses of "tradition" do not represent the only or, indeed, the major impact of late imperial culture on modern China.[4] This traditionalism, as officially approved or at least officially tolerated during recent years, coexists, as we shall see, with an earlier but still modern heritage of antitraditionalism involving equally modern notions of "backwardness" and "feudalism," with these latter two terms used to characterize various beliefs and practices derivative of late imperial culture, including expressions of traditionalism such as the Hakka temple.

An especially important dimension of the late imperial legacy was the cultural and economic sophistication of ordinary people in China. Extending well beyond the scholarly elite, popular standards valorizing managerial and technical competence in agricultural and nonagricultural livelihoods; in controlling family, community, and the larger network of social ties; and in understanding, confronting, and manipulating money, credit, contracts, and other instruments of economic life were well developed in the highly commodified environment of late imperial times. These standards, and the skills they supported, had major implications for the directions taken by social and economic change among Chinese during the modern era. China's rapid economic development in recent decades forms the acknowledged or unacknowledged backdrop for much of recent China anthropology, be it written by non-Chinese or Chinese anthropologists. Yet in much of this literature it is hardly noted that China has had a commodified economy for centuries, so that the contribution of China's own history to its present-day economic culture often goes unrecognized. Connected to the theme of cultural sophistication is that of groups and institutions as products of social management in interaction with basic orienting ideologies. Chinese organizations did not maintain themselves simply through momentum supplied by tradition, but rather they depended on leaders, managers, and social activists for their continuity. On the one hand, entities such as the family, the lineage, the religious association, or the territorial community are organized on the basis of commonly accepted social, religious, or economic beliefs and standards. On the other, management and leadership often determine the shape such groups take, the extent of their prosperity and solidarity, and whether they survive at all. Their innovations may also add to the fund of beliefs and standards upon which their group and others draw.

The areas of concern I have highlighted here reflect my impressions of the people I have lived and worked with during extended stints of fieldwork in culturally Chinese environments over a period beginning in 1964 and extending through 1990. My earliest fieldwork was in southern Taiwan in 1964–65 and followed by more sojourns there. My later fieldwork was in mainland China villages, first in Hebei in 1986–87, then near Shanghai in 1990, and, finally, in Sichuan, also during 1990.[5] All of these field settings were to varying degrees rural, thus making the interpenetration of late imperial culture with subsequent cultural trends perhaps more apparent than would be the case if I had worked in newer urban districts in Taiwan or China. The Taiwan fieldwork was undertaken when anthropologists from the United States were not permitted to carry out such research on the China mainland, but the locations of my subsequent field studies reflected deliberate choices on my part. Although the political separation of Taiwan from mainland China is now very real, albeit hotly contested by the mainland government, the island certainly was part of China during the Qing, until it was taken over by Japan in 1895. Before then, Taiwan's overwhelmingly Han Chinese population was formed largely by immigration from the nearby mainland provinces of Guangdong and Fujian. Thus the Taiwan Han Chinese were located in the southeastern portion of the empire, both in terms of the island's geographical position and with respect to the region of the Chinese mainland from which their ancestors came. Hebei, of course, is in north China, Shanghai is near the eastern coast, and Sichuan is on the western side of the area where the Han Chinese population is distributed within the larger empire. Thus my fieldwork represents my interest in working at sites in the northern, southern, eastern, and western areas of the old empire. Each locale was a small rural community, and certainly not taken to be representative of a much larger region. Rather, my intent was to inquire through fieldwork about commonalities among the Han Chinese as a whole. In all four communities local society was still shaped in important ways by late imperial culture, although in the context of obvious and rapid cultural change. My idea was that features shared by all four fieldwork communities could legitimately be considered generally characteristic of the Han Chinese. As it turns out, my fieldwork did show me a common Han Chinese culture. Features of religion, kinship, the family, economic relations and management, and numerous other aspects of life combined to form a shared cultural pattern.

My concern with late imperial culture developed early during my embrace of both anthropology and the study of China. This was during the late 1950s, when anthropological interest in China surged even as fieldwork in the People's Republic of China was banned to U.S. and other social scientists. At that time China anthropology was still largely engaged with issues of research and interpretation derived from fieldwork and analysis carried out before World War II or during that conflict in areas of China not under Japanese occupation. Given the fact that until the Communist victory the vast bulk of the rural Chinese continued to live in a cultural setting overwhelmingly of late imperial vintage, it is not surprising that late imperial cultural patterns were the focus of major anthropological questions concerning matters such as community, class, family, and kinship. Such issues continued to shape and inspire China anthropological research in the decades following World War II and the

Communist victory, when anthropological research was of necessity confined to Taiwan and Hong Kong and would not resume in mainland China until the end of the 1970s. Prior to this closure, work on the China mainland by anthropologists such as Fei Xiaotong (Fei Hsiao-tung), Morton Fried, Francis L. K. Hsu, Lin Yuehua, Cornelius Osgood, G. William Skinner, and Martin Yang all strongly engaged late imperial culture, as did the somewhat later documentary-based writings of Maurice Freedman, even though these scholars were also interested in contemporary culture change.[6] Nevertheless, the availability of ethnographic data and analyses concerned with late imperial culture was one encouragement for further research along the same lines. Another was that with research restricted to Hong Kong and Taiwan, and with the direction of social and cultural change there presumably vastly different from that in mainland China under Communist rule, the extent to which research on modern developments in these two small areas could contribute to larger understandings of China was at that time felt by many in the field of Chinese studies, if not anthropology, to be quite limited.

By focusing on "traditional" aspects of life, those engaged in research on Taiwan and Hong Kong felt that their work would be of immediate relevance to the larger field of sinology, for the field reports of these anthropologists marked contributions in areas such as popular religion, family and kinship, and community organization that enhanced understanding of the late imperial culture of China as a whole.[7] In the 1960s and 1970s these perspectives on late imperial culture were based upon research in Hong Kong and Taiwan settings where that culture still significantly shaped local life. During my first fieldwork in southern Taiwan, for example, I was exposed to religious, family, and economic arrangements matching what I had earlier seen described in works pertaining to late imperial times, including Arthur Smith's *Village Life in China*. So when I was asked to write the introduction to a reprint of that book (included in this volume as chapter 1), my own recently completed fieldwork in Taiwan informed what I had to say. Although I had yet to do fieldwork on the mainland, the fact that Smith's work dealt with rural north China meant that in using my own fieldwork findings from Taiwan to illuminate his text I was able to focus my remarks on what I could take to be Han Chinese rather than simply local cultural characteristics. In other words, what applied equally to south Taiwan in the 1960s and to Shandong Province in north China during late Qing must represent powerfully rooted components of late imperial Han Chinese culture (disregarding broader commonalities reflecting East Asian patterns or even the human condition as such). Obviously, that village in south Taiwan was then representative of traditional culture only in certain respects. Yet in numerous others the village also bore the marks of the island's turbulent history, with enhanced political control and efforts at modernization beginning before the 1895 onset of Japanese occupation, and accelerating under Japanese colonial control and during the following period of Chinese Nationalist rule that started in 1945.

Such changes in Taiwan, like those in Hong Kong under the very different circumstances of British colonial rule, provided extremely valuable data for anthropologists and other social scientists interested in culture change, modernization, or colonialism, but research along such lines always had to contend with the prevalent climate of Chinese studies, in which findings pertaining to contemporary developments in either territory could readily be characterized as "different" from what was going on in mainland China, and therefore somehow of diminished significance in the China research field. Anthropologists wanted to deal with China, but in the massive shadow of the unapproachable People's Republic—where it seemed that rapid social change was moving in directions quite different from those in the areas where anthropologists were doing their fieldwork—the only larger "China" that could be described was that of the late imperial society and its twentieth-century derivatives in parts of the old empire not under Communist control.

Resumption of fieldwork in mainland China by the late 1970s coincided with the emergence of new anthropological interests and theoretical orientations, and under the influence of both developments the earlier fascination with "traditional" or late imperial culture among China anthropologists—especially those based outside China—has largely given way to concern with contemporary society and the modern forces shaping it. Interestingly, with the revival of anthropology in China itself, that country's anthropologists have focused much attention on late imperial culture in their writings on family, lineage, popular religion, and other areas of inquiry that often follow from themes first engaged outside mainland China during the Taiwan–Hong Kong era of anthropological research.[8] But these Chinese scholars certainly are also attentive to developments during the Communist era, and in this latter respect they are closely aligned in their interests with the dominant international trends in China anthropology.[9] In recent years, linked to the accelerating pace of economic development and dislocation in China has been similarly rapid social and cultural change, such that keeping up with the latter is a challenge for anthropological researchers. Despite these developments, however, late imperial culture remains a subject of professional concern to China anthropologists, in terms of research, teaching and expected expertise. Even more important is the uncontested understanding in China anthropology that the legacy of late imperial China continues as a major influence on Chinese culture today.

The three chapters in Section One of this book deal with Han Chinese late imperial culture during Qing, with how that culture continued to influence China after the collapse of the empire and its institutions, and with some of the forces changing this culture. Chapter 1, which in its original version was my introduction to Smith's book, here introduces late imperial culture and society, focusing on life in local communities and on the institutional arrangements and cultural forces linking local communities to each other and to the Qing imperial state. Chapters 2 and 3 were originally written following my fieldwork at the three sites in north, east, and west China. Chapter 2 continues the introduction to late imperial culture, with an increased emphasis on how the shared features of that culture incorporated a cosmic vision such that people were conscious of their place within their communities and larger local settings as well as within a Chinese imperial domain, which itself was seen as an integral component of a total cosmos also including heaven and an underworld. This was a form of identification with nation and empire rejected, ironically, by the new elite nationalism that emerged in reaction to China's defeats and humiliations by European imperialism and mercantilism beginning in the mid-nineteenth century, with the United States and Japan later joining in. The nationalistic rejection of tradition by the modern elite and some of its consequences for Chinese culture and society are taken up in the second part of chapter 2 and in chapter 3. One important component of elite antitraditionalism was a view of late imperial culture as "backward" in many respects, and responsible for China's weakness in the face of imperialistic aggression. Identification of this theme in elite antitraditionalism is important for many reasons, but in this book I stress how this view has tended to strongly deny the very cultural and economic sophistication of ordinary people that was part of the late imperial legacy. Antitraditionalism's notions of backwardness and superstition were epitomized in its vision of the "peasant," yet another modern invention, as discussed in chapter 3. With antitraditionalism providing an important perspective on late imperial culture, displays of traditionalism have been suppressed until recently, and elements of this culture that might more positively accord with ideas of progress or other notions of modernity have not been given the emphasis they deserve. Thus management, commodification, and contract remain key areas of consideration in the essays that follow.

Section Two of this book consists entirely of chapter 4, which deals with family organization and its changes under Communist rule in the Hebei village where I did fieldwork in 1986–87. This chapter provides an overview of Han Chinese family organization and development, and its frame of reference is based squarely on my analysis of family life in the southern Taiwan village where I had done fieldwork more than twenty years earlier (Cohen 1976). Although this framework was originally developed for interpreting these Taiwan data, the ability to apply it without much difficulty to families in north China was for me a very strong indication of the commonalities of Han Chinese culture. Chapter 4 goes beyond that framework, however, in considering in some detail changes in family organization since the onset of Communist rule. In examining these changes there was another lesson, that change involved a complex interplay between old and new elements, with the corporate family or *jia*, for example, continuing to be of significance throughout the Communist era—despite going through important changes—with even family division contracts of a kind directly derivative of late imperial times continuing to be written. Continuities such as those pertaining to the *jia* were to be seen within a context of major changes in marriage, residence, and other areas of family life such that the entire process involved ongoing interaction between old and new elements rather than the former simply giving way to the latter.

Section Three of this book (chapters 5 to 7) turns to lineage, a subject attracting less attention nowadays than previously, but of traditional interest to anthropologists, including those focusing on China. Lineage and other kinship matters need consideration in any work seeking to look at Chinese culture and society in the round, for far too much of Chinese social life clusters around kinship issues for these to be ignored or treated lightly. The patrilineal lineage or "descent group" was a basic formation in Chinese society, and in recent decades it has reemerged as such in rural China. In China people may feel they are related through shared patrilineal descent from an ancestor, but this does not necessarily mean that they are members of the same lineage. Likewise they may identify themselves as members of a particular local community, such as a village or village neighborhood, but this identification may not involve kinship elements. It is only when community elements and patrilineal kinship elements coincide that a lineage can be identified. Another manifestation of links based upon acceptance of common ancestry could be the ancestral halls found in many larger towns, briefly noted earlier; often these halls were collectively built and subsidized by rural lineages in the surrounding area and focused on an ancestor they believed they shared. Insofar as a "group" can be identified this would comprise those periodically worshiping or meeting together in the hall. Such a group might be better identified as a "congregation" rather than a lineage or any other residentially based community, it being understood that from within lineages or other kinds of local communities congregations could also form during religious undertakings. There were also religious associations of many kinds, some with their own temples, and each of these also comprised a congregation: it was quite common for a person to belong to various congregations at the same time, some involving the kinship religion of ancestor worship and others focusing on the gods of Chinese popular religion. All such congregations were groupings that could be involved in social, economic, and political activities, as well as in religious matters. Another factor to consider is corporate ownership. Many but certainly not all congregations in late imperial times were anchored to corporations owning land, other income-producing assets, or at least a temple serving as the congregation's religious focus. A congregation supported by corporate wealth was better able to arrange elaborate religious rituals and feasting for its membership and play a larger role in the affairs of the local community. So just as a lineage was only one kind of local community, so did it produce members for only one kind of congregation, and it might or might not have corporate holdings. But because a lineage was a community, lineage membership was a condition of daily life in religious, economic, and social terms. Also, because a lineage was a residential community it could not be as readily dissolved during the height of the Maoist suppression of "feudal superstition" as could a religious congregation which was not at the same time a local community. Since the post-Maoist liberalization of the Communist state's religious policy, many lineages remaining in place during the Maoist era have resumed religious activities.

The essays in Section Three depart from the earlier model of lineage organization in southeastern China developed in the first instance by Maurice Freedman (1958, 1966), whose powerful impact on the field of

Chinese anthropology, even to the present, can hardly be overestimated. Thus interaction with the Freedman model, positive or negative, remains characteristic of much of China anthropology, at least insofar as matters connected with late imperial culture and society are concerned. Although the first essay expands upon that older model with reference to the interconnections between lineage and family organization, the following essays on lineage organization in north and east China represent original modes of analysis I have developed in ethnographic confrontation with lineage arrangements vastly different from those made familiar by Freedman and others. Thus this section provides an analysis of lineage as a component of Chinese culture rather than as a characteristic of southeastern Chinese social organization. While these essays show regional variation in lineage arrangements, at the same time they confirm how in each region there was considerable variation in lineage size, wealth, and organization. Finally, by showing how the lineage was widely distributed, they confirm again its general importance in Han Chinese culture.

In chapter 5 the large, well-endowed lineages of southeastern China are viewed from the vantage point of the corporate aspects of the family. This chapter was originally written before I had an opportunity to do fieldwork in mainland China. It represents an effort to make the best of anthropology's confinement to Taiwan and to Hong Kong, where lineages of the kind introduced to a large anthropological audience by Freedman, writing on this subject mainly on the basis of documentary research, were still found largely intact in Hong Kong's rural New Territories. This chapter explores the implications for the corporate family of membership in lineages so well endowed with land and other holdings that they in effect subvert the corporate solidarity of member families. Drawing upon my own Taiwan data to fill out the family's characteristics as a corporate group, I relied on Freedman and on the work done by anthropologists in the New Territories to bring lineage corporate features into the discussion.

Chapters 6 and 7 were written on the basis of fieldwork in two mainland China villages. Although my main focus at both sites was contemporary society, the research behind these chapters can be characterized as "historical anthropology," for when I was in Hebei Province in 1986–87 and then in Shanghai County in 1990, it had already been many years since lineages in the Hebei village ceased to function as congregations. In the village near Shanghai, where lineages seemed to have never developed socially significant corporate or congregational characteristics, they had lost many of the important community attributes that had previously identified them as lineages. In these villages, most lineage activities ended by 1955, when the still new Communist government fully collectivized agriculture. However, given the dominance in China anthropology of the southeastern model of lineage organization, I wanted to take advantage of my location in these field settings to explore what had been the characteristics of lineages there and how these might relate to the findings in Taiwan and Hong Kong that had earlier loomed so large in anthropological writings. As with the family, I wanted to take advantage of my research in diverse settings to develop a comparative understanding of lineage arrangements and patrilineality as fundamental orientations in Han Chinese culture. Thus largely on the basis of informant interviews, supplemented by whatever relevant written sources I could find, I was able to develop the analyses of north China lineage organization found in chapter 6. Among the major challenges to received wisdom posed by the north China lineages was their ability to display considerable congregational solidarity even in the absence of significant corporate holdings, thus inviting reconsideration of the southeastern lineage "model" with respect to its emphasis on the importance of corporate property. Chapter 7's consideration of lineage arrangements in eastern China shows how groups without corporate holdings or much organizational solidarity and even lacking congregations could nevertheless constitute themselves to the extent that recognized leadership positions were defined within the lineage context; here, the lineage is of greatest significance as a level of community organization. In an addendum to this chapter, I briefly consider lineage arrangements in a Sichuanese community, and I am especially concerned with how lineages were organized in the context of the dispersed residential patterns characteristic of this area in west China.

Section Four (chapters 8–9) brings together two essays that resulted from my most recent project, the study of the historical anthropology of Minong (as Meinong Township was known during Qing and until its name was changed in 1920), in southern Taiwan. Within this particular community setting the first essay deals with commodification as a fundamental attribute of late imperial economic culture and, among many other things, addresses the role contracts played in this commodified environment. The second focuses on contracts and other transaction documents in order to explicate their vital role not only in society and economy, but also in the very process of social reproduction. None of the twenty contracts and other documents presented and analyzed in this second essay duplicates the far smaller number used in the first. These two essays represent an exploration of anthropologically fresh terrain, concerning the conduct of practical affairs and the competence of ordinary people in late imperial China. They link with the earlier essays and powerfully confirm that China's modernity has deep roots in its own traditions.

The two chapters in Section Four represent the practice of historical anthropology to a far greater extent than do the preceding essays on lineage. The historical dimension of the lineage essays is based primarily on oral reports by informants, with relatively little backup from local documentary sources. Yet historical anthropology as illustrated by the essays in Section Four is not in the first instance the product of archival research, for it requires long-term fieldwork at a particular site for which ample documentation is also available. Indeed, it is the anthropologist doing this fieldwork who must obtain the documents from a wide variety of sources, usually through borrowing, copying, and returning papers, the most important of which are the various documents of their ancestors still held onto by local families. It thus requires considerable fieldwork simply to create the archive, which will have its greatest value precisely in that it can be linked to the ethnographic findings also resulting from that fieldwork. For such historical anthropology, documentation should be informative regarding intimate social relations of the kind that anthropologists otherwise seek to identify and describe through ethnographic study (as illustrated in this book especially in chapter 4). Historical anthropology of this kind cannot be done everywhere. Late imperial China was notable for the importance of written documents in everyday life, with the result that Chinese sites are potentially advantageous for historical anthropological research. Unfortunately, given China's tumultuous history during recent centuries, documents such as land transfer contracts, family division agreements, temple records, family or association account books, and genealogies have not always survived, nor are they always available in quantities sufficient to provide the basis for a detailed exploration of social relations and cultural patterns within a community setting. It appears that Taiwan may be better off than much of mainland China in this respect, for although that island has certainly had its share of suffering, it at least escaped certain recent calamities, such as the protracted land campaigns of World War II and the subsequent Nationalist-Communist civil war, not to speak of the vast destruction of documents on the mainland after the Communist victory, as during the land reform campaigns and the Cultural Revolution. In any event, in Taiwan's Meinong Township and surrounding areas many documents predating the Japanese occupation had survived and were preserved in the homes of their owners. These could be usefully supplemented by the household registration data the Japanese began to gather early during their rule, in 1906. For Meinong Township in particular, the availability of the even earlier plot-by-plot cadastral survey carried out by the Japanese in 1902 is especially notable both because it comprises a description of Qing-era land relations for every plot in the present-day township and because the original cadastral survey books for most of Taiwan were destroyed in the mid-1980s to make way for newer documents in the government storage facility where they had been kept (but this was well after the Meinong records used in my research had been copied from the original files).

These final chapters, written only recently, nevertheless are based primarily on fieldwork carried out jointly with Professor Burton Pasternak in Meinong Township in 1971–72 (Pasternak 1983). We were interested in both the contemporary society and in Meinong's earlier history and development. I was especially concerned with the Qing period, such that familiarity with the field site on the basis of participant observation, and conducting many interviews focusing explicitly on Qing rather than later developments in Meinong society went together with a far greater reliance on documentary materials than is usually the case during anthropological fieldwork. Japanese sources such as the cadastral survey and the household registration data provide context to the Qing-period contracts and other documents used in these chapters. These documents are part of a much larger body of such materials, most of which were borrowed from their owners and copied during the 1971–72 fieldwork, but in later years I obtained additional material of this sort during shorter trips to Meinong, most recently in 2002.

Chapter 8 brings into focus within the setting of my historical study of the Meinong community the theme of economic sophistication that runs throughout this book. Linked to this sophistication was the high value placed on superior managerial capabilities, all in the context of the deeply rooted commodification generally prevalent in late imperial culture. Commodification during this period was not the product of an industrial economy hell-bent on producing items for sale, but rather it was a dimension of late imperial economic culture involving the creation of things to be bought and sold, some on the basis of preindustrial production, to be sure, but others through the definition and transfer of different kinds of access rights, such as to land or via corporate shares. As such, this late imperial commodification was not disruptive of social relations but, on the contrary, depended on such relations to serve as the protective framework within which commodity transactions could take place.

In chapter 9, I focus attention on a crucial aspect of Meinong's commodified late imperial economic culture, the documents that facilitated, legitimized, and provided evidence of major transactions. Most of these documents are contracts, long considered important indicators of "modernity" and contrasted to "traditional" or "backward" economic relationships based upon "status," which is presumably inherited. In spite of the fact that contracts were endemic to late imperial economic and social life, their importance was until recently vastly underestimated if not denied altogether. This was under the impact of modern antitraditionalism, which held that because Chinese traditional culture was backward and feudal it could not have been characterized by the wide use of such symbols of modernity as contracts. In fact, the use of contracts went far beyond land and other real estate transactions and commerce. Contracts were involved in matters such as family division, certain kinds of marriage and adoption, the setting up of various shareholding corporations geared toward worship of gods or ancestors, and the sale or bondage of human beings. But not all documents fixing transactions were contracts: some were more like affidavits, and others were authoritarian depositions regarding the distribution of property. In any event, there was a heavy reliance on the documentation of transactions. This documentation involved the mobilization of social relations, including ties of kinship or common membership in a lineage, community, or congregation. The main parties to the transaction and those participating as middlemen or witnesses were connected to each other through such ties, thereby increasing the likelihood that the transaction would be executed as described in the document. The significance of such ties becomes more apparent in light of the fact that the vast majority of land-related contracts were "white," or unregistered, and only a small minority were the "red" contracts registered with the local government office. So the propensity for contractual behavior—whatever the impact of government regulations—was a fundamental attribute of late imperial economic culture. Surely, this economic culture is one legacy of obvious import to contemporary China.

For those with less background in Chinese studies, it might be advisable to read the chapters in this book in the order they are arranged. Others can proceed according to their own interests.

Late Imperial China and Its Legacies

CHAPTER ONE

Introduction to Arthur H. Smith's
Village Life in China

Village Life in China is one of the vital sources for data on Chinese society during the late nineteenth century; the book deals with rural life at a time when the growing impact of the West was still only minimally felt over most of China's countryside. When Arthur H. Smith lived and traveled in China, the Qing dynasty still held sway, although it was to topple only a few decades later, in 1911. Most of what Smith observed was "traditional" Chinese behavior and social organization, the product of over two millennia of development during which the Chinese subcontinent attained a degree of political, economic, and social integration perhaps unparalleled among preindustrial civilizations. Smith's work, then, is valuable reading for anyone concerned with China, including the present-day Chinese People's Republic, for he deals with the culture and society from which much of life in China to this day derives.[1]

Smith's book is not what anthropologists and sociologists would call a "community study." Rather than comprehensively describing a single village, Smith deals with rural society in general, as he observed it mainly in the northern province of Shandong. Nevertheless, much of what he observed pertains to basic patterns of organization in Chinese society: the ways in which social, economic, and political relationships crosscut village boundaries and fixed villages within larger social arrangements.

The book's first chapters deal with the physical appearance of the countryside and its villages. In most of China the population lived in concentrated settlements: hamlets, villages, towns, and cities. The spatial dimension provided a crucial framework for social organization. Territorially defined social units were arranged hierarchically such that they were integrated into the nation as a whole. As spatial and settlement units, local areas were organized roughly as follows: in a larger village or in a town or city, the basic unit would be a ward or a neighborhood, and in a smaller village or hamlet the unit would be the entire settlement itself. Such basic-level units were formally organized community entities; in its simplest form, the organization might be expressed by nothing more than a common ritual or religious focus on a shrine representing Tudi, the "earth god" or the "local god" (see Smith, pp. 99–100),[2] with such a focus defining the territorial community as a religious congregation. In communities that were more prosperous, advantageously located, or with especially influential members, religious organizations might be much more complex, boasting large temples with a clearly defined group of managers; secular organizations could also be more clearly defined and undertake a variety of activities.

Such basic community units usually were components of larger territorial entities, with several small hamlets or village neighborhoods forming a larger village organization. It seems safe to say that in the case of larger villages subdivided into neighborhoods, the major organizations, with functions most vital to village life, were those that encompassed the village as a whole. But even in a concentrated village settlement the organizational importance of the component segments might, in what was probably a minority of cases, outweigh that of the higher-level unit. Smith refers to this in passing: "If the village is a large one, divided into several sections transacting their public business independently of one another, there may be several temples to the same divinity" (pp. 99–100). The hierarchy of local units usually involved more than two levels: in the countryside regional communities comprising several villages were important in rural life, with a shared temple often serving to identify such a multivillage community; and it was commonly the region occupied by such a community that people identified as their "homeland" or "ancestral home" (xiang, guxiang). Multiple levels of community and regional organization were especially characteristic of larger towns and cities. While there also must have been cases where the small size and isolated location of a settlement precluded its involvement in such local hierarchies, such circumstances almost by definition had to pertain to only a very small minority of China's population.

Local settlements, irrespective of the degree of their internal complexity, were fitted into hierarchical structures of yet larger scope; these centered on towns and cities that supported larger populations and were the sites of markets, commercial and manufacturing establishments, and other specialized economic activities. Thus, since the surrounding villages were dependent upon such a town, it formed a central point for intervillage activities of many sorts. A market town, therefore, usually served as the focal point of a region composed of many villages. Just as there was variation in the number of organizations and their functions at the village segment, village, and village cluster levels, so were there differences in the extent to which there emerged important organizations encompassing a region centering on a market town. There might be nothing more than a town-based temple serving to define the entire region ritually, or there might be comprehensive region-wide organizations with important economic and political functions. Although the strategic economic significance of a market town frequently meant that the villages in its hinterland maintained social and economic links with each other via their common access to this town, it was sometimes the case that such a town rather was seen as a desired economic asset by competing village cluster communities who might at times even confront each other violently so as to gain control over it.

Towns and cities can be ordered into yet another hierarchy, using certain economic and social functions. In an ascending scale, larger towns and cities served as marketing and distribution centers not only for the farming villages surrounding them, but also for smaller market towns. There was a hierarchy of marketing areas of ever-increasing size, then, and the central towns or cities exhibited economic complexity and diversification on a scale commensurate with their marketing functions. Such towns and cities were also the locales for the activities of those powerful men with economic and social interests over wide areas of the country. A region consisting of a market town and its surrounding villages, or simply one of several village clusters within a larger marketing area, however, seems to have been the largest region whose population could form a discrete and organized social unit that recognized itself as a community and where there was common participation of the general population in a wide variety of activities, and therefore "face-to-face" familiarity among the community's members.[3]

At each level in a local spatial hierarchy, the inhabitants were themselves fitted into what might be called a sociological hierarchy. There were a variety of attributes that tended to position an individual and his family at or near the apex of such an arrangement. Wealth, especially in the form of land, was surely one; literacy, recognized managerial ability, and spare time to devote to public affairs were other attributes. In addition to its more mundane manifestations, one's high position within a local hierarchy was expressed by a greater approximation to the standards of *li*, often translated as "ritual," or "propriety." In the elite literary tradition, *li* denotes concepts developed by Confucian thinkers concerned with the ethics of human relationships, society, and government. Ethnographically, *li* designates the elite style of life, compounded of many elements: patterns of behavior and belief; education; material possessions; and the full elaboration of funerals, ancestral worship, and other ceremonial or ritual expressions of ethical ideas such as filial loyalty, obedience, and others.

It is not surprising that among the Han Chinese, settled across an area of subcontinental proportions, there were local variations in customs, attire, and even in aspects of social organization; what is remarkable is the near uniformity of the usages of *li*, although there was some variation in this respect also. Nevertheless, an elite style of life of basically one pattern was practiced over wide areas of China by the men (and their families) who were near or at the apex of their local hierarchies. During the Qing dynasty, and doubtless much earlier, the close connections between the practice of *li* and wealth, power, and prestige were as much incorporated into local custom as were those patterns that might vary from one local region to another. Added to the role of *li* in local hierarchies was that of the examination system itself. Success in the examinations—the achievement of a government degree—had the effect of raising one's position in a local context, while at the same time it gave a person a new status with respect to the government. Degree holders, the "literati," were thus members of the upper strata of local elites at the same time that they comprised a nationwide class.

The system of social stratification was manifested at all levels of the hierarchy of social and spatial units. Within each neighborhood of a village, for example, some men were more influential and powerful than others, and to a greater extent tended to partake of an elite style of life. These men—the elite components of each village neighborhood—as a group formed the villagewide elite. It is true, of course, that not every part of a village boasted men of equal wealth, learning, and power, so that two persons, for example, occupying apical positions in their respective hierarchies might not be social equals in terms of the village as a whole. Thus, while the men with the greatest social status within each village section dealt with each other and jointly managed village affairs, within this group there was a further hierarchical ordering of relationships. The same situation was present with respect to village clusters or to the market town and its surrounding villages; the various component communities contributed men who formed a regionwide elite, within which there were those men who had the highest social status and the greatest influence on the affairs of the region as a whole. It was at this level that local elites interlocked to form a nationwide elite stratum. Membership in this group was on the basis of different combinations of attributes such as great wealth, academic rank, and a past or present position of importance in the government bureaucracy. Persons in this group were powerful in their local regions, but their power was fed by the potential or actual nationwide scope of their personal, commercial, and political interests and contacts.

In the integration of society at the national level, the bureaucracy and the administration it manned played a crucial role. The many references in Smith's book to yamens, yamen runners, magistrates, and lawsuits give powerful testimony to the ongoing impact of government administration on rural life. It is of some interest, therefore, that in most of China the *xian* (county or district) was the smallest administrative unit for which a yamen was established. *Xian* varied greatly in area and population, some including only a score or so villages, while others encompassed hundreds of villages and many market towns. In general, however, a *xian* magistrate had under his jurisdiction a very large number of people indeed. According to official statistics, cited by Hsiao (1960: 5), there was an average of 100,000 people for each magistrate in 1749 and 250,000 in 1819. The ability of the complex and highly centralized Qing bureaucracy to function with such a minimal administrative establishment at the local level was due precisely to its close interconnections with the local social hierarchies described earlier. Magistrates, forbidden to serve in their home districts, would carry out their administrative duties with the cooperation of the local elites in the region to which they had been assigned. Through its intimacy and social equality with the district magistrate, including a similar or identical style of life, the local elite was plugged into the national political system (see Smith, p. 95). The district magistrate, from his point of view, required the cooperation of the local elite in order to fulfill his administrative responsibilities. In this fashion local social hierarchies, national elites, and the imperial administrative system combined and interlocked to provide a framework for Chinese society as a whole. There were persons with positions of power and influence at many points within this system; they would deal with their equals and superiors as representatives of the units within which they occupied superordinate positions; at the same time, they would have to reconcile the interests of their own groups with those of equivalent or higher-level units, and with their own personal ambitions.

What the operation of this system meant from the point of view of the individual is aptly summarized by Smith: "In China the power is in the hands of the learned and of the rich" (p. 94). China was unlike many other preindustrial agrarian societies in that, with very few exceptions, the highest positions in society were, in theory at least, open to anyone (to any man, that is) who might achieve them. Only at the very bottom and at the pinnacle of the nationwide arrangement of social classes was membership hereditary. There were, then, a small number of "mean people" (*jian min*) who held "despised" occupations and were ineligible for participation in the government examinations. Within the very top social strata was the nobility, including the emperor, his family, and the imperial clan. The vast majority of the population belonged to neither of these social categories: ordinary villagers and elite alike were in a situation where a person's social and economic status could change. There was a definite pattern of upward mobility involving the accumulation of wealth and scholarship; a family's movement up into the elite would be followed by movement, down again, unless circumvented by continuing fiscal and scholastic successes on the part of subsequent generations. To be sure, a Chinese who would fit into a Horatio Alger story was a rare person indeed; nevertheless, families were always going up or down. Those not eliminated by poverty would manage eventually to improve their position, and for those on top, the constant struggle to maintain their status eventually met with defeat.[4]

A good portion of *Village Life in China* in fact deals with the way rural life was involved in this fluid social situation. Chapters 9 and 10 provide an excellent description of the arduous program that had to be followed by all desiring a coveted academic degree. One's own native village, if it supported its own school—and quite a few villages did—could be the starting point of a career that, if one succeeded at each juncture, could result in attainment of the highest academic honors, and in entrance into the imperial bureaucracy. A careful reading of Smith's description of the village school curriculum shows the very same texts were studied, and by some students mastered, in villages, towns, and cities throughout China.

The successful operation of a uniform system of education at the immediately local level throughout the Chinese empire, which by mid-Qing contained about 400 million people, was an achievement unmatched by any other preindustrial agrarian society, and it is safe to say that even today there is no comparably standardized educational system extending over such a wide area and involving such a large population—except, perhaps, in China itself. This is not to say that all the Chinese received even the first few years of a "classical" education. The facts emphatically were otherwise. Within the population at large, girls and women were largely excluded from formal education, precisely because they were not eligible to enjoy the advantages it afforded. Even for boys, education required money and time, both of which were in short supply in a nation fed by small-scale intensive agriculturalists. In wealthier literati households, however, many girls were schooled in reading and writing, some even to levels equivalent to those attained by accomplished male degree holders. But such education for women represented not so much a family's effort to improve its social standing but rather a statement of its achieved social position, and for such achievement high levels of male literacy were required.

As Smith emphasizes repeatedly, education was geared toward preparing students for participation in the nationwide series of competitive examinations. Competition was extreme because the stakes were high indeed; at all levels those who succeeded were vastly outnumbered by those who failed. Smith, viewing this situation from the perspective of the village school, remarks unfavorably on the fact that lack of ability or the pressure of other circumstances prevented the large majority of entering students from learning enough even to make an initial attempt at the examinations (Smith, pp. 75–76). The possibility of having a son succeed in the examinations was indeed a major inducement for parents to hire a tutor or send their son to the village school. But what was at work at the local level in reality was a system of generalized education precisely because most students never reached the point where they were prepared to compete in the examinations.

Although Smith is skeptical of the practical usefulness of the orthodox education, the fact remains that it disseminated throughout China basic literary skills, which were of use in many ways. By the latter portion of the imperial period, China was a society where written records and documents were of crucial importance in practically all spheres of life. Literacy was required not only for scholarship and official administration, but also for successful farm management and commerce, and it was extremely useful if not essential for those wishing to assume a greater than ordinary influence in the local affairs of their neighborhood or village. Written material was thoroughly incorporated into ceremonial and religious activities; indeed, the written word was in itself often an object of religious veneration. In many parts of China villagers considered the random disposal or destruction of paper with printing or writing to be a shameful or even sinful act; special receptacles were set aside where such paper might be reverentially burnt and, thereby, received by a deity. Thus, the very strategic role played by the written word included, but clearly extended beyond, the literacy required for examination competition and the operation of the national bureaucratic administration. At best present among only a small number of women, literacy to one degree or another was rather widespread among men, even though only a minority had full control over the classical texts and were able to write in the elite style. Many men, however, recognized at least a minimal vocabulary, and education at home or in school had equipped a significant number of men throughout the countryside sufficiently to undertake the literary tasks required in Chinese rural life.[5]

Thus the importance of local schools, as basic purveyor of literacy to the population, was reinforced by many factors. Success in the examinations was surely the greatest reward of education, and the bureaucracy made this reward possible by defining the course of study necessary for such an achievement. Completion of even the first few stages of this course, in any event, provided advantages, so that investing in the education of a village boy was not simply a risky proposition focusing entirely on the examination system. Since ultimate success in the examination system was the most desirable benefit, among many others, there was created through the local-level educational system a direct and highly significant link between the village and the imperial state. Through this system there was provided an avenue for the dissemination of state-approved texts ideologically orthodox in content. It is safe to say that persons with above-average ambitions and intellectual endowment were strongly motivated to occupy themselves fully in the mastery of such material. The educational system, with its built-in possibilities for advancement, was therefore a means of political and social control. At the same time, this system not only provided recruits for the bureaucracy, but also precisely the teaching personnel needed to maintain the system itself. Thus, at the local level, teachers were drawn from among the large group of men with sufficient education to act as tutors or to head village schools. Some of these men had degrees, others were still competing in the examinations, and some, presumably, had given up hope for academic success. There was a market relationship here, and those families or groups who could offer better wages would obtain the services of men who were academically better qualified (see Smith, pp. 51–52). As Smith's description of the "Strolling Scholars" and their going from school to school in an effort to sell paper, pens, ink, and other such supplies amply demonstrates, several years of education in itself might not suffice to save a man from poverty. The important point, however, is that education could be put to use in both local and national contexts.

While competition in the examinations was confined to a comparatively small proportion of the rural population, everyone participated one way or another in the economic struggle. I have noted that Chinese society was "fluid" in the sense that there were very few groups of persons with special hereditary prerogatives or disabilities. One reflection of this fluidity in the economic sphere was the fact that some of the most crucial relationships were contractual or market dominated. This extended to the control of land itself, a matter of greatest significance in a preindustrial agrarian society. During the Qing period, land was overwhelmingly in the private domain, with the family and not the individual as the most important unit of ownership. There were neither the vassal-lord or serf-and-manor relationships prominent in certain periods of European history and replicated or closely approximated in various Asian regions, nor the highly developed patterns of communal tenure common to many preindustrial societies. In Qing China, a family had land to cultivate if it was purchased or obtained through patrilineal succession, or if it was tenanted through a contractual agreement with the owner. Land was indeed the crucial commodity; landlessness meant poverty, and while the village family in most cases led a more comfortable life if they owned the land they worked, even tenancy gave them some status as members of their home community, as well as at least minimal economic security.

The attitude that land was a favored form of investment was held in common by those who prospered through agriculture or through riskier but usually more remunerative commercial ventures. When wealth, however obtained, was translated into land within one's home community, there was relatively greater assurance not only of a predictable income for one's family, and an estate for one's posterity, but also of increased status and influence in local affairs. Because land meant power in rural China, it was an expression as well as a source of wealth. Land was one of the most important commodities involved in Chinese economic relationships, and it was also one of the most expensive. This was true monetarily, to be sure, but equally true in terms of the social impact of land transactions. Land transfers and their consequences were what Smith had in mind when he notes that "the insecurity of human affairs is nowhere more manifest than in the tenure of Chinese property. Families are going up or coming down all the time" (p. 204). In general, the outright sale or pledging away of a plot of land was a direct statement of the changing economic and social fortunes of both parties to the transaction.

The harsh competitiveness implicit in such a situation was not the only element in Chinese economic relationships involving land. Contracts embodying cooperative arrangements could also be negotiated. For example, common in many parts of China were societies or associations (*hui*) formed by several persons who would contribute money for the purchase of a plot of land; often, some of the income would be earmarked for purposes such as the construction or maintenance of a bridge, a school, a temple, or the like. If there should be a surplus income it would often be distributed to the original owners and their descendants; the group of members, then, were in effect shareholders in a corporation. Also of a similar corporate nature were the large localized and landowning groups of kinsmen bearing the same surname. Such groups were especially well known in south China, but in fact were found throughout China; Smith calls them "clans," while anthropologists have preferred to use the technical term "lineage," which can also refer to local groups of kin who might not own property collectively. Precisely because of the great monetary and social costs involved, land transactions did not loom large in the daily run of economic affairs within a local community. This situation may have prompted Smith's remark that "all the available land in the greater portion of China is wholly out of the market" (p. 39). As we have seen, he was aware that there was indeed a land market, one that had a crucial bearing on rural life.

Commodification at a relatively high pitch, as associated with land transactions, also found expression in other, more frequent, types of activities. With respect to commercial life in general, it hardly seems to have been encumbered, during Qing, by the low status assigned merchants in the ancient Confucian writings (see Smith, p. 32). Chapter 7 is a good description of the busy life led by the keeper of the *zahuopu*, or village shop; we note that in some cases this store may also be the headquarters of an enterprise trading with a much larger rural population through participation in the periodic markets held in nearby towns. A firm of this sort might serve as an outlet for a general assortment of wares at the village level while selling a more specialized line of village-produced commodities at the markets. Such a firm would be enmeshed in a complicated network of economic relationships stretching over a wide area of the countryside; this was not an uncommon situation in the commercial world, and far more complex arrangements were possible. Frequent business failures attest to the competitive nature of commerce during Qing. Enterprises might attempt to secure their positions through dealings, sometimes illicit, with government officials, or through the judicious use of contacts of various kinds. A merchant's complex bookkeeping arrangements, using multiple account books (Smith, p. 35), exemplified one of the means he employed to protect his business from outside interference as well as from within. Different sets of records could be made selectively available depending on whether it was officials, his own employees, or even members of his own family who wanted to see them, although the example of bookkeeping described by Smith may have been a bit more involved than was usual. Agriculture was similar to commerce in that most cultivators also managed the economic affairs of their farms. Farming was in the hands of small-scale operators who were responsible for the disposal of the produce of the fields they owned outright or tenanted. Tenants, of course, were obligated to pay their landlords stipulated rents, while assessments of many kinds could be levied on tenants and owner-cultivators alike (some tenancy contracts called for the landlord to pay part or all of the land taxes). Plantationlike arrangements in which larger numbers of resident workers would be employed for comparatively long periods and given room, board, and wages in cash or kind were known, but quite uncommon. There were no explicit cultural or political obstacles to such arrangements, but they were less efficient and profitable than land rental precisely because the widespread use of contracts enabled landlords to specify high rents and avoid the complex managerial problems that running a plantation would entail.[6]

Managerial responsibility, then, devolved upon the cultivator irrespective of the form of tenure. Agricultural wage labor was limited to a comparatively few "long-term" (*changgong*) workers, hired usually by better-off farmers to assist in field labor, and to the far more numerous workers hired during the transplant, harvest, and other busy agricultural seasons. This "short-term labor" (*duangong*) might consist of local farmers in need of extra cash, landless residents of the region, or migratory workers.

In any event, it seems clear that most of the rural population participated in agricultural production not as paid laborers, but as tenant or owner farm proprietors. They were faced with problems of credit, marketing, hiring, rental contracts, and many others; to the best of their ability, they had to manipulate the social and economic environments, as well as the physical. Farmers were thus involved in precisely the same universe of economic relationships as were the merchants. Competition was implicit in the process whereby some families would advance economically and others go down in an environment where the margin of survival was in any event quite narrow; the pervading poverty that so impresses Smith may have been more pronounced in those regions of north China with which he was most familiar, but it is safe to say that it was an actual or potential fact of life for most Chinese. Credit was an area of economic life where competition was explicit and readily observable. Smith (pp. 152–54) describes how it was very common for Chinese to borrow or lend, so the heavy demand for limited resources led to high interest rates in the credit market.

Competition for credit, again, was coupled with the cooperative patterns found in other aspects of the economy. By organizing a "cooperative loan society" (Smith, chapter 14), participants could distribute indebtedness among themselves in such a way as to obtain some protection from market credit rates by exercising joint control over terms of interest and repayment. Although, as Smith shows, loan societies might differ according to how funds were deployed among the membership, they all shared the basic principle that the pooled periodic contributions of all members be made available in rotation to each member at time. It must be kept in mind that those participating in a loan society were sufficiently well off economically as to enjoy each other's confidence. Cooperative arrangements could also be employed for participation in the open credit market. The "mountain societies" that organize pilgrimages to Mount Tai in Shandong—or at least worship its important deities, (pp. 103–4)—the funeral assistance "leagues" (p. 141), and the "New Year Societies" (p. 156) are but some of the organizations where the pooled funds of the membership were set aside to earn interest on the credit market before being applied to the specific purposes for which the organizations had been set up. The joint ownership by "ordinary farmers" of funeral and wedding paraphernalia is an example of the pooling of funds for capital investment, as is the "Bowl Association" (p. 141), whose members purchase bowls for rental to families sponsoring feasts such as for weddings or funerals. Such varieties of individual and group investment described by Smith in each case involve relatively minute sums by the present-day standards of contemporary developed economies. In the late imperial Chinese context, however, the amounts involved were substantial as far as those party to the transactions were concerned. The economic patterns of lending, borrowing, and investment on an individual or group basis involved a very considerable proportion of the population. This brings us back to the earlier point that the phenomenon of economic managerialism was widespread. Indeed, merchant and farmer alike had to develop a degree of fiscal acumen to survive in the Chinese world.[7]

The academic and economic routes toward advancement overlapped in many ways, including forbidden and illegal practices described by Smith, such as payoffs and cheating during the examinations. A legitimate means of directly translating wealth into an official title, or into a position in the bureaucracy, was through direct purchase. The Qing government obtained funds through the sale of academic titles, and sometimes government posts as well, primarily during periods of acute fiscal crisis, as was the case during both the initial and terminal phases of the dynasty. Yet a string of examination successes was still considered the most prestigious means of achieving higher academic rank and appointment to the bureaucracy, with the highest (*jinshi*) degree consistently obtainable only on the basis of examination performance. Here, too, there was a connection with economic factors, for the equipment, tuition, and leisure required for an academic career had to be paid for. Finally, if wealth could support scholarship, the reverse might also be true, for a higher position among the elite certainly increased opportunities for economic gain.

The importance of ceremonialism and feasting in Chinese society is accurately reflected in Smith's book. Competition in the marketplace, or cooperation based upon particular contractual understandings, comprised a sphere of economic life that was intimately connected with socioeconomic mobility. But even as families moved up or down, they continued to participate in broad networks of social relationships, although even these might change with growing wealth or poverty. These relationships were defined in terms such as kinship or community and thus were able to survive, at least up to a point, the divisive tendencies generated by socioeconomic stratification and mobility. Ceremonialism and feasting not only served to affirm feelings of social solidarity, but were also of considerable economic importance. When a village sponsored a fair, or an individual family a wedding or funeral, participation was on the basis of social ties of many sorts. The excellent food served to guests was in most cases a far cry from their usual fare, and as far as subsistence is concerned, food consumed during ceremonial occasions probably played a very significant nutritional role. Reciprocity was a key element in such feastings; the roles of guest and host were constantly reversed so that social relationships defined patterns of economic flow, mainly in the form of foodstuffs, but also involving many other commodities. The ceremonial sphere of the economy, like the social relationships upon which this sphere was based, provided the continuity and predictability that in many ways served to ameliorate some of the harsher and more competitive aspects of life.[8]

Smith's book contains much vital information regarding what was a crucial unit in social and economic life: the family (*jia*).[9] If China was a familistic society, it was so mainly in the sense that the family as a unit was geared to the protection or advancement of its members. The family obtained its livelihood through the coordinated effort of its members, and it was also a unit of consumption. While most families were primarily engaged in agriculture, as economic and social groups they were patterned from the same mold as families whose members might be engaged in any combination of agricultural, commercial, or handicraft activities, or even as those families which boasted wealth, learning, and elite status. From Smith's description, several of the most important features of Chinese family organization can be seen. The Chinese family was male-centered, most emphatically with respect to authority, residence, succession to property, and a pronounced preference for male offspring. While it is true, as Smith indicates, that women could find ways of expressing their opinions and influencing events, it was mainly the men who directed family affairs, especially those pertaining to farm management or other major economic activities, and the family's overall relationships with the outside world. Although the father's position of authority was assured from the moment he began to head an independent family unit, his wife would obtain a degree of authority in her own right only after the passage of many years. Her position was weakest when she was still childless (sonless); when she bore a son it improved. When a daughter-in-law came under her direction her position grew even stronger, and by the time she entered into advanced age her authority began to approximate that of her husband, especially in farming families. If her husband's death was the earlier, full power within the family might sometimes fall into her hands.

The family was a group of kin related through marriage, descent, or adoption. The economic basis of the family was its estate, owned jointly by male family members and exploited in common by the family as a whole. Usually, the most significant property in the estate was farmland, but there were other items such as residences, household effects, farm buildings and equipment, livestock, and the like. If the family was engaged in commerce or other nonagricultural activities, the shop and other assets would likewise be part of the family estate. Associated with joint ownership of the estate was the common budget kept by family members. Persons working family fields or managing the family shop would contribute the earnings to a common fund managed by the family head, who was usually the father, on behalf of the family as a whole. Persons working outside for wages were expected to do likewise if they earned a surplus above agreed-upon requirements for subsistence and personal expenses. The family thus was a cohesive unit economically as well as socially. In terms of family dynamics, poverty meant the absence of a viable estate and a concomitant weakening of family solidarity.

With this in mind, Smith's description of family "division" becomes understandable. In China, marriage as such did not lead to the emergence of a new family; rather, it meant the absorption of an additional woman into her husband's family unit, although in a minority of cases it was the man who married into his wife's family (most likely if that family was sonless). New families were created through division of the family estate; with the division of family holdings there occurred the termination of many of the social and economic obligations that bound the family together. Each of several brothers, for example, might now be the heads of independent families and related to each other as close kin, to be sure, and cooperate in a variety of settings. But they no longer had obligations as members of the same family, such as eating from a common kitchen, pooling income, or coordinating their labor under the supervision of the family manager.

Such changes are rightly emphasized in Smith's excellent description of family division (pp. 251–52). Family division brought into sharp focus the dominance of males within the family system. It was the men who shared in the partition of the estate, and in most cases it was a matter of brothers obtaining equal shares. A married brother would use his share as the economic foundation of the new, smaller family he now headed, while it was a common pattern for an unmarried brother temporarily to continue to maintain a joint estate with one of his married siblings or with his father. There was, therefore, a cyclical process by which family formation through division was followed by expansion and then division again.

Smith's description gives the impression that families in the majority of cases were quite large by the Western standards of his time and generally included more than one married couple. Such large and complex families were indeed to be found, and most closely approximated Confucian-associated ideals of numerous male offspring for the perpetuation of the family line and maintenance of family unity across several generations. In fact, at any particular time the large family ideal was expressed only in a minority of cases, and in any event, it was inevitable that most larger families would split into smaller units at one point or another. An observer in a village would find that most families were small; some would include parents (or one surviving parent), one son, his wife, and their children; others would be limited to parents and unmarried children and would thus be similar in size and composition to most families in industrialized societies. Especially among the less well-to-do, family size would be restricted not only because of divisive tendencies within the family organization, but also because of high infant mortality rates. To carry on the ancestral line was a major tenet of Chinese ideology, and male infant mortality was one of the factors leading many families to resort to the adoption and marriage practices (Smith, pp. 190–91) by which males could be incorporated into the family from the outside. Nevertheless, the fact that family development cycled between simpler and more complex forms means that membership in a complex family (the "joint" family including parents and at least two married sons and their children) was far more common a phase in a person's life history than might be inferred simply on the basis of the relative representation of such families in a community at any time.

Thus variations in family size and complexity were expressed in individual life histories as variations in the frequency and, more important, the duration of membership in complex families. In general, the richer a family, the more likely it would approximate the ideals of large size and continuity over several generations. In demographic terms, this meant that economically more comfortable families were more successful in raising their children to maturity. There were additional factors involved in the connection between a family's economic situation and its size and complexity. The Chinese family was under a constant tension produced by the conflict between unifying forces on the one hand, and those making for fragmentation on the other. The major divisive force was generated by the equal rights to the family estate held by brothers, who had the choice of staying together or dividing into smaller family units. The continuation of family unity was encouraged by situations where the advantages, especially economic, derived from such unity outweighed those forthcoming for some or all parties concerned in the event of division.

The organization of the family was such that success in the economic struggle was to a large extent achieved precisely through the effective coordination of the economic activities of family members. A common budgetary arrangement made the income of individual family members available for the family as a whole. If total family earnings were sufficient, they could be used to enrich the family estate further by expanding current agricultural, commercial, and other enterprises, or by developing new ones. Some forms of investment, especially in land, were more secure but less remunerative than others. Families often adopted a diversification scheme as they attempted to advance economically; this would include investment in several directions, and the diversification of the economic activities of family members as well. If such schemes succeeded in further advancing the family, the economic rationale keeping the brothers together would be strengthened at the same time. Therefore, it can be said that the more a family succeeded, the more pronounced would be those forces keeping it together. Contrariwise, if a family began to decline economically, the brothers would be increasingly encouraged to look out for their individual interests by claiming their share of the estate and striking out on their own, and each brother's wife would all the more press him to demand family division. It can be seen, then, that wealth had a relationship of both cause and effect with respect to large and complex families. Although the economic characteristics of a family might be one of the factors prolonging family duration, division was eventually the fate of all families where several parties held rights to the estate jointly. Self-interest and the greater commitment of men to their own wives and children served at one point or another to compromise and then destroy the patterns of sharing and coordination required for the continued successful operation of a large and complex family.

Managerialism, which in China was so much a part of economic and social life, was strongly manifested within the family context. The family head had first to manage the careers of his sons if he hoped to launch his family on a course that would preserve it intact and hopefully enrich it. If the economic struggle was a function of the fluid status system in Chinese society, an individual's impetus to participate in the struggle to a large measure was generated by the pattern of family relationships. The family head's efforts to diversify family economic activities often involved grooming some sons for nonagricultural careers while expecting others to remain on the family farm. Smith (pp. 65–66) gives an example of this diversification process at an early stage when he contrasts boys chosen to receive formal education and therefore allowed to devote their time to study with those from the same families who, destined to follow farming, must give priority to laboring in the fields. Within the family framework there were a variety of occupations possible, involving agriculture, handicrafts, commerce, and a scholarly or official career. The common theme was the constant search for opportunities in as many directions as feasible. With the maturation of sons, their marriage, and their entrance into economic life, the managerial responsibilities of the family head shifted to coordinating his sons' activities for the benefit of the family as a whole, and to preserving and supervising the sharing practices that made the family an economic unit. Earnings usually were given to the family head for safekeeping and for redistribution to family members as needed. His position within the family and his own interests made the father the most appropriate person to carry out this managerial role. Formally, there was nothing to lead a father into closer alignment with one son as opposed to the others, and in any event his interest in preventing a family breakup would encourage him to act in such a way that inequities in the distribution of family resources would not appear. Family management could be transferred to another party as a result of the father's incapacitation, advancing age, or death. His wife, if competent, might take over; more often, one of the sons became the new family head. Such a man was in a difficult situation; he had to reconcile his commitment to the welfare of himself, his wife, and his children with his role as manager of the larger family's economy and custodian of its finances. Often, such conflicts of interest were irreconcilable and led to family division.

Although the ethnographic portion of this volume ends with a description and discussion of "family disunity," Smith includes patterns of conflict extending beyond the confines of individual families. Conflict forms an important theme throughout the book, and within this general category a distinction can be drawn between those conflicts that in a sense were aspects of the social system, and those that took the form of an assault upon the system itself. With respect to the former type, there were present institutions and procedures for conflict resolution. Smith repeatedly refers to the county office (*xian yamen*) in its capacity as a court of law presided over by the county magistrate and to the omnipresent "peace-talkers" who helped settle disputes within local communities.

The utility of these and similar institutions was not evident in all cases of conflict, however, for even when Chinese society as a whole was in reasonably good working order, certain individuals and groups stood in varying degrees of opposition to the system itself. Among those at the periphery were many of the "village bullies" described by Smith (chapter 20). For the poor and landless, violence, or the threat of violence, was clearly one means, albeit risky, of survival within a community. In ordinary times, persons undertaking such a course of action would require a certain degree of aggressiveness, stamina, and courage. Another option would be to accept the minimal economic support and social recognition that within a local community was available to the poorest class. But local communities were able to tolerate only a limited number of "bullies" and would be willing to provide the margin of survival to only so many of the landless and destitute. When these swelled in number and were pushed beyond the limits of the communities' endurance, they were not all able to become "bullies," and probably did not desire to do so; however, they could and often did seek through violent means to relieve their plight.

It is undoubtedly true that China as a whole was at a stage of crisis when Smith made his observations, yet Smith is probably least reliable with respect to his evaluation of the scope and nature of China's difficulties. The source of his unreliability is revealed in the book's last chapter, where Smith, a dedicated missionary, expresses his hope that there will emerge in China a version of his own religion and society. By idealizing his own tradition, he distorts the reality of China's. In this light Smith's sometimes very disparaging remarks regarding various aspects of Chinese civilization and society, especially the intellectual tradition and the character of village and family life, can be appreciated. Smith thought he had the solution to China's problems; in many cases, however, his solutions define the problems rather than the reverse. It must also be remembered that Smith's very presence in China and the special "extraterritorial" privileges he enjoyed were the result of the humiliating treaties inflicted upon the Qing government by the Western powers. Smith was as much a product of Western society as were the soldiers, businessmen, and politicians who had brought China to her knees during a period of Western commercial and colonial expansion. We should not be surprised, therefore, to find Smith, like many other Westerners, expressing the often-contemptuous attitudes of a conqueror. But it was not only some Western imperialists who showed such contempt, for when Smith was making his observations, a particular form of nationalism was beginning to emerge among China's new modernizing intellectual and political elites. These elites (whose attitudes are discussed in greater detail in the following two chapters) held that China's weakness in the face of Western (and Japanese) aggression could largely be attributed to the characteristics of Chinese culture, so they could hardly disagree with Smith's statement that "To infer from any phenomena of Chinese life that the Chinese do not need a radical readjustment of their relations is to judge most superficially" (p. 269).

The "radical readjustment" indeed occurred, and within an ideological framework largely of Western origin, to be sure, but hardly the one proposed by Smith. It may be that Smith's perception of China's difficulties was informed by an acute awareness of that country's vulnerability to internal and external threats, for which it continued to suffer dearly during the half-century following the original publication of *Village Life in China*. In any event, China, no longer so vulnerable, stands once again as a cohesive society of subcontinental proportions, while it still remains the nation boasting the world's largest population. I suspect this feat of integration has been facilitated by the heritage of unity about which *Village Life in China* provides such precious information.

CHAPTER TWO

Being Chinese

The Peripheralization of Traditional Identity

Embedded in China's late imperial culture was a representation of that country's social and political arrangements so strongly developed as to convey to the Chinese people a firm sense of their involvement in them. Indeed, China's society and polity were represented as dimensions of the cosmos itself. Being civilized, that is, being Chinese, was nothing less than proper human behavior in accordance with cosmic principles. It therefore is ironic, and for much of the Chinese people problematic, that the modern Chinese nationalism articulated since the beginning of the twentieth century by China's new elite has involved a forceful and near-total rejection of the earlier traditional and culturally elaborated sense of nationhood. Those who today identify themselves as Chinese do so without the cultural support provided by tradition. Some, having rejected that tradition, are unable to replace it with an alternative cultural arrangement for a nationalism that provides a satisfactory form of identification. The vast majority of China's population neither rejected tradition nor saw it as incompatible either with modern nationalism or with national modernization. Yet this majority has seen its traditional forms of identification with the nation derided as backward and actively suppressed by China's modern political and intellectual elites, whose views on other matters range from the left to the right of the political spectrum. China's traditional elites were cultural brokers, for their high status in society was based upon nationally accepted standards that were also validated by local culture. In contrast, the pronounced cultural antagonism separating the new elite from the masses has represented a barrier between state and society, one hardly conducive to the construction of a form of modern nationalism that would engage, reinterpret, and derive support from the traditional consciousness of national identity. In recent years there are signs of a reemerging cultural consensus, involving elements deriving from late imperial culture as well as new cultural patterns, some linked to the appearance of a mass-oriented consumer society. But it remains to be seen if or how these new elements in Chinese culture will be used to bridge the gap between ordinary people and the state.

Common Culture and National Identity

In late imperial times there was in China a common culture based upon shared behaviors, institutions, and beliefs. The existence of a common culture requires only the geographic distribution of certain traits in a way that defines what earlier generations of anthropologists called a "culture area," but China's common culture was also a unified culture in the sense that it provided standards according to which people identified themselves as Chinese. Taking this Han or ethnic Chinese culture as a whole, there can be no doubt that the historical trend in premodern times was toward increasing uniformity. By the end of the imperial era the Han Chinese had hardly attained a state of total homogeneity, but the extent to which the Han Chinese shared a common culture was considerable in comparison with many traditional empires or states, and all the more impressive given the size of the Chinese empire and the very small proportion of non-Han within it.

Diffusion and acculturation account for much of the replication of many aspects of social organization, economic behavior, and religious ritual and belief throughout the Han population. Some of this diffusion was brought about simply by migrations, there being some very large-scale population movements even as late as the Ming and Qing dynasties. In many cases Han Chinese immigrants simply swamped earlier settlements, while in others Han Chinese of varying social backgrounds gained the upper hand when interacting with natives. Their agriculture was far more productive than the slash-and-burn cultivation often encountered in the south, for example. Again, the entrepreneurial orientation built into traditional Chinese family organization could facilitate Han economic dominance and thereby form the basis for the emergence of a Han local elite that would transform local culture. The Chinese imperial state played a paradoxical role in these migrations. When it was strong it controlled regions extending far beyond areas where large Han populations already were in place, and therefore provided a security umbrella for Han movement toward the frontiers. When the state was weak or divided the resulting wars and chaos also drove large numbers of refugees to seek new homes in distant regions.

Although China is often described as having been unified despite its significant linguistic diversity, I am more impressed by the fact that in late imperial times perhaps two-thirds or more of the Han Chinese population used as their native tongue a variant of Mandarin. Among the Han, extreme linguistic heterogeneity was mainly characteristic of the southeastern coastal provinces in an arc extending roughly from Shanghai through Guangdong and into Guangxi. Furthermore, "Mandarin," known in China during Qing and earlier as the "official language" (*guanhua*) because it served as the imperial bureaucracy's lingua franca, was in fact the basis of a nationwide *written* vernacular used in novels, some operas, and certain ritual texts recited during rural and urban ceremonies of popular religion.[1] This was linguistic unity at a high level, facilitated by the descent of later forms of spoken Chinese from a common earlier language; by the educated elite's use of a common script and an elaborated style of classical writing that in a simpler version was widely employed in business contracts and other everyday documents; and by the widespread circulation of printed texts representing all prevalent writing styles. Printed texts conveyed much information that was absorbed into popular lore; they also served as vehicles for the transmission of opera and other performances that portrayed a history of China, which also described its current polity and society.[2]

On the basis of my own field research in four widely separated Chinese villages, I can confirm that even where differences in spoken language were most obvious, the Han Chinese shared traits so numerous as to readily place them in a culture area easily distinguished from those of nearby state civilizations in Asia. My earliest fieldwork, in the 1960s, was in the southern part of subtropical Taiwan. During 1986 and 1987 I carried out field research in the northern province of Hebei, notable for its long, cold winters. My final stint of long-term fieldwork was when I divided the first half of 1990 between research in villages in east and west China, one near Shanghai and the other on the Chengdu Plain of Sichuan Province. These villages are thus found in what were the northern, southern, eastern, and western regions of agrarian China during late imperial times. If considered as they were before the changes they have undergone in the past fifty years or so, they provide evidence in the form of near-total identity that key features of family organization were common to Han society throughout China. These include a patrilineally oriented and male-centered arrangement of marriage, authority, and social and economic roles that reflected the family's character as being as much an enterprise as a domestic group. Among the characteristic roles were those of family head (*jiazhang*)—the senior male and the family's formal representative to the outside world—and family manager (*dangjia*), in charge of family work and earnings. Although there was a clear social distinction between these two roles, in small families the father would fulfill both. As he advanced in age and his family size increased, the position of family manager was frequently taken over by one of his sons. Brothers had equal rights to family property, the dominant form of ownership, but they were also obligated to pool their earnings as long as the family remained intact. The distribution of this property among them was a key element in family division (*fenjia*), which also involved the setting up of separate kitchens for each of the new and now economically independent families. The four villages also amply confirm that other features already generally noted as characteristic of late imperial China were indeed embedded in village life. There was a high degree of premodern commercialization and commoditization; land was commonly bought, sold, and mortgaged, and contracts, written and oral, played an important role in village life. It was in this context that families and the family farm were distinctly entrepreneurial and market-oriented to the extent permitted by their resources. Contracts even entered into intimate family relationships and conflicts, as in the businesslike partition documents that were signed by brothers about to form separate households. (See chapter 9 for more on contracts in one rural community during late imperial times.)

Among the more obvious of the other factors behind the spread and reproduction of Han culture across China was the state's ability to define a national elite through an examination system requiring the mastery of a standard curriculum. These examinations both generated candidates for the bureaucracy and created an even larger class of degree holders whose status gave them positions of influence in their home communities at the same time that it confirmed their social equality with the bureaucrats. Cultural integration was also fostered by China's well-developed traditional economy, which has long linked large regions in marketing arrangements, supported a high degree of urbanization, and involved large-scale circulation of merchants and commodities. Like the examination system, the economy provided a means to validate local elite status through participation in wide-ranging extralocal relationships.

The question remains as to how the participation of elites in a national culture led to this culture's deep penetration into local society. It has been suggested that a key element in China's unified culture was acceptance of particular standardized rituals.[3] Through participation in such rituals one was Chinese, that is, civilized. The use of ritual to validate cultural status is indicative of the Chinese focus on proper behavior rather than on proper ideas, on orthopraxy rather than orthodoxy. Although correct ideology was hardly insignificant for the state and for the scholarly elite,[4] there can be no doubt that ritual, or *li*, loomed very large in Confucian thinking, and it was a major concern of the Master himself. From the elite Confucian (or later neo-Confucian) perspective, *li* was indeed a civilizing force. The term referred both to ritual and to proper behavior, and in the latter sense it can most appropriately be translated as "etiquette." By late imperial times both the term and its different referents had been fully absorbed into the vocabulary and thinking of ordinary people throughout China.

Ritual and etiquette are very different kinds of behavior. Ritual behavior is distinct from that of daily life and involves actions held to be instrumental either on the basis of the particular theory, goals, or beliefs linked to the ritual itself, or simply as confirmation that the ritual is being properly performed. Etiquette, on the other hand, is precisely the regulation of everyday behavior according to standards accepted as proper. From the point of view of state Confucianism there was a strong emphasis on etiquette as well as ritual, for in the final analysis both were held to be based upon ethics and also to be means of inculcating ethics, and such ethics were themselves validated as being elements of a total, morally good cosmic order. It was as important that filial piety, for example, receive proper expression during a funeral as it was for children to demonstrate filial piety by respecting their living parents. Indeed, the Chinese term *xiao* means both "filiality" and "mourning." Thus proper morality meant full adherence to *li* in all senses of the term. Moreover, it was understood that not everyone could live fully in accordance with these standards, and that those most able to do so would serve as exemplars for the rest of society.

It may be difficult to judge the extent to which China's scholarly elite, who understood the state Confucian theory of *li*, related it to their style of life. Nevertheless, there is little doubt that in late imperial China there was an impressively homogeneous elite lifestyle involving, among many other things, classical learning, avoidance of physical labor, styles of dress and home furnishings, decorous behavior, and full adherence to *li* as ritual. The elite population was distributed throughout China and it spanned the divides between commercial wealth, landholding, and status based on the possession of an examination degree. This elite has long since passed from the scene, which may be why, in much of the anthropological literature, its local impact on culture and society tends to be underestimated, and in some cases ignored altogether. To the extent that late imperial Chinese culture survived to come under the scrutiny of anthropologists and other fieldworkers—especially in China before 1950 and in Taiwan and Hong Kong even into the late 1960s—it is a culture stripped of its elite component and that tells only part of the story. Yet among the now-departed elite, the learned and the wealthy in the cities and in the countryside alike, the *li* of etiquette and the *li* of ritual were as one.

Ordinary people had neither the leisure nor the financial wherewithal to live in full accordance with the standards of *li* as etiquette. For most of them, however, *li* as ritual certainly was in their grasp. Ritual has a beginning and an end, and the most important life-cycle rituals did not occur with great frequency in any one family. They were indeed expensive, but it appears that in any region a particular ritual was available in packages of varying cost, such as one-, two-, or three-day funerals; or—in Hebei—one- or two-palanquin weddings. Again, throughout China guests invited to the feasts invariably accompanying such rituals would make cash contributions that often helped subsidize these events. In any case, the differences between rituals related more to their scale than to the presence or absence of key elements. As Evelyn Rawski has shown,[5] the same basic ritual ingredients were present in the funerals of emperors and ordinary farmers. Furthermore, such rituals were expensive for villagers precisely because they represented the closest approximation to elite standards of *li* such people could manage. Thus in much of China the use of palanquins by bride and groom was common to both elite and ordinary weddings. For most people this was purely a ritual vehicle, while for the elite its use was merely one element in the etiquette that generally governed their lives. Again, even among farmers the formal wedding attire of bride and groom was based upon elite versions; the groom, especially, wore a formal gown of the kind that a member of the elite might wear under a great variety of circumstances. The food consumed by ordinary villagers during the banquets associated with weddings, funerals, and festivals was a far cry from their usual fare, and to varying degrees it approximated ritual and nonritual elite culinary standards.

Rituals firmly linked China's common people to a national culture through their emulation of local elites. This process was facilitated by the local-level social mobility that by late imperial times was institutionalized in many different ways, as through partible succession to family property, the pronounced commodification of land and other valued goods, the examination system, and the strong deemphasis of hereditary status discrimination implied by all of these. As to the elites, even those living in rural communities were immersed in much larger social networks based on marriage, commercial ties, the examination system, and many other elements. The social universe of the elite was united by a culture largely colored by both etiquette and ritual precisely because involvement in that culture had to be based primarily on norms recognized and accepted in China as a whole.

Despite the operation in China of strong forces making for cultural unity, there remained readily apparent differences in language and custom. In recent years among anthropologists there has been a reawakening of interest in such regional differences in Chinese culture, or, indeed, in Chinese regional cultures. One source of variation pointed to with increasing frequency is the absorption of elements from earlier native cultures.[6] There can be no doubt that aboriginal traits have entered into Chinese culture, and that at one time or another this has occurred everywhere in the country, with the Han Chinese being the product of a fusion of cultural elements. Variations, however, are not explained by asserting or even demonstrating the aboriginal roots of the Han Chinese, for this begs the question of why some such traits made it into the Han mainstream (or even into Han tributaries) while others fell by the wayside. Another problem is that not all variation can be attributed to particular aboriginal influences. Under circumstances of premodern communications it is almost inevitable that variations will develop, given that rural populations generally remain rooted in their locales for long periods of time. In his original study of marketing in rural China, G. William Skinner proposed that the "standard marketing community" was a kind of semiencapsulated catchment area within which a particular localism might emerge and differentiate the marketing community even from the one next door.[7] Certainly villagers I spoke with in Hebei during 1986 and 1987 could readily note how their marriage customs differed from those of nearby communities, with which they in fact had marriage ties; they seemed to thoroughly enjoy describing how these differences had to be reconciled when marriages were negotiated. Earlier, I encountered precisely the same situation in Taiwan, where the residents of the southern-most Hakka villages on the Pingdong [Pingtung] Plain married in ways somewhat different from people in Hakka villages less than twenty miles to the north, so that compromises had to be made to allow the frequent marriages between those who lived in these two areas.

Whatever their origins, there were many regional variations in Chinese culture far more pronounced than those just noted, and these were reflected in the four villages where I have worked. The south Taiwan village was a Hakka-speaking community and, as among the vast majority of Hakka, female footbinding had never been practiced. In each of the other villages, by contrast, such footbinding had been almost universal, so that these villages were fully representative of what had been the dominant Han pattern in late imperial times. Although the practice and especially the distribution of footbinding have yet to be given the full scholarly attention they merit, this custom would appear to have been firmly established throughout much of urban and rural China during the Qing dynasty.[8] In late imperial times absence of footbinding was characteristic of Hakka speakers living in southern Taiwan, who overwhelmingly traced their descent from mainland China ancestors who came from the northern Guangdong Hakka heartland, especially present-day Mei and Jiaoling counties. However, during the imperial period footbinding had begun to be practiced by at least some elite families in these counties and among Hakka speakers in adjoining areas of Fujian, especially the bigger cities there, suggesting that the oft-noted Hakka nonindulgence in this habit might reflect the fact that the Hakka regions were just beginning to assimilate a cultural element that had been spreading in China through a centuries-long process of diffusion. Footbinding among the Cantonese also seems to have been restricted to the elite, but it was nevertheless practiced far more widely than among the Hakka. The Cantonese therefore lent credence to the otherwise erroneous but widespread Western notion that this was an upper-class custom only. In much of China only socially marginal women such as unmarried servants had natural feet, and if for no other reason mothers would bind their daughters' feet to ensure their eligibility for marriage. In most areas where footbinding was practiced it was forced upon women as being as essential a manifestation of "proper" or "civilized" status as was a ritually correct marriage or funeral. In these areas, in other words, a woman's being Chinese required that she have bound feet. Thus if some of the rituals and practices associated with being Chinese were in fact found throughout the Han population, others may have had a more limited distribution. The consciousness of being Chinese, therefore, can be distinguished from specific attributes associated with that state of being in any particular region.

Following along lines suggested by Skinner, we might usefully consider the extent to which the generation or preservation of differences was the flip side of the creation of uniformities in late imperial Chinese culture. Anthropologists, after all, have long been interested in how particular groups actively construct (or at least manipulate) their cultural milieu in order in some cases to assert their unique identity and in others to create claims for acceptance within a larger group. That differentiation and integration may occur concurrently, especially in complex societies, should hardly come as a surprise. This, of course, is what the "ethnic" factor in American politics is all about. In China, differentiation was encouraged by the fact that local communities (however defined and at whatever scale of organization) had their own parochial interests to consider. Such interests could be protected or advanced by local elites, community defense organizations, and by many other means, while a major focus of community religion was the enhancement of local welfare.

Place of origin was one of the major ascribed statuses in Chinese society.[9] Common place of origin served as the basis of organization for merchants and others away from home, and such people were expected to contribute to the welfare of their native communities should they succeed on the outside. In general there was, among the Chinese, a deep and very sentimental attachment to the localisms—whether customs, food, or local products—of their home communities. Furthermore, it was well understood and accepted by the Chinese state that each district had its own customs, descriptions of which were standard entries in officially authorized local gazetteers. At all levels of society, and among those serving or representing the state, it was considered that one dimension of being Chinese was to have a place of origin somewhere in China. It was therefore as important for a region to have its own personality as it was for it to manifest its Chinese character. Regional differences, whatever their origin, were not as such discouraged by the state's local representatives. Although efforts were made to eliminate local behaviors considered uncivilized or heterodox, it was not the aim of the state to impose total conformity, precisely because the only available model for such conformity was the national elite culture that commoners were not expected to be able to emulate.

It is therefore clear that the state's co-optation of localisms or regional practices went much deeper than I have suggested above. Once a community—generally at a scale of local organization well above the village level—had an established local elite conforming to China-wide standards of etiquette and ritual, the stage was set for the reinterpretation of many local practices as Chinese. Almost by definition, this local elite would be involved in the examinations, in the classical education they required, and in commercial, social, and political relationships extending well beyond the community. It would be or would develop into a native elite, with a gradual turnover in membership resulting from the operation of the Chinese institutions that made upward or downward social mobility almost inevitable. Social mobility, as well as the hope for upward mobility, would be factors encouraging cultural interchange between the elite and ordinary people. In conjunction with the development of this elite many local customs would disappear, some deliberately suppressed and others falling by the wayside. There would also be a massive penetration of Han cultural traits, a process that might very well have been under way prior to the appearance of such a local elite and that may have facilitated the latter's development.[10] The area would thus experience the evolution of a syncretic culture to a point that it became acceptably Chinese. One important sign of such a local culture's acceptance would be the transformation of some surviving (or invented) local traits into the identifiers used by the local elite to glorify their place of origin within China. Rather than being covered up, acceptable localisms were incorporated by the state and the elite into Chinese cosmopolitanism.

The Bai or Minjia people who live in the southwestern province of Yunnan provide an excellent example of this process. The Bai became anthropologically famous as the subjects of Francis L. K. Hsu's book *Under the Ancestors' Shadow*, a study of a community portrayed as culturally Chinese.[11] The case of the Bai is especially significant because the cultural absorption of their area into China began only after the Ming conquest late in the fourteenth century, yet by the end of the Qing dynasty the transformation of at least some Bai-speaking communities into Han Chinese was well under way—indeed, for most practical purposes, it may have even been completed. In these communities education was based on the same curriculum used elsewhere in late imperial China; the Bai boasted local elites with wide-ranging commercial ties to other parts of the country, and their enthusiastic participation in the examination system receives prominent mention in Hsu's monograph. Although much aboriginal culture had given way to Han practices, the area was still bilingual, a fact perhaps related to the relatively late arrival of the Han and to the presence of a large settled rural population prior to Han penetration. In any event, what was left of Bai culture had by the end of the Qing dynasty been redefined as Chinese local customs, the practice of which was proof of being Chinese. Thus it is not at all surprising that Bai speakers thought their language was a "Chinese dialect."

A remarkable feature of late imperial Chinese culture was that it linked being Chinese to a firm consciousness of participating in a nationwide system of political, social, religious, and symbolic relationships, with even localisms being transformed into statements of such relationships. The power of the imperial state received direct cultural confirmation in many ways. During the Qing dynasty the subordination of the Chinese people to this state was given blatant expression by near-total compliance with the requirement that all men adopt the Manchu tonsure, shaving their foreheads and arranging what was left of their hair in a queue.[12] Even though rejection of this requirement was thus made an easy symbol of rebellion, by the end of the dynasty this hairstyle had become a more general signifier of being Chinese, as evidenced by the reluctance of many men to change it after the dynasty fell. Another example of submission to state hegemony is the equally ubiquitous use of imperial reign titles, which served to identify years in the Chinese system of dates. As they were everywhere else in China, dates were indicated in this fashion in southern Taiwan. I know from copies of old contracts and account books in my possession that in many cases the reign years continued to be used during the first five years or so of the Japanese occupation of Taiwan, which began in 1895, and that it was only after about seven or eight years that the transition from the Qing Guangxu to the Japanese Meiji reign period was complete. This Taiwan example also indicates that the use of reign titles was a more general statement of being Chinese.

Few Chinese if any did not know about the examination system, which generated the country's degree-holding local elite and provided candidates for its bureaucracy. Degree holders were ubiquitous in city and countryside alike, and if no degree holder resided in a particular village there certainly would be some nearby. Although the examinations hardly presented realistic opportunities for social advancement for the majority of China's population, examination system lore deeply penetrated popular thinking. In many parts of China it was customary for a midwife, having delivered a village woman's son, to express the hope that he would obtain the highest rank (*zhuangyuan*) the system had to offer.

China-wide links were embedded in the symbols of the ancestral cult, as in the use of "hall names" (*tanghao*) linking surnames to places of origin in the old north China heartland of the Han, or in the identification of prominent figures in Chinese history or myth as founding ancestors. Even variations in language could be described in terms pointing to links between regional and national identification. In the rural area of Sichuan where I did my fieldwork, the local form of Sichuanese (itself a Mandarin dialect) was contrasted with that spoken in Chengdu, the provincial seat about fifty miles away, and with the traditional standard Mandarin largely based on the dialect of Beijing, the capital both during Qing times and at present. The speech of Chengdu was known as the "little official language" (*xiao guanhua*), that of Beijing as the "big official language" (*da guanhua*).

The gods of popular religion, in their relationships to one another and to mortals, identified local communities with the organization of the Chinese state and the cosmos. The Jade Emperor, as the supreme ruler of the universe, represented a personified version of the abstract Heaven worshiped by the living emperor, but he was also seen to be the latter's divine equivalent. In the Jade Emperor's court were the major gods and goddesses of the Chinese popular pantheon. In his supernatural bureaucracy the City Gods and other tutelary deities carried out their duties on earth, each with jurisdiction over a particular area. In the underworld, the ten magistrates of hell judged and punished the dead in courts that were images of the offices (yamen) where mortal bureaucrats carried out their work. Heaven, earth, and the underworld were united in an arrangement modeled on that of the human imperial order.

Popular images of the Jade Emperor and his bureaucracy on earth and in the underworld appear to have been relatively standardized throughout China. This standardization was encouraged and promoted by the state and represented one aspect of its deep involvement in popular religion. City God temples, for example, were focal points of this religion; yet they also were official, and it was required that at each administrative seat such a temple be constructed, together with those dedicated to Confucius and Guan Yu, the patrons of the civil and military wings of the bureaucracy and the degree-holding class in general. Perceptions of the Jade Emperor's court varied, however, precisely because different communities and regions placed their own particular patron deities and other local gods in positions of prominence, thus linking the religious representation of local society to the larger cosmic system. The court—be it divine or in

Beijing—was an arrangement of personal relationships and thus a most appropriate source of protection for the individual or the community. The gods of the divine bureaucracy and court represented a major component of the supernatural entities and forces constituting Chinese popular religion; ordinary people were in constant contact with these gods, so that involved in their religious beliefs was an intimate image of the Chinese state, one far closer to home than was the actual government of mortals.[13]

Consciousness of being a full participant in the total political, cultural, and social arrangements of the Chinese state and Chinese civilization was what being Chinese was all about. The symbols, rituals, and lore evoking this consciousness were embedded in local culture, so that being a complete person by local standards was also being Chinese. This late imperial Chinese consciousness was reinforced by a cultural system that both defined the cosmos and monopolized perception of it. The natural, the supernatural, society, the state, and the universe were subsumed within a total cosmic plan that left little if anything unaccounted for. It is no wonder that those who because of poverty or for other reasons were unable to live or to succeed in accordance with local standards could be attracted to various "heterodox" beliefs, and that many of these beliefs implied rejection not only of locally dominant sentiments, but also of the larger cultural design that made proper people Chinese.[14] Similar reactions were to be forthcoming from the new elites of the late nineteenth and early twentieth centuries, for whom the cultural and social arrangements of the late imperial period likewise provided little or no comfort.

Anticulture and Nationalism

The very fact that for elite and ordinary people alike being properly Chinese involved acceptance of an all-encompassing cultural arrangement led to a major crisis in self-identification, occurring first among the bureaucratic and scholarly elite during the onset of the Western powers' assault on China in the nineteenth century. For increasingly large numbers of people Chinese culture simply did not work; since this culture conveyed a China-centered definition of the cosmos rooted in China's own history, it had little relevance to the unprecedented conditions created by Western domination and the large-scale introduction of new technology, institutions, and ideas. For those most immediately involved in these novel circumstances, such as students in the new schools, treaty port merchants and workers, and many others, the cultural crisis was acute. Many must have felt that they were living in a cultural vacuum that could only be filled both by the creation of a new cultural design and by a redefinition of being Chinese.

These were the conditions leading to the emergence of the cultural realignments and cleavages that have remained characteristic of modern Chinese society. The new definition of being Chinese is firmly rooted in nationalism, in a conception of China as a nation-state with interests that must be protected and advanced in competition with those of other nation-states. Modern Chinese nationalism is hardly an ultimately cosmic orientation, as was the traditional sense of Chinese national identity which placed China at the center of the universe. The emergence and growth of modern nationalism rather was prompted by the conviction that China was weak, and indeed in many ways inferior to other nation-states. One of the original slogans of this new nationalism, that China must become "prosperous and strong" (*fuqiang*), is still commonly associated with Chinese nationalist sentiment today. The new Chinese nationalism was not at all defined within a larger cultural framework. In this respect it was also very different from the earlier form of Chinese identification, and also unlike many versions of the Western nationalism that precipitated the new Chinese national orientation. This meant that Chinese nationalism could spread across the widening cultural divide separating traditionalists—who even at the time of the Communist victory still constituted the vast majority of the rural and urban populations—from those involved one way or another in the modernizing sectors of society. Chinese of varying cultural inclinations could identify with the increasingly common anti-imperialist and antiforeign movements of the early twentieth century. In more recent years, China's successes in science, sports, warfare, and other endeavors have been as much a source of pride for ordinary farmers as for nontraditional urban intellectuals.

Among these intellectuals and some other segments of the population, however, there emerged and continues to thrive an important connection precisely between nationalism and an at times almost ferociously iconoclastic antitraditionalism. Although perhaps anticipated by the mid-nineteenth-century Taiping Rebellion and beginning to develop during the final years of the Qing dynasty, nationalistic antitraditionalism received its first forceful expression during the May Fourth Movement that exploded in 1919. One extreme but nevertheless instructive example of the antitraditionalism of the May Fourth era is Qian Xuantong's letter to Chen

Duxiu, who later would be one of the founders of the Chinese Communist Party. The letter reads in part as follows:

Dear Mr. Chen:

In an earlier essay of yours, you strongly advocated the abolition of Confucianism. Concerning this proposal of yours, I think that it is now the only way to save China. But, upon reading it, I have thought of one thing more: If you want to abolish Confucianism, then you must first abolish the Chinese language; if you want to get rid of the average person's childish, uncivilized, obstinate way of thinking, then it is all the more essential that you first abolish the Chinese language.[15]

Qian went on to suggest that the Chinese language be replaced by Esperanto in order to save the country. He appears hardly to have been concerned with the extent to which his program might be supported by China's masses, since in his view they were the problem.

With the Communist victory and the establishment of the People's Republic in 1949, nationalistic antitraditionalism achieved unprecedented dominance, with its best-known and most extreme expression during the severely iconoclastic Cultural Revolution (1966–76). Yet this orientation has been common to Nationalists, Communists, warlords, intellectuals, and other political groups and movers who have been prominent in modern China and have often fought for control of the country. The Nationalists, for example, began their "Superstition Destruction Movement" in 1928–29 and sponsored organizations that were to oversee the elimination of the gods and temples of popular religion.[16] Iconoclastic nationalism sees China's tradition to be the source of its weakness. This nationalism provided China's modern political and military elites and its intelligentsia with ideological underpinning for their cultural remoteness from the much larger traditional sector of the population. Other state elites, such as Japan's, have fed their nationalism by embracing their tradition or indeed inventing a glorious version of it. The Chinese invention, backed by the state and by elites who in many cases may otherwise have been hostile to their government, has been rather different. This invention is "feudalism": traditional culture defined as totally unacceptable. The very logic of this form of Chinese nationalism, based as it is on rejection of the past, impels its adherents into a search for a cultural construction that must be totally new but must also work, a search that continues to this day.

One such construction, blending iconoclastic nationalism and Marxism-Leninism and enforced as state ideology, has proved unable, in the

People's Republic, to provide an alternative to local, albeit changing, versions of the traditional culture. As anyone who has done fieldwork in rural China knows, traditional but sometimes modified religious practices remain very much alive, although their scale and the frequency of their performance are strongly conditioned by the local and national political climate. As noted above, however, nationalism has indeed taken hold. On the basis of my own fieldwork in China, it appears to me that this nationalism involves a single-stranded tie between the individual Chinese and his or her country, and is amazingly devoid of elaborated cultural content.[17] The modern national holidays, for example, have little cultural meaning and elicit no special behavior whatsoever except for that arranged by local cadres. The contrast with the lunar New Year and other traditional festivals could not be greater.

I see no necessary contradiction between a consciousness of national identification grounded in an elaborate cultural construction and a more recently developed nationalistic consciousness. In many parts of the world, modification of the former and its linkage with the latter have been employed by elites to mold a powerful and deeply penetrating nationalism used to mobilize the population—for better or worse. That such a fusion has not been involved in the creation of modern Chinese nationalism might be viewed with relief in light of the uses to which some variants of state-cultural nationalism have been put in modern times.[18] On the other hand, that in contemporary China rulers interact with those whom they rule in the absence of an elaborated shared cultural framework has had particular consequences. Traditional culture, in its entirety "feudal" and "superstitious," has presented no constraints whatsoever with respect to the policies that China's rulers have implemented, although the goals of such policies have not always been successfully realized.

A case in point would be religion. Religion has come under the strongest pressure from the state, which at times has resorted to general persecution, as during the now-discredited Cultural Revolution. In more recent times the formidable hostility to religion must be viewed in the context of the official distinction between *zongjiao* and *fengjian mixin* (feudal superstition). The former term is usually translated as "religion," and this is eminently appropriate since *zongjiao* is precisely the Chinese pronunciation of the kanji neologism originally invented by Japanese westernizers to translate the term "religion." However, current Chinese usage, especially in the context of "religious freedom," restricts this term to officially recognized "religions" institutionalized in the form of state-organized and state-regulated national associations.[19] All else is feudal superstition (*fengjian*, in its modern meaning of "feudal," is also a term introduced from Japan), and this includes the popular gods of heaven, earth, the underworld, the ancestral cult, the house doorpost, the kitchen stove, and so forth. In other words, what is well known to be the basic traditional religious system of the Chinese people and a major component of the cultural arrangement providing them with national identification is in contemporary China excluded from the domain of officially tolerated religion.

Contemporary state hostility toward Chinese popular religion has been fed by the earlier intellectual antitraditionalism associated with the May Fourth Movement and by Marxism-Leninism. Hostility toward so-called feudal superstitions is hardly confined to ideologically sophisticated and committed Communist Party members, but is also characteristic of urban intellectuals of varying political persuasions living at home or abroad. A similar hostility was also displayed by the Chinese Nationalists when they controlled the mainland and for much of the period following their retreat to Taiwan. The obviously outstanding feature of the religious beliefs and practices attacked as "superstitious" is their embeddedness in the very structure of social life, such as in the family, lineage, or village community. Attacks on "superstitions" represent efforts by those who are cultural outsiders (by birth, self-definition, or both) to control and remake society. These efforts on the part of Communists and non-Communists alike have been undertaken in the context of a hostility so pronounced as to warrant consideration of the entire historical process as cultural warfare. The war of the elite and the Chinese state against popular religion resulted in the stripping from China's cities and countryside of most of the colorful physical manifestations of traditional culture. This assault, involving the destruction or conversion of temples, shrines, ancestral halls, and a wide variety of other structures and monuments having important local cultural significance, began during the final years of the old dynasty and was well under way when China was under Nationalist and warlord rule, but under the Communists it was carried out with unprecedented intensity and thoroughness.[20]

Because political relationships in modern China have had no shared cultural framework they have been largely expressed in the form of naked commands, obeyed because of the formidable state power they represent and irrespective of their consequences, cultural or otherwise. Hegemony in modern China received no commonly accepted legitimization through culture; rather, it was represented by the culture of the barracks, a culture of compliance, slogans, posters, and mobilizations conveying messages and commands rather than meaning. This form of flat, cultureless culture was most emphasized during the various movements or campaigns (*yun-dong*) that were especially characteristic of the first three decades of the Communist era, and perhaps achieved its strongest expression during the Great Leap Forward of 1959–61, in the form of the mess halls that were meant to eliminate family commensalism. Yet during the first thirty years of the People's Republic, the culture of the barracks consistently had been a major theme in the Communist reorganization of economic and social life: factories, stores, and other organizations were often numbered rather than given names, and the basic designation for almost any kind of organization was *danwei*, or "unit," another term derived from Japan and originally used in a military context.

The past two decades, marked by reforms that have seen the retreat of the state from areas of social, economic, and even religious life, have been characterized by the reappearance of cultural diversity. Popular religion has experienced a remarkable revival; some previously hostile intellectuals are now attracted to "tradition" as a source of meaning for their lives, and this religion is now usually tolerated but hardly embraced by the state.[21] A new popular culture—much of it derived from the West, Taiwan, Hong Kong, Japan, or South Korea—also has taken hold; it is expressed in styles of clothing, music, and other consumer elements having little relevance either to state ideology or to a cultural redefinition of Chinese identity.

The state has achieved impressive physical compliance with its directives. However, the absence of cultural links between China's population and its political elites at all levels of government and party organization has led to the ironic consequence that the state has had little or no success in realizing its ideological or cultural goals. After the Communist state spent three decades attacking popular religion, a lessening of state surveillance in this area resulted in its widespread reappearance. The inability of the state to implement deep cultural change had as its cause the alien quality of the new elements it sought to have take hold among China's masses. Furthermore, the period the Communist Party has been in power has been marked by so many policy changes and reversals that there has been no consistency in what the government has tried to have people do or believe. No effort has been made to introduce or negotiate cultural change within a framework of common understandings. Perhaps such negotiation is now impossible, even in the unlikely event that the state would want to participate in it, given the formidable cultural gap that is now apparent to all. Indeed, to the extent that the power-holding elite and ordinary people—at least those in the increasingly prosperous professional and entrepreneurial classes—are beginning to resemble each other it is because both now participate in the new cultural and consumption patterns emerging precisely in the absence of major state interventions, with such patterns having few or no readily apparent implications for Chinese nationalistic sentiments. With the revival of popular religion, another pattern of coparticipation that has emerged is the shared involvement of ordinary people and local government or Communist Party officials in activities such as community rituals or ancestor worship, representing far more the growing identification of these officials with local interests than any trend of accommodation on the part of the government or Communist Party as such.

The possibility that traditional Chinese culture might positively be involved in the creation of a modern national consciousness is more than hypothetical, for Taiwan provides an ironic example of just such a process. On that island the forceful expression of antitraditionalism occurred under circumstances rather different from those of the China mainland. Until seized by Japan, Taiwan had long been part of the Qing state, and its overwhelmingly Han Chinese population largely comprised immigrants from nearby mainland provinces and their descendants. During the period of their colonial rule (1895–1945), the Japanese understood all too well that incorporated into the culture and religion of their subjects was a strong identification with the totality of Chinese society. During World War II, the Japanese authorities, increasingly fearful of the form Taiwanese loyalties might assume, launched an assimilation campaign aimed at ensuring that the island's people stayed on their side. One important component was an assault on popular religion: the destruction of temples, shrines, gods, and other physical manifestations of this religion was on a scale to be surpassed only during the Cultural Revolution on the mainland two decades later. In Taiwan, however, such religious structures were quickly rebuilt after Japan's surrender, when there was a strong revival of popular religious practices. These practices, together with many other traditional elements, increasingly were redefined as identifiers of "being Taiwanese" in the context of the growing hostility between the local population and the mainlander-dominated Nationalist government that had fled to the island by the time of the Communist victory.

It is not surprising that the Nationalist political and intellectual elites who came to Taiwan brought with them an antitraditionalism quite similar to that of their mainland enemies, for they all shared the May Fourth heritage. By the time they reached the island, however, the Nationalists' hostility toward traditional popular religion and culture had assumed more muted forms of expression: restrictions were placed on the frequency and costs of religious celebrations, and these were indeed denounced as superstitious and wasteful, but there was no repetition of the temple busting they had carried out on the mainland. More important was the fact that on Taiwan the lines were drawn differently. With traditionalism transformed into being Taiwanese, the Nationalists lost ideological control; attacks against tradition justified in the May Fourth spirit of "progress" were invariably reinterpreted by those adhering to such traditions as assaults of mainlanders against Taiwanese. In turn, politically active Taiwanese intellectuals became increasingly, and conspicuously, involved in popular religion, even though many had originally been as alienated from traditional beliefs and practices as had mainlanders of similar background. In contrast to its fate on the mainland, traditional Chinese culture on Taiwan was transformed into a modern assertion of national identity, but in this case the identity was Taiwanese and the nationalism was linked to the movement for Taiwan independence. Against this background, the Taiwan government's attitude toward popular religion was transformed. This was dramatized in 1980 when President Chiang Ching-kuo, the government's leader, presented an image of Mazu, one of Taiwan's most important deities, to her major temple on the island.[22] In Taiwan, at least, one legacy of the May Fourth era has finally come to an end. It remains to be seen, however, what effect the legitimization of popular religion will have on the continuing tension between competing Taiwanese and Chinese identities.

On Taiwan and on the mainland, the nationalism that is the common framework for the expression of Chinese identity remains culturally incomplete. For a large proportion of the population in the People's Republic, especially in the countryside, nationalism coexists with a sense of being Chinese still conditioned to varying degrees by traditional orientations. Because these people continue to be told by the state that their traditional outlook is objectionable, the cultural content of their nationalism is sparse indeed. Ironically, it is precisely this culturally impoverished nationalism that facilitates its providing a thin veneer of common identification for traditionalists, nontraditionalists, and antitraditionalists alike. Especially among many of the latter, on the mainland, in Taiwan, and abroad there is the further problem that *being Chinese* is no longer buttressed by a firm sense of cultural participation in *something Chinese*. The result is an ongoing crisis of "identification" that has deeply colored intellectual discourse in China during the twentieth century and that, to this very day, is expressed with an intensity no less than that of the May Fourth era more than eighty years ago. In sum, for much of China's population, being Chinese is culturally much easier today than it ever was in the past, for this identification no longer involves commonly accepted cultural standards. Existentially, however, being Chinese is far more problematic, for now it is as much a quest as it is a condition.

CHAPTER THREE

Cultural and Political Inventions in Modern China

The Case of the Chinese "Peasant"

The gods? Worship them by all means. But if you had only Lord Guan
and the Goddess of Mercy and no peasant association, could you have
overthrown the local tyrants and evil gentry? The gods and goddesses are
indeed miserable objects. You have worshipped them for centuries, and
they have not overthrown a single one of the local tyrants and or evil gentry for you! Now you want to have your rent reduced. Let me ask how
will you go about it? Will you believe in the gods or in the peasant association?

—Mao Zedong, 1927, quoted in MacInnis,
Religious Policy and Practice in Communist China

At the time of Liberation there were many temples in the villages of
northern Jiangsu, such as the Grandma Temple, Fire God Temple, Guandi
Temple, and Temple of the God of Wealth. At the time of land reform [ca.
1950] these were abolished and all superstitious sects and secret societies
were banned. But ideas of ghosts and gods are deeply rooted among the
people, and all kinds of superstitions are rampant. . . . The Yellow Stone
Brigade once had a temple of the "Old Man Yellow Stone." . . . It was destroyed during the War of Liberation. . . . But the place where the temple
had been is still considered to be sacred by the local peasants. . . . A myth
suddenly surfaced in February and March 1979, saying that Old Man
Yellow Stone had returned and would offer treatment to the sick. It is
said that about thirty thousand people came from the local county,
nearby counties, Shandong and Henan provinces, and even riding on mo-
torcycles from Shanghai.

—Field study report, 1983, cited in Luo Zhufeng,
Religion Under Socialism in China

Like the now-defunct Leninist-Stalinist states of central and eastern
Europe, the Chinese Communist government has sought to base its
legitimacy on the creation of a "new" socialist society, one in which a
pervasive and fundamental reorganization of the economy would, of
Marxist necessity, lead to the emergence of a new culture, indeed to the

emergence of a new kind of person. In order to create such a new society, and to supply the justification for its creation, it is also required that the "old" society be defined in such a way as to provide the basis for its thorough rejection. All Communist states have thus faced the enormous burden of two major tasks of cultural construction: there must be both a totally objectionable "old regime" and a new liberated society. Furthermore, the characteristics of the old society have to be formulated in sufficiently convincing detail such that they come to form a meaningful negative image assimilated into the consciousness and cultural outlook of the ordinary person. At the same time, the assertion that there is now a new society must be backed by cultural innovations that take a firm and positive hold among the masses.

Communist states thus have taken upon themselves tasks of cultural creation so comprehensive as to comprise assertions of their cultural infallibility. Yet it is precisely the enormity of Communist cultural ambitions, as backed by the politically enforced monopolization of cultural production at the national level and by the claim to be the sole legitimate source of cultural meaning, that in fact has led Communist states to be revealed as so amazingly culturally impotent. These states have been able to construct impressively well organized arrangements of political and economic control, such that decades of Communist rule certainly have produced changes in many areas of social and cultural life, some linked to the severe disruption of the transmission of religious and other pre-Communist traditions. Therefore, it is all the more obvious and remarkable that their major cultural projects have been such failures. Although China's Communist government remains in power, cultural developments in that country since decollectivization and other reforms were instituted more than two decades ago bear some resemblance to those during the Soviet Union's terminal Gorbachev era and to the circumstances following the collapse of the other Communist regimes in Europe. The Communist states in Europe, China, and elsewhere in Asia demanded of their subjects both compliance and cultural change, and for many observers of Communist societies it sometimes has been difficult to distinguish one from the other. If the energetic and frequently disastrous reemergence of long-dormant ethnic and religious forces in former Communist Europe initially took many observers by surprise, so did, for example, the widespread and increasingly public revival of popular religion in much of China.

But in China the Communist state continues to assert its cultural dominance even though it remains unable to give it viable cultural expression. In China, furthermore, there had already emerged a major crisis of cultural integration and national identity during the century prior to the onset of Communist rule: the Western assault on and penetration of China, the collapse of the old dynasty, the emergence of new urban working and professional classes, and the rise of a new intelligentsia were among the developments linked to the construction of a particularly Chinese style of elite intellectual nationalism that was severely antitraditional and iconoclastic. We saw in the last chapter that by rejecting and condemning the traditional culture of the Chinese masses—even though this culture provided a strong albeit premodern awareness of national identity—the new elite lost an opportunity to participate in the construction of a modern popular nationalism providing elaborated cultural linkages between the individual and the state. In the absence of a successful effort to forge a meaningful and elaborated common cultural framework for the expression of Chinese identity, contemporary China is characterized by an obvious lack of cultural consensus between city and countryside, state and society, intellectuals and the public, and between many of these intellectuals and the state. Such divisions among the population remain even while the new popular culture, increasingly incorporating China's rapidly expanding consumer-oriented economy, is now creating new connections and commonalities in terms of food, clothing style, mobility, household appliances, and the like. If anything, many of these most recent changes tend to position those experiencing them within a framework of a shared East Asian or even global popular culture, and they do not appear to involve significant symbols or statements of Chinese identity as such.[1]

During the early decades of the twentieth century, China's intellectual elites did indeed engage in cultural invention. Increasingly under the influence of Marxism and Marxist categories, both Communists and non-Communists began the construction precisely of an image of the old society that had to be rejected, an image that was to be refined and promoted to cultural orthodoxy after the Communist victory. Key to this image was the redefinition of traditional Chinese culture and of the vast majority, especially in the countryside, who still adhered to it. For the elite, China's rural population was now "backward" and a major obstacle to national development and salvation. For them, rural China was still a "feudal society" of "peasants" who were intellectually and culturally crippled by "superstition."

Through the transformation of "farmers" into "peasants," "tradition" into "feudalism," and "customs" or "religion" into "superstition" there was invented not only the "old society" that had to be supplanted, but also the basic negative criteria designating a new status group, one held *by definition* to be incapable of creative and autonomous participation in China's reconstruction. To be sure, there were variations in the depiction of the peasant condition: as noted by Charles W. Hayford, if in some of the new modern writings the "peasants" were "superstitious, ignorant, and inert," in others "they were no longer to be blamed for China's weakness, but to be pitied as a victim of soluble oppression."[2] Furthermore, a much smaller group of intellectuals had a somewhat more positive view of the cultural circumstances of China's rural inhabitants. Notable examples were the participants in the folklore studies movement of the 1920s, some of the active organizers of rural reconstruction and development projects, such as James Yen and Liang Shu-ming, and anthropologists and sociologists such as Fei Hsiao-tung (Fei Xiaotong), Lin Yuehua, C. K. Yang, and Martin M. C. Yang.[3] For such intellectuals who had worked in villages, especially the anthropologists and sociologists, it was clear that the society, customs, and beliefs they investigated had positive meaning and considerable importance for the rural Chinese.

Except for the anthropologists and sociologists, again, even many of these intellectuals were hostile to village popular religion and encouraged the destruction or conversion of local temples and shrines; they, like the others, hardly appear to have been inclined to view the reconstruction of rural Chinese society and its reintegration into a renewed national cultural framework as a process that would draw upon the existing culture of the countryside. In any event, to the degree that they might sympathize with rural lifeways theirs was the minority view, and the notion of the peasantry as a culturally distinct and alien "other," passive, helpless, unenlightened, in the grip of ugly and fundamentally useless customs, desperately in need of education and cultural reform, and for such improvements in their circumstances totally dependent on the leadership and efforts of rational and informed outsiders, became fixed in the outlook of China's modern intellectual and political elites. For such elites governing China, or seeking to assume power over it, this image of the peasant confirmed their own moral claim to an inherently superior, privileged position in national political life, and their conviction that populism or popular democracy were utterly unacceptable if China was to avoid chaos and achieve national strength.[4] Indeed, such elite sentiments have been aptly characterized as involving a strong strain of antipopulism.[5] Thus

Mao Zedong and other Communist intellectuals were hardly the only ones believing that the physical, political, and economic liberation of the peasantry required its cultural destruction.

Key terms employed in creating a negative perception of China's "peasants" were among the many loanwords from Japanese that entered China in especially great numbers during the late nineteenth and early twentieth centuries, words that have played such an important role in shaping the modern Chinese vocabulary.[6] In addition to "feudal" (*fengjian*), there is *nongmin*, precisely the term usually glossed as "peasant." In some cases (i.e., *fengjian, nongmin*) the Meiji-era Japanese modernizers drew upon classical Chinese texts for the kanji terms they would use in their translations of works from the West, while in others they created their own neologisms. In all cases, however, these terms entered both written and spoken Chinese as "modern" words, inherently abstract and readily available for the assignment of new meaning precisely because they were largely unencumbered by any traditional cultural baggage that might interfere with their use in the context of visions of contemporary China. Although Hayford already has documented the transition from "farmer" to "peasant" in the English-language writings of both Chinese and Western observers of rural China,[7] there was a parallel change in Chinese, with a wide variety of words giving way, perhaps first in intellectual and political discourse, to the categorical *nongmin*.[8]

The conceptual transformation of the population of China's countryside from farmers into peasants was a reversal of the sequence of events involved in Western perceptions and scholarship concerning rural Europe, whose modernization was seen to turn peasants into farmers.[9] In Europe the end of the peasantry was linked to the formation of modern nation-states, and to growing rural-urban ties in the context of industrialization, the modernization of communications and agriculture, and the spread of formal education. In China, however, Western influence and pre-Communist industrialization and modernization had their greatest impact in the cities, especially the major foreign-dominated "treaty ports," such that the effect was the modern creation of the severe rural-urban contrasts that in the Western imagination, as formed by historical experience, are seen to be characteristic of Europe's premodern era. The different Western and Chinese experiences have been well summarized by F. W. Mote:

The idea that the city represents either a distinct style or, more important, a higher level of civilization than the countryside is a cliché of our Western cultural traditions. It has not been so in traditional China. . . . [The] sharp division into distinct urban and rural civilizations disappeared very early in China, although it remained characteristic of much of the rest of the world until recent times and produced distinct urban attitudes in other civilizations. The conditions allowing such attitudes in China seem to have vanished by the beginning of the imperial era, so long ago that a sense of that kind of urban superiority has not remained.

Chinese civilization may be unique in that its word for "peasant" has not been a term of contempt—even though the Chinese idea of a "rustic" may be that of a humorously unsophisticated person.[10]

Whatever the Chinese word for "peasant" that Mote may have had in mind, his observation underscores the significance of the adoption of the new term *nongmin*, precisely in the circumstances of the emergence and deepening of the cultural divide between the new urban-based intelligentsia and China's vast rural hinterland. This divide represented a radical departure from tradition: Mote and others have shown how especially during the later imperial era (Ming and Qing dynasties), China was notable for the cultural, social, political, and economic interpenetration of city and countryside.[11] But the term *nongmin* did enter China in association with Marxist and non-Marxist Western perceptions of the "peasant," thereby putting the full weight of the Western heritage to use in the new and sometimes harshly negative representation of China's rural population. Likewise, with this development Westerners found it all the more "natural" to apply their own historically derived images of the peasant to what they observed or were told in China. The idea of the peasant remains powerfully entrenched in the Western perception of China to this very day. The term is commonly encountered both in journalism and in academic discourse, and even in reference to the contemporary rural scene, which in many areas of the country is characterized by rapidly expanding highway networks, increasingly mechanized and in some cases increasingly prosperous family farms, growing economic diversification, and modernization in many other respects, and by the long-term urban employment of migrants from the rural sector. Yet for many Chinese and Westerners alike, "peasant" has been a purely cultural category since its first appearance in modern China. There were always many "peasants" who were not farmers; the fact that this is increasingly the case does not yet appear to have altered perceptions of the countryside.

The staying power of this idea is at least in part attributable to the powerful reinforcement it has received since the establishment of the Communist government. Incorporated into its official and administrative classification of China's population is the distinction between peasants and other categories of persons, such as "workers" (gongren) or "urban residents" (jumin). Until a little more than two decades ago, there was the further differentiation of the peasantry into "classes," as determined during the land reform campaigns first carried out in areas of the country under Communist control even before their final victory over the Nationalists. On the basis of their pre-Communist economic circumstances villagers were classified as "poor," "middle," or "rich" peasants, or as "landlords," and among the various peasant classes there were further subdivisions. Once assigned, these "class labels" largely remained fixed until the end of the collective era, with a person born after land reform inheriting his or her father's class designation. During the various political campaigns, those with "rich peasant" or "landlord" labels could be subject to public humiliation and condemnation, while the "poor and lower-middle peasants" were defined by the Communist state as the new rural political elite.[12]

Prior to the arrival of the Communists there certainly were wealthy landlords, and many if not most villagers were very poor indeed. But the imposition of class categories on the basis of supposedly objective economic criteria was fundamentally an administrative act. Borderline cases sometimes had their class standing revised after appeal, and those with advantageous kinship or other social ties sometimes received a better class label than they might otherwise have expected. Even though the antilandlord "struggle" sessions encouraged by the land reform cadres working in villages throughout China did in some cases lead to violence and to killings, the fact remains that with the elimination of these class labels, community, economic, and kinship ties once again came to form intricate social networks linking villagers of previously "good" and "bad" class backgrounds. This was quite evident in all three mainland China villages where I have done fieldwork, with social reintegration given public manifestation during occasions such as weddings, birthday celebrations for the aged, funerals, and death anniversaries. Both the rituals and banquets involved in such events were characterized by the easy participation of persons who, during the collective era, would not risk being seen as involved with each other. What has been reported for a village in south China was equally true in the three villages where I have worked: "even the old landlords, now retired, could, for the first time since the land reform of the fifties, casually mingle with other villagers."[13] For most people, the old rural class labels hardly had been productive of culturally deep and meaningful class consciousness, notwithstanding the fact that their imposition did lead to real resentments and antagonisms that have not been easy to forget. Yet these labels—a major factor in the practical affairs of daily life for more than twenty-five years—did provide powerful reinforcement to the idea and reality of the peasantry as an overarching status group comprised of different kinds of peasants.

In terms of these labels, landlords were not peasants. But by 1959, landlords and the various classes of peasants were all peasants—*nongmin*—in contradistinction to "workers" (*gongren*) or "urban residents" (*jumin*), the more inclusive term. This distinction between "peasant" and "urban resident" is inherited through the mother and was originally given legal standing in order to control migration from the countryside to the cities. But even in the far less restrictive social and economic environment of present-day China, it remains in force and is based purely upon household registration. During the collective era being an urban resident provided access to certain commodities at subsidized prices, employment with retirement and medical benefits, and a wide variety of other preferential treatments, and in recent years urban registration status has continued to be highly desirable in light of the better job and educational opportunities associated with it. Being a peasant, therefore, is to be disadvantaged, and the resentment felt by those so registered, and their envy of urban residents, has been widely reported.[14] Peasants in modern China now have second-class citizenship, thus, ironically, giving legal confirmation to the second-class, "backward," culture they earlier had been identified with.

At the same time, the increasingly obvious and economically significant occupational diversity of these statutory peasants has led to some being assigned labels that outside observers might take to be oxymora, such as peasant entrepreneurs, peasant merchants, or peasant businessmen.[15] Many of these "peasants" now live in the cities or in the smaller towns that have been rapidly developing since decollectivization and the other economic reforms of the past two decades. In the course of my fieldwork in still overwhelmingly agricultural villages in Hebei and Sichuan provinces, I noted that most families with farms also had additional income in the form of wage labor or some kind of family enterprise, with the importance of such nonfarm earnings steadily increasing. Furthermore, with the expansion of China's cities, state-owned urban factories and other organizations have been taking up farmland. With such a transfer of land, the organization involved sometimes must agree to hire a certain number of people from the village providing it. This procedure represents one of the very few avenues for status change open to ordinary people, and in the village near Shanghai where I also did field-work it involves entering on the household registration form of the person hired the notation "peasant changed to urban resident" (*nongmin zhuan jumin*) and the date of change.[16] In that village land transfers had reduced village-managed land to only a small fraction of what it had been twenty years earlier, such that by 1990 the majority of villagers had been reclassified as urban residents. Nevertheless, the demand for urban resident status and the associated employment has always been higher than the supply provided by any particular land transfer, so that with each new opportunity care is taken by village leaders to distribute the status transfers on a one-per-family basis. As a result, most village families in 1990 had mixed memberships of "peasants" and "urban residents," at the same time that the majority of those who were still "peasants" worked in village-run factories or ran their own nonagricultural enter-prises.[17]

If the Western heritage played a role in the formation of the Chinese concept of the peasant, that concept in its developed form continues to have an impact on Western scholarship. In Western studies of contempo-rary rural China the term "peasant" is commonly employed, as already noted, but it is rarely defined. Although much of this scholarship resem-bles Chinese usage in that the presence of a peasant category is assumed, it does not usually involve any explicit expression of negative attitude re-garding the beliefs or practices of the so-called peasant. Nevertheless, such writings cannot avoid suggesting that there must be some special at-tributes making peasants different from other kinds of people, although they do not suggest what these are. Titles of books or articles certainly convey a very different impression if "peasant" is replaced by another word, such as "farmer." Note these examples from works published dur-ing the past two decades: "State and Farmer in Contemporary China," "China's Farmers," "The Re-emergence of the Chinese Farmer," "State Intervention and Farmer Opportunities," or "Farmer Household Indi-vidualism." Of course, "farmer" will not do. It hardly suggests the en-counter with a primordial "other" that gives use of the term "peasant" such dramatic punch; it is even functionally inappropriate given precisely the occupational diversity that inevitably forces the "peasant" into a cul-tural mold, the subjective evaluation of which is by default left to others.

More firmly in the Western tradition of the comparative study of rural society is the effort to redefine the peasant in functional terms free of the cultural associations provided by European history. In this context the peasantry is seen to comprise the subsistence-oriented agriculturists of premodern societies, a portion of whose output is skimmed off by overlords in the form of rent, taxes, or tribute. Farmers, in contrast, are produced by modernization and characterized by their involvement in a commercialized, market-oriented economy.[18] The peasantry's production is based on survival requirements and the demands linked to their social and economic status, that of farmers on economic rationality in response to market conditions. But such a distinction hardly does justice to the great variety of agrarian circumstances in the world both today and indeed in many premodern societies. Furthermore it has not succeeded in placing the peasantry in a culturally neutral context. As Polly Hill puts it, "Despite the absurd waste of effort that has gone into attempts in the past fifteen years or more [as of 1986] to qualify *peasant* appropriately, its power to confirm our primitive ideas of an amorphous, undifferentiated mass of tillers of the soil, labouring against overwhelming odds to provide sufficient food for their families, remains undiminished."[19]

Yet the functional approach remains important as far as China is concerned. It is involved in the controversy over whether there was growth or stagnation in the pre-Communist Chinese rural economy during the twentieth century and late imperial times. Those with the more optimistic view take the Chinese agriculturist to be a farmer, a rational economic optimizer in a market context. The pessimistic perspective, however, sees peasants trapped by economic stagnation and struggling to survive under increasingly harsh circumstances.[20] At issue in this debate is not the presence or absence of commercialized agriculture, for all agree that by late imperial times it was widespread. The question, rather, is the extent to which this commercialization involved commodity markets fully open to the participation of the ordinary cultivator. Those involved in this controversy have shifted analysis from peasantry as a category to a focus on the real problems faced by rural Chinese and the means they employed to deal with them. In this sense all agree that those in the countryside were rational actors whose predicament was circumstantial rather than cultural.

Another tradition of analysis moves even further from the Chinese construction of peasant "backwardness" by focusing on those features of late imperial culture and society that may have been assets in China's later modernization. This focus restores a cultural approach, but it is the "economic culture" of late imperial society as a whole; it denies the salience of the peasant-nonpeasant cultural and functional distinctions, thus placing the appraisal of China's heritage for modernization precisely in the late imperial context of rural-urban interpenetration and integration. This approach thus represents a refutation of the entire "peasant, feudalism, feudal superstition" bundle, for it seeks to identify just those cultural advantages brought to bear by the many people of rural background who have made such important contributions to the rapid economic development of Taiwan, Hong Kong, and, more recently, mainland China.

Key to my own approach to Chinese economic culture is the fact that family organization provided the common framework for the ownership, management, and exploitation of the enormous variety of income-producing assets present in what was indeed the highly commercialized economy of late imperial China, especially during the Qing dynasty. The characteristics of the Chinese family system were such that personal and conjugal-unit (*fang*) property was clearly subordinate to that owned by the family (*jia*) as a unit. Brothers held basically equal rights to the family estate, which they would distribute among themselves during family division (*fenjia*)—the procedure whereby a large family with married brothers, their wives, and their children would form separate and independent smaller family units. Thus, it is safe to say that in China, insofar as property was not held by other kinds of corporations, it was overwhelmingly held by families. There was also a cultural distinction between the roles of family head (*jiazhang*), based on seniority and gender, and family manager (*dangjia*), based on competence and also—somewhat less uniformly—on gender. The family economy was characterized by the pooling of income from the earnings of family members and family property, so families commonly adopted strategies of asset diversification and personnel diversification for purposes of sheer survival or, hopefully, to advance their fortunes. Such diversification might for the poor simply mean seeking whatever work outside the family might be available, but often diversification involved the investment by farm families in nonagricultural enterprises such as shops, and the assignment of family members to run then. These well-documented features of family organization are among those that served both to define the family as a corporate economic actor and to position it to deploy whatever resources it had available so at to best succeed in the highly competitive economic environment of late imperial times. My own fieldwork in different areas of mainland China and in Taiwan confirms that historically this common pattern of family organization operated in very diverse geographic, environmental, and economic settings.

The extent to which agriculture was based upon subsistence crops as opposed to those mainly suitable for sale is thus far less relevant to family organization than the more general commodification of assets of many kinds, including land or particular rights to land. The fact that land itself could readily be negotiated through sale, rent, or mortgage is well known. However, it is also a well-documented fact that a single plot of farmland could be defined as two or even three commodities, especially in areas of central and southern China; most common was the distinction between subsoil rights and surface rights, each of which could be independently marketed. Linked to this commodification and contributing to its expression were the availability of credit and the widespread use of contracts and other commercial papers. These were important in the formation of various kinds of corporations: some were based upon share holding and in the countryside these included lineages, religious associations, and many others. Indeed, some of the corporations organized by ordinary villagers paid out per-share dividends, often annually, on the basis of profits realized from rental of corporation land. While the corporations might impose restrictions on the transfer of shares, or ban it entirely, the shares themselves were family property. In any event, some corporations did allow for the sale of shares, which therefore represented yet another kind of commodity. Thus in some cases a corporation's assets included shares in other corporations.[21]

"Commercialization" is a kind of buzzword in much social science literature. As noted, it implies a movement away from a "peasant" subsistence-oriented economy to one in which expanding market relationships tend to break down tight-knit rural communities and turn cultivators into the rational managers of farm enterprises. The term also conveys a sharp distinction between the worlds of agriculture and commerce, with the former largely comprised of intimate social relationships, and the sentiments reinforcing them, while in the latter dealings with strangers play an obviously important role. As far as late imperial China is concerned, the distinction between farming and market-dominated relationships breaks down even within this framework of commercialization, given how Chinese farmers indeed were widely involved in the commercial disposal of their crops. Nevertheless, use of this term in effect assigns to particular cropping patterns what is really an arbitrary cultural significance, perhaps based upon assumed parallels with the Western experience. I suggest that "commodification" far more accurately conveys the economic realities faced by Chinese in and out of farming, and helps explain their culturally easy movement from farming into commerce should other circumstances facilitate it. Such commodification is discussed in chapters 8 and 9 with reference to one community in late imperial China.

An economic and cultural environment where assets were generally commodified spans the divides between subsistence and commercial crops, farms and shops, and cities, towns, and the countryside. Likewise, the diversified activities of individual families could also span these divides, such that it was common for shops and firms to be run by families also owning farms and having some of their members working them. The strategy of diversification of family economic roles and assets was common to ordinary people and traditional elites alike.[22] There was structural equivalence between a very poor rural family in which one brother might work a tiny plot of tenanted land and another was forced to hire out as a worker for other farmers; a somewhat better-off family in which one brother worked the fields they owned or rented while another managed the small family store; and a powerful elite family in which one brother might be an imperial degree holder, another the functional landlord in charge of the family's rural holdings, and yet another in the role of merchant running the family's impressive urban commercial enterprises. The overall commodification of assets provided the cultural context in which a common pattern of organization could characterize families sustaining or attempting to sustain themselves under a great variety of economic circumstances. Being generally commodified, a wide variety of assets could take the form of family property, thus establishing one basic link between marked economic heterogeneity on the one hand and uniformities in family organization on the other. Linked to this commodification was the relative unimportance of hereditary economic and political statuses, such as those that might define serfdom or caste membership in other parts of the preindustrial world. Therefore there was considerable social mobility in late imperial society, such that even for an increasingly prosperous family the almost inevitable occurrence of family division would commonly lead to the impoverishment of later generations, while in the generally risky economic environment of that time a great variety of factors could cause a family's economic ruin. Family strategy might lead to favorable occupational and economic mobility among the family's members, while a family's bad luck might have consequences that were functionally similar but economically disastrous or even fatal. In this context, imposition of the historically burdened Western contrasts of town and country, shopkeeper and peasant or merchant and landlord serves only to distort the realities of the Chinese economic tradition.

All families were enterprises insofar as they strove to obtain or preserve and manage assets that formed the basis of the family estate and to distribute among family members the product of these assets. A traditional focus in the Chinese family, therefore, was on flexible and entrepreneurial management geared to making the best of available family resources and local economic opportunities, hence the importance of the family manager role. With collectivization imposed on the Chinese countryside by 1955, a period of about twenty-five years followed during which the rural population was in effect almost entirely transformed into wage earners for the communes, production brigades, and production teams. During this period the rural family still retained its corporate character, but family property amounted to little more than housing and furnishings, and the scope of the economic activity of family members was almost entirely restricted to that assigned and managed by the collective organizations (see chapter 4). Decollectivization and economic reforms in China during the past two decades have paved the way for the reemergence of a variety of autonomous units in China's economic life. Most notable, especially but not exclusively in the countryside, has been the resurrection of the Chinese family as a major economic actor. China is now fed by the output of millions of family farms. These families, however, once again presented with what might be characterized as relatively open or unencumbered economic and social space, have rapidly expanded into other areas of entrepreneurial activity, contributing to the growing availability of goods and services and helping to give rise to the massive development of the new "small towns" that have received so much attention.[23] Likewise, the development in recent years of a massive "floating population" that is of rural origin but working or seeking work in China's major cities and yet without urban registration status also in part reflects family diversification strategies.[24]

This diversification commonly involves the departure of able-bodied men from the farms, with their wives or daughters staying behind, with the result that there has emerged a so-called feminization of agriculture. At the same time there are also forces at work tending toward the "masculinization" of agriculture in areas of the country, as increasing numbers of young unmarried women work in coastal export-oriented districts, with the young men remaining in their home communities.

An approach to Chinese economic culture emphasizing the family as a corporate unit creating, deploying, and managing its human resources and property in a highly commodified environment in order to provide for family survival or enhance family welfare better explains the continuity between late imperial culture and modern economic trends than does one focusing on the supposed inability of families to adapt to modernization because of their backward peasant status. The importance of the family as an enterprise in the modern economic development of Taiwan, Hong Kong, and, now, the China mainland is with respect to the capitalization and management of family-run firms far different in function, organization, and technology from those characteristic of earlier times. But the attributes of these new economic units are certainly not incompatible either with the tradition of rational management or with that of commodification.

In China, the invented peasant, associated with growing rural-urban differentiation, has given way to the statutory peasant, a result of administrative fiat. But this administrative peasant is now to be found in a context of rapid economic development, especially in some areas of the country, that is blurring the very rural-urban gap that encouraged the birth of the idea of the peasant in the first place. Nevertheless, in China the idea of the peasant as comprising a distinct and backward cultural category shows no sign of losing its force. That China's peasantry is for cultural reasons not fit to participate in political democracy is at least one point on which the country's Communist leaders agree with elites who in other respects form an opposition. These elites include many of those who as students demonstrated at Tiananmen, and certain of the established intellectuals who supported them, some now in exile leading what they call a democracy movement. If, as I have suggested, the creation of the peasant in China was related less to the circumstances, potential, and culture of the country's rural inhabitants and more to an elite antitraditionalism that formed a moral claim to political privilege and power, then it is not at all surprising that Chinese elite attitudes remain consistent.[25] The "peasants" may do what they will, but the real issue is elite conceptions of their own role in China's polity and society.

The Family

CHAPTER FOUR

North China Rural Families

Changes During the Communist Era

C hanges and continuities in family organization were among my major concerns when I began field research in Yangmansa, a farming village in northern China's Hebei Province.[1] It soon became clear to me that under Communist rule family life had hardly undergone total transformation. Rather, as I will show, innovations during the land reform, collective, and postcollective eras have combined with older practices to produce family arrangements that variously express the interests of individuals, married couples, and larger family units as these both adapt to and help shape rapid economic and social change in China.

Yangmansa, a village in Xincheng County, is about ninety kilometers south of Beijing and six kilometers east of Gaobeidian, the county seat that is a stop on the Beijing–Guangzhou railroad. Yangmansa is thus on the North China Plain, which experiences long and cold winters. The present-day village represents the fusion through natural expansion of Yangmansa and Jumansa, two villages that were therefore readily amalgamated administratively shortly after the Communist victory. With 3,303 people and 648 registered households, Yangmansa as a whole was far too large for intensive interviews of all families, and I therefore chose to focus on what had been the old village of Yangmansa, where there were 280 registered households and 1,175 people.[2] During most of the collective era this section of the present-day village comprised the first four of Yangmansa Brigade's thirteen production teams. But the entire village, encompassing old Yangmansa and old Jumansa, was my arena for general field investigation. I use "Yangmansa" when referring to old Yangmansa, unless otherwise noted.

In this area of Hebei the main crops are winter wheat and spring maize, known respectively as "fine grain" (*xiliang*) and "coarse grain" (*culiang*), a terminology closely reflecting the cultural hierarchy of tastes, at the very bottom of which are "miscellaneous grains" (*zaliang*) such as sorghum and millet, now of only minor significance. Present cropping arrangements (in 1986–87) depend on deep well irrigation, which began in 1958 and attained its current dominant proportions about twelve years later. Earlier this had been an area of rainfall agriculture with two annual crops of maize and a small amount of high-risk wheat, which could not survive the all-too-frequent droughts.

In 1948, following nasty battles in Gaobeidian, the Nationalist army retreated from the vicinity and the Communists entered, as they tightened their noose around Beijing. Earlier during the civil war there had been some fighting in Yangmansa, and the village suffered dearly during the 1937–45 war with Japan, whose forces contended with the Communist Eighth Route Army and with occasional Chinese Nationalist guerrilla units for control of the region. Indeed, the twentieth-century violence began precisely in 1900, when villagers participated disastrously in the Boxer uprising. I could trace the village's turbulent history farther back to the arrival in the mid-seventeenth century of the Manchu conquerors, whose seizure of territory for assignment among themselves as "banner lands" extended to this part of Hebei.

However, rather than provide detailed historical background I only want to make the point that this village cannot be considered a remote backwater. In addition to its involvement in violent phases of China's recent history, it has also been exposed to other changes such that, for example, since the late nineteenth century villagers could walk or go by cart to the Gaobeidian station and from there by train to Beijing. Thus it is clear that the continuing importance of traditional elements in family organization as described below cannot be attributed to inertia or functionless survival facilitated by isolation from the mainstream. Rather, they remain of importance precisely due to their relevance to present-day circumstances.

After 1948 political and economic changes in Yangmansa resembled those elsewhere in rural China, and here I focus on matters relevant to the family. During the 1949 land reform those labeled "poor peasants" or "lower middle peasants" were about equal in number to "middle peasants," with 2 percent of the population classed as "rich peasants" or "landlords." Following the confiscation and redistribution of land mostly belonging to "landlords" or "rich peasants," the basic unit in agriculture remained the family farm. Only about half the village families joined the lower-level cooperatives organized in 1953, but in 1955 there began the full collectivization of agriculture and other enterprises that lasted until 1982. During most of this twenty-seven-year period larger Yangmansa (including Jumansa) was a production brigade with thirteen, or at times fourteen, production teams. As in rural China as a whole, the teams were the basic farm units; each was assigned its own land, organized farming activities, and was the accounting and distribution unit for its members. Except for small "private plots" or "retained plots" (ziliudi) allotted each family, control of farm management and farm labor had been transferred from family to team. Collective arrangements did fluctuate, however, especially during the Great Leap Forward (1959–61) and the early stages of the Cultural Revolution (especially 1966–69).

With decollectivization in 1982, land previously assigned to the production team was equally allocated to team members. Due to variations in team holdings and population, the size and quality of the per capita distributions differed somewhat from one team to another. Distribution was per capita irrespective of age, sex, or marital status, with land assigned on the basis of existing family units. The procedure was to divide a large block of land into as many plots (each usually a narrow strip) as there were team members. Lots were then drawn by each family's head, who on that basis would be given as many adjacent plots as there were members in his family eligible to receive land. Each family thereby obtained several larger plots assigned according to the terms of fourteen-year leases. This process was quite appropriately called "contracting production to the household" (baochan dao hu), for it marked the restoration of family-based agriculture.

The Family

Before the end of my first full day in the village it was already evident to me that local families, with their recently renewed economic and managerial autonomy, still had many traditional features, by which I mean features characteristic of late imperial family organization. During the preliminary fact-finding interview with village cadres I asked about local forms of property and was told that there was "state property and family property." The lack of reference to individual property could only be explained in terms of continuities in property relationships extending back into late imperial times, when the family was the major property-owning unit. Traditionally, however, there had also been an important form of personal ownership, and after some prodding on my part the cadres did acknowledge that there was also "women's property," known in this region as *tixi*, which by definition is held on an individual basis.[3] On that day neither the cadres nor I mentioned the husband-wife unit's property (*fangchan*) within the larger family, but in the course of my fieldwork it became clear that this relatively less significant but equally traditional class of property was still locally recognized. Discussion of *tixi* was followed by a description of family division (*fenjia*), whereby new families are created through equal distribution of family holdings among brothers, with a family division contract usually written to record and confirm the agreement. Furthermore, postmarital residence was virilocal or, in a few cases, uxorilocal, and the family economy was characterized by income pooling. Such features of local family life as noted by the cadres amounted to nothing less than a description of traditional family organization, one that matched my findings in a Taiwan farming village more than twenty years earlier (see Cohen 1976).

During fieldwork I saw that there indeed had been important changes in the family, even though traditional elements such as those mentioned above still loomed large. Considering first reasons for continuities, it is obvious that although the Chinese state has used its formidable power to promote dramatic changes in society and economy, as with the imposition of severe restrictions on family size,[4] it has continued to accept or tolerate certain customary procedures in family and social life. Thus if family property (*jiachan*) remains vital in present-day family organization, it is given no recognition in the state legal code. Likewise, family division procedures hardly accord with China's inheritance code, which stipulates that sons and daughters have equal rights of inheritance with respect to their parents' property (Ocko 1991). But all this is quite irrelevant to local and traditional practices, for just as parents as individuals or a unit do not own the property targeted by the inheritance code, neither do their daughters have rights to the family estate. When I pointed out these inconsistencies to the cadres, they noted that these are the local procedures and that anyone dissatisfied could sue in court, something that had never been done. De facto tolerance of such traditions reflects government's reluctance at all levels to interfere with domestic arrangements for residence and consumption in the absence of an infrastructure providing viable alternatives. There was indeed such interference during the 1959–60 Great Leap Forward, with the establishment of the public mess halls now firmly linked by villagers to the severe food shortages and other disasters of those years.

If key family arrangements were maintained during the collective period, when the family otherwise lost much of its earlier economic autonomy, it is hardly surprising that they remain significant in present-day Yangmansa's decollectivized and relatively freewheeling economic environment. The family unit is still the *jia*, defined through prior family division, succession to the family estate of a single son (who in a few cases may be an adopted heir) or, on occasion, by daughter-husband succession through uxorilocal marriage. Even though *jia* organization has changed such that frequently a *jia* now includes several economically autonomous households, the traditional definition of a *jia* as a family unit is locally recognized in many ways. For example, the *jia* continues as the unit for invitations to wedding or funeral banquets: as they arrive guests present cash gifts recorded on the spot in ledgers later used by their hosts to determine their own social obligations.[5] Invitations are issued and contributions recorded in the name of the *jia* head (*jiazhang*) even if another family member should attend as *jia* representative. If not resulting from single-son or uxorilocal marriage succession, a *jia*'s headship is determined by *jia* division (*fenjia*), following which each new *jia* makes a separate contribution.

In local social relationships what is important is *jia* membership. It is irrelevant if members of one *jia* are listed in the government registers (*hukou*) as belonging to different administrative households. Missing from the village registers and separately registered elsewhere are men (and a few women) working outside the village in state-owned units and therefore eligible to "eat state grain" (*chi guojiade liangshi*).[6] While the majority live in the village and commute to work, some reside in dormitories provided by their units and return home only periodically or during the agricultural busy season. Whether living in the village or outside, they are full members of their village-based *jia*.

Property

Property is the family's traditional foundation as a corporate unit. In pre-Communist times, such family property, including land, vastly outweighed in significance what individuals privately held, with corporations such as temples, lineages, or religious associations the only major nonfamily property owners in rural China. After the Communists gained

control, land reform campaigns—as during 1949 in Yangmansa—if anything served to increase the importance of family property for the rural
population as a whole. Families classed as "landlords" or "rich peasants"
had their holdings drastically reduced, but this meant that the far larger
number of "poor peasant" family estates underwent expansion. Likewise, with their land confiscated and redistributed to the "poor peasants," the traditional corporations lost significance as property owners.

Only a few years after land reform there was full collectivization in
1955. Land held as family property was entirely eliminated except for the
small "private plots," which remained under family cultivation. Yet the
family continued as a corporate unit even under such vastly changed circumstances, for the economic relationship between the collective era's
production teams and the team workers was defined on the traditional
basis of the family as major property holder. As is well known, the distribution of team income was through workpoints. A team member working at particular tasks such as plowing, harvesting, and so forth was
awarded a designated number of workpoints. Once a year the total
workpoint accumulation of all team members was divided against the total worth of team income available for distribution to determine an individual workpoint's value. Cash or grain was then distributed on the basis
of each team member's workpoint earnings.

Although individuals earned differing numbers of workpoints, such
earnings were considered by their families and by team cadres to be family property, or *jiachan*. Thus a family's workpoint earnings were combined and paid directly to the family head. A woman who married out
prior to the annual distribution could not take her workpoints with her;
they were treated precisely as *jiachan* and remained in her natal family's
account until distribution. Likewise, during family division (*fenjia*) workpoints accumulated up to then were not allocated among brothers or
other eligible males in accordance with their respective and necessarily
different earnings, but rather were treated as an undifferentiated family
holding, the division of which, like other family property, had to be negotiated.

One man, a team accountant during the collective period, described
how team cadres and members took it as given that workpoints were
family property:

Every person had a workpoint registration book [*jigongber*]; the workpoint
recorder [*jigongyuan*] recorded in his own book on a daily basis everyone's workpoint earnings. Once a month the workpoint recorder recorded in the workpoint

registration book of each commune member [*sheyuan*] the number of workpoints that person had earned. The family was the unit for receiving workpoints. If a family divided, they reported to the team and separate accounts were set up. If a family divided in the middle of the year, they told the team how to distribute workpoints earned prior to division. They never calculated on the basis of individual earnings, but rather they always lumped all workpoint earnings together and then divided them; the workpoints were family property [*jiachan*].

His remarks confirm that because workpoints were family property, women marrying out lost rights over them, as with their natal family's other holdings:

A woman who married out did not take her workpoints with her. Rather, her earnings were given to her natal family after her marriage. The woman would not demand workpoints; rather she would want money and dowry. Even within the same brigade, women marrying from one team to another didn't take their workpoints with them; also, even within the same team they didn't transfer workpoints [although this last would pose no administrative problems].

The increase in family-controlled assets after decollectivization has reinforced the family as a corporate unit, and a woman's virilocal marriage still represents transfer of her family membership from one such unit to another. Although it is now common for parents to provide a son with a new house in anticipation of his marriage, the same hardly applies to daughters who marry out. When a village woman told me that her daughter and son-in-law were building a new house, I asked if she would help them financially. Her answer was that "if I have a daughter-in-law I can't give any money to my daughter. When we get old we will have to depend on our daughter-in-law; we can't go to our daughter's home." Fear that such use of family money might damage relationships with her daughter-in-law obviously reflected the fact that mother and daughter-in-law were members of one family corporation, while the daughter now belonged to another. In another family, a married woman who developed a serious mental illness was indeed returned to her natal home to live under their care, but her husband arranged to pay them four hundred yuan yearly to cover their expenses, since his wife remained a member of his family. As in the past, the many social and economic links created by marriage are connections between fundamentally independent family units.

If family property still comprises by far the greater part of all holdings, other kinds of property also accord with traditional patterns. Husband and wife are still a property-owning unit (*fang*) with possessions (*fangchan*, as noted earlier) distinct from family property and not liable to distribution during family division. Kept mainly in their own bedroom or, especially nowadays, their own house, such *fang* belongings include furniture and other items originally provided as dowry or directly by the husband's family at the time of marriage.[7]

There is also woman's property, usually money (*tixi* or *tixiqian*), and, as observed earlier in Taiwan, it is obtained in a variety of ways. Symbolically most important is money publicly given to the bride during her wedding. In Yangmansa this involves the *shangbai* ceremony, during which the bride's father-in-law introduces to her other members of her new family; each person called places money on a table in front of which the bride stands, thus confirming her new family's recognition of her property rights. Another source of *tixi* is the bride's retention of some money originally sent by the groom's side for her clothing and other purchases connected with the wedding. Also, some brides have money earned as wages before marriage. The amount retained, if any, is determined by her parents, in light of their own family's needs. If the bride's parents allow it, premarital *tixi* may accumulate into a tidy sum. After marriage she keeps this money; her husband knows or assumes she has some but may be unaware of the exact amount. However, this property really represents the autonomy of the husband-wife unit within a larger joint or stem family, and upon family division the property is merged with the husband's share of family property. Given the secretive nature of these holdings, however, it is quite possible and not uncommon for a woman to hold onto some of her private funds even after family division. In larger joint families some men give family funds to their wives, who add this cash to their private holdings.[8]

Marriage

Present-day marriage reflects the rejection of some traditional customs, the modification of others, and the introduction of new procedures. Until the Communists arrived, marriage retained the arrangements of late imperial times. Such marriages were facilitated by go-betweens (*meiren* or, if a woman, *meirenpo*), as is still common today. However, in contrast to contemporary procedures, they were then arranged entirely by the two families concerned, and the bride and groom usually did not see each other before their wedding day.

A major exception to the practice of keeping bride and groom away from each other prior to marriage was *tongyangxi*, or "little daughter-in-law" marriage. One villager's description was typical of the comments made about marriage of this kind:

It was not common before liberation; but there were cases. They had this sixty years ago [as of 1986]. The girl was sent at seven or eight to the boy's side. The girl's side would have to be especially poor. The boy's side would not necessarily be in bad circumstances. When these girls reached sixteen to nineteen they were married. They would just wear the same clothes and that would be enough. There were only a few cases in this village. Liang Zhiping's mother was a *tongyangxi* [Liang Zhiping's daughter was born in 1932]. She came to the man's side when she was ten, and married when she was sixteen or seventeen. A *jiaozi* [palanquin] was used during the wedding, but she simply went around the village.

The reference to the palanquin merely circling the village rather than going between the families of groom and bride was one expression of the fact that such marriages did not create strong ties of kinship between these families, if any at all. Indeed, because in such marriages the groom's family tended to be far better off than the bride's, the former was not inclined to see the development of important kinship ties with the latter. These might be of little benefit for the groom's side and could be taken by them as posing a possibly threatening burden when their resources, though relatively more ample than those of the bride's natal family, were nevertheless quite limited.

In most cases, therefore, *tongyangxi* marriage was avoided. Rather, a son or daughter ready for betrothal attracted go-betweens, who sought to arrange marriages between families "of equal standing" (*men dang hu dui*), although poorer families would in any event welcome matches with wealthier ones. After hearing from the go-between, two families interested in proceeding further arranged to determine if there was horoscopic compatibility for the proposed marriage. It was first up to the family preparing for their son's marriage to provide the potential bride's side with his *bazi*, the "eight characters" showing the year, month, day, and hour of birth; if his matched her *bazi*, then negotiations could move on. In fact, the interpretation might be influenced by each family's judgment as to the desirability of the match. One man described the process as follows:

First, the groom's side wrote the *bazi* on a red piece of paper given to the go-between, who brought it to the bride's side; if the bride's side found it acceptable they sent a similar document to the groom's side. Sometimes the bride's side faked a good fit if they saw that the groom's side was an attractive match. If there were any doubts, either side placed the paper into the alcove of the kitchen god and waited three days. Any unfortunate or unlucky incident during this period could be used as a pretext to cancel the match without anyone losing face.

Under Communist rule the earliest changes in marriage involved the undermining of such traditional procedures of spouse selection. They were among the many marriage customs attacked as "feudal superstition," but they also lost relevance due to the marriage code the new Communist government announced in 1950 and implemented in the village during the following several years. The code's requirement that the couple directly concerned decide marriage was quite energetically publicized by local cadres, in contrast to provisions pertaining to equal inheritance or freedom of divorce.[9] One man involved with the early marriage reform campaign recalled how "we first worked with members of the Communist Youth League to tell them about the new law. Then we did propaganda mobilization; we would go to the families about to get married and tell them about the new law." This massive and intimate intervention by agents of the state did lead to new practices whereby prospective spouses would first meet and indicate their consent to the match.

Successful state intervention was facilitated by the tension and anxiety of bride and groom anticipating "blind marriage" to someone possibly physically unattractive or in other ways undesirable. Women feared a new and harsh family environment, and, especially, confrontation with a classically hostile mother-in-law. One man described how "women wanted to see the kind of man they were marrying. If they discovered that their husband was no good they might cry. In the past they had to try to secretly look at the boy's side [check out him and his family]; now, [after the marriage law was publicized] . . . daughters demanded to see the boy's side." Another villager noted that "after the new marriage law, women were the first to demand to meet the man's side." Family heads could not easily resist such demands. One woman told me how "at the time of the new marriage law, if boys or girls were not satisfied they complained to the government. Also, parents were afraid that if they made an unacceptable match, the boy or girl would run away with someone else."

The code was also reinforced by its requirement that there be a marriage license, applied for in person by the couple concerned, so as to confirm their consent. In Yangmansa the couple go to the township office (which earlier had been the commune office), a procedure incorporated into the local sequence of wedding rituals and timed to occur just before the couple joins others from the bride's side at the relatively lavish betrothal banquet hosted by the groom's family. Thus what the state requires for the legalization of marriage has been absorbed into local practice as a new element in ceremonies of betrothal. According to one villager, "we already had this procedure by 1960; it developed very quickly."

While the man and woman now play an important role at all stages of spouse selection and must agree to their marriage, family involvement remains important; the large majority of marriages still owe their origin to the activities of go-betweens, and sometimes parents reject a go-between's proposition even before consulting their son or daughter. "Free love," which in the Chinese context simply means that husband and wife became acquainted and romantically attached on their own, or at least apart from any actions by their families, is still rare. According to my survey of old Yangmansa families, of 185 women marrying in since 1965—the year of the first "free love" marriage in this part of the village—only 14 of the 155 women for which this information is available married out of "free love."[10]

For villagers, "free love" marriages are notable because most take place in spite of family opposition. By definition, "free love" marriages involve individual considerations that, in rural society, will likely be in conflict with familial economic, social, and political concerns of little relevance to the independent romantic attachments of young men and women. Thus the very few "free love" marriages approved at the outset by the families on both sides are if anything even more sensational, although many families finally consent to avoid a total break with a son or daughter determined to marry. One woman described her son's 1984 "free" marriage as "easy." "Both sides agreed," she said, and "all the village knew and talked about this."

Opposition began in 1951, just one year after the marriage code was announced, with the first free love marriage in the larger village (in old Jumansa). Against her own family's wishes a woman married a man from a neighboring family and went with him to the army camp to which he had been assigned. When they returned, her parents refused to see them, but later they did reestablish ties. A far more recent free love marriage in 1983 involved a woman in old Yangmansa and a similar story of parental rejection followed by reconciliation. In this case I was able to get her mother's account, which is of interest in that it highlights some considerations leading to family opposition. The woman had been living for a time with her mother's sister's family (yijia) in another village; she got to know a man from a nearby family who was the third of seven brothers. According to her mother, when my daughter and the man who is now her husband were discussing marriage we [her parents] found out and were opposed. I was opposed because there were too many brothers in that family and therefore it would not be in good economic shape [because each brother represents yet another claim on family property]; I also felt that the village was too far away and that my daughter was too young [she was seventeen at that time; the marriage was not registered until three years later]; also, free marriage is really quite outrageous [*tai buhaoting*], for there is no go-between. But she nevertheless fled to her *yijia*, where she got married; we did not know at the time, for it was my own sister [the girl's mother's sister (*yiyi*)] who married her off [*ba ta gei pinle*]. After she married we broke off relationships, but after a period we restored them. Now she has two children and is in very good health; they are getting ready to build a house.

In arranging marriages there is an obvious connection between the use of a go-between and the expression of family interests. The go-between functions as a sort of clearinghouse for finding a spouse that suits family needs. Of equal importance, the go-between represents an elaboration of the social ties reinforcing commitments entered into by both families party to the marriage, for a go-between who arranges a marriage is held responsible for its success. Should problems arise among spouses or their natal families, the go-between is frequently called in to help settle them. Since a go-between will have had prior social ties with both families, conflicts damage or destroy not only the social connections between the two families party to the marriage, but also those each has with the go-between and her family. Because the go-between's involvement increases a bad marriage's social cost, it is commonly believed that her participation enhances the likelihood that a marriage will succeed. The importance of the go-between explains why even in cases of family-approved "free love" marriages a go-between is called in to arrange details after the couple have met and decided to marry on their own.

There was no room for a go-between in the most recent—and most sensational—case of free love marriage in the face of family opposition. During my fieldwork a village man whose childhood bout with polio left him with paralyzed legs and dependent upon a hand-driven tricycle to get about began discussing marriage with a woman who had no physical disabilities but was very much in love with him (both were from old Jumansa families). Not surprisingly, his family was delighted, for it was the usual fate of a man in his circumstances to remain single, while hers was bitterly opposed. By the time this development came to my attention the woman had already broken ties with her natal family and moved into her future husband's home, where he lived with his parents. Several weeks later they obtained their marriage certificate from the township government office, and then after about another two weeks there was a simplified marriage ceremony in his home. Whether or not there will eventually be a reconciliation between the woman and her parents remains to be seen.

The requirement that bride and groom consent has led to the introduction into the sequence of activities preceding marriage opportunities for young men and women to meet. These meetings are by now standardized in local custom, which, as already noted, also continues to provide parents with opportunities to reject proposed marriages. After the go-between gets preliminary expressions of interest by both sides, the main elements comprising the present-day method of spouse selection are the first "meeting" (*jianmian* or *huxiang jianjianmiar*); the second meeting to "talk things over" (*tanhua*); the "small betrothal" (*xiao dengji*); the "large betrothal" (*da dengji*); and, finally, the wedding (*jiehun*).

The go-between arranges the introductory "meeting." If the families are from different villages, the young woman goes with members of her family and the go-between to where the young man lives. Should the woman's family have kin in that village, they meet in their house. In the absence of such relatives their encounter can take place in the go-between's home, if it happens to be in that village, but in any event they do not meet in the young man's home. Alternatively, they can meet in her village, either in the go-between's house, should it be there, or in her own home. In addition to the go-between and the young woman, participating family members minimally include her mother. Older brothers and their wives may also be present, but her father rarely attends. The young man, however, comes unaccompanied. The following description of what then follows exemplifies what I was told by many villagers:

After the boy arrives, coming alone or brought in by the go-between, if it is the girl's house, he and the girl look each other over as everyone else is talking about this, that, and the other. Then the girl leaves; then her parents leave together with her older brothers and everybody else, leaving the go-between and the boy alone. The go-between then asks the boy, "how do you feel about the girl?" [*ni kan ta zemeyang?*]. If the boy says "no good" [*buxing*], he leaves and then that is the end of the matter; if he says, "she's all right" [*chabuduo*] and then leaves, the go-between asks the girl's side what they think. If they say "*buxing*," then it is over. Under such circumstances, if the boy had said "*chabuduo*," the go-between has to notify his family that it is off and will go to their home and so inform whoever might be there when she [or he] shows up.

After this first encounter, more often than not one or both sides reject the match; but if the woman's family indicates continuing interest, the go-between so informs the man's side and arranges for another meeting to "talk things over." This second meeting, unlike the first, usually results in an agreement to the match. Although potential bride and groom have an opportunity to talk alone, this event also gives her side an opportunity to size up the economic and social circumstances of his. A typical description of this meeting is as follows:

For this, the girl goes with one or both of her parents to the boy's side, also accompanied by the go-between. The go-between sets this meeting up. They are greeted by the boy's parents, who offer them tea. The go-between tells boy and girl to "talk to each other" [tanhua], and at this point both sets of parents and the go-between leave the room, where the boy and girl are now alone. Then the two of them talk; when they have finished the girl goes out to where her parents are waiting. After the girl and her parents return home they ask her what she thinks, and she will say either "yes" [keyi] or "no" [buxing]. The boy's parents will ask him the same question. For each of these meetings the boy or girl will consult with his or her parents, and if the latter disagree the boy or girl usually will go along with their decision. Most first meetings do not result in a match, but most second meetings do succeed. Matches can be rejected by parents or by their children, and mainly it is the latter who do so.

During the next one or two days the go-between determines how each side feels about the match. If one side rejects it and the other accepts, the go-between has to notify the latter as to the former's response. Agreement by all concerned to move on to the next event represents a major but not irrevocable commitment to marriage, for this means that the go-between is now expected to consult with both families as to the timing of the "small betrothal" (xiao dengji), the successful conclusion of which fixes the marriage. This event also takes place in the young man's home and usually involves more people: the young woman is accompanied by her parents, her older brothers and their wives, and her paternal uncles (shushu) and their wives (shenshen). For the "small betrothal" the man's family prepares a banquet with what by local standards are among the finest dishes of meat, fish, vegetables, and steamed bread (mantou). Participation is quite appropriately called "eating the betrothal meal" (chi dinghun fan), for with very few exceptions it is precisely when the guests from the woman's side partake of this meal that their commitment to the match is indicated. For them not to participate, then, represents their last opportunity to reject the match in a way that still causes minimal long-term social damage. One person described such an occurrence to me as follows:

This group [of guests] looks over the family's circumstances. If they approve, then they take the meal prepared by the boy's side; if they don't approve, they don't eat. It is a good meal, and if they don't approve, the boy's side will be left with it. The girl's side will give an excuse of some sort and then leave. If they are satisfied, they eat and go home.

In the large majority of cases the meal is indeed consumed, allowing for the commencement of betrothal gift transfers prior to the departure of the guests. First there is the "exchange of handkerchiefs" (*huan shou zhuar*), during which the young man gives the woman a handkerchief wrapped around money or a wrist watch; if cash, the sum is usually 100 yuan, and can range from 70 to 150 yuan. The woman also gives the man a handkerchief, this one containing a pack of cigarettes or a fountain pen (this a gift worth no more than about four yuan). Later, the now-betrothed couple leaves first, with the young man escorting his fiancée to the nearby county seat of Gaobeidian where, for about twenty yuan, he buys a bolt of cloth to be used for making each of them a pair of trousers. This purchase is by now a well-established custom locally described as "buying a piece of cloth for two trousers" (*mai yikuai bu, liangtou fu*). The woman's parents and other guests stay a bit longer and may begin preliminary discussions with the man's family concerning the forthcoming marriage. After shopping in Gaobeidian, the couple returns to Yangmansa; as they approach, they separate and go to their respective homes, with the woman taking the bolt of cloth.

The next event is the "large betrothal," or *da dengji*, which includes another meal hosted by the groom's side. As with the "small betrothal" banquet, the food is of the highest quality by village standards. As noted above, the "large betrothal" is now linked to marriage registration, hence it is also commonly referred to as "obtaining the marriage certificate" (*ling jiehunzheng*). Usually the woman's party first goes to the groom's house. Then the young couple goes to the township government's civil affairs office (*minzhengban*) to register for their marriage license; when they arrive firecrackers are set off and they distribute candy to those present. With this certificate, they are in fact legally married, even though from the local point of view it is their betrothal that is now fixed. Meanwhile, the rest of the woman's group remain at the boy's side, "simply waiting to eat," as one person put it. Arriving with the young woman are one or both parents (usually both), her older sisters and brothers, the latter's wives, and also the wives of her father's older and younger brothers (*shenzi* [or *sher*], *dama*); these comprise the key group of close kin expected to be in her party, but others, such as her older sisters' husbands (*jiefu*), may also go along. They bring sweets and perhaps other gifts such as fruit. After the meal the couple once again sets off for Gaobeidian, on a trip that is both recreational and an expedition to buy more clothing for the future bride; but this time the purchases are not of material, but of ready-made apparel and shoes. Although the man pays for everything, with money supplied by his family, none of these expenditures counts toward the payment the woman's family expects to later receive from the man's side. Indeed, villagers were emphatic in stressing that during the "large betrothal" there is no discussion of subsequent wedding-related expenditures.

During the period between the "large betrothal" and the wedding the couple periodically meets for outings that resemble dates, such as visits to the flourishing but now temple-less "temple fairs" (*miaohui*). They also socialize during the traditional holidays, especially the lunar New Year and the Fifth Month and Mid-Autumn festivals, with the woman usually staying for a few days at her future husband's home. Such visits are known as "welcoming the daughter-in-law" (*jie xifu*) and involve the man going to her home, escorting her to his, and then escorting her back again. Gifts are presented by both sides but, once again, the groom bears the heavier burden of gift giving, as one woman's description makes clear enough:

Each time the boy goes to [her home] to welcome her he must bring lots of gifts: pastries, liquor, candies, and fruits. The girl also brings gifts with her for the boy's side, but not as much. She stays each time for between two and four nights. When the boy escorts her back home, he again must bring gifts; fewer than when he welcomed her, but still a lot.

Another large outlay of funds by the man's family is for the new house they build for him and his wife. Construction will certainly have been completed at some point before the wedding, and in some cases before betrothal or even before the parents begin consulting go-betweens concerning their son's marriage. Prebetrothal house preparation increasingly is seen as necessary for a good match, for it shows commitment by the man's family to endow his marriage.

Discussed so far are components of marriage representing sharp modifications of traditional practices. In addition to the increased involvement of the young people themselves in decisions regarding marriage, as during their first two meetings, the economic burden of marriage has decisively tilted toward the man's side. The groom's family serves as host during the two betrothal banquets, at other events prior to the wedding, and during the wedding itself. The small and large betrothals do figure in descriptions of traditional marriage in Beijing and the surrounding Hebei area, where they are referred to as "*xiaoding*" and "*dading*," but each involved the man's family sending gifts to the woman's side. The gifts could be brought by a family member or by the go-between, but in any event it would be the woman's family that would prepare a feast for the gift bringers (Ma Zhisu 1981: 220–21; Takeda 1935: 13–20; Yang Derui 1973). Neither these terms used in the literature nor their current forms (*xiaodengji, dadengji*) were mentioned by Yangmansa villagers when describing pre-Communist practices;[11] however, they did note that after agreement to a match there were two major events before the wedding: presentation (*guoli*) by the man's family of betrothal gifts (*pinli*), and the transfer of the marriage agreement documents (*guotie*). The betrothal gifts varied in value and quantity corresponding to the wealth of the families involved, but they generally included some jewelry and clothing the bride would wear on the wedding day. Subsequent exchange of documents involved a "marriage solicitation" (*qiuhun*) from the man's family and a "marriage assent" (*yinghun*) from the woman's; these included the horoscopes (*gengtie*) of bride and groom, upon which basis the wedding date would be fixed. In Yangmansa, as far as I was able to determine, the man's family did not host the woman's at any point prior to the wedding, but published sources on practices elsewhere in Hebei do describe prewedding visits to each other's home by the families of bride and groom so as to check out the other side's economic circumstances.[12] In any event, the contemporary pattern in Yangmansa represents a major reorientation of prewedding activities—and a shift of the burden of expenditures—toward the male side.

This shift characterizes subsequent phases of the sequence culminating in marriage, but before turning to these I want to consider factors that may have been involved in such changes. The importance of women's increased economic value already has been proposed by Parish and Whyte in their pioneering study, which focused on the southeastern province of Guangdong. That area and, it would appear, much of rural China has been characterized by a movement of marriage costs to the male side quite similar to what happened in Yangmansa. Parish and Whyte suggest that "in Kwangtung [Guangdong] as elsewhere women are now performing a larger share of agricultural work than they used to. Since family income now depends overwhelmingly not on landholdings but on the number of laborers and their level of earnings, women's labor should be more important to the family economy than formerly" (1978: 187).

Parish and Whyte's findings were with respect to the collective era, and in Yangmansa, as in Guangdong, it does appear that the most significant increase in women's economic value occurred as a result of collectivization, when women became workpoint earners at the same time that family property (*jiachan*) was reduced to housing, its furnishings, and the like. The economically important factor was no longer land but labor. The workpoint system itself created strong pressure on all families to mobilize every able-bodied family member for work, for all workers had to be assigned tasks and awarded workpoints. Workpoints were created by labor, not by its products, such that a family keeping its women at home would suffer a loss of income relative to those more fully deploying family members.

In north China, including Yangmansa, women's participation in agriculture during the collective era represented a far sharper break with older patterns than in the Cantonese-speaking and Hakka-speaking areas of Guangdong, where women traditionally had done more farm work than those in other parts of the country. The important difference was the prevalence in the north of footbinding, which in Yangmansa ended only in 1930 or just before, even later than in nearby areas.[13] Earlier, footbinding had been almost universal in this region, contradicting the commonly held belief that this practice was confined to China's elite or upper classes. This was in sharp contrast to the Cantonese-speaking areas of Guangdong, where the practice was limited to elites, and footbinding was even rarer among Hakka speakers in that province and in adjacent regions. Although Yangmansa women with bound feet could perform some farm work, doing so was painful and represented a desperate response to a shortage of male labor. One woman, who was born in 1922 and had her feet bound when she was about seven years old, described women's work under such circumstances as follows:

Women had to stay home and cook and take care of the house, sew, and so forth, and could not leave the house [*bu chu damen*]. Only men went shopping at the market; women did not go out. However, during the busy season women with bound feet would work in the fields if they were from families where otherwise there was not enough labor available. Other women only worked at home. But the bound feet would interfere with the work and be painful; also women with bound feet could not carry water. Mine was the last generation of women with bound feet.

Another villager recalled how

Until then [the end of footbinding], all women rich or poor would have their feet bound; this would be done when they were five or six years old. Some women still went out to the fields even if they had bound feet. Richer families didn't send their women into the fields; poorer families did. They could only do lighter work, not heavier tasks. They could not go out during the rain; they could not get their feet wet. However, at that time all fields depended on rainwater; [deep well] irrigation began only after liberation and started with the cooperatives.

Government intervention beginning in late 1927 stopped footbinding. For about two years women inspectors from the county government slapped a fine on the head of any family with a child whose feet had recently been bound, so that by 1930 the practice had ended. Thus when the Communists took control of the area less than twenty years later, it was not easy for the women who already had bound feet to enter into farming. Furthermore, the first generation of women to grow up with unbound feet came of age only at about the time of the Communist victory, such that elimination of this form of crippling really should be seen as setting the stage for later changes in women's economic roles under Communist rule.

If collectivization encouraged women's large-scale participation in field labor, with it also came the reduction or outright elimination of forms of domestic labor by which women traditionally had made major contributions to family earnings. In addition to doing almost all household work and caring for children, women were importantly involved in drying, grinding, and otherwise processing maize and wheat, the major crops. Perhaps even more important was their contribution to family enterprises that, supplementing farm work, significantly enhanced family income. Chief among these were oil pressing (*zha you*; from peanuts, beans, and sesame seeds) and cloth weaving (production of *tubu*, homespun cloth), with women and men involved in the former and women providing almost all labor for the latter. Most families were involved in one or both of these kinds of work; one estimate from an especially knowledgeable villager is that more than 60 percent of families wove cloth and as many as 90 percent pressed oil. "Only richer households didn't do this work," he added. Families engaged in these activities throughout the year. These types of work represented diversification of family economies and a movement away from agriculture; they were adaptations to the confinement of women to their homes and to farming that was restricted by long winter slack seasons, and was always risky in any event. Moreover, for many families agriculture served mainly to provide subsistence. The product of these family industries was either sold in the village to purchasing agents or directly retailed by family members in the village or in nearby market towns. As one man put it, "families had to have these sidelines [*fuye*]."

It is thus clear that traditionally women had important economic roles in spite of footbinding and other manifestations of severe gender discrimination. With the onset of collectivization their roles did indeed change, but so did those of the men, for all family enterprises came to an end, including those where men's labor had been important. Weaving cloth in the home was forbidden, as was pressing oil. The latter, like farming itself, was taken over by the production teams. Thus, with the minor exception of whatever small income and supplementary food might be provided by the tiny "private plots" allocated to and directly cultivated by each family, there was a major change in the nature of all income-producing labor undertaken by men or women. The value of the family's labor was now determined almost exclusively by its ability to produce workpoints, even though women generally were given only 80 percent of the workpoints received by men ("older men" also received 80 percent, "older women" 60 percent, I was told). Thus the changing economic role of women during the collective era was characterized not only by their enhanced participation in agriculture, but also by the almost total involvement of both men and women in work assigned them by their production team.

Because land and other income-producing property or enterprises were no longer available, labor power in fact became the family's only asset, albeit one given differential value according to the varying wealth—i.e., the varying value of workpoint earnings—of teams differing from each other in terms of both total and per capita earnings. With such collectivization, the family was still a corporate unit, but its corporate assets now included only housing, furniture, and other such "private" property on the one hand, and precisely its membership rights in a production team on the other. Also, marriage remained overwhelmingly virilocal; as of old, this meant for most women a transfer of membership from one family corporation to another. But a woman's entrance through marriage into such a corporation, stripped by collectivization of its land and other holdings, no longer gave her access to family assets, a portion of which she and her husband would later come to control through family division or through simple succession in the event her husband was an only son. Such a family now had as its only economic assets the labor of its members and the relative value of their workpoints; obviously, this was equally true of the woman's natal family. In other words, marriage now involved transfer of labor power from one family to another under conditions where labor was the family's only remaining major economic asset. I suggest that this circumstance, rather than the enhanced participation of woman in agriculture per se, was behind the pronounced shift of the economic burden of marriage to the male side, the side that received the labor.[14]

The strongest evidence of this shift was described by Parish and Whyte, with particular reference to Guangdong, as a transition from indirect dowry—where payments from the groom's side to the bride's were matched or even exceeded in value by what the latter sent with the bride as dowry—to brideprice, involving payment by the groom's family with little returned as dowry by the bride's (1978: 180–87). Their findings apply to Yangmansa during the collective period, when it was common for the betrothal payment from the man's side to be large enough to provide for all the woman's side's expenses as well as for an additional sum retained by her natal family. This betrothal payment, known as *caili*, was delivered to the woman's family at some point after the "large betrothal" feast. All villagers with whom I discussed this matter agreed that *caili* was not a matter of negotiation: the woman's family simply demanded a payment that the man's side had to provide. A family used income derived from marriages of daughters to pay for weddings of sons; hence families with many sons tended to demand greater betrothal payments for their daughters, although at any point in time there was a range within which demands were made. I was told that during the collective era there was a steady increase in *caili* costs: in the late 1950s they ranged from 40 to 50 yuan, ten years later between 80 and 90 yuan, in the early 1970s 100 to 200 yuan, and by 1978 between 400 and 500 yuan.[15]

Caili payments were not an innovation of the collective era and were found in Yangmansa even prior to Communist rule, but then only the poorest families demanded such payments (in cash or grain). Among villagers old enough to remember, even those whose families had been classified as "poor peasants" during land reform made comments such as "in the past there was no *caili* among ordinary farmers," "before liberation no one wanted *caili* except for poor people," or "some wanted *caili*, others didn't; if the girl's side was poor they would want *caili*, but if they had money they wouldn't want any; most didn't want *caili*." Such payments were rare enough for one man to tell me that "*caili* began six or seven years after liberation," which would be at the beginning of collectivization. In Yangmansa the important distinction was between those families demanding *caili* in addition to the betrothal gifts of clothing and jewelry noted above, and the majority of families accepting only the latter. *Caili* payments were received only by the poorest of the poor families, those with little or no land or other assets. Their circumstances, although linked to extreme poverty, bore a certain resemblance to those characterizing all farm families during the collective era, insofar as their only corporate family resources were the labor of family members and the reproductive power of family women.[16] During the collective period the transformation of *caili* into a standard payment increased the share of marriage costs borne by the man's side, which even traditionally had been larger than the contribution of the bride's family. The prevailing traditional arrangement, except for the poorest families, was that expenditures by the two sides, involving both direct and indirect dowry, were largely geared to the endowment of the new married couple. The major changes during the collective era were that the endowment function of wedding exchanges was now almost entirely taken on by the groom's family at the same time that the bride's family received a *caili* payment, a large portion of which they retained.

Caili aside, weddings during the collective era maintained the arrangement of economic transfers characteristic of earlier times. This earlier pre-Communist pattern involved, first, the groom's side supplying the bride with clothing for her to wear on her wedding day, as already noted. Then, usually the day before they received the dowry, the groom's family sent the *cuizhuang*, gifts for the bride's side that, if the term is to be taken literally, were meant to "press for dowry [delivery]." The *cuizhuang* was his family's major presentation and included pork, husked rice, wheat flour, bean curd, chickens, and mung bean pancakes. The dowry, delivered the following day, generally would include "one table of furnishings" (*yizhuozi jiahuo*), consisting of two trunks with clothing for the bride, a mirror, a vase, a clock, a *penjing* (miniature landscape), a teapot, and cups. This was the standard dowry; poorer families gave "half a table of furnishings" (*banzhuozi jiahuo*): one trunk with some clothes, a small hand valise, a small makeup kit for the bride, a tea set, and a mirror.

The dowry was more valuable than what the bride's family received from the groom's. Villagers insisted that, except for the poorest families, the woman's side spent more than the man's. As one man put it, "the woman's side got lots of face by sending as big a dowry as possible," and that if "the man's side spent 200 yuan, the woman's would spend 500." He thus described a proportional distribution of wedding expenses that accords with what Gamble (1954: 383) reported for elsewhere in Hebei in the 1920s. However, because the groom's family also had to prepare and furnish the "new room" (*xinfang*), which would serve as the couple's living quarters, their total contribution to the endowment of the new married couple generally exceeded that of the bride's side. I was told that the standard set of furniture provided by the groom's family for the "new room" would include two closets, a small table with three drawers, a larger square table, and two chairs. This set was purchased or, if the family had its own lumber, made for them by a hired carpenter. Poorer families might supply only a portion of this set. What went into the "new room" as endowment was clearly defined as such: whether contributed directly by the groom's family, or coming in as dowry with the bride, new room furnishings were *fangchan*, or conjugal unit property.

On the morning of the wedding day the groom went by palanquin to fetch the bride. Wealthier families hired a second palanquin for the bride's use when the wedding party returned with her; in most cases (80 percent, according to one estimate), however, the palanquin used by the groom now took the bride, and he would return on horseback or in a horse cart. Before the groom's arrival the bride's face was made up and a square piece of red cloth—the *gaitou*, or "head cover"—placed over her head. She then stepped into the palanquin and was taken to the man's side. Upon reaching the groom's home bride and groom first "worshiped heaven and earth" (*bai tiandi*) or, rather, their representation on a red strip of paper placed in front of an offering table. The bride remained standing while the groom kowtowed. Then the bride was led into the "new room," but just as she was about to enter, the groom used a steelyard (*chenggar*) to remove her *gaitou*, which he then threw onto the roof, all the time not looking at her face. The bride entered the "new room," combed her hair, adjusted her makeup, washed her face, and then reemerged for the *shangbai*, at which point the groom and others present for the wedding saw her face for the first time. The *shangbai*, or "paying respects to the senior generation," involved the bride's ritual introduction to her husband's senior kin. Upon being introduced, each of the "collateral kin" (*pang xueqin*)—including older and younger brothers of the groom's father, father's sisters, those sons of the latter older than the groom, the groom's older brothers, and their wives—placed a cash gift for the bride on the offering table, while none were received from the groom's "lineal kin" (*zhi xueqin*), his parents and grandparents. The cash gifts became part of the bride's private fund (*tixi*), for this presentation of *shangbai* gifts was the local version of wedding rituals—widely distributed in China—that helped endow a woman with private property and at the same time publicly affirmed her right to have it.[17] Following *shangbai* the bride returned to the "new room," where she remained for the rest of the day; that evening younger relatives and other guests crowded into the "new room" and teased bride and groom, often not departing until late into the night.

The next day bride and groom paid a "return visit" (*huimen*) to her natal family, where there was another *shangbai*, this time the groom's introduction to his wife's kin. They gave him cash gifts, but he was expected to give these to his wife, reflecting the fact that as a man he was not supposed to have private cash holdings, with those held by his wife in reality representing a conjugal fund to which he also gained access at the time of family division. The *huimen* was a one-day affair, with the couple going back to the groom's family that afternoon or evening. The final major event in the wedding ritual was "third day's worship" (*baisan*), worship of the groom's ancestors and visits to his close senior agnates three days after the wedding. The couple first worshiped the family's ancestral tablets, if they had any, or their ancestral scrolls. These scrolls or tablets ordinarily were kept in storage and displayed and worshiped only for three days during the lunar New Year; *baisan* appears to be the only other occasion when they were brought out (see chapter 6 for more on ancestor worship in Yangmansa). Finally, the bride was escorted by her husband to the homes of his senior agnates, where she received additional cash gifts.

Both sides held wedding feasts; the groom's family staged a feast for relatives and friends on the wedding day, while the bride's family invited fewer guests to a banquet the day before. Villagers insisted that unlike present-day weddings, families rich and poor did not serve meat in pre-Communist times, but rather bean curd, steamed bread (*mantou*), other wheat-based foods, and vegetables, with wealthier families providing higher-quality fare. As at present, and in conformity with a China-wide pattern, arriving guests presented cash or gifts; these were recorded in a ledger later used by the host family to determine their own contributions when responding to invitations from families that were now their guests, as noted above. A family sponsoring a wedding feast was said to *banshi*, "to hold an affair," which meant inviting a wide range of kin and friends to a banquet with as many as thirty or forty tables (usually eight persons per table). Most people were asked to attend on the basis of relationships earlier expressed by invitations received from them, usually for weddings and funerals.

Poorer families could opt for *bubanshi*, or "not to hold an affair," in which case a few persons from the bride's immediate family and close kin would be invited by the groom's side to a banquet of two or three tables only and no record of contributions would be kept. *Bubanshi* implied retreat from the activation of existing kinship networks and instead a simple acknowledgment that new core social ties had been created by the marriage. Because invitations to *banshi* weddings represented continuing activation of social ties, these ties would be considered terminated if an invitation was not received. With recourse to *bubanshi*, a family avoided inviting relatives and friends without breaking social relationships. Thus, I was told, if a family chose to *banshi*, the number of guests invited would not significantly depend upon its wealth, but rather on the number of lineage agnates (*jiazu*) and affinal kin (*qinchi*) to whom they were obligated. These were most abundant for families belonging to larger lineages and where the senior generation parents had many married siblings as well as many married sons and daughters. Villagers agreed that *banshi* was the preferred and more common arrangement in the early twentieth century; one man estimated that only 20 or 30 percent of Yangmansa weddings were *bubanshi* before the region came under Japanese occupation and at the same time suffered severe droughts. During those bad years, however, as many as 80 percent of village weddings were *bubanshi*, with bride and groom "going by bicycle or palanquin in the early dawn before the sun rose and simply pasting a piece of paper inscribed with 'double happiness' [*shuangxi*] on their gate."[18]

With Communist rule came the innovations in spouse selection already described. However, remaining intact was the basic structure of the wedding itself, by which I mean the ritualized movements between the homes of bride and groom, the wedding feasts, and the gift giving, notwithstanding the fact that, as we have seen, in the flow of wealth between the families of bride and groom, and in the amounts involved, there were notable changes during the collective era. Strong pressure by the new Communist authorities to end the use of "feudal" palanquins led to the substitution in the late 1950s of horses and then bicycles, which remained the standard vehicles for conveying bride and groom into the 1980s. Traditional attire for bride and groom gave way, as did all clothing, to the "Mao jackets"[19] and Western-style trousers of the collective and postcollective periods, although new sets of clothing were still purchased for marriage. At different times large banquets were discouraged, as were explicitly religious elements such as worship of heaven and earth or the ancestors. Yet at least some families surreptitiously continued religious observances, even though the village's temples and shrines and its ancestral tablets and scrolls had all been destroyed by the end of the Cultural Revolution, if not earlier.

Contemporary marriage (during my fieldwork in 1986–87) still shows the changes of the collective era, but with decollectivization there have been further modifications, especially of betrothal payments and dowry. As before, with marriage the bride's family loses a worker, and the groom's side still bears most of the wedding cost. However, since decollectivization family corporate property has reemerged as a major factor influencing marriage, and the family has regained much of its economic autonomy. Families are now free to develop additional sources of income while in most cases continuing to farm. Women are even more important for their contribution to family income under circumstances of overall rapid economic development. There is now a greater focus on diversification, with women caring for the fields, pigs, poultry, and children, while men work outside the home in commerce or as wage earners and help with farm work during the busiest periods. All this has led to a notable increase in living standards compared with the collective era and increasingly to a focus on consumption enhancement rather than on mere subsistence.

Linked to growing prosperity and to the fact that women now marry into families where labor is no longer the sole asset has been yet another major change in the relationship between betrothal payments and dowry. In recent years (since about 1984–85) it has become less common for the bride's natal family to retain a portion of the funds given by the groom's side; rather the former increasingly must spend their own money on dowry. Furthermore, the *caili* payments—which were in the 800 to 1,200 yuan range while I was in the village—are beginning to go down in value, reflecting how through marriage and then family division a woman once again obtains access to her husband's portion of a family estate, which can include property and other holdings of value. In other words, bride-price has largely been displaced by a combination of direct and indirect dowry, direct dowry being that portion given by the bride's own family, as added to the *caili* from the groom's side now functioning as indirect dowry insofar as these funds are no longer retained but rather are used for dowry purchases. These developments mark a return to the earlier precollective pattern of transactions between parties to a marriage, where the focus of payments was on the endowment of the married couple, with better-off families providing their daughters larger dowries, even though present-day transactions have far greater value than those of the past.

It is now generally held that *caili* from the man's side should at least cover costs of the bride's clothing, while her family should pay for other dowry items. An important demonstration of the commitment of the bride's side is inclusion of a black-and-white television set or a large stereophonic tape recorder. Most recent dowries include a tape recorder (costing more than 400 yuan), perhaps because the village is already saturated with black-and-white television sets. Also, color television sets are now the prestigious dowry item, but they are in short supply and, costing well over 1,000 yuan, they are still (as of 1987) too expensive for inclusion in a standard dowry. (By the late 1990s color television sets were common in rural and urban China.)

Wedding cost data do show both sides contributing. A father describing his daughter's November 1986 wedding said that the groom's family provided 800 yuan as *caili*, while the total value of dowry provided by the bride's side was 2,255 yuan, as follows: bicycle, 170 yuan; sewing machine, 197 yuan; wristwatch, 80 yuan; tape recorder, 435 yuan; sofa, 100 yuan; large clothes closet, 200 yuan; two trunks, 60 yuan; clock, 50 yuan; four sets of bedding, 300 yuan; "daily use items," including tea set, 100 yuan; nylon coat, 128 yuan; nylon pants, 41 yuan; three sets of women's matching jackets and trousers, 160 yuan; mattress, 37 yuan; woolen rug, 50 yuan; undergarments, 110 yuan; protective winter overcoat, 37 yuan. Of the money spent for dowry 1,000 yuan was from the bride's own earnings; she had worked in the village-owned shoe factory. At first she gave her father all her wages, but then, he said, "I told her to keep some of the money for her wedding." Both families are relatively well off and well placed, and the bride's savings represented a deflection of what ordinarily would be considered family funds, one her natal family permitted and was quite able to afford. Thus her father jokingly remarked that the money she was allowed to keep was "not exactly the same thing as *tixi* [women's private fund], but amounts to the same thing; this is open [*gongkai*, as opposed to secret] *tixi*." On the groom's side the largest expense was not *caili*, but the new couple's house, which cost 5,200 yuan, with another 1,000 yuan for furnishings, new clothing for the groom, and other items. Although contributions of either side to the new couple's endowment vary depending on economic circumstances, the contribution of the groom's family is in any event much larger than the bride's.

As during the collective era, *caili* payment from the man's family is forthcoming at some point after the betrothal banquet but before the wedding, and is used by the woman's side for major purchases of her clothing, usually in Beijing. Nowadays there are two ways to make such purchases. The first is known as "*baogar*," or "[the bride's side] undertaking full responsibility." This involves the man's side making a comprehensive payment to the future bride's family covering costs of wedding attire and clothing for her dowry; an expanded form of *baogar* includes payment by the man's side for the bride's entire dowry. With either version of *baogar* the woman goes with her relatives to Beijing for a few days to buy clothing. She is accompanied by women senior to her but in her generation, her sisters-in-law and her older sisters. A brother may also come along to help bring the purchases home. The expanded *baogar* was the first to emerge, during the collective era, for it was the basis upon which the demand for *caili* was made. The second procedure is "*bubaogar*," or "not to assume full responsibility"; the man's family makes no comprehensive payment, but rather the young couple themselves do the shopping, spending about a week in Beijing, with the man bringing money provided by his family. While in Beijing the couple begins their sexual relationship, if they had not done so earlier. Although yet to have their wedding, they have been legally married since they obtained their marriage certificate during the "large betrothal" ceremonies, as described above. That the *bubaogar* pattern has only recently emerged (as of 1987) and is increasingly dominant is another manifestation of the renewed emphasis upon the joint contribution of the families of bride and groom to the new couple's endowment, for with *bubaogar* all other items of dowry are paid for directly by the bride's side. One person described the transition from *baogar* to *bubaogar* as follows:

After some days [following the "large betrothal" banquet], the go-between consults with the girl's side as to the timing of the marriage. She consults with the parents and with the girl herself. The go-between then informs the boy's side as to the schedule; the boy's side just agrees, they have no say in the matter. After determining the date, the girl and her parents consult and then decide on the amount of money they want from the boy's side. This is the *caili*. This money is used to buy clothing. This is called *baogar*, and means that all purchases are taken care of by the bride's side. The boy's side simply pays out the money. With *baogar*, the girl goes shopping with her older brothers, older sisters, older brothers' wives, etc. The older brother goes to help bring the purchases back home. For such purchases people go by train to Beijing, or at least to the Zhuoxian county seat; they don't go to Gaobeidian [the nearby Xincheng county seat, a much smaller town], which doesn't have good enough clothing. If *bubaogar*, then the boy and girl go shopping by themselves, with the boy bringing with him all the cash that they will use; this money will be about the same amount as for *baogar*, and also is the *caili*. Many marriages still are *baogar*, but even with *baogar* the girl's side in most cases will spend money of their own. If *bubaogar*—that is, when they go to Beijing to buy clothes—then the girl's side definitely will have to spend additional money. In the past, *baogar* was more common, and it was more common for the girl's side to earn money. It was much less common in the past for a couple to go to Beijing themselves to buy clothes. In the past it was more common for the payment from the man's side to cover all of the woman's side's expenses. Now, for all marriages the girl's side will spend some money of their own for dowry.

As to the connection between dowry and the change from *baogar* to *bubaogar*, one village woman put it this way:

Now about 40 percent of marriages use *baogar*, and 60 percent of the couples make the purchases on their own. This is the proportion during the past two or three years; before, during the collective period, *baogar* was far more common. And it also was more common to give a portion of the *caili* to the bride's family for their own use. Now the woman's side loses money, as a richer family will give their daughter more dowry, a poorer one less; this has developed in the last three or four years. For clothing, the man's side pays; for the other items in the dowry the woman's side pays. The most important thing is if there is a television set or a tape recorder. Nowadays, most dowries have a tape recorder but not a television set.

The trend toward *bubaogar* also shows the growing importance of "conjugalism," by which I mean a greater focus by married couples on their own interests and pleasures, as distinct from and sometimes opposed to those of the larger family.[20] Movement in this direction already was apparent during the collective period, when there began the couple's postbetrothal visits and outings as described earlier. While it is obvious that *bubaogar* represents an acceleration of this trend in that this form of dowry purchase allows the couple a few days of freedom and holidaying in Beijing, there is also an important economic element involved, for it is now the couple that controls the *caili*. That this can have interesting consequences was first brought to my attention when one woman, while describing *bubaogar*, said the following:

The boy and girl go to Beijing for up to a week, where they buy clothes for the girl, for wearing on the day of her wedding and also for later. At this time the boy can also buy clothing for himself. They can also spend time going around in the city. One trip and one payment may not be enough. In most cases, when there is one cash payment there will not be anything left over after making purchases for the bride. In a few instances, however, there will be a surplus. This money is kept by the bride; it is her *tixi* [private fund] and is used to purchase necessary items after she and her husband divide [later, from his larger family].

That *caili* under conditions of *bubaogar* can be converted into a woman's private money represents its total transformation from "brideprice" used to compensate her family to an endowment fund for the couple's exclusive use. For as *tixi*, this money is removed from family control and kept by the woman. As the quote above indicates, and as noted above, her "private money" in reality is the fund that she holds for herself, her husband, and their children. While this conjugal unit is part of a larger family the money must be held by her, for her husband's access to funds is within the context of the larger family's pooling of all income: money that passes through his hands can only be family money, such that his wife alone can represent the economic interests of their smaller conjugal unit. As elsewhere in China, the true status of woman's "private money" is thus revealed at the time of family division, when her funds and other "private" assets she might have are merged with her husband's share of the old family estate to form their new one.[21] If the conjugal unit's growing independence represents a "modernization" of family life, the expression of such independence through use of *tixi* shows the importance of traditional elements in the process of family change, with such elements contributing to a family whose "modernity" has local historical roots.[22]

What we may characterize as consumerism is an additional force impinging on marriage practices. Consumerism has no ideological value in terms of what is encouraged by the state (at least as of 1986–87), but it has growing importance in these increasingly prosperous times. There is a strong desire, again, to be modern or, rather, to be no less modern than others, especially in the context of the marriage market (thus tape recorders or television sets are now standard in dowries). The most interesting example of this trend occurred while I was in the village during the 1986–87 winter wedding season. I saw then a rapid and seemingly total transition from bicycles to cars or vans to convey the bridal party to the groom's side. This change was precipitated simply by one family setting the new local standard, and given the deliberately public nature of wedding processions, the pressure on everyone else to follow suit was enormous.

At the same time, more traditional forms of ceremonial consumption are reinforced by contemporary affluence, and for weddings this means bigger and better banquets, held in direct conflict with state propaganda to economize (again, as of 1986–87). But, as noted above, the option to economize is well known in the traditional distinction between *banshi*, "to hold an affair," and *bubanshi*, "not to hold an affair." One man, after describing how during the Japanese occupation people were afraid to sponsor large banquets, added that "now there is *bubanshi* because to *banshi* is too much trouble." While many weddings now do involve *banshi*, it is easy to confuse or conflate a traditional strategy for economizing with ostensible adherence to state pressure against "waste," since the latter would be the same as *bubanshi*. For example, when a man with six sons decided that the wedding of the last would be *bubanshi*, he expressed his desire to economize under circumstances in which *banshi* required inviting guests from a kinship network grown massive even by local standards. Yet it was easy and indeed convenient for him to express such domestic concerns in the ideological idiom propagated by the state. On the other hand, the existence of this traditional distinction also makes it easier for families to respond to state pressures to economize, for they are able to do so on the basis of well-established local conventions. But even *bubanshi* wedding banquets are getting larger, expanding from the three-table affairs of pre-Communist times and the collective era to seven, eight, or even more tables. The November 1986 marriage noted above was *bubanshi*, yet on the day before the wedding the bride's family had eight tables for about sixty guests (plus the hosts), and the groom's family invited about the same number of people the next day. The groom was the fifth son; the wedding of the fourth had been *banshi*, with seventy tables, for well over five hundred people. For the most recent wedding the bride's family did not keep a written ledger of contributions, while the groom's family did; they showed it to me, and in comparison with the ledger of the fourth son's wedding, which I also saw, it was a thin volume indeed. The intent of recording all social obligations in a ledger might seem to contradict that of *bubanshi*, to reduce the number of guests, but it would appear that the expansion of *bubanshi* banquets has required broadening the definition of a family's core kin, under circumstances of

TABLE 4.1
Women Marrying In, by Type of Marriage and Type of Wedding, Yangmansa, 1943–1987

	1943–47	1948–52	1953–57	1958–62	1963–67	1968–72	1973–77	1978–82	1983–87[a]
Total number of marriages	16	24	16	24	14	30	45	48	62
Number of marriages for which information is available	8	16	11	14	10	21	41	40	55
Percentage of marriages for which information is available	50%	67%	69%	58%	71%	70%	91%	83%	89%
Arranged marriage with full banquet	5	8	3	6	1	5	15	18	24
Arranged marriage without full banquet	3	8	8	8	8	16	21	17	24
Arranged marriage with traveling marriage	0	0	0	0	0	0	1	1	2
Free love marriage with full banquet	0	0	0	0	0	0	0	1	2
Free love marriage without full banquet	0	0	0	0	0	0	1	2	2
Free love marriage with traveling marriage	0	0	0	0	1	0	3	1	1

[a] Figures for 1987 are for January and February only.

rapid change such that no new standard has emerged. Thus both *banshi* and *bubanshi* ledgers now record obligations of reciprocity, but to different sets of relatives and acquaintances. "Not to hold an affair" is still a means of restricting the number of guests invited without damaging social relationships, but it no longer relates to the scale of betrothal payments or dowry.

Wedding banquets are notably absent in "traveling marriages" (*lüxing jiehun*), during which the bride and groom honeymoon in Beijing or elsewhere for a week or more. Although after they return there is a meal for the bride's family and closest relatives, it is small even by the standards of present-day *bubanshi* feasts. The first such marriage recorded in my survey was in 1973, and although my coverage is not complete, it is unlikely that there could have been many earlier cases. In any event, I have records of only six such marriages between 1973 and 1987 involving Yangmansa men still living in the village. Yangmansa women account for several more, and although my data do not allow for a more precise figure, it is clear enough that these marriages have never been very common. Parish and Whyte (1978: 258–59) note that there were such "traveling marriages" in Guangdong during the collective era; their presence in north China as well certainly testifies to their assimilation into a national culture of "modernity," wherein the focus on the interests and pleasures of the couple themselves is especially pronounced. In Yangmansa, however, such marriages have coexisted with the increasingly dominant *bubaogar* dowry arrangement noted above, whereby the young couple in any event will be by themselves in Beijing or elsewhere. Hence the relative rarity of traveling marriages in Yangmansa does not testify to a continuing conservative deemphasis of conjugal interests in favor of the larger family. What is important, rather, is that in a locally acceptable fashion these marriages free the couple and their families from responsibility for organizing weddings and hosting banquets.

Table 4.1 shows the quantitative data I was able to gather concerning the types of marriages and weddings discussed so far. It can be seen that my data—even when restricted to women marrying in—are far from complete, especially for earlier periods. Nevertheless, the table does provide some information of interest. First, it shows that the option as to whether or not to hold a full wedding banquet (*banshi* or *bubanshi*) has consistently been present. As noted earlier, villagers asserted that *banshi* weddings were strongly dominant during the early twentieth century, until the war with Japan reached Hebei. They also noted that recourse to *bubanshi* was far more common during the earlier years of the collective era, in part reflecting economic distress and difficulties in obtaining the food required for a large banquet, and in part in response to political pressure. *Banshi* weddings became more common later in the collective period, when economic conditions improved. This trend has continued, and since 1983, the first year of full decollectivization, there has been an equal distribution of either option (26 of each kind among the 55 out of 62 marriages for which this information is available, including in each category two "free love" marriages). A family's wealth and political position is one factor in their decision whether or not to "hold an affair," with families of higher standing in these respects far more frequently opting for *banshi*, even for the weddings of fifth and sixth sons. But, as suggested above, a son's position relative to his brothers is also important. Thus, since 1983, the first full year of decollectivization, 12 of the 21 marriages of only or first sons were marriages with *banshi* (11 arranged, 1 free love), 5 were arranged without *banshi*, while the remainder involved various combinations of free love and traveling marriages. During this period all 15 of the marriages of second sons were arranged, and of these 9 were *banshi* and 6 *bubanshi*. In contrast, only 5 out of the 19 marriages of sons with at least two older brothers were *banshi* (including 1 free love marriage), 12 were *bubanshi*, and 2 involved the other forms.

The continuing importance of family considerations is also suggested by the fact that four of the ten traveling marriages shown in Table 4.1 were arranged marriages, entered into with full family approval and with go-betweens linked to each family through prior social ties. All four involved eldest or second sons (two each), while three first or second sons and three third sons were grooms in the six "free love" traveling marriages. Thus arranged traveling marriages are most common precisely for men who would otherwise be under the strongest pressure for a *banshi* arrangement. These data, although sparse, do suggest that—whatever other considerations may be involved—traveling marriages may represent a family's appeal to "modernity" and the importance of the pleasure of the newly married couple so as to avoid both the expense of "holding an affair" and the negative consequences of not fully activating the family's social network by resorting to *bubanshi*. However, the remaining six traveling marriages were also "free love" marriages; they therefore represent the fullest expression of modern marriage forms, in which the freedom and independence of the couple are the decisive factors. However, these marriages fall into a special category as far as local society is concerned: they either involved couples who met and were married while working outside the village, or they were entered into in the face of opposition by one or both concerned families. Likewise, family approval was forthcoming with respect to the remaining eight "free love" marriages, for which there was either a full wedding banquet or at least the smaller meal called for under the *bubanshi* arrangement. In most and perhaps all of these marriages a go-between was relied upon to finalize arrangements and, at the same time, to validate the marriage in terms of local procedures. Taken together, traveling marriages and those involving "free love" still represent only a very small proportion of all marriages, and an even smaller proportion result from independent decisions on the part of bride and groom irrespective of family interests.

While the continuing interest of families in their children's marriages is demonstrated by the use of go-betweens, the dominance of arranged marriages, and the economic transactions involved, some marriage forms are especially strong expressions of family strategy. Family interests are obvious in "*huanqin*," or the "exchange" of daughters, who marry each other's brothers so that each family makes its own purchases for the new couple and avoids heavy betrothal payments. I was told that such marriages were relatively common during the collective period among families with many sons and daughters. A "two-family exchange" (*liangjia huanqin*, shortened to *lianghuan*) is a direct swap, while a "three-family exchange" (*sanjia huanqin* or *sanhuan*) is a circular transaction. In one 1973 example a family head's eldest son and eldest daughter were involved in a three-way exchange. His daughter went to Beizhuang (a village in the adjacent Zhuo County); the Beizhuang woman went to Niujiafa (like Yangmansa in Xincheng County, near the market town of Fangguan, heavily frequented by Yangmansa villagers); and the Niujiafa woman came to Yangmansa. In a 1977 example, a man's second daughter was exchanged for the wife of his fourth son (out of six); this latter woman was from a nearby village and had four brothers. In such *huanqin* marriages the women usually all go to their husbands' homes on the same day. With the far greater prosperity of the postcollective era *huanqin* is still practiced, but now largely by older men in their late twenties or early thirties who, for one reason or another, had been unable to marry in their early twenties and are thus increasingly undesirable as spouses. Such a man's family will exchange his younger sister for one in another family in similar circumstances.[23] *Huanqin* seems to have been arranged exclusively with families from outside the village, since the data at my disposal would readily reveal instances of intravillage *huanqin*—at least since the onset of the collective period—if there had been any.

By keeping sons home and yet avoiding betrothal payments, *huanqin* in many cases provided an alternative to uxorilocal marriage, in which betrothal payments are likewise avoided, but only by having the son move into his wife's natal home. In earlier times uxorilocal marriages were quite rare, with one man estimating that in this part of Hebei they accounted for well under 1 percent of all marriages. In Yangmansa I know of only one case, involving a man born in 1913 who married into a Beijing family and then divorced and returned to the village, all before the arrival of the Communists in 1948. That this was an uxorilocal marriage entered into with a city family is probably why it was undertaken at all. In such an urban environment local lineages with a strong sense of solidarity presumably did not characterize the social landscape, quite unlike circumstances in the Hebei countryside, as shown below in chapter 6. As far as the countryside is concerned, I was told repeatedly that the strong opposition of agnates was the main factor blocking such marriages. As a villager put it, "a man married uxorilocally might not make it and be kicked out by members of his wife's lineage." Closer agnates were especially hostile, because uxorilocal marriage precluded *guoji*, or the form of agnatic adoption whereby the patrilineal nephew of a man without sons inherits his property and sees to his proper worship as an ancestor (see below). Agnates aside, a family with an uxorilocally married man was looked down upon by its neighbors, and the man himself was the object of even greater contempt. Nevertheless, such marriages were recognized as a variant form, as demonstrated by the fact that there were well-known local procedures through which they were arranged, especially the use of a contract detailing the man's severing of ties with his natal family, any payments due the latter from his wife's family, and whatever might be his rights with respect to the property of the family into which he was marrying. Such were the characteristics of uxorilocal marriage as described by one elderly villager: "the man's side sent only the man and a contract; all expenses were borne by the woman's side."

Uxorilocal marriages are still infrequent, albeit more common than in the past. In Yangmansa seven women and ten men had such marriages since the first post-Communist marriage of this kind in 1961, the most recent in 1986 (this includes three marriages where both bride and groom were from the village). In contrast, from 1961 through February 1987

212 village women and 213 village men married virilocally, thus accounting for all remaining marriages. Only after eight years—in 1969—
was there the second uxorilocal marriage of the Communist era, but since
then such marriages have been consistently rare, there never being a year
with more than two. Uxorilocal marriages express family interests, usually in conjunction with varying combinations of demographic, political,
or economic hardship. For a family whose daughter is party to uxorilocal marriage, the demographic hardship is the absence of sons (or the
presence only of impaired sons, unable to marry), as was characteristic of
all but one of the families with uxorilocally married village women. The
exception was the 1961 uxorilocal marriage. The woman involved had a
married brother; but her own husband was a Beijing factory worker, and
she could not join him in that city because her "peasant" status precluded
such a move, so her husband still spends most of his time in Beijing and
joins his wife only on weekends, holidays, and during the busy season.
This marriage was an adjustment to the Communist state's controls over
population movement and did not directly reflect family concerns, such
as parental support, which otherwise typify uxorilocal marriages in the
village. Therefore the 1969 marriage was the first during the Communist
period that expressed local acceptance of this uxorilocal procedure as a
family strategy.

As far as men are concerned, the demographic hardship is their membership in a family whose very many sons represent too much of a good
thing, yet this leads to uxorilocal marriage only when exacerbated by political or economic problems. The problems were political for one family
with six sons. According to their father:

We were "rich peasants" [a "bad" class label], and during the Cultural Revolution we had difficulty finding girls to marry our sons. The oldest son worked and
married outside. [He is a middle school graduate who was assigned a job in Beijing.] The second and third sons married into their wife's families. . . . The older
brothers were able to marry outside because the [class] status of their children
would be inherited through the mother in that case; if the marriage is into the
husband's family, then it is inherited through the father. The basis of this is the
household registration.

This man's three youngest sons all married virilocally, after the political
pressure had relaxed. In another family, the uxorilocal marriages of three
out of seven sons reflected their family's poverty, exacerbated by their father's early death. Also poor was a family in which two out of three sons

married uxorilocally, and yet another where one of three so married. Thus, just four village families provided nine of the ten uxorilocally married men. The tenth case, one in which the man married into another Yangmansa family, provides a powerful example of how economic and demographic factors can encourage uxorilocal marriages, as described by this man's wife:

I married uxorilocally because one of my brothers died young and the other is retarded; in my absence, there would be no one to take care of the parents. As to my husband, his parents died young, and he was left with a younger brother. He had no assets, however, and was unable to build another house [for his own use after marriage]. If he didn't marry uxorilocally, he would have no hope of getting married. He left the original house to his younger brother.

With uxorilocal marriage all expenses connected with the man's moving into his wife's home are borne by her family. Furthermore, the man's obligations to his natal family, such as support for parents or contributions for the weddings of siblings, are terminated. Likewise, the man marrying uxorilocally relinquishes rights to a share of the family estate. This was true traditionally, during the collective era, and has remained the practice after decollectivization. Therefore, men marrying uxorilocally during the collective era, like women marring virilocally, gave up rights to workpoint earnings. The collective era team accountant quoted earlier with reference to women giving up workpoints upon marriage also noted that "the same was true for uxorilocal marriages; the man didn't take his workpoints with him."

As in the past, uxorilocal marriages commonly are fixed through written contracts specifying the man's rights after he has become a member of his bride's family. I was able to copy the text of one such contract, dated 1982, which reads as follows:

The parties to this contract of everlasting loving harmony, Guo Min and his daughter Shuxiang, and Wang Deshui and his son Jingpo, noting that as Guo Min has as his only offspring his daughter Shuxiang and that as his health is not good and he finds work difficult, and that as Wang Deshui has five sons, and that as the eldest, Jingpo, will go to the family of Guo Min and live there, have therefore today invited [the several] family heads from both sides to consult and arrange for their becoming the families party to the marriage. In accordance with the principle of self-initiative in marriage for the formation of a bond of affection the two principals consent to this marriage, which, in spite of their limitations, ought to be based on the way of Communist morality, with the parents supported from beginning to end, with joint participation in production, joint consultation over matters, mutual respect and love, and the establishment of a fine, harmonious, and happy family. After the parents have attained their hundred years [i.e., have passed away], all bequeathed property will be succeeded to by Jingpo and Shuxiang, and none of the affinal or agnatic kin are to interfere. Concerned that later there will be no evidence [of this agreement] we write out this contract as confirmation. Each of the two families party to this contract will retain one copy.

Family heads [*jiazhang*]of both sides:

Guo Wenan	Wang Deshui
Guo Wenze	Guo Min
Wang Xuelu	Guo Chun
Wang Zuoyun	Guo Zhi, amanuensis
Guo Zongzhang	

1982/3/25

That the signatories to this contract are identified as *jiazhang*, or family heads, and not as *huzhu*, or household heads, confirms the continuing importance of the *jia*—and not the administrative household—as the relevant social unit with respect to traditionally derived patterns of social action. All signatories were residents of old Jumansa [the area of present-day Yangmansa that was not the focus of my family surveys and interviewing], so that the contract pertains to an uxorilocal marriage not contained in the data given earlier. Among the signatories were the heads (Guo Min and Wang Deshui) of the families of bride and groom; also Guo Min's brothers (Guo Chun and Guo Zhi), Guo Min's father (Guo Zongzhang), and Guo Zongzhang's father's brothers (Guo Wenan and Guo Wenze). Wang Xuelu and Wang Zuoyun signed as Wang Deshui's close agnates, senior to him by two and one generations respectively. Although I was unable to determine their precise relationship to him, they are probably his father and the latter's father's brother. Guo Min's brother Guo Zhi, who served as amanuensis, was at that time the Yangmansa Brigade (now Village) vice party secretary, which may account for the effort to phrase the contract in terms reflecting Communist Party ideology. But the contract's purpose was to satisfy the far more traditional requirement that closest agnates consent to an uxorilocal marriage and thereby waive their rights to property that, given Guo Min's lack of a son, they could otherwise claim. Here, they sign on to a contract in which succession rights are explicitly assigned to the bride and groom in conformity with traditional expectations that only with such contractually explicit designation do uxorilocally married men acquire rights to the property of the family they have married into. We may take the fact that both bride and groom are specified as heirs to be a concession to the modern inheritance laws of China, a specification that protects family holdings from legal claims by the groom's family in the event that he would be predeceased by his bride. At the same time, by signing the contract Wang Deshui's agnatic kin confirmed that his son had undergone a fundamental change of status, such that he no longer had claims to his natal family's estate or a son's obligation to support his parents in their old age, pay their funeral expenses, or worship them as ancestors. Also, his responsibilities as an agnate—for example his participation in weddings and funerals—were significantly reduced. All signatories to this contract are family heads representing in each case their family as a corporate unit; because the contract represented agreement that Wang Deshui's son Wang Jingpo transfer through uxorilocal marriage from one family to another, it is not surprising that neither groom nor bride appear as signatories. That this contract with respect to its major intent and in terms of the wording of its last two and most important sentences derives from late imperial practices can be confirmed by comparing it to the Qing-period uxorilocal marriage contracts presented and discussed in chapter 9.

This contract marked the resolution of what had been a matter of some contention for, as of old, Guo Min's agnates had opposed the marriage. They preferred recourse to *guoji*, the traditional means of providing a man without sons a male heir. *Guoji* can be translated as "agnatic adoption," but the term's meaning is more accurately rendered as "to cross succession lines," for the focus is not on the transfer of parental care for an infant or young child, but rather on the obligations of the adopted heir to care for his adoptive parents and worship them after they are dead. Through the fulfillment of these duties he succeeds to their property. Because of such obligations, a person transferred from one family to another in this manner should be aware of his responsibilities. Hence infants or very young children are not qualified for *guoji*, a procedure commonly understood to be quite distinct from infant adoption (*baoyang*). As described by one villager, "To *baoyang* means to give an infant to another family in adoption; the child does not know its real parents. In order to *guoji*, the person should be old enough to know what is going on. If it is a baby that is involved, to adopt a younger brother's son is *baoyang*, not *guoji*." *Baoyang*, as defined above, was and is quite rare. During the Communist era a childless couple adopted a baby boy from a hospital in 1975. The two other occurrences of non-*guoji* adoption during this period represented responses to special circumstances. In one case a man—following his wife's death and prior to his remarriage in 1963—gave his young son and daughter in adoption to his older brother. In another a villager took in his two grandsons and one granddaughter after their father had been murdered in 1986 by his wife and her lover (these two were apprehended and executed the same year, just before I arrived in the village). As to *guoji*, it was (and still is) firmly embedded in the genealogical links between agnates, with brothers having the strongest claims on each other's sons. The local understanding of the genealogical basis of such claims was spelled out for me as follows:

> *Guoji* was the preferred means of getting a male into the family; if a son was not available from a man's brothers, then there would be *guoji* from among the sons of the *shubai xiongdi* (men with a common paternal grandfather). If there were two brothers but only one son among them, then that son would take care of both; they [the other agnates] still would not allow uxorilocal marriage. Another way would be for a man's son's son to *guoji* to the man's brother who had no sons. The principle of *guoji* is for son number so-and-so to *guoji* to son number so-and-so [i.e., a man's second son goes to this man's brother, who is also a second son]. There was *guoji* in the past and it is still practiced now.

Prior to the Communist era *guoji* reinforced virilocal marriage, insofar as daughters without brothers were not kept home. It also functioned to keep property under the control of agnates at the same time that it provided those without sons some assurance of support in their old age. That the claims of both sides party to a *guoji* transfer were based upon genealogical ties, precisely reckoned, was but one manifestation of the importance of such ties in local society, where they more generally served to define important spheres of interaction as well as lineages and lineage branches (see chapter 6). Because *guoji* involved access to another family's property, strict adherence to genealogical guidelines also served to identify those obligated to *guoji* and thereby to prevent conflicts among agnates over control of such assets.

Under Communist rule, since the appearance of uxorilocal marriages in the late 1960s, *guoji* has become the less favored option for families without sons. My own survey has in fact detected only five instances of *guoji* since 1948, with four of these taking place in the 1960s or later. That *guoji* now plays a supplementary role in conjunction with uxorilocal marriage was revealed in especially stark terms by the most recent case, in 1986, when a married man twenty-nine years old became the heir of his elderly paternal uncle. Earlier, the latter had been living with his uxorilocally married daughter and her husband, but they together with their children left him and moved to the husband's natal village, an action described to me as "family division" (*fenjia*) by Yangmansa residents. While the 1948 *guoji* was still of the "classical" type and obtained an heir for a man whose four daughters had married out, all later *guoji* excepting the one in 1986 concerned completely childless men or couples who took adult agnates as their heirs. In other words, the function of *guoji* has changed from providing successors to men without sons to providing the childless with heirs who will look after them in their old age. Yet these five cases of *guoji* do testify to the continuing importance of the genealogical orientation. Three involved eldest sons becoming the heirs of oldest brothers and one an eldest son being made heir of an eldest paternal granduncle. The one exception was a late 1960s *guoji* where an eldest son was made heir to his father's younger (and only) brother. Although the circumstances behind this deviation from expected procedures are not clear to me, they were probably related to the fact that it occurred after the eldest son and his two brothers had already divided into separate families and their parents had long since passed away. Far more than in other cases of *guoji*, it was now up to the brothers themselves to decide who would gain control over their paternal uncle's property.

Family Division

In the past the distinction between family unity and family division was clear-cut. In a unified family, married brothers lived together such that the family was an integrated unit with respect to residence, consumption, pooling of income, and the coordination of family labor. There were a few cases in which brothers lived apart, but this simply reflected family diversification involving outside employment or establishment of family enterprises at some remove from the main family residence in the village; tight economic integration was nevertheless maintained. In any event, upon division each brother—together with his wife and children—lived as an independent economic unit, sometimes in a separate house but far more frequently in a portion of the old home, which was now a multifamily residence. The new expectation, which took hold during the collective era and is now dominant, is that each son will have his own house by the time he reaches marriageable age. The demand for separate housing reflects a rising standard of living and a desire for both the additional space and the greater freedom from everyday parental interference provided by such an arrangement. A newly married woman living together with her husband in their own home is relieved of much of the burden imposed by interaction with her mother-in-law. For these reasons, and also because premarital construction of a house represents a guaranteed endowment of the new couple by the man's family, such new housing is now required if a man is to successfully compete in the marriage market.

This new trend has been encouraged by the availability of house sites (*zhaijidi*) allocated by the village government. Only males at least eighteen years old are eligible, and usually a man requests a site for his son and seeks to demonstrate that their present living quarters are too cramped. In applying for a house site the household head must write a letter to the village (*cun*) government (in the past to the production brigade), I was told, but the one letter of application I saw was held by the village head (*cunzhang*) and addressed to both the village government and the village Communist Party branch. Permission is given only after the village government and party branch decide that the applicant indeed requires more space. Should village permission be obtained, the letter is forwarded to the township government and party organization, where there is a deputy party secretary (*dangfushuji*) who has to approve each application. After permission is granted, the village is notified, and a housing site will be assigned on land set aside for such purposes, but this site will not necessarily be near the applicant's original home. A site cannot exceed 0.3 mu (18 square meters), and all are about that size. The old production teams remain the relevant units for purposes of housing site distribution; sites within a team's territory are assigned to that team's members, and this is one of the very few contexts in which such team affiliations still have some contemporary significance. A successful applicant gets the site for free. Other sites, larger or more favorably situated, are for sale. Some, formerly held by *wubaohu* ("five-guarantee households"),[24] reverted to the village when the last household member died. Others, such as those located by the side of the main road (now being paved with asphalt) and recently put up for sale by the township government to families wishing to build stores or other commercial structures, are connected with recent economic expansion.

Early residential separation is involved in a new pattern of family development, which in brief outline runs as follows. Shortly before or after a son's marriage his family builds him a new house. He and his wife live there after marriage, but they and his parents are still in one family economy, for they continue to eat together and pool family funds and other resources. After a few months or a year, however, the new couple in most cases will *danguo*, or "go it alone." *Danguo* involves separation in eating and economic life, but it is not the same as family division or *fenjia*. With *danguo* certain domestic responsibilities, such as funding the marriages of younger siblings, are still shared, and there remains at least the potential for reunification in the face of economic adversity.[25] Furthermore, I was told that during the *danguo* phase a woman still retains her private fund (*tixi*) to protect these resources from any future claims that might be made by the larger *jia*, it being understood that a woman can continue to control her private fund under various circumstances, as long as she does not tell her husband. During the collective period, a son's independence under conditions of *danguo* related primarily to workpoint distribution, as described by the former team accountant. "When someone lived *danguo*, workpoints would be separately registered, as would workpoints that had previously been earned [during that year] before *danguo*. If someone was already living *danguo*, then the subsequent family division only involved the division of property."

Whether or not preceded by *danguo*, family division (*fenjia*) remains the final event in a family's corporate history. Given that *danguo* involves separation, but prior to the final determination of certain rights and obligations concerning property and family members, it is common to characterize *fenjia* as "clear-cut division" (*fenqing* or *fenqingchu*), that is, the settlement once and for all of the distribution of family assets and obligations. In ways almost completely identical to the Taiwan practices I have described elsewhere (Cohen 1976), *fenjia* follows traditional procedures in Yangmansa, with men from outside the family invited to participate in order to facilitate agreement on property distribution and perhaps other matters frequently involved in family division, such as care of parents or support of younger siblings. If those party to division—usually brothers and their father, if he is still alive and active—have reached agreement concerning most issues, they may formalize division without participation of outsiders, or sometimes even without a contract, or they may only invite relatives such as close agnates or their mother's brother. However, the more difficult the division, the greater the necessity for assistance from those who because of their higher standing in local society are able to force agreement. Such outside participants commonly include the village head (*cunzhang*) and the village party secretary. In addition to hammering out an agreement they help prepare a written family division contract if one is thought to be needed. In some cases only these outsiders are signatories, with the parties directly involved mentioned in the text of the document, while in others both outsiders and the brothers or other parties involved (usually paternal nephews) will sign. However, the parents of sons dividing only occasionally appear as signatories.

As already noted, this procedure of family division—including participation of outsiders, distribution of family property and family responsibilities, and preparation of division contracts—is China-wide (among the Han Chinese), with obviously deep historical roots. As elsewhere, it was well established in Yangmansa during late imperial times—and doubtless much earlier—and continued to represent the final phase of family development throughout the Communist era, as it does at present (1986–87). In the pre-Communist Republican era, as during the old dynasty, those frequently invited to help families divide on the basis of their higher political and social standing also tended to be wealthier and more fully literate. One Yangmansa man, a landlord before the arrival of the Communists, had also been in demand as a family division expert. He told me how later he had to teach the new "poor peasant" leaders to write division contracts since his own "bad class" background now prevented him from providing such services.

With elimination of family-owned land and enterprises through collectivization, remaining family assets included small "private plots" (ziliudi) assigned by the collective as well as residential sites, housing, and furniture. But introduced with collectivization were workpoints, and those earned by family members formed a new kind of family property. The old team accountant provided interesting details as to how workpoints figured in family division negotiation. His remarks confirm that workpoints—no matter who in the family earned them—were indeed family property to which all parties to division had claims:

During family division the matter of workpoint distribution was discussed. When the mediator [zhongren] heard family opinion and proposed a division scheme [tichu fang'an] this would include the matter of dividing workpoints. Workpoint distribution could also serve as a basis of conflict. For example, if two brothers had been living together and prior to division had earned different amounts of workpoints, they might nevertheless decide to split the workpoints equally between them. If the brothers were on good terms, one who had accumulated more workpoints might give some to a brother who had earned fewer. If they were not on good terms they might make an equal division. The general pattern was for brothers to divide workpoints equally, even though earnings of necessity were different.

With respect to married brothers, if one was only recently married so that his wife had earned few or no workpoints, while the other's wife had been earning workpoints throughout the year up to division, the division was nevertheless equal between the two brothers. If the oldest brother had two children, for example, and the second none, then they might agree to distribute joint workpoint earnings on a per capita basis. The same applied to the support of parents if they should stay with one of the sons. If the sons divided and left the parents by themselves, workpoints accumulated prior to division might be distributed on a per capita basis, but after division it would be up to the family members to decide how to distribute the burden of parental support.

With family division, the division of workpoints was just like the division of property; the people involved would inform the team accountant as to the distribution agreed upon, and he would adjust his accounts accordingly. These matters were not included in the family division contract [*fenjiadan*], however, because as soon as they agreed they would notify the accountant.

While in Yangmansa I was able to see and copy only four family division contracts, all from 1986 and far fewer than I had hoped would come my way. My own survey revealed that during the collective era between 1956 and 1981 there were forty-three cases of family division (final division, not including the more numerous instances of "going it alone"). Villagers recalled that fifteen involved division contracts and twenty were oral agreements, while circumstances regarding the remaining eight were unclear. After decollectivization, from 1982 through 1986, another fifteen contracts were written, but this time in contrast to only nine oral agreements, with two cases not clear. The trend toward an increase in the proportion of family divisions with written contracts may be linked to increasing prosperity since the break-up of the collectives. With more property, more is at stake when families divide; people are more inclined to protect through written agreements holdings obtained through division. Also, assurances traditionally included in division contracts concerning care of parents have assumed greater importance since decollectivization, which saw the elimination of previously free or heavily subsidized medical services.

The four contracts that I did obtain provide varying perspectives on what remains at issue in the postcollective era, when family division is usually preceded by "going it alone," and when among the claims negotiated or recognized are those of each son for a portion of land based upon the original per capita distribution that ended the collective system. Even though this initial distribution of collective lands still remained fixed at the time of my fieldwork, such that changes in family membership through births, deaths, or marriages did not lead to reallocations, there was still the strong perception among villagers that land was indeed state-allocated and subject to reclamation. Awareness of the fragility of rights to farmland as family holdings, reinforced by the original principle of per capita allocation of collective land, and by the practice of "going it alone" after marriage, may be behind the increasing importance of per capita distributions of family-farmed land when sons "go it alone" and then divide. Such circumstances may also help to explain why farmland distribution often is totally ignored in division contracts, as in three of the four I was able to copy.

Yet the four contracts also illustrate the continuing importance of totally traditional criteria in family division agreements, as reflected in the division of family property only among sons and in their equal rights and their postdivision responsibilities to parents and unmarried siblings. Such traditional elements loom large in contemporary family division contracts from other Chinese communities. This was the case in a Shandong Province village, where Eric T. Miller was able to collect copies of fourteen family division contracts, all dating from the Communist era. In his discussion of them (Miller 2004: 43–50), he provides extracts and in a few cases the full text of these agreements, which can be compared to those from Yangmansa that follow below. The Yangmansa division contracts also should be compared with those from a community in Qing-era southern Taiwan whose texts are given and discussed in chapter 9. Despite the large differences in space and time, it can readily be seen that the Yangmansa and Taiwan contracts are products of the same late imperial culture. That the Communist state now requires children to support retired parents obviously provides a certain powerful reinforcement, but in Yangmansa this requirement is met only by means of the traditional support obligations of virilocally married sons (i.e., those with a claim to the family estate), uxorilocally married daughters, and unmarried children still members of their parents' family.

One contract is fairly typical of those written after decollectivization in that the focus is largely or exclusively on the distribution of residential holdings, with farmland either ignored or brought into the picture only under special circumstances. However, the contract is notable for its detailed focus on the exact dimensions of the division of the family's one residential site:

The parties to family division—Xu Chengjun, Xu Chengjie, Xu Chengnian, Xu Fuchang:

We four parties, being [three] brothers and their paternal nephew [their deceased oldest brother's son], following discussion by the entire family, shall allocate control of our parents' property among the four of us. The parent's residential plot shall be divided into four portions. The front plot on the western side goes to

Chengjie; from south to north its length is 24.2 meters; its southern edge is 18.85 meters wide; its northern edge is 19.35 meters wide. The front plot on the eastern side goes to Fuchang; from south to north its length is 30.7 meters; its southern edge is 24.2 meters wide; its rear [northern] edge is 23.7 meters wide. The rear plot on the eastern side goes to Chengjun; its southern edge has a length of 30.7 meters; from east to west it has a length of 22 meters. The rear plot on the western side goes to Chengnian; from south to north it has a length of 24.4 meters; its front edge has a width of 19.35 meters; its rear edge of 23 meters is bounded by Chengjun['s plot]. The excess land on the western side of Chengjun['s plot] goes to Chengjie. Distributed together with these newly divided residential plots and houses are the trees [located thereupon]. The fifteen large trees go together [with the plots whereon they are located] and there shall be no transfers or compensation [so as to equalize their distribution]. Each party consents to the above conditions and will not go back on [this agreement]. If anyone does renege word of mouth provides no guarantee, and this contract is put into writing as evidence.

> Parties to the contract: Xu Chengjun, Xu Chengjie, Xu Chengnian, Xu Fuchang
> Guarantors: Yang Gui, Xu Weitian, Wang Hongchen
> Amanuensis: Wang Zengcai
>
> 1986, second month, nineteenth day

During fieldwork in Yangmansa, elsewhere in mainland China, and on Taiwan I was told often enough that with substantial property involved or with strong and conflicting claims among the parties to family division there will be a written rather than an oral contract and the participation of more outsiders. Also, the more serious the original disagreements, the higher the social and political standing of the outsiders participating and the greater the detail in the resulting document. As indicated in the above contract, the outsiders helping the family to divide were indeed important figures in that family's social universe: those listed as guarantors (*zhong-baoren*) who helped hammer out the agreement were the village (the old production brigade) party secretary, the village head, and the mother's brother (*jiujiu*) of the three siblings. In addition to this characteristic mix of locally prominent persons and key relatives there was the amanuensis (*daibiren*), who had been the old production team's accountant and was known to be experienced in writing division contracts.

In this particular division the value of family holdings was hardly especially high relative to other village families; but none of the parties involved had obtained separate house sites, and in the absence of any prior clear-cut allocation of residential arrangements each party's rights to the one plot they had possessed in common was spelled out in considerable detail. Each of the three brothers had followed the now-typical pattern of separating from their parents shortly after marriage and taking up residence in a house the latter had built for them; but in this case, the three houses were all on the one plot that their father had obtained from his. Farmland is not mentioned in this contract because with decollectivization in 1982 it had already been distributed to all the sons, born respectively in 1947, 1949, and 1952. When they received this land through per capita allotment, all three were already married and living apart (*danguo*).

In this and the other three Yangmansa contracts, and in many Qing and post-Qing division agreements that I have seen from the mainland or Taiwan, the father does not appear as signatory, reflecting the quite traditional idea that family division is an act of *succession*, not *inheritance*, with those involved exercising claims to family property through birth or adoption. In some division contracts, as shown in chapter 9, the father does indeed sign on, together with his sons, often as an expression of the fact that he has jumpstarted the division process by demanding that his sons divide the family while he, the father, is still alive and has the power to play an important or even decisive role in the outcome. Usually, however, the father does not sign because he as an individual has no claim to this property, while his prior claim as family head is obviated precisely by the act of division that deprives him of this role. We will see in chapter 9 how in traditional land sale contracts it was common for only the seller, middleman, and witnesses to be signatories. The buyer did not sign, but instead took possession of the contract (together with earlier contracts, if available), which thus served as deed of ownership. Likewise, in traditional family division contracts the father often does not sign, but his sons usually do; in two of the four 1986 Yangmansa contracts only the witnesses and the amanuensis signed, although in each the names of the brothers directly involved were in the text. In any event, each son gets a copy, which serves as deed of ownership. The circumstances of family division are such that a particular brother's possession of his share in the family estate is confirmed by the division contract containing the signatures or at least specific mention in the text of all brothers or other parties with claims to this estate (sons of deceased brothers, for example). In a sale, the seller by his signature as family head confirms alienation and transfer from one family estate to another, while confirmation of family division does not need the father's signature, nor even mention of his name, since now he has no family to represent. Yet the above contract, as well as the three introduced and discussed below, result from family division indeed involving the father as an active participant, insofar as some of those party to the contract, usually younger unmarried sons, remain with him. In the above case, still living with his grandfather was the fourth signatory, the unmarried nineteen-year-old Xu Fuchang, the deceased oldest brother's only son and therefore his sole successor. The grandfather assumes control of his grandson's portion of the old housing site until such time as the latter marries, at which point the grandparents most likely become the "collective dependents" (see Cohen 1976: 74–75, 213) of all successor households. With his sixty-six-year-old grandfather disabled, and his grandmother, at sixty-eight, well past the age when women retire from most work in and out of the house, the unmarried grandson farmed the land still held by his grandfather, again on the basis of the earlier per capita distribution of production team land. Included in this land was the portion allocated this grandson's sister—still unmarried at twenty-three—who also lived with her grandparents and did most of the cooking and housework.

The dimensions of residential plots are left unstated in the following contract, for the eldest of the two brothers involved had already been allocated his own house site:

We, the parties to this family division, the two brothers Hu Zhenming and Hu Zhenxian, no longer desire to live together, and each of his own free will wishes to establish his own family. For this reason we have asked that our *zushu* [lineage father's elder brother, i.e. senior generation lineage agnate] Hu Shiping serve as witness [*zhongzhengren*] with respect to the division of our family's two residential land sites, these being the old plot and the new plot. The new plot goes to Hu Zhenming, including the four-room [*jian*] house and its furnishings. The old plot goes to Hu Zhenxian, including all trees; furthermore, our two parents will assist [Hu Zhenxian] in building a five-room house, one room of which will serve as the living quarters of our two parents until the end of their years. At that time this one room will go to Hu Zhenxian, and Hu Zhenming is not to interfere. Also, after the marriage of Hu Zhenxian the living expenses of our two parents will be borne by we two brothers. Each year they will be supplied one thousand catties [*jin*] of grain; each brother will be responsible for 500 catties, out of which fine grain [*xiliang*, wheat] will comprise 300 catties and course grain [*culiang*, maize] 200 catties; each brother [will provide the parents] monthly pocket money to the sum of five yuan. Both the provision and the washing of [the parents'] clothing will be the responsibility of the two families [*jia*, i.e., of the two brothers, now divided into two families]. Fearing that verbal understanding is unreliable, we now execute this contract as evidence [of our agreement].

Mediator-witness: Hu Shiping
Amanuensis: Hu Shijie
1986

This contract was written when the father of the two brothers party to family division was sixty-one years old and their mother fifty-three; it is one in which the brothers directly involved did not add their signatures to the document. As stated in the contract, the witness and the amanuensis were chosen because they were agnates obligated to help when so requested; other than the latter's contract-writing expertise, neither had elite political or social status in the village. The eldest son married in 1984 and after eleven months moved to his own house, built with family funds and resources on a residential plot allocated by the village. Thus family division took place only a few months after the eldest son's departure. According to the mother, this family division confirmed by contract meant that "we have divided completely, everything is clear [*qingchu*]." The older son and his wife already had a young child, while the younger son still lived with his parents, so that the division of farm land into two equal portions amounted to a per capita distribution not dealt with in the contract. The division also reflected the traditional equality of brothers as far as succession to the family estate is concerned. This distribution does not, however, accord with the original land allocations that came with decollectivization, since the eldest son was still single at that time, and the youngest of his sisters had yet to marry out.

Much of this contract deals with postdivision obligations. After division, the still-single younger son continued to reside with his parents, commuting daily to a salaried job in the nearby town of Gaobeidian, but spending time at home when farmwork was most demanding. As do most unmarried children living with their parents, this son gave all outside earnings to his father or mother. Thus when the contract notes the obligation of the parents to help this son build a new house, most if not all of the money needed will have come from the latter's earnings. Noting this parental obligation underscores the fact that at this point, prior to the son's marriage, the parents remain in control of the family and its economic affairs, even though neither has signed the contract. Furthermore, by specifying parental responsibility for the construction of their younger son's house, the contract frees the older son from any obligation to contribute. Likewise, it explicitly denies him any claim to this house. This stipulation cannot be understood other than in terms of the totally traditional requirement that after family division all resultant families retain collective responsibility for the future marriage expenses of any unmarried brothers and sisters. In present-day Yangmansa such a responsibility includes providing a son or brother with a new house. However, as in the above contract, and also in full accordance with traditional patterns, these responsibilities can be met through alternative agreed-upon arrangements, and the house specified in this contract was already being built when I visited the parents in early November 1986.

This contract also documents how with their second son's marriage the parents no longer have authority over him as a member of their family; they continue to live with him, but now in a room specifically identified as part of his estate. Likewise, rather than having claim to this son's earnings by dint of his membership in their family, they are jointly supported by both sons, as specified by the contract in some detail.

In the next contract the existing distribution of residential plots again forms the basis of division, without specification of their dimensions or location. Once more, postdivision support of the parents is a major concern, and they still live with their youngest son, not yet married, at the time of division. But this contract reveals another possible arrangement of the transformation of parents from senior members of their own family into collective dependents of families headed by their sons. Rather than staying with one son after division, as specified in the preceding contract, the parents get a room in each son's house, thus ending even in terms of residence their membership in an independent family. In the previous contract the parents agree to help their youngest son build his house, thus relieving his older brother of responsibility to support an unmarried younger sibling, while in the contract that follows the obligations of older to younger brothers are in spelled out in detail:

Determination of a contract for family division

Concerning the family division of the four brothers Hu Zhenyu, Zhenxue, Zhenfu, and Zhengui.

Zhenyu: the buildings, property, and trees in the compound where he presently resides go to him. From within there will be removed one poplar tree, which will be given to the parents for sustenance in their old age.

Zhenxue: the buildings, property, and trees in the compound where he presently resides go to him.

Zhenfu: the buildings, property, and trees in the compound where he presently resides go to him.

Zhengui: the buildings, property, and trees in the compound where he presently resides go to him. When he rebuilds his house, his three older brothers Zhenyu, Zhenxue, and Zhenfu will each give him 150 yuan. When he marries each of his three older brothers will give an additional 150 yuan.

Each of the four brothers will give 15 yuan a month for the old-age support of their parents, whose medical expenses will be borne equally by the four brothers. The parents will reside where they please, and in each compound there will be a place for them to live.

As evidence [for the above], a contract is set out in writing.

Witnesses [*zhengren*]: Hu Zhendong
    Hu Shirong
    Hu Shiliang
Amanuensis: Hu Shixian

1986, third month, thirteenth day

The father was sixty-three years old and his wife fifty-seven when this contract was written. The witnesses and the amanuensis were agnatic kin, none with prominent formal leadership positions in the village, but all were among the village's more prosperous families and recognized for their managerial know-how. The amanuensis was the accountant at the village-owned electroplate factory. The youngest son, then nineteen, worked in the shoe factory, also village-owned, and, as usual, turned his salary over to his parents. With his three married older brothers party to this agreement, it represented negotiation of the impending final phase of a long process of residential and economic dispersion. This process was described to me by their mother; because it illustrates the relationship between housing, marriage, and division, I summarize her remarks:

Each of the sons separated after getting married. For the first son, we first built him a house and then he married [in 1979]. The house was built three or four years before he married, and he lived there with his paternal grandmother [*nainai*] before he married. At that time we had not yet begun to negotiate his marriage. For his marriage, the go-between arrived on the eighth lunar month, and he was married on the twelfth month. His house was distant from this one that we, his parents, live in, and the house site was issued to them by their team. He separated after one year of marriage; living far away, it was not convenient to eat together. All the furnishings in the new house went to the son.

The period from the second son's marriage [in 1982] to separation was seven months. From completion of the new house to marriage was two years. In those two years he lived alone in the new house. It also was on a house site issued by the team and distant from this one. Again, the go-between arrived on the eighth lunar month, and the marriage was on the twelfth month.

For the third son, there was one year from completion of his new house to marriage [in 1985]. Again, the house was distant from that of his parents and on an allotted site. Between the arrival of the go-between and marriage there was one year. When the go-between arrived they already had begun to build the new house. Marriage was during the eleventh lunar month, separation the following third month.

In each case people came to help with the separation. They helped divide the grain and the land. The oldest son just started eating separately; with the second son, they began to use four people to help them divide the property: Hu Shirong, Hu Shixian, Hu Shiliang, Hu Zhendong. They came to help because they are known as people who can help others solve problems. The same four people came to help with the division of the third son. One of them, Hu Shixian, wrote the division document. This actual division contract [*fenjiadan*] was written only on the occasion of the third son's division. But all four sons have a copy of this document, for it is an understanding as concerns all of them, and involves agreement that each of the three already separated will contribute fifteen yuan per month to their parents. The fourth son gives his earnings to his mother and also asks her for money when he needs some.

Much of the final contract to be introduced here refers to matters already familiar from the preceding documents. Unlike in the others, however, the assignment of residential plots does not simply reflect preexisting arrangements, and there is explicit mention of the distribution of some farmland:

Family division contract

In obedience to our mother's command and because living together as one family is no longer convenient, we the parties to this division contract, Yang You, Yang Chuan, and Yang Qing, by common consent will equally divide our holdings into three portions. Each [of us] will establish his own family and [by executing] the clauses [of this contract] relevant to property, etc., we will once and for all clearly divide [everything].

1. To the east of the wall of the supply cooperative there is one residential plot with a three-room [*jian*] house, and this goes to Yang You. The residential plot bequeathed to us by our ancestors has two houses, each with three rooms; the western section of this plot goes to Yang Qing, and the eastern section goes to Yang Chuan. Each of the three brothers will prepare a one-room residence for mother to live in. Nobody can refuse to do this. From among the trees originally growing in the compound bequeathed to us by our ancestors, ten will be selected and given to mother for her ownership.

2. The three portions of responsibility land [*zerentian*, land allocated with decollectivization] now held by mother [the three portions being those allocated per capita to the mother, her deceased husband, and her unmarried daughter] will be distributed among the three brothers, with each given one portion to cultivate. Every year each person will give our mother and younger sister grain, to the amount of 250 catties of wheat and 100 catties of maize. After our younger sister's marriage, the amount of grain to be supplied [to mother, who will then be alone] will be adjusted.

3. Each of the three brothers will give mother a monthly payment of ten yuan for her living expenses. The medical expenses of our mother and younger sister as billed will be equally borne by the three brothers, as will all other expenses of mother and younger sister. Three willow trees behind the house will be selected for use as longevity timber [i.e., for mother's coffin].

4. When younger sister marries all expenses will be borne equally by the three brothers. After this family division should there be any regrets among the sons, or wrangling over misunderstandings [of this agreement], the matter will be attended to by the middleman [and guarantor]. Fearing that a verbal understanding is unreliable, we now execute this division contract as evidence [of our agreement].

Family division guarantors [*zhongbaoren*]: Hu Shiying, Yang Tian
Parties to the family division contract: Yang You, Yang Chuan, Yang Qing
Amanuensis: Hu Yulian
Common era [*gongyuan*] 1986, third month, sixth day

The contract details support for the mother, fifty-seven years old at the time of division, and her youngest daughter, fourteen. Living with the mother, whose husband had died the previous year, were this daughter and her youngest son, twenty-one. This contract was written in anticipation of the rapidly approaching transformation of mother and daughter into the collective dependents of the three brothers; while the eldest had married in 1979, the second and third were already betrothed and married before the end of the year in which the contract was written. One witness was an agnate; the other witness and the amanuensis held longstanding salaried positions—involving management responsibilities—in Gaobeidian, the nearby county seat, and their families were among the wealthier ones in the village. These families were close neighbors whose ties to the family now dividing had historically been reinforced when all three were in the same production team.

Circumstances behind the allocation of residential plots were different from those encountered in the other contracts, in that the first house noted in this document, built two years earlier on an allocated site, was given to the eldest son, although originally it had been intended for the second. The latter subsequently obtained a salaried job in Beijing, where he lived except for brief returns to the village; at the time of division he was already betrothed to a woman from that city. Although he continued to live in Beijing after his marriage in early November 1986, he planned at some point to return to the village; this man had no intention of giving up his rights to the family estate. Prior to division, the mother and her youngest son and daughter lived as a household: they held the farm land allocated to them on a per capita basis, as well as that allocated to her late husband and to the son in Beijing. With division and the marriage of these two sons, the portions allocated to them through decollectivization came under the direct control of their own new families, and they are not dealt with in this contract. What is specified, however, is land representing allocations to the deceased father, the mother, and her youngest daughter. With the latter two now collective dependents, the land is distributed among those supporting them, which involves the assignment of additional land to each of the three sons.

With residential dispersion and even the emergence of economically independent households now commonly preceding family division, formal *fenjia* might be seen merely as a kind of tidying up, as a final adjustment among married sons of property rights and continuing responsibilities such as the support of parents or siblings not yet married. However, that *fenjia* remains important enough to require procedures and often contracts of the kind discussed above should alert us to the continuing importance of the *jia* as a social and corporate unit even when it is no longer a unit in residential or economic terms. The *jia* receives recognition in the larger community as, for example, the unit for participation in weddings and funerals. But for its members the *jia* also comprises a social unit, one characterized by casual and diffuse economic ties such that brothers, their wives, and their children frequently eat at each others homes, or during the busy periods of the farm season combine working and eating arrangements. These shifting and variable ties contrast with those following division, when each of several brothers formally declares the independence of his own family and the relationships between brothers are finally transformed from those of family members into those of relatives. In contemporary Yangmansa the *jia* represents a flexible arrangement among separate households united by common corporate interests. While it is true that for most *jia* residential separation represents a phase in the transition to full social and economic independence, the very flexibility of *jia* arrangements allows for the possibility of other outcomes, including the maintenance of considerable economic integration. That *jia* arrangements are adjustable accounts for the *jia*'s continuing importance. Although there have been massive and obvious changes in rural social life since the onset of Communist rule, the enduring significance of the *jia* is manifested in property relationships and division practices such that these are highlighted as being among the most conservative elements in local society. These continuities reveal the ongoing importance of the family as a corporate unit that under appropriate circumstances can organize itself as an enterprise with the potential to provide important benefits for its members. In the uncertain world of rural China, people do not seem inclined to totally abandon such arrangements.

Family Structure and Development

Because the *jia* has maintained itself as a corporate unit whose foundation is family property, it is not surprising that Yangmansa family composition still reflects arrangements traditionally characteristic of Chinese family units. Tables 4.2 and 4.3 show that simply on the basis of residential households, terms long used in the literature concerning Chinese family structure still apply: most Yangmansa households can be identified as "conjugal," "stem," or "joint," that is, as containing respectively only one married couple, two married couples in each of two generations, or two married couples in one generation (with the exception of single-person households, the absence of one spouse due to death or divorce does not change the typology used here).[26] The three family forms of course represent stages of family development given that sons remain with their parents and are joined by their wives, and the family continues to grow in size and complexity until there is family division. However, not everyone fully participates in such processes of family change, especially insofar as they involve marriage and patrilineal succession: in some cases married couples fail to have sons, and in others people are unable to marry due to poverty or some physical liability. Table 4.2 shows how because of these and other factors influencing family development one household is composed of three unmarried brothers; seven out of fourteen single-person households are listed as independent *jia*, for in each an elderly person survives without the support of sons; there are also ten households where brothers, paternal uncles, or other solitary relatives have been taken in. Such solitary couples or individuals would be far more numerous if not for the relief traditionally offered those without sons by the *guoji* form of agnatic adoption and, more recently, by uxorilocal marriage.

Most people in Yangmansa do live in households that reflect family development processes based upon the availability of sons for marriage. These processes have been changing, however, such that the overwhelming majority of conjugal households express the trend toward early residential separation of parents and sons that took hold in the collective era and has continued since. Even when viewed with respect to *jia* rather than household relationships, the trend toward simplification remains apparent. Table 4.3 shows that if about 72 percent of all households are conjugal, 53 percent of all households are conjugal at the same time that they are independent *jia*; of these latter 146 households, 13 were not the

TABLE 4.2

Yangmansa Households by Form and Composition, March 1, 1987

Household form	Household composition	Household status	Number of households	Total membership
One person	Full	*Jia*	7	7
One person	Full	Dependent	7	7
Brothers	Full	*Jia*	1	3
Conjugal	Full	*Jia*	129	538
Conjugal	Full + brother	*Jia*	3	18
Conjugal	Full + brother + maternal gm	*Jia*	1	5
Conjugal	Full + paternal gm	*Jia*	1	5
Conjugal	Father	*Jia*	2	5
Conjugal	Mother	*Jia*	7	19
Conjugal	Mother: divorced	*Jia*	1	3
Conjugal	Full: uxorilocal	*Jia*	2	9
Conjugal	Full	*Danguo*	30	114
Conjugal	Full + paternal uncle	*Danguo*	1	5
Conjugal	Full + grandchildren	*Danguo*	1	6
Conjugal	Full	Dependent	15	33
Conjugal	Full + grandchildren	Dependent	1	4
Conjugal	Mother	Dependent	2	4
Stem	Full	*Jia*	22	150
Stem	Full + mother	*Jia*	3	22
Stem	Full + brother	*Jia*	2	15
Stem	Full + mother's brother	*Jia*	1	10
Stem	Father	*Jia*	3	14
Stem	Mother	*Jia*	15	86
Stem	Mother + mother's brother	*Jia*	1	6
Stem	Mother with son (widower)	*Jia*	2	7
Stem	Mother with divorced son	*Jia*	1	4
Stem	Full: uxorilocal	*Jia*	2	12
Stem	Father: uxorilocal	*Jia*	2	6
Stem	Mother: uxorilocal	*Jia*	1	5
Stem	Full	*Danguo*	3	17
Joint	Full	*Jia*	2	17
Joint	Full + mother	*Jia*	1	9
		TOTALS	272	1,165

NOTE: A household is "full" if it contains all persons defining its form. In a full conjugal household there will be husband and wife with or without unmarried children; a full stem household will contain father and mother, with or without unmarried children, but with one married son or daughter (if uxorilocal) and that person's spouse; a full joint household has parents with at least two married sons and their wives with or without the unmarried siblings of the sons and with or without the sons' unmarried children. In conjugal or stem households where a spouse is absent (due to death or divorce), the remaining spouse is identified as "father" or "mother." Other than unmarried children, who for the purposes of this table are not shown, the "+" sign indicates the presence of a household member in addition to those defining its form. For example, a stem household described as "full + mother" includes a man, his wife, his son, the latter's wife, and the man's mother.

TABLE 4.3

Yangmansa Households: Distribution by Structure and Jia Relations,
March 1, 1987

Household category	Number of households	Percentage of all households	Total membership	Percentage of total population
One person: *jia*	7	2.57%	7	0.60%
One person: dependent	7	2.57%	7	0.60%
Brothers: *jia*	1	0.37%	3	0.26%
Total	15	5.51%	17	1.46%
Conjugal: *jia*	146	53.68%	602	51.67%
Conjugal: *danguo*	32	11.76%	125	10.73%
Conjugal: dependent	18	6.62%	41	3.52%
Total all conjugal	196	72.06%	768	65.92%
Stem: *jia*	55	20.22%	337	28.93%
Stem: *danguo*	3	1.10%	17	1.46%
Total all stem	58	21.32%	354	30.39%
Joint	3	1.10%	26	2.23%
TOTALS	272	100.00%	1,165	100.00%

result of family division, but rather of single-heir succession in nine cases, uxorilocal marriage in three, and divorce in one. This leaves 133 conjugal households, or 48 percent of all households that are independent *jia* as a result of division. Also resulting from division are about another 7 percent of all village households that comprise conjugal households made up of collective dependents (mainly parents with some unmarried children). Thus about 55 percent of all village households are conjugal in form and result from family division. That there are also collective dependents in seven of the single-person households—each consisting of an elderly parent living apart from his or her sons—is perhaps the strongest evidence of how for younger people the importance of residential privacy in some cases overrides earlier or competing notions of filiality and parental care.[27] However, even in terms of household composition the corporate *jia* is strongly in evidence, as manifested by the fact that about 30 percent of the village population lives in stem households and that three households are indeed joint in form. At the same time, the now-common occurrence of "going it alone" (*danguo*) means that in terms of *jia* (rather than household) form there is a somewhat higher degree of complexity. Table 4.3 shows that thirty-two conjugal and three stem households are *danguo* rather than independent *jia*, such that they comprise nine joint and four stem *jia*, as detailed in Table 4.4. The member-

TABLE 4.4

Yangmansa Households "Going It Alone" (Danguo), by Jia Form,
Jia Membership, Household Form, Household Condition, and
Household Membership, March 1, 1987

Jia form	Jia membership	Household form	Household condition	Household membership
Joint	17	Conjugal	Full	3
		Conjugal	Full	4
		Conjugal	Full	5
		Conjugal	Full	5
Joint	15	Conjugal	Full	4
		Conjugal	Full	4
		Conjugal	Full	4
		Conjugal	Full	3
Joint	11	Conjugal	Full	4
		Conjugal	Full	3
		Conjugal	Full	4
Joint	10	Conjugal	Full	4
		Stem	Full	6
Joint	12	Conjugal	Full	3
		Conjugal	Full	3
		Conjugal	Full + grandchildren	6
Joint	9	Conjugal	Full	4
		Stem	Full	5
Joint	9	Conjugal	Full	3
		Conjugal	Full	3
		Conjugal	Full	3
Joint	16	Conjugal	Full	3
		Conjugal	Full	5
		Conjugal	Full	3
		Conjugal	Full + paternal uncle	5
Joint	9	Conjugal	Full	3
		Stem	Full	6
Stem	9	Conjugal	Full	5
		Conjugal	Full	4
Stem	9	Conjugal	Full	5
		Conjugal	Full	4
Stem	9	Conjugal	Full	4
		Conjugal	Full	5
Stem	7	Conjugal	Full	4
		Conjugal	Full	3

	Joint	Stem
Number of jia with danguo	9	4
Total membership	108	34
Membership as percentage of village population	9.27%	2.29%

TABLE 4.5

Yangmansa Jia: Distribution by Structure and Household Relations,
March 1, 1987

Jia form	Number of jia	Number of households	Percentage of all households	Total membership	Percentage of total population
Dependents		25	9.19%	48	4.12%
Single person	7	7	2.57%	7	0.60%
Brothers	1	1	0.37%	3	0.26%
Conjugal	146	146	53.68%	602	51.67%
Stem	59	63	23.16%	371	31.85%
Joint	12	30	11.03%	134	11.50%
TOTALS	225	272	100.00%	1165	100.00%

ship of all joint and stem *jia* accounts for more than 44 percent of the village population, as shown in Table 4.5, which takes the *jia* rather the household as its main point of reference.

A comparison of 1987 family arrangements with those of earlier periods reveals both changes and continuities. Tables 4.6, 4.7, and 4.8 show the distribution of household structures at different times. In these tables I have arranged the data according to both household form and the class labels assigned during the 1949 land reform campaigns. The three tables are based upon my own survey, which incorporated, corrected, and expanded the 1964 individual household census forms and the household registration books that were current as of November 1986. My focus on the household rather than the *jia* allows for far more precise comparisons across time, even though it also conceals the new *jia* relationships that took hold as "going it alone" became increasingly prominent during the collective era. Arranging the 1950 family data (Table 4.6) according to class label should help clarify the extent to which pre-Communist family development was conditioned by differences in landholdings. In order to explore the degree to which differences linked to class label in 1950 had relevance to later family development I also classify households or derivative households in 1964 (Table 4.7) and in 1987 (Table 4.8) by class label; although these labels were abolished in 1979, I use them for the purpose of continuing the comparison up through the time of my fieldwork. It is to be expected that differences in family form associated with economic differences before land reform would continue to have an impact—at least for a period—on subsequent patterns of family development. There may be a more subtle relationship between class label and

TABLE 4.6

Yangmansa Households, by Structure, Size, and Class Label,
December 31, 1950

Household structure	Class label					
	Landlord	Rich peasant	Middle peasant	Poor peasant	Unknown	Totals
INDIVIDUAL						
Number of households	0	0	0	4	0	4
Total membership	0	0	0	4	0	4
Average membership	0.00	0.00	0.00	1.00	0.00	1.00
Membership as percentage of class or total population	0.00%	0.00%	0.00%	1.17%	0.00%	0.61%
CONJUGAL						
Number of households	1	1	20	54	3	79
Total membership	5	6	80	246	16	353
Average membership	5.00	6.00	4.00	4.56	5.33	4.47
Membership as percentage of class or total population	41.67%	100.00%	28.99%	72.14%	76.19%	53.81%
STEM						
Number of households	1	0	17	15	1	34
Total membership	7	0	131	91	5	234
Average membership	7.00	0.00	7.71	6.07	5.00	6.88
Membership as percentage of class or total population	58.33%	0.00%	47.46%	26.69%	23.81%	35.67%
JOINT						
Number of households	0	0	6	0	0	6
Total membership	0	0	65	0	0	65
Average membership	0.00	0.00	10.83	0.00	0.00	10.83
Membership as percentage of class or total population	0.00%	0.00%	23.55%	0.00%	0.00%	9.91%
ALL HOUSEHOLDS						
Number of households	2	1	43	73	4	123
Total membership	12	6	276	341	21	656
Average membership	6.00	6.00	6.42	4.67	5.25	5.33
Membership as percentage of total population	1.83%	0.91%	42.07%	51.98%	3.20%	100.00%

NOTE: Middle peasant households include one conjugal household where only the mother is present and another with the father's brother; in one stem household there is the father's brother and in another there is only the father. Among poor peasant conjugal households there are two where the father's brother is present; in four stem households there is only the mother and in one only the father.

family development in that a family's economic circumstances could also reflect differences in managerial capability or with respect to other skills continuing to confer advantage during the collective era, and perhaps even after decollectivization.

Table 4.6 shows household arrangements as of the end of 1950, before Communist rule had a major impact on family development. The household composition survey upon which this table is based used as its earliest reference point the 1964 individual household census forms. Even though I was able to enlarge and correct the 1964 census data, and to extend my own coverage to this earlier period, it is most probable that I missed a few 1950 households that left no members or descendants to be picked up by the census carried out fourteen years later, perhaps including households containing only isolated individuals or those comprising elderly couples with no children or only with daughters who had all married out of the village before 1964. I do know that one landlord household (husband, wife, three sons, and two daughters, with the oldest child born no earlier than 1930) is missing from this table because the family head was arrested in 1949 and the other members relocated. Had they remained in the village they might very well have attained stem form by 1950. Yet I have some confidence that my 1950 figures are quite close to the mark: a man who had been a land reform cadre told me that during the late 1949 land reform campaign there were 1,800 people (his rounded figure) in all of Yangmansa Village (including Old Yangmansa and Jumansa), or 54 percent of its present (1987) population of 3,303. My own total of 656 people for the end of 1950, which pertains only to Old Yangmansa, amounts to 56 percent of its 1987 population of 1,165.

In this table little can be revealed with respect to families classified as "landlords" or "rich peasants," since these accounted for only three households. Likewise, the fact that I was unable to determine the class labels of what in 1950 amounted to four households containing about 3 percent of the village's population detracts very little from the finding that there were major differences in levels of attained family complexity between households labeled "middle peasant" and those labeled "poor peasant," with households falling into these two categories together accounting for 94 percent of the village population. "Middle peasants" were defined as households not needing to sell their labor and in most cases completely or partially deriving agricultural subsistence from land they owned. "Poor peasants" owned little or no land and were forced to rent land or obtain their livelihoods by selling their labor to others. Middle peasants, therefore, were members of family corporations where the possession of family property enhanced solidarity—that is, delayed family division—to a greater extent than among the land-deficient poor peasants. This greater solidarity is manifest with respect to each category of family form shown in Table 4.6. Almost one quarter of the middle peasants were members of joint households, and only middle peasants had such households; with another 47 percent members of stem households, the 30 percent in conjugal households represented a distinct minority of the middle peasant population, with the data suggesting that most if not all middle peasant households would attain and for a relatively longer period preserve joint household form given the presence of two or more sons. The contrast with poor peasant households is striking: all one-person households had the poor peasant label; the large majority of households with this label were conjugal, such that among the poor peasants the distinct minority was formed by the 30 percent who were members of stem households. Among these families early division appears to have been the prevalent pattern; I was told of several cases of family division immediately following marriage, such that younger unmarried brothers remained with their parents in households that were still conjugal. Yet those designated middle peasants were hardly a privileged stratum in pre-Communist local society; they were ordinary farmers, albeit ones better off than those with the poor peasant label.

That households classified as middle peasants should be characterized by such high levels of complexity once again confirms the by now well-established rebuttal of the much earlier contention that the joint family was the preserve of elites or "gentry."[28] However, the presence of such complex families among common people raises the question what might encourage brothers or sons to delay family division. Research in Taiwan and elsewhere suggests that land adequate for familial self-support was not the only factor encouraging solidarity, and that the enhanced economic interdependence of people in families able to diversify away from farming could be a more powerful force keeping them together (Cohen 1970a, 1976, 1992). Economic diversification was indeed a well-known family strategy in Yangmansa, and its major expression appears to have been the oil pressing and weaving enterprises noted earlier in this chapter as important additional sources of family income. The connection between such diversification and enhanced familial solidarity was well understood in Yangmansa, and the following is but one example of what many people told me concerning this matter:

About 80 percent of cash income came from these sidelines [oil pressing and weaving]. Before liberation, therefore, it was especially advantageous to keep the family together. There could be a good division of labor; it was more efficient. Some would work in the fields, others could sell products [of family enterprises], and yet others could cook. Each family had an especially skilled worker for the family sideline; a family also would choose especially capable people to sell their products outside. Yangmansa had these sidelines for many years before liberation.

However, middle peasants were best able to keep their families together, suggesting that they were in a better position to diversify. Because they owned land they were entirely or partially free from the burden of rent and could more readily invest in the materials and equipment that diversification required, either through the use of their own funds or through loans for which they, unlike the landless, could provide collateral.

Another issue was good management. The accumulation of funds for diversification or for the purchase of more land required that family consumption be kept under strong centralized control. In a stem or joint family, the combined labor of the larger family allowed for an accumulation of funds beyond the means of families in which there was only a married couple and younger children. One woman described the importance of family management as follows:

In the old society husbands were stupid and gave all their earnings to their parents; they didn't give their wives any money. The *popo* [husband's mother] would be especially economical or miserly, and would calculate every penny. They would save everything they could to buy land and houses. The landlords and rich farmers in those days became that way because they saved every penny and spent bitter days. Once, Xu Chengxin's mother went to a relative's house to burn paper money [ritual money for the gods or the ancestors]. This was just before the fifteenth day of the eighth lunar month [i.e., the Mid-Autumn Festival], but the head of that family said, "Let's not buy meat; let's rather spend the money on a hoe, so we won't have to borrow one anymore." This was one of the three days during the year when meat was eaten. Meat was also eaten on the lunar New Year and the fifteenth day of the fifth month. But the sons and daughters-in-law were not opposed, because this miserly economizing was for buying things that they later would get [with family division].

While there may have been other factors placing those later known as middle peasants in a more advantageous position for successful diversification, the important point is that prior to the arrival of the Communists the entrepreneurial corporate family was well established in local society. Land and diversification were associated with familial complexity, and with the imposition of collectivization in 1955 both were removed from the family domain.

From Table 4.7 it appears that by the end of 1964, after almost ten years of collectivization, the transformation of villagers into work-point earners had made a major impact on family development. Among those

TABLE 4.7

Yangmansa Households, by Structure, Size, and Class Label, December 31, 1964

	Class label					
Household structure	Landlord	Rich peasant	Middle peasant	Poor peasant	Unknown	Totals
INDIVIDUAL						
Number of households	0	0	0	7	2	9
Total membership	0	0	0	7	2	9
Average membership	0.00	0.00	0.00	1.00	1.00	1.00
Membership as percentage of class or total population	0.00%	0.00%	0.00%	1.65%	7.69%	1.06%
CONJUGAL						
Number of households	1	1	43	59	3	107
Total membership	6	8	184	271	16	485
Average membership	6.00	8.00	4.28	4.59	5.33	4.53
Membership as percentage of class or total population	42.86%	100.00%	48.81%	64.07%	61.54%	57.19%
STEM						
Number of households	2	0	24	22	1	49
Total membership	8	0	177	145	8	338
Average membership	4.00	0.00	7.38	6.59	8.00	6.90
Membership as percentage of class or total population	57.14%	0.00%	46.95%	34.28%	30.77%	39.86%
JOINT						
Number of households	0	0	1	0	0	1
Total membership	0	0	16	0	0	16
Average membership	0.00	0.00	16.00	0.00	0.00	16.00
Membership as percentage of class or total population	0.00%	0.00%	4.24%	0.00%	0.00%	1.89%
ALL HOUSEHOLDS						
Number of households	3	1	68	88	6	166
Total membership	14	8	377	423	26	848
Average membership	4.67	8.00	5.54	4.81	4.33	5.11
Membership as percentage of total population	1.65%	0.94%	44.46%	49.88%	3.07%	100.00%

NOTE: Middle peasant households include five conjugal households where only the mother is present, one with only the father, and one where there is also the father's brother. One middle peasant stem household has married couples in three generations, in six there is only the mother, in four only the father, in one the wife's parents have entered the household as has a brother's son in yet another. Among poor peasant conjugal households there is one where only the father is present, and eight with only the mother; in two of these latter households and in three other poor peasant conjugal households there are also relatives in addition to parents and their children. In nine poor peasant stem households there is only the mother, in six only the father, and in one of these latter the father's brother is present. Only the father is present in the stem household where the class label is unknown and only the mother in one of the conjugal households in this category.

with the middle peasant label a trend toward simpler household structures is apparent, with conjugal and stem household membership now almost equal. Households attaining joint form did not stay together for long; the one 1964 joint household (where there were three surviving generations of married couples, such that it had been stem in 1950) turned joint in 1962 and divided in 1966. However, by 1964 residential separation after marriage was becoming increasingly common, and it may be that the joint family endured for as long as it did because one of its members held an outside salaried position, which in the context of collectivization was about as close to "diversification" as a farm (production team) family could get. But even in 1964 middle peasant households on the whole still seem somewhat more complex than those in the poor peasant category; all one-person households are among the latter, and conjugal households still account for about two-thirds of all poor peasant household membership.

By 1987 residential separation after marriage and then "going it alone" were well-established elements in the family development cycle, with the simplification of household structure now generally characteristic of the village population. Table 4.8 shows that "class" origin seems to have lost all relevance as far as conjugal and stem household distribution is concerned, with members of conjugal households accounting for about two-thirds of the total "middle peasant"–derived population and for about the same proportion of those of "poor peasant" background. In other words, with the vast majority—about 94 percent—of the village population divided equally among the membership of poor and middle peasant households, conjugal household distribution in either class-label category was almost identical to that of the village as a whole. The 1987 distribution of conjugal households does reflect a villagewide trend toward household simplification, such that the 66 percent of the village population who were members of conjugal families in 1987 can be compared with the lower proportions of 57 percent in 1964 (Table 4.7) and 54 percent in 1950 (Table 4.6). However, this village trend is based upon changing characteristics of family development in the "middle peasant" category, for a comparison of Tables 4.6, 4.7, and 4.8 shows that among "poor peasants" there has been no such trend toward simplification of household structure: with members of conjugal households comprising 76 percent of the "poor peasant" village population in 1950, 64 percent in 1964, and about the same percentage in 1987, the trend, if anything, has been—in a minor way—toward greater complexity.

TABLE 4.8

Yangmansa Households, by Structure, Size, and Class Label, March 1, 1987

Household structure	Class label					Totals
	Landlord	Rich peasant	Middle peasant	Poor peasant	Unknown	
INDIVIDUAL						
Number of households	0	0	4	11[a]	0	15
Total membership	0	0	4	13	0	17
Average membership	0.00	0.00	1.00	1.18	0.00	1.00
Membership as percentage of class or total population	0.00%	0.00%	0.73%	2.37%	0.00%	1.46%
CONJUGAL						
Number of households	5	4	89	91	7	196
Total membership	17	14	360	348	29	768
Average membership	3.40	3.50	4.04	3.82	4.14	3.92
Membership as percentage of class or total population	100.00%	100.00%	65.57%	63.50%	78.38%	65.92%
STEM						
Number of households	0	0	26	30	2	58
Total membership	0	0	159	187	8	354
Average membership	0.00	0.00	6.12	6.23	4.00	6.10
Membership as percentage of class or total population	0.00%	0.00%	28.96%	34.12%	21.62%	30.39%
JOINT						
Number of households	0	0	3	0	0	3
Total membership	0	0	26	0	0	26
Average membership	0.00	0.00	8.67	0.00	0.00	8.67
Membership as percentage of class or total population	0.00%	0.00%	4.74%	0.00%	0.00%	2.23%
ALL HOUSEHOLDS						
Number of households	5	4	122	132	9	272
Total membership	17	14	549	548	37	1165
Average membership	3.40	3.50	4.50	4.15	4.11	4.28
Membership as percentage of total population	1.46%	1.20%	47.12%	47.04%	3.18%	100.00%

NOTE: Included among landlord conjugal households is that of an elderly couple who returned to the village following the husband's release from prison in 1969. Seven households went extinct between 1964 and 1987. In these households sons had remained unmarried or there had been no sons, or no children at all; other than one with the landlord label, all were poor peasant.

[a] In order to simplify the table I have included here one poor peasant household with three unmarried brothers.

It appears that since the onset of Communist rule changes in the environment for family development have had less of an impact on "poor peasant" households. Since "middle peasant" households, or those deriving from them, have tended to increasingly approximate "poor peasant" households with respect to complexity, there is also the possibility that at least some of the factors now encouraging more simplified forms of household organization are the same as, or functionally equivalent to, those to which "poor peasant" households had been exposed since even before the Communists arrived. I have already noted how in pre-Communist times early separation, even before marriage, was common among landless farmers (i.e., those later to be labeled "poor peasants"). My research in Taiwan, near Shanghai, and in Sichuan, like that in Hebei, reveals how rapid division, often involving seriatim separation of sons, was widespread among families that neither owned nor had long-term access to land through tenancy contracts. Such families depended upon wage-labor of one sort or another for survival, but their survival over the long term was most problematic; even if minimal subsistence was secured, poverty might postpone marriage or prevent it outright, leading to a family's extinction. The landlessness and wage dependence characteristic of poor families in pre-Communist times were replicated with respect to all village families during the long collective period (1955–82), with the important difference that collectivization provided at least minimal protection from severe economic deprivation. Nevertheless, the fact remains that through collectivization the family was stripped of almost all corporate assets, and its income was now based upon workpoints earned outside the family context. We have seen that even under such circumstances of collectivization the family continued to be constituted as a corporate *jia*, but this was an economically weak *jia* and, like weak *jia* among the pre-Communist poor, it was far less able to prevent the early separation of sons.

Although such a "replication" hypothesis does not account for all factors behind the present-day trend toward family simplification and conjugalism, it does suggest that collectivization of itself was sufficient to importantly change the balance between forces promoting complex family unity and those making for its fragmentation. Unity certainly was enhanced by a family's having more valuable corporate assets and by its ability under such favorable economic circumstances to diversify family holdings and the economic activities of family members so as to provide family income while striving to maximize family interdependence and minimize risk. Collectivization largely eliminated differentials in family wealth and family economic interdependence insofar as these were based upon family property and family-managed work, although within the collective framework working against economic equality were political considerations such as "class" designation and party membership and demographic factors such as the ratio within a family between workpoint earners and consumers. Nevertheless, by the end of the collective era the dominance of the conjugal household certainly testified to the "equalizing" impact of collectivization on family organization.

Collectivization also provided the context for changes in *jia* relationships as these increasingly came to differ from those expressed in household residence arrangements. During the collective era, in the absence of significant economic autonomy for individuals or families, the *jia*'s continuing importance as a framework for closer cooperation was less obvious than during the period following decollectivization, when renewed economic freedoms resulted in increases in income, a rising standard of living, and many new opportunities for cooperation within the *jia* context. Because decollectivization gave families freedom to develop enterprises, which through good management helped maintain family unity, there have emerged two contrasting tendencies in family development. For most families the pattern of residential separation followed by "going it alone" and then by family division continues as during the collective era, with considerable variation in the economic and other relationships among the different households of a single *jia*. However, in a small number of families there has been an increase in economic and residential solidarity, with residential dispersion and *jia* division delayed such that joint families do emerge and maintain themselves for periods of time. Thus with an almost-traditional integration of economic and residential arrangements, the three joint families shown in Table 4.8 represent one extreme in a postcollective continuum in *jia* organization, the other extreme, as we have seen, being little more than informal arrangements among largely independent households who have yet to formally divide.

In these joint families, as in the far more common conjugal households, family income is pooled. Likewise, the role of the family manager (*dangjia*) remains vital and is distinguished from that of family head (*jiazhang*), even though in most cases one person, usually the father, holds both. The family head's position is defined by his seniority, and his name serves to symbolize the family as a whole, while the family manager is in charge of the family's economic activities on and off the farm. In an economically integrated *jia* only death or family division can deprive a man of the first role, but senility or incompetence can force him to turn over the second to another family member, usually one of his sons. Under far more common present-day circumstances, where several economically independent households remain within a unitary *jia* framework, each household has its own *dangjia*. Thus, the preexisting distinction between *jiazhang* and *dangjia* turns out to have been well suited for the transition to *jia* that are residentially and economically dispersed.

One of the three families had attained joint form only as the result of the second son's marriage in 1987. With both sons supplementing family income through earnings from periodic temporary wage labor, this family's economic profile hardly differs from those of many conjugal or stem families and households. The other two joint families have the kind of tight-knit organization commonly associated with families of this form, with a division of labor between the farm and other family enterprises, and with the increased importance of the family manager. For such families that have successfully diversified into nonfarm or specialized farm enterprises the fact that good management has led to higher than average income seems to be a major factor behind the determination of family members to stay undivided.

Thus diversification characterizes Hu Shirang's family of nine people, including his wife, two sons, two daughters-in-law, and three young grandchildren (two daughters have married out). Hu Shirang and his oldest son are state cadres and work in different organizations outside the village. Their salaries are supplemented by income from the enterprise managed by the second son, who has hired eight women workers to make rugs for export. The two daughters-in-law cook and work in the fields, and also help with the rug business when they have time. Hu Shirang's wife looks after her grandchildren but also contributes to family income by making children's clothing for sale with her sewing machine. In this family, one of the wealthier in the village, overall management of economic matters is in the father's hands; but on a daily basis his wife takes care of family money, receiving all family earnings and disbursing family funds as required.

This family certainly displays pronounced solidarity. One son acknowledged that there are some conflicts, but, he says, they talk them over and the trouble passes. The relationships between Hu Shirang's wife and her daughters-in-law, the brothers, and their wives are all good, he insisted. If even one of these were to go bad, the son noted, the family would have to divide. Both brothers said that under present circumstances they are better off than if they were to divide the family, for their parents do a lot for them. The family now has two houses. The eldest brother lives in an older four-room house; although it has furniture, a black-and-white television set, and other amenities, he, his wife, and their children only sleep there. Other activities are in the new eight-room house, which has a color television set. A high degree of family integration is maintained in spite of the fact that the old and the new houses are rather far apart. This is of some significance in that the dispersion of family members as a result of separate and distant housing is frequently asserted to be a factor in family division; it may indeed be a contributing factor, but one that can be counteracted by others promoting family unity. In any event, the "old" house was built only ten years ago, but this family says that in a few years they will tear it down, for it "no longer is in style." The site for the new house is larger and better placed than those usually distributed without charge upon application, for it was purchased from the team for 3,800 yuan.[29]

Likewise characterized by diversified endeavors, good management, and relatively high income is the family of nine headed by Xu Chengxin, which includes his mother, wife, three sons, two daughters-in-law, and one grandchild. Assertions of family solidarity are readily forthcoming; one son says, for example, "we have a responsibility to the old people" not to divide, and that "this is a peaceful large family." This family, as Hu Shirang's, still works all land obtained during decollectivization yet now derives most of its income from nonfarming sources. These include salaried "temporary" jobs (*linshigong*) held by the oldest and youngest of the three sons, who daily commute to work in the nearby county seat of Gaobeidian.[30] Xu Chengxin and his second son work at home, where they make sheepskin coats that they personally sell in various northern and northeastern cities, such as Beijing and Dalian, during the farming slack season. The two daughters-in-law cook and do other household work under their mother-in-law's supervision, and also perform most farm tasks required during the many slack months. During busy season, however, all able-bodied adults in the family help on the farm. In this family Xu Chengxin controls the money and decides on major expenditures; even his wife must ask him for funds, as do his sons and daughters-in-law.

These two joint families appear to be worlds apart from most Yangmansa families, in which parental authority and larger family solidarity have been weakened by the independence of the husband-wife unit. This independence is fostered by the process whereby parents build new houses for their sons, who thereby establish residential autonomy, in some cases even prior to marriage, concurrent with or followed by the assertion of economic autonomy through "going it alone." This pattern of early residential dispersion took hold during the collective era and has continued to characterize family arrangements even after decollectivization. Since decollectivization, however, the reemergence of betrothal payments and dowry as indirect and direct endowment of bride and groom means that such payments now support their residential separation from the groom's family. It can be added that another sign of weakening parental authority is the growing equality between mother-in-law and daughter-in-law, a trend already apparent during the collective era. In the pre-Communist period, conflicts between mother-in-law and daughter-in-law were characteristic of their relationship in a unified family, for family solidarity was supported by the mother-in-law's authority over her sons' wives and therefore encouraged such friction. In other words, such conflicts were not detrimental to family unity but in fact were symptoms of such unity. Now, however, separate housing lessens these conflicts, but if they remain severe they lead to early family division.

The dominant pattern of family development in Yangmansa appears to contrast with that characteristic of families maintaining solidarity such that they assume and for a period maintain joint form.[31] In reality, however, the two patterns represent different sides of the same coin, by which I mean the transition from a survival and subsistence orientation to a desire to enhance life comforts in terms of both material possessions and greater freedom from the social constraints of life in large, complex families. Privacy and a degree of independence are now desired, but so is the greater wealth to be obtained by continued large family unity under good management. It remains to be seen if the option for life in a large family will survive under the impact of the Chinese state's program for population limitation, or in the face of growing consumption-oriented individualism and the popular culture nourishing it.

Lineage Studies

CHAPTER FIVE

Lineage Development and the Family in China

Until recently lineage organization loomed large in the anthropological study of Chinese culture and society, so much so that Jack Goody characterized this research as reflecting what had been the "dominating concept" of the lineage within social anthropology as a whole (Goody 1990: 52). Although attention to lineage organization was largely inspired by the works of Maurice Freedman (1958, 1966), this particular focus emerged in the context of a major growth of anthropological interest in China that occurred precisely when fieldwork was restricted to Taiwan and Hong Kong. As noted in the Introduction, the "Taiwan–Hong Kong era" of China anthropology began in the early 1950s, and only in the late 1970s did fieldwork at mainland sites resume. Since Freedman's largely library-based studies focused on the southeastern provinces of Fujian (Fukien) and Guangdong (Kwangtung), they had immediate relevance to the field research of anthropologists in Hong Kong's New Territories, originally part of Guangdong, and in rural Taiwan, the large majority of whose inhabitants were the descendants of immigrants from Fujian or Guangdong.

One consequence of the preoccupation with late imperial China during the Taiwan–Hong Kong era was that the developing anthropological picture of this China, especially as regards those intimate social and cultural patterns that only fieldwork can reveal in a comprehensive yet detailed way, was in fact based upon ethnographic evidence overwhelmingly derived from only tiny portions of what had been the Han-dominated "China Proper" of the old Qing empire. Yet because Taiwan and Hong Kong were obviously different from each other in many respects, anthropological research at these sites did provide room for comparative analysis, such that Freedman in his 1966 volume regretted how in his 1958 work he had neglected to use valuable Taiwan data. This chapter represents an effort on my part to apply perspectives gained through research in Taiwan to a discussion of the highly developed lineages of the kind that were found in the New Territories and in other areas of mainland southeastern China. In contrast to what had developed in Taiwan during the relatively short history of Han Chinese settlement on that island, such mainland China lineages were powerful and well endowed and had a long history and a relatively large and compact membership. In his original analysis Freedman (1958: 131–33) showed that on the China mainland such lineages coexisted with smaller and weaker lineages and with agnatically mixed settlements, such that he was able to suggest a continuum of lineage complexity, ranging from "type A" to "type Z." Type A lineages were the simplest; they were landless, relatively small, and without a central ancestral temple or well-defined leadership. Lineages at or near this "A" end of the continuum were in the New Territories side by side, as it were, with powerful lineages approximating type Z (Strauch 1983). In Taiwan type A lineages were common, as were more complex forms, but none appear to have attained the complexity of type Z. The well-known characteristics of type Z lineages included larger concentrated lineage communities, large corporate estates, segmentation, well-endowed ancestral halls, and clearly defined ruling elites.[1]

In lineages approaching the type Z end of the continuum, patterns of family organization, residence, marriage, and adoption differed in important ways from those of other rural communities, as did other aspects of everyday social life and the rituals highlighting them. As suggested by Freedman's construction of a continuum, these differences were neither cultural nor regional, since Freedman's point was that type Z lineages did not comprise the entire countryside of the New Territories nor any other part of rural China. Many of these differences, I will show, instead reflected the impact on social life of the collective landholdings of lineages and lineage segments.

A type Z lineage was, among other things, a community, but it was one rather different from most Chinese communities in that the individual family was far more closely linked to other families. The family in such a lineage had as a portion of its family estate shares in the corporate holdings of different lineage segments or of the lineage as a whole. Furthermore, because of the high tenancy rates in such lineages, the chances were that for most families such shares made up the entirety of their family holdings. The obvious contrast here is with a village where corporate lineage development was weak or not at all in evidence. In the latter village there was a direct relationship between the family and its own estate. Such a family, although having many vital ties with other families in the community, was in a fundamental way an isolated economic unit, one whose survival was largely an expression of its immediate control and management of the productive resources it owned or otherwise had access to, such as through contractual tenancy. The contrast between such a family and one in a type Z lineage could not have been greater. A family in a type Z lineage owned abstract shares in a lineage common property, and commonly also rented lineage land, so that its livelihood to a large extent was linked to the management of this lineage corporation and to the standing of the lineage in society at large. Such a family had intimate links with its agnates, created through the common benefits they enjoyed by dint of their membership in a larger collectivity. Therefore, I would suggest that in the strong Chinese lineage there was a blurring of what in other community contexts was a very clear demarcation between the family on the one hand and wider society on the other.

As is well known, benefits of lineage membership could include cash dividends paid shareholders in lineage corporations, distribution of pork and other food, and, perhaps most important, preferential access to land for rental. Again, education tended to be more widely available in lineage communities, as was the protection afforded by local militia. Although the particular array of benefits might differ from one type Z lineage to the next, what all such lineages had in common was the availability of corporate wealth that could be used for a variety of purposes, opening up possibilities that were not present in a village whose wealth was largely under the control of individual landlord or farming families.

Because of the nature of lineage segmentation and differences in the population of the various lineage branches, some families obtained more income from their share holdings than did others. Such circumstances, although resulting in important wealth differentials within a lineage, did not as such change the basic connection between family estate and corporate holdings that I have suggested. Thus, although it might commonly be the case that the majority in a type Z lineage were members of poor tenant families (see R. Watson 1981), such families had as their only assets whatever their shares in the main lineage estate might have been. Among such families, therefore, it could be expected that the demarcation drawn between family and lineage was weakest. Likewise, it is also to be expected that the wealthiest families benefited most from their shares in the lineage and segment corporations, as well as from their private holdings. Because of their larger private estates, richer families tended to be more sharply defined as individual economic units; at the same time, their personal wealth gave them the influence and social standing that placed them in a leadership position with respect to the lineage as a whole. While in all communities the social and political activities of the elite had several dimensions—directing community affairs, representing the community to the outside world and the outside world to the community, and protecting their own interests—in a type Z lineage these various roles of the elite were held within the context of their control over corporate resources.

Later in this chapter I will have more to say about the relationship between a family's wealth and its involvement in lineage leadership. But first I would like to consider several characteristics of type Z lineages that reflected the impact of corporate arrangements on the ties between families. It has been shown in the literature often enough how families in an agnatically mixed community were linked through affinal, matrilateral, and other ties to families in other villages, and to families in their own community both through agnatic ties and as neighbors. In sharp contrast, the social network of the male villager in a type Z lineage was largely restricted to members of his own agnatic community. In his study of one lineage in the New Territories, Potter (1968: 27) describes the "*su-po hsiung-ti* [*subo xiongdi*], or the group of agnates descended from a common grandfather," as the "unit in which the members have frequent and intimate obligations to each other." Such a social network was very different from that defined or reflected in agnatically mixed communities by the *wufu*, or mourning circle, both in terms of mourning obligations and with respect to social relationships in general. Although there were variations in local practices, the *wufu* defined what was essentially a true bilateral kindred, albeit one with an often strong agnatic bias (see Baker 1979). Again, Rubie Watson describes social relationships in another New Territories lineage as characterized by a "general reticence toward and avoidance of affines" (1981: 598). If such affinal ties lost much of their significance in a type Z lineage community, at least as far as the men were concerned, it can be added that even in the creation of such ties as there were, family autonomy might have had to give way to lineage interests. Since powerful lineages often were in conflict with each other, marriages of course were determined in part by the prevalent pattern of interlineage hostilities and alliances (Baker 1968, 1979).

Another manifestation of the close connections between the lineage and the family was with respect to adoption, which in most of China was a domestic act expressing family interests. As James L. Watson (1975a) shows, the situation could be quite different in a strong lineage. Although according to his interpretation a child from outside the lineage might be preferable from the point of view of the family wanting to adopt, for the lineage such acceptance of outsiders posed an obvious threat to the lineage's control over its corporate resources (also see Wolf and Huang 1980: 208–11). In the lineage studied by Watson, the ceremonial requirements regulating adoption of an outsider were such that the recruitment of a new family member in this fashion was a humiliating and desperate act. Although the fact that such forms of adoption were possible at all represented a compromise between lineage interests and the most fundamental interest of a family in its own reproduction, we see in the very existence of such a compromise powerful evidence of lineage intrusion into the family sphere.

The relative weakness of the family as an independent unit within the lineage population was not expressed simply by the greater authority held by the lineage leadership or by the lineage as a collectivity. Given the shared interests of agnates, there was an agnatic solidarity that weakened that of the family unit. Interesting evidence for this in many type Z lineages was the so-called "bachelor house," a structure often attached to an ancestral hall. Such houses served as the sleeping quarters for unmarried young men and were the subject of an article appearing more than fifty years ago in the *American Anthropologist* (Spencer and Barrett 1948) that describes them in a village in the Pearl River delta. Later they were noted again in a work dealing with Guangdong Province during the collective era (Parish and Whyte 1978). Although to my knowledge they are not mentioned in any of the published Hong Kong field studies, they indeed were to be found in all the major New Territories lineages (J. Watson, personal communication). Parish and Whyte report such houses in eight villages, again mainly in the Pearl River delta, but they add that they made no systematic inquiry as to the overall distribution of such structures within their total sample of Guangdong communities (1978: 231–32, 393). I take the bachelor house to represent the extension to a larger group of agnates of what otherwise would be family-centered relationships and solidarities. Such extensions clearly followed the distribution of corporate holdings, for Spencer and Barrett report that these houses might be attached both to lineage and to branch ancestral halls, adding that the "bachelor house itself is important in creating a sense of family [*sic*] solidarity and in promoting a close bond between the individual members of one generation in the clan" (1948: 473).

Spencer and Barrett also note that an informant had heard of some villages with special houses for unmarried girls and young women (1948: 477), and Parish and Whyte confirm this, as does Topley (1975). Such "maiden houses" also represented the intrusion of the larger agnatic group into the domestic sphere. I suggest that they also were linked to the development of the female networks, whose importance is stressed by Rubie Watson (1981); she describes how in at least one type Z lineage village affinal ties found expression almost exclusively through the movement of women, both in ceremonial and in more mundane contexts. Likewise, I follow the lines of analysis suggested by Topley (1975) and see in these maiden houses one of the preconditions for the development, especially in the region of Guangdong's Shunde County, of strong sororities linked to antimarriage movements and other expressions of female solidarity. As Topley shows, there were various factors encouraging female alliances, but agnatic solidarity, by weakening family control over women, helped form the environment that made it easier for them to unite and to reject the family system as a whole.

The merging of familial and larger agnatic economic and social interests in corporately well endowed lineages also led to the emergence of hereditary or castelike social patterns, in which circumstances of birth played a far larger role in status definition than was the case in most late imperial Han Chinese communities. In the literature on type Z lineages, there commonly are references to two major categories of relationship between members of a dominant lineage, on the one hand, and persons of inherited subordinate status, on the other. In one category were hereditary slaves in wealthy lineage households, and in the other satellite villages whose members characteristically were in a position of hereditary subordination to the dominant lineage controlling the land. In two important papers James Watson deals respectively with each category of hereditary inferiority; in both he summarizes earlier data that, taken together, indicate quite convincingly how there was a common association between type Z lineages, hereditary slaves, and satellite villages (J. Watson 1976, 1977). It would appear that type Z lineages generated, as it were, such relationships of hereditary superordination and subordination. While slaves might have belonged to individual families, their low social status was with respect to the lineage community as a whole. In this sense all lineage members were their masters, and only because of their servile position were they accepted as low-status members of an otherwise agnatically exclusive community. The slaves' acceptance of their status was the price they paid for whatever advantages and security community membership provided, while for the dominant lineage it was the deep interpenetration of agnatic and family relationships that defined nonagnatic relationships within the territorial community in terms of hereditary subordination. Likewise with the satellite villages: although in the first instance the relationship here was between landlord and tenant, both parties often were constituted as corporate groups. The satellite villages might comprise one or more smaller lineages whose corporate resources consisted precisely of their tenancy rights, a situation that had built into it a structure of permanent subordination. Under such circumstances the more narrowly defined contractual agreements characteristic of ties between landlord and tenant in much of China gave way to a hereditary relationship, in which status definition on both sides transcended family boundaries and was vested in the agnatic group.

Although the ethnographic record cites many instances of the displacement or extinction of lineages, they obviously were much longer-lived than individual families. The very process of family reproduction had built into it family extinction, for a family that succeeded in realizing the goal of many sons brought to maturity and marriage set the stage for its own demise through family division. Unlike the family, the lineage in accumulating wealth did not of necessity face the destructive impact of partition. The contrast between even that most unusual family meriting imperial state recognition for having achieved the goal of "five generations under one roof" and type Z lineages was especially marked, for a long history of development was required for a lineage to take on the particular type Z characteristics. Thus the "social mobility" of entire lineages was very different from that of individual families. Since I have tried to show how ties between families took on special features in the context of a strong lineage community, I now turn to briefly consider how such a lineage might influence upward and downward mobility of its member families.

It has been suggested frequently enough in the literature that lineage- or segment-endowed schooling provided lineage village families, or at least the men among them, greater opportunities for advancement through learning than was the case in communities where lineages were not well developed. The corporate community as a whole benefited from degree-holding status achieved by members of any of its constituent families. Likewise, the inability of particular families to maintain their status as degree holders across the generations could, as far as the lineage or lineage branch was concerned, be offset by the scholarly achievements of other agnates. Although commentators on social mobility as a whole have sometimes not carefully drawn this distinction between lineage and family, major elements involved in the relationship between lineage organization and advancement through education are well understood (Beattie 1979). Of course, there was an important connection between education and wealth in late imperial China. But in turning now to social mobility through success in commerce, land accumulation, and other economic undertakings, I will suggest how there might have been a seemingly paradoxical relationship between a family's advancement, on the one hand, and its social involvement with its lineage, on the other.

In her paper on economic differentiation within the New Territories' Teng lineage, Rubie Watson notes that in 1905 49 percent of "Teng owned" land was held by "lineage ancestral estates" and another 36 percent was in the hands of a mere six families (1981: 596), with the remaining 15 percent presumably distributed as small holdings among other lineage families. From her data, and from earlier discussions (i.e., Freedman 1958: 51ff.), it is clear that high social standing and power within a lineage, including a controlling power with respect to the management of lineage and segment property, were associated with independent family wealth. I refer to wealth not in the form of shares in a lineage or lineage branch corporation, but as consisting of directly owned family assets such as land or other enterprises fully liable to subsequent distribution through family division. In other words, precisely among families playing a leading role in lineage and lineage branch affairs was there the greatest development of those independent family estates that encouraged a focus on family interests, rather than those of the larger agnatic community. These circumstances raise the otherwise counterintuitive and indeed paradoxical expectation that those social relationships suggested as especially characteristic of type Z lineages would receive less emphasis among such families of greater wealth. Thus, Rubie Watson contrasts in general terms the farmers, men who "were encapsulated within the lineage," with the merchants and landlords, whose success "was in large part due to their many contacts with non-agnates," and she describes in detail how affinal ties were well developed among the rich and gave way to a strong agnatic bias only among other lineage members. However, she also notes that in weddings nonparticipation of male affines characterized the ceremonies of rich and poor alike (1981: 599; Spencer and Barrett 1948: 474). Among the rich there thus was an important distinction between what can be characterized as public and private domains of kinship behavior. There could be no such distinction as far as the poor were concerned, because their family interests were largely or entirely defined by their rights to larger multifamily corporate holdings.

The separation of the rich from their less fortunate agnates received architectural expression. Rubie Watson notes that "the large houses of the wealthy were clustered in a special part of the village," and it is likely that in such homes joint families could develop. Also, that younger members of richer families did not sleep with their agnatic age-mates in the "bachelor houses" or "maiden houses" is suggested by Spencer and Barrett, who describe how "if the individual family owns a fairly large house with several bedrooms, the unmarried men of the household need not take up residence in the men's house" (1948: 475). The noninvolvement of the rich in such lineage or lineage-segment dormitories for young men and women is confirmed by James Watson as far as the large New Territories lineages are concerned (personal communication).

It is not surprising that the wealthy controlling elite of a type Z lineage resembled in their behavior the similarly dominant strata of other Chinese communities. What is of interest is that in departing from the social patterns followed by the majority of their lineage agnates, the behavior of such wealthy families more closely approximated that of the majority of Chinese who were not members of strong lineages. Thus it seems clear that for a member of a well-endowed agnatic corporation upward economic mobility required more than remaining "encapsulated within the lineage"; rather, it necessitated the same array of strategies used by other Chinese attempting to advance their fortunes, strategies significantly involving the coordinated deployment of family members. However, the possible impact of the special circumstances connected with membership in a type Z lineage community on such mobility strategies and on social mobility rates deserves consideration.

One such set of circumstances involved the corporate resources of the lineage and its segments and the strategies employed by individual families so as to gain privileged access to them. It is well known that the relationship between individual family wealth and the endowment of separate ancestral estates was such that within the larger lineage community smaller groups of more closely related agnates had at their disposal additional sources of wealth in the form of separate ancestral corporations. Richer families donated land to set up ancestral corporations focusing on more recent ancestors, thus denying many lineage agnates share-holding status. This procedure, which gave rise to differentially endowed lineage "segments," certainly was not confined to type Z lineages, and has been widely documented both for the mainland and for Taiwan (see Pasternak 1972). Nevertheless, in type Z lineages segmentation was most pronounced. Establishment of ancestral estates defining lineage segments involved transformation of family property into corporate holdings of larger agnatic groups. These estates, if preserved intact, also represented removal of land from the open market, that is, land available for purchase by individual families as they advanced themselves economically and socially. Such land removal was most apparent in type Z lineages, where it resulted from the particular connection between mobility strategies of individual families and endowment of new ancestral corporations. Among the rich, having achieved positions of controlling influence in the community through the private accumulation of wealth, the endowment of new corporations made most sense as a mobility strategy where well-endowed corporations were already in place. As far as ordinary villagers were concerned, the adverse effects of downward mobility were ameliorated somewhat by dint of the protection and rights to land afforded by continuing membership in lineage and lineage segment corporations. For the wealthy, however, a response to the potential damage forthcoming from family division was the creation of new ancestral estates. Precisely because the large lineage community had corporate wealth available for those who would control it, the creation by wealthier lineage members of new corporations can be seen as a means of assuring their continuing control or influence over the older ones as well.

Addendum

This article was originally published in 1985 in a "conference volume" of collected essays. That book's introduction was written by Arthur P. Wolf, who commented on each of the following contributions. In addressing my piece, he made it clear that he did not buy what I had to say: "The principles on which Cohen's argument is based seem self-evident, but I am not convinced that his conclusions are correct" (Wolf 1985: 8). He went on to note the prevalence of uxorilocal marriage in certain type Z lineages as evidence contradicting my analysis, and wrote that "we cannot assume that because a lineage is poor in property it is weak in social solidarity." The uxorilocal form of marriage was not considered or even mentioned in my article as first published, but my argument certainly would lead one to anticipate that in a type Z lineage agnates would resist the entrance of outsiders into the lineage community through such marriage arrangements. Irrespective of the anthropological literature at large, which does tend to focus on the solidarity-enhancing impact of lineage corporate holdings such that lineages with little or no property are seen to be less socially cohesive, nowhere in this article do I state or assume a necessary, positive association between lack of lineage property on the one hand and weak lineage social solidarity on the other, although such an assumption may have been implicit in Freedman's analysis. In any event, consideration of the characteristics of type A lineages is something totally separate from an exploration of the social implications of heavy endowments in lineages of type Z, which is what this essay is all about. My own later findings pertaining to lineage organization in Hebei and near Shanghai, introduced in the following two chapters, relate precisely to the issue of lineage solidarity in contexts where lineages had little if anything in the way of corporate holdings.

More recently, Wolf appears to have had a change of heart, perhaps on the basis of additional research in China. His brief description of the Wu lineage in Hu-shih [Hushi], Fujian, identifies it as a classical type Z lineage and links it to other lineages of that type as follows:

Outrage at the prospect of a small plot of land being sold to an "outsider" points to an essential feature of big inland lineages like the Wu lineage. They were total communities. Education and economics and residence and religion were all forcibly united and made to depend on kinship. The members of the Wu lineage lived together, worshipped together, and fought together. Those who studied, studied in the lineage school, and those who farmed, farmed lineage land. . . . The essential fact is that by renting lineage lands to lineage members at favorable rates, the elite managed to use group property to buy personal loyalty. They were able to do this because like all successful inland lineages, the Wu lineage owned a huge estate. My informant estimated that taken together the estates held by the various branches of the lineage included more than eighty percent of the arable in the valley in which Hu-shih is located as well as extensive tracts of arable in neighboring valleys.

It is not surprising that the only uxorilocal marriages my colleagues found in Hu-shih had occurred after the revolution. In a powerful, hierarchical lineage like the Wu lineage families were not free to arrange their children's marriages as they pleased. Marriage, like everything else, was a lineage affair, and most of the lineage had no interest in giving strangers access to its resources. (Wolf 2000: 11–12)

Everything that Wolf says above confirms my own characterization of the social features of such type Z lineage "total communities," to use his term, even though in this article he neither casts backward glances at nor cites what he, I, or Freedman had written earlier. Here Wolf correctly identifies the near-monopolization of land ownership by lineage or segment corporations as key to the lineage's massive impact on family life, in part via its controlling elite, not to speak of the pervasive lineage influence on less intimate community affairs. In contrast to his earlier remarks concerning my essay, he now sees how this control extends to marriage, and how absence of uxorilocal marriage is precisely a result of type Z lineage practices. Additional evidence confirming the bundle of associated traits connected with type Z lineages, in consequence of large concentrations of corporately owned land and the controlling power over these assets held by lineage elites, can be found in later works by Rubie Watson (1985, 1990).

CHAPTER SIX

Lineage Organization in North China

North China heretofore has been only minimally involved in the modern anthropological analysis of Chinese patrilineal kinship, which has focused largely upon the southeastern regions of the country (as described in the previous chapter).[1] Yet north China merits our attention; here lineage organization prior to the Communist era comprised a social structure, symbolism, and arrangement of ritual that call into question the line of anthropological inquiry that had focused almost exclusively on the linkages between a lineage's corporate resources and its social cohesion, for the north China data provide additional perspectives on the sources and representation of kinship solidarity in a lineage context. The characteristics of lineages in Yangmansa (the village introduced in chapter 4) appear to have been typical of this broader north China pattern and considerably different from those associated with the southeastern Chinese model that has dominated the anthropological literature. Although many elements of northern lineage organization are found also in the southeast and elsewhere in China, they are combined in the north into a distinctive arrangement of cemeteries, graves, ancestral scrolls, ancestral tablets, and corporate groups linked to a characteristic annual ritual cycle. I deal first with the expression in Yangmansa of key features of the north China pattern, but also draw on other sources to fill out the picture and establish its broader regional relevance.

The north China data reveal a dimension of agnatic kinship previously not seen as significant in lineage organization. In what I call the fixed genealogical mode of agnatic kinship patrilineal ties are figured on the basis of the relative seniority of descent lines, so that the unity of the lineage as a whole is based upon a ritual focus on the senior descent line traced back to the founding ancestor, his eldest son, and the succession of eldest sons.[2] This form of kinship reckoning can be contrasted with what I call the associational mode of patrilineal kinship. The latter involves the assertion of common descent from a founding ancestor and hitherto has been held to be the kinship basis of lineage organization in late imperial China. In the associational mode all lines of descent are equal, and this equality provides the foundation for the subdivision of the lineage into hierarchies of genealogically based branches or segments. Furthermore, access to corporate resources held by a lineage or lineage segment is based upon the equality of kinship ties asserted in the associational mode. In north China, both modes of kinship could coexist within a lineage framework and be involved in expressions of lineage solidarity. I suggest that in north China the fixed genealogical mode most readily served as an expression of solidarity in the absence of significant corporate holdings.

Throughout the era of the People's Republic, Yangmansa's complex and resilient social organization has shown marked continuities with the past, even though local social relationships are no longer characterized by the economic and political alignments of pre-Communist times. Kinship ties of one sort or another still loom large as a major link between families (as of 1987), and they provide individuals one framework for interacting with other members of the local community. A prominent area of kinship connection is based upon patrilineal descent, which before Communist times received organized expression in the form of lineages that to varying degrees were corporate. These lineages are still major reference groups in village life, although they no longer possess corporate holdings or display their solidarity by feasting together or through common worship at the lineage cemetery. Indeed, it appears that even earlier the economic pressure, regional political turmoil, and outright warfare characteristic of much of the first half of the twentieth century in this part of China all served to reduce the scope of such lineage undertakings. Nevertheless, the contemporary social significance of lineage ties is apparent in many ritual contexts, as during weddings, funerals, and the lunar New Year, and is also more generally apparent with respect to various kinds of cooperative relationships. Thus it is not surprising that expressions of consciousness of lineage membership still loom large in everyday conversation. Fellow lineage members are most casually and sentimentally referred to as *jiali* (family), and when considered appropriate the more formal term *jiazu* (lineage) is used with reference to one's own group or to others. Within the village context a local lineage can also be referred to

TABLE 6.1

Yangmansa Lineages

Lineage	Lineage families	Lineage	Lineage families
Chang	19	Wang (1)	8
Chen	2	Wang (2)	106
Guo	46	Xu	67
He	17	Yang (1)	30
Hu	75	Yang (2)	57
Li	40	Zhang	4
Liang	6	Zhao	4
Liu	11	Zheng	8
Ma (1)	20	Zong	4
Ma (2)	126		

NOTE: The Ma, Wang, and Yang surnames are each represented by two lineages. In each case, the two lineages with the same surname trace descent from different founding ancestors and are independent of each other with respect to ritual and other expressions of agnatic kinship. Figures on lineage families are based on the township household register, which indicates families as of 1982.

as "the Xu," "the Hu," and the like. Members of one's own lineage are clearly distinguished from others bearing the same surname,[3] and from *qinqi*, the term used for affines and matrilateral kin. With its nineteen lineages (see Table 6.1), Yangmansa's pronounced agnatic heterogeneity is similar to that characterizing many north China villages. The trend since even before the establishment of Communist rule has been toward the residential mixing of members of different lineages, although families from the larger lineages do tend to cluster in particular areas of the village.

Lineage membership in Yangmansa in some cases also involves affiliation on a smaller scale with a lineage branch or segment. The story told by several members of the Xu lineage is that they are the descendants of three brothers who came from Beijing. Therefore, as one man put it, "the Xu are now divided into three branches [*zhi*]." Another person from this lineage referred to the three branches as *pai*, an equivalent term. A man from the Hu lineage used the phrase "*si damer*," or "four great branches" (literally, "four great gates") when he described its four subdivisions, each tracing descent, again, from one of four brothers who settled in Yangmansa. The larger Yangmansa lineages are thus subdivided into sections based upon genealogical branching rather than asymmetrical segmentation. The latter form of internal lineage differentiation was especially characteristic of landed, wealthy lineages in southern China and involved agnates defining themselves as a subgroup within the larger lineage by highlighting an ancestor they shared in common; this ancestor might be the focus of a new ancestral temple and a separate set of rituals, with a special landed estate sometimes purchased or contributed for their support. Other lineage members would be excluded from this subgroup.[4] On the other hand, affiliation on the basis of branching is a matter of levels of genealogical reckoning and as such does not involve any assertion of exclusivity based upon corporate holdings of one sort or another. The literature on south China lineages indicates that such branching, based upon the genealogical equivalency of brothers sharing descent from a common ancestor, provided the connections of common kinship even in those lineages where agnates were otherwise separated into subgroups through pronounced asymmetrical segmentation. Such a kinship orientation represents associational kinship in its genealogical aspect.[5]

In Yangmansa, however, lineages can also be subdivided into branches based upon the nonequivalence of lines of descent. A branch tracing its origin from the eldest son of the founding ancestor is seen to be in a relationship of ritual superiority to those branches deriving from the younger brothers. Members of different branches are thus related to each other not only in terms of common descent, but also on the basis of permanent horizontal ties between senior and junior descent lines. Because these ties are totally defined by genealogical position they cannot in principle be modified by asymmetrical segmentation or by other factors external to kinship. Therefore, I place such agnatic connections within what I call the fixed genealogical mode of kinship. A fixed genealogical orientation of this kind certainly is appropriate in present-day Yangmansa, where it provides one set of referents for the assertion and negotiation of social relationships in a context where every family is strongly motivated to look after its welfare by participating in a network of relationships involving many kinds of social ties.

Graves

As noted above, Yangmansa's lineages were characterized by the coexistence of the fixed genealogical and associational domains of kinship. In the past, burial grounds were a key element in the symbolic and ritual assertion of common descent, and they thus expressed lineage unity in terms of associational kinship. In Yangmansa and north China generally the common graveyards of lineages contrasted with the dispersed burials characteristic of much of south China. Graveyards in this north China pattern constituted the major symbols of agnatic affiliation that were on permanent public display, again different from the characteristic south-eastern China focus on ancestral tablets kept in special temples or, at least, prominently placed in the main room of a family residence or a compound housing several closely related families. Below we shall see how in Yangmansa ancestral tablets and scrolls were treated differently. As to the graves, in a Yangmansa lineage cemetery they were arranged in a roughly triangular fashion to reflect genealogical relationships. Hus-band and wife were buried side by side, with the site of their internment usually covered by a single mound of earth in the traditional north China style. The first ancestor's own grave formed the triangle's apex. The arrangement of graves below that of the first ancestor was on the basis of descending generations, so that the trend of lineage membership to in-crease through time led to the typical triangular shape of these cemeter-ies. The "ancestral grave" (*zufen*) at the apex did not contain coffins, but rather a stone, brick, or wooden board on which was carved the names of the founding ancestor and his wife.[6] This founding ancestor and his wife were the parents of the man belonging to the first generation buried in a particular Yangmansa cemetery, and their bodies were buried in their original lineage cemetery. By symbolically providing the founding ances-tor with a second grave the new cemetery was able to provide a ge-nealogical representation of the lineage's more remote origins. Therefore, an ancestor with two graves simply could be the connecting link between the two burial grounds of one lineage, or this ancestor might link the graveyards of two separate lineages.

By 1987 the major Yangmansa lineage cemeteries were gone, but it ap-pears that they were filled even before their leveling during the Commu-nist era. Thus, according to one man from the Xu lineage, "there were about ten generations in the Xu common cemetery; and since then there have been about another ten generations." Likewise with the Hu lineage, whose "graves originally were together in Yangmansa; but at a very early date the common graveyard filled up." However, my Hu informant went on to note that "they still used the same arrangement, but on a smaller scale." Among the Xu, similarly, "when the common cemetery was filled up the Xu would place the later graves elsewhere; they would take a wooden tablet with the father's name and bury it in front of the new graves." Thus, when the lineage common cemeteries no longer were able to contain later generations there was a proliferation of smaller burial sites, and for each of these there was the designation of an ancestral grave. The establishment of new ancestral graves continues to be linked in Yangmansa to the start of new burial areas. In earlier times this centrifugal tendency might have been circumvented through the purchase or donation of additional grave land, such that wealthier lineages might have been in a better position to preserve intact a cemetery that continued to provide a total genealogical charter. In Yangmansa, to my knowledge, no lineage made such a move in the decades immediately prior to Communist rule. The power and social significance of lineages therefore might have been weakening even in pre-Communist Yangmansa, a possibility certainly not ruled out by the deteriorating economic, social, and political conditions in northern China during the first part of this century.

On the other hand, the overflow of graves onto smaller scattered sites is not as such a symptom of a decline in lineage solidarity; each new site had its ancestral grave that in the past provided the link to the common lineage cemetery. Furthermore, the common cemetery remained the only physical expression of agnatic solidarity on a larger scale. This solidarity could be expressed ritually at the common cemetery even if it no longer contained all lineage graves. The important thing was whether it contained "senior" graves of sufficient generational depth to provide the lineage a shared reference point. The phenomenon of overflow takes effect only after the interment of several generations of lineage members. In contrast, true segmentation or fission, involving ritual statements of separation, could be manifested by the inauguration of a new cemetery at any point, either before or after overflow. Although graves in north China figure into the representation of lineage sociology in ways strikingly similar to the role played by ancestral tablets in the south, there is the obvious difference that graves require relatively large plots of land in order to fully provide such representation. A related point concerns the ancestry stories mentioned earlier. That the Hu and the Xu tell how the ancestors of their respective lineages arrived in each case as several brothers means that in both cemeteries the graves of these brothers and their wives must have comprised the second generation, the first being represented by "ancestral graves." The second generation is thus fully embedded in what was for each lineage a statement of its corporate and genealogical solidarity. Within the public cemetery context brothers in this generation cannot provide a focus for asymmetrical segmentation, or even for genealogical branching.

In north China there were ways to begin a new cemetery that involved ritual separation from an older one. Gamble describes one such procedure in Dingxian (Ting Hsien), central Hebei, and also the alternative, the common practice in Yangmansa. Thus he first notes how when "a family graveyard had been filled the geomancer was called in to find a new burial plot with auspicious influences that would add to the family welfare" (Gamble 1954: 393). He then goes on to describe the other possibility:

In order to maintain the continuity of the generations some families exhumed their parents' bones and buried them in a position of honor at the top of the new graveyard. Whether this was done or not depended on the will of the clan [i.e., lineage] and the decision of the geomancer. Neither would allow anything that would break the auspicious influence of the old graveyard. If the decision was against moving the parents' bones a small symbolic coffin was often buried in the new graveyard. Then the current head of the family and his wife would be buried at the top of the plot, his sons and their wives in the next row, and his grandsons and their wives in the third row. (Gamble 1954: 393)

While I do not know if the "symbolic coffin" Gamble mentions contained an ancestral tablet, the principle of two graves for the connecting ancestor is in any event involved. This connection is broken by disinterment and reburial, and it is not surprising that objections could be forthcoming from members of the original lineage and the geomancers they employed. Fission asserted dominance by demonstrating the ability of those proceeding with it to act independently. It breached lineage solidarity, and in Gamble's comment that lineage approval was required I think we may have his report of what in fact was acceptance of a fait accompli on the part of those who at first may very well have been opposed to such a move by an agnate.

In the contrasting southeastern Chinese circumstance it is in principle possible to define a new segment at any genealogical point, for the focal ancestral graves are hardly fixed in a cemetery position. Rather, these graves are notable for being placed individually in particularly auspicious locales, selected by specialists in accordance with the principles of Chinese geomancy (fengshui, or "wind and water") such that only immediate descendants will benefit from the location (Freedman 1958: 77–78; 1966: 118–38). In the north, the selection of a new grave area also required the expertise of a geomancer. However, this new burial area would also be defined as such with a new ancestral grave that asserted the genealogical connection with the older burial site. Subsequent burials at the new site would be with reference to the deceased's generational relationship to the ancestral grave and to his relative seniority within his own generation. It is true that in the north, as in the south, geomancers were called in at each burial to decide a grave's depth and the coffin's exact placement in it. But in the north these considerations regarding particular burials were overshadowed by the genealogical principles of placement, which assured that every burial would demonstrate the deceased's position within a larger agnatic framework. Within these limits, the positioning and burial of a coffin remained a serious matter, such that in Yangmansa and elsewhere in the north, as in the south, the mother's brother, for example, was expected to be present at her funeral, inspect the process of her burial, and make exacting and often angry demands that it be done properly.[7] Thus efforts in the north to assure geomantically proper burial could be quite compatible with practices that made cemeteries the representations of lineage solidarity.

Tablets and Scrolls

North China cemeteries provided a genealogical focus that in much of China, including Guangdong, Fujian, and Taiwan, was furnished by ancestral tablets placed in homes or ancestral temples. Therefore it is not surprising that in Yangmansa the roles of ancestral tablets in ritual and in social representation were quite different from their roles in southeastern China. In Yangmansa ancestral tablets and ancestral scrolls were the physical representations of the fixed genealogical mode of kinship. There had never been ancestral temples in this village, and even tablets, on which were inscribed the names of the agnatic ancestor and his wife, were relatively rare. All were owned by individual families, not by lineages or other multifamily groups, and were known as "ancestral tablets" (*zupai*) or "ancestral boxes" (*zuxia*). The former term was also used for the inscribed tablets buried in the ancestral grave. Ancestral tablets tended to be found only in better-off households, while most families had ancestral scrolls. The scrolls were known as *jiapu*, a standard term in modern Chinese for "genealogy." In fact, these scrolls illustrated genealogical relationships in a manner that replicated the arrangement of tablets. Apical ancestors would be at the top, their names written in small rectangles drawn so as to resemble ancestral tablets; below were the names of the various descendants arranged in horizontal rows by generation. Next to the name of each male descendant would be that of his wife. With each person's name there would also be indicated, I was told, his or her year, month, and day of birth, age at death, and year of death. Although in Yangmansa all scrolls and tablets were destroyed during the

Cultural Revolution and at least as of 1987 had not been reintroduced, some survive or have been restored in other north China villages.[8]

In contrast to the practices reported for southeastern mainland China and Taiwan, where tablets were on permanent display in homes or ancestral halls, tablets and scrolls in Yangmansa were kept under wraps for the entire year by the families owning them. They were brought out—the scrolls unrolled and displayed on a wall—for a three-day period beginning with the last day of the old lunar year, when there was the initiation of a period of ancestor worship. At that time the ancestors were "invited" (*qing shen*) to join the families of their patrilineal descendants, who "received" them (*jie zuzong*); their visit ended on the second day of the new lunar year with the "seeing off" of the ancestors back to their graves (*song zuzong*).[9] Scrolls were also brought out from storage by the groom's family during his wedding, when bride and groom would worship his ancestors, as described in chapter 4. Otherwise, only during the lunar New Year were the scrolls in view.

The particular constellation of tablets and scrolls in a family's possession depended on the family head's genealogical position in the lineage and on the family's wealth (or on its previous wealth, given the high rate of social mobility generally characteristic of Chinese villages in premodern times). Thus in Yangmansa the important distinction, as one person put it, was that "poorer people had ancestral scrolls, richer ones had ancestral tablets." Among the former, the scrolls could vary in age and in the amount of genealogical information they contained. Some families owned scrolls passed down through the generations, and these documents would be updated as deaths in the families possessing them were recorded. Other scrolls were relatively new, having been purchased by families as preprinted "forms" that they would fill in from scratch with the names of more recently deceased family members and their immediate ancestors. These scroll forms, I was told, "were cheap, but more expensive than the ordinary 'lunar New Year prints' [*nianhua*]" with which homes were annually redecorated. (By the 1990s, if not before then, such scroll forms were again widely available in north and northeastern China.)

Within Yangmansa the most elaborate arrangement of tablets and scrolls described for me involved special rooms that were set aside as "ancestral halls" (*zuxiantang*). These halls contained ancestral tablets arranged according to generation, above which there would be an ancestral scroll presumably showing earlier generations. Each tablet was enclosed in its own container, hence the term "ancestral box." Such rooms, with their collections of tablets and scrolls, were in the homes of several individual families in Yangmansa. All appear to have been wealthy, and my major source for this information had himself been a rather rich landlord in pre-Communist times. Although a fully laid out ancestral hall obviously was a powerful assertion in a lineage context of a family's dominant position, such a hall's involvement in ancestral ritual followed the standard pattern. As my informant said, "only during the lunar New Year would people open up the ancestral hall, uncover the tablets, and worship them; at all other times the room would be kept locked."

Ritual succession in the senior line was a major factor determining the distribution of tablets and scrolls. Ancestral scrolls were passed down in the senior line, such that the succession through the generations of eldest brothers to one ancestral scroll led to its containing the longest and most complex genealogical statement. As one man put it, "the ancestral scroll of the senior line is the longest, with as many as nine generations; this is the longest that I remember seeing."

Confirmation of the eldest brother's ritual seniority through his special right to the ancestral scroll must be distinguished from the jural and economic equality of male siblings, each of whom had an equal claim against the family estate. As elsewhere in China, family division (fenjia) required first that all male adults (usually married brothers and their father) agree to divide. Second, they had to concur regarding the composition of the group of mediators they would invite to serve as witnesses, facilitate agreement among the parties directly involved, and, in most cases, write out the partition contract detailing the distribution of property (and liabilities). The third requirement was that the meeting of male family members and mediators in fact result in a partition agreement, which in a small minority of cases was not the outcome at the first try. This entire procedure is still followed in present-day Yangmansa in many but not all cases of family division, and it bears a remarkable, near-total identity with family division practices I observed earlier in southern Taiwan (see chapter 4, above). Fundamental to this procedure is the opportunity it gives each brother, as the equal of his male siblings, to assert his claim to family property. Each instance of successful family division represents a negotiated agreement, in some cases achieved relatively easily, but often enough forthcoming only after an hours-long (or even days-long) meeting marked by bitter disputes. Although the usual result is an equitable division, there are occasions when the equality of brothers may be less visible from the details of the agreement—for some men strike a better bargain than others—than from the instituted means, deeply rooted in customary practice, employed to achieve them. The jural equality of brothers as to family property stands in marked contrast to the eldest brother's ritual superiority within the larger agnatic descent group.

Yet it was as a result of family division that this superiority was given expression. The oldest brother would succeed to possession of the family's original ancestral scroll. Each of his younger brothers would at this point have the opportunity to purchase his own new scroll form. Some of my informants insisted that younger brothers almost universally did so, while others asserted that it was not uncommon for junior siblings, especially if they were poor, to go without them. In any event, there is agreement that a younger male sibling starting a new scroll would fill it in to indicate a direct line of descent only one or two generations above his father. One man described the practice as follows: "upon family division, the oldest son would get the original ancestral scroll; the younger brothers would start new ones but with no more than three generations, to the paternal great grandfather." He and other villagers also noted that the genealogy on a younger brother's ancestral scroll did not include his own siblings or those of his parents and paternal grandparents. The scroll now held by the eldest son, on the other hand, was a fuller record of descent from a common ancestor, one periodically updated to include both lineal ancestors and collateral lines.

Succession to the more elaborate ancestral tablets and ancestral halls described above was also through the senior descent line. When a wealthy family divided, the brothers, almost by definition, would be of roughly equal economic standing. In principle, this economic equality was not compromised by the eldest brother's accession to stewardship of the ancestral hall. Indeed, the ritual framework defining his control of the ancestral hall stressed its separation from whatever economic assets might have been his share of the original family estate. As I have noted, this hall was kept locked except for the few days of the lunar New Year period, when it was available to all appropriate agnates for the purposes of ancestor worship. Thus the eldest brother, again in principle, was but the custodian of a physical expression of agnatic solidarity and the religion of ancestor worship that could not be used for other purposes.

Genealogical position received recognition independent of economic factors. An eldest brother (or an only son) was known as the "successor son" (*xiachuanzi*), the man who received from his father an ancestral scroll or tablets. Within a lineage, successor sons were ranked genealogically in terms of their relative seniority of succession. Thus for each of a lineage's major branches, as described earlier in this chapter, there was a successor son said to have an especially detailed genealogy. The senior successor son in the lineage as a whole was also known as the "eldest of the senior branch" (*zhangmen laoda*). He was in the descent line of eldest sons going back to the eldest son of the founding ancestor. I was told that "he would have the most complete ancestral scroll." Another man, speaking of his own descent group, mentioned the person "who was the senior successor son of the local Xu lineage; he had the largest ancestral scroll; this kind of successor son had respect in the old society, he had considerable prestige." Genealogical position was the precondition for translating wealth into a position of ritual eminence through the construction of a hall that was the focus of ancestor worship during the lunar New Year period. As one person put it, "the oldest brother had to have wealth and to have been the senior descendant for several generations before he could set up an ancestral hall. An older brother in poorer circumstances would simply hang an ancestral scroll on a wall, and this would be equivalent to a rich person's ancestral hall."

Wealth could facilitate an even more elaborate arrangement in the form of an "ancestral temple" (*jiamiao*, literally "family temple"). Although not represented in Yangmansa, buildings of this kind, set apart from residential quarters and containing ancestral tablets, would appear in the north China context to be most similar to the ancestral temples that were well known in southeastern China. In some cases, however, differences with the south remained in that particular families, not lineages or lineage segments, might own even these northern structures. "Only very rich people had them," I was told. Ancestral worship even in these temples was limited to the lunar New Year: "on the first day of the lunar New Year people would go to worship [*bai*] at the ancestral temple. One person was especially in charge: they would light candles, burn incense [*shao xiang*], and prostrate themselves [*ke tou*]." Nevertheless, I shall suggest below that with the construction of such a temple the pattern of New Year's ancestor worship might undergo important changes.

New Year

During the year just four occasions provided lineagewide contexts for ancestor worship and associated visiting and feasting in Yangmansa: the

Ghost Festival, the Cold Clothing Festival, lunar New Year, and Qingming. The Ghost Festival (Guijie) on the fifteenth day of the seventh lunar month was generally concerned with comforting or at least placating the dead; this included worship and the burning of ritual money at ancestors' graves. The Cold Clothing Festival (Hanyi), on the first day of the tenth lunar month, involved worship at the ancestral graves and the burning there of "winter clothing paper" (hanyizhi), so that the departed ancestors in the underworld would be assured of protective covering during the coming winter months so notable for their severity in north China. The focus on both occasions was on the continuing interaction between the living and the dead and involved expression of the former's ongoing obligation to support and comfort the latter. In terms of lineage organization, the Ghost and Cold Clothing festivals were significant in that they underscored lineality, that is, the ties between the living and their closer direct patrilineal ancestors. The lineage as a collectivity was not emphasized; rather it was the "descent" element of the "descent group" that was highlighted (also see Gamble 1963: 250).

The sociological focus during the lunar New Year celebrations shifted from lineality to what might be termed "networking," characterized by much visiting among agnates. During such visits there was the major ritual expression of the fixed genealogical mode of kinship. The heightened interaction among lineage members was keyed to rituals of ancestor worship that each family would arrange on its own, together with many other activities during this period. On the last day of the old year the "receiving of the ancestors" (jie zuzong) involved graveside rituals followed by the display of ancestral scrolls and tablets. The scrolls were taken from storage, unrolled, and placed on a wall above an offering table, while the tablets would be revealed with the removal of the covers from the containers in which they had been kept throughout the year. On the first day of the New Year, before dawn, the ancestors were first presented with an "offering of dumplings" (shang jiaozi gong) that was then consumed by the family during an early morning banquet.[10] Later that day the ancestors were given an offering of sweets and fruit (shang dianxin gong). On the second day there was a "red" or meat offering (shang hong gong), which likewise was later used to supply the family's feast. On the third day, following a final burning of incense and prostration (ke tou) by family members, the tablets were once again covered and the scrolls rolled up. This, together with another trip to the ancestral graves, marked the "sending off of the ancestors" (song zuzong) for another year.

The first and third set of offerings to the ancestors reflected their sharing in the exclusivist family commensality characteristic of New Year feasting throughout much of China. These lunar New Year activities were preeminently a family affair, and the presence of guests in the home or at meals was strongly discouraged (Cohen 1976: 113; for north China, also see Yang 1945: 90–91). An important modification of this restriction in Yangmansa was that brothers who had already divided into separate families would nevertheless gather at the oldest brother's home at least for the first two major feasts of the New Year period; this man would continue to host these meals until he and his younger brothers were rather advanced in years, when each family would dine separately. On the other hand, visiting other village families on the first day of the year (*chuyi*) was customary. Thus the offerings to the ancestors at that time reflected their participation in the ritualized socializing known as "making New Year calls" (*bainian*), for the ancestors were given "treats" of a kind appropriate for that day's many visitors. These visitors were received by senior family members who stayed at home. Visiting was not restricted to male agnates, although men and women would go about the village in separate groups, with the first day of the New Year being an opportunity for a woman to present a new daughter-in-law to other members of her husband's lineage. Yet while even unrelated neighbors might call at each other's homes, it was considered proper to call first upon agnates, who clearly had priority, and then village neighbors. Relatives and acquaintances outside the village might be visited later during the New Year period, with married women returning to their natal families on the second day. Nevertheless, in Yangmansa, and apparently in much of north China, the visits on the first day were dominated by the circulation of agnates among each other's homes, such that this marked one of the two annual ritualized expressions of lineage solidarity.

Among agnates it was common for men of the same generation (*tong-beide ren*) to *bainian* together. I was told that this was "only for convenience," which may have been my informant's way of stating that the rituals of ancestor worship, and those emphasizing genealogical relationships among the living, did indeed focus on generational position within the lineage. When visiting the home of a fellow lineage member agnates would first worship the ancestors (*lao zuzong*) by offering incense and then prostrating themselves before the tablets and scrolls. Then they would perform the same acts of prostration in offering their respects to living members of generations senior to them. Senior generation men also visited the homes of generationally junior agnates, where they confined ritual activities to worship of the ancestors. As one man put it, "the person with the most complete ancestral scroll would get everybody to *bainian* the scroll even if he himself was of a junior generation." However, I was also informed that agnates visiting the home of a member of the same generation could not *bainian* as far as that person was concerned, but rather had to "apologize" (*peili*) to him for being unable to ritually pay such respects, even if he were senior to them in terms of actual age. It was not the successor son who received ritual recognition from members of his own generation, but rather the scroll and the tablets over which he had custody. The ritual superiority of the "successor sons," manifested through the transmission of scrolls and tablets, was thus limited by the countervailing expression of the equality of members of the same generation. Indeed, generation took precedence over age to the extent that those junior in terms of the former nevertheless had to prostrate themselves before agnates who might in fact be much younger than they (also see Smith 1970: 149–50).

The connection between ancestor worship and "making New Year calls" highlighted the lineage as a sphere of especially intense social interaction, one given powerful religious and ritual support. In this context there was not the distinction that could emerge in south Chinese lineages, where worship in ancestral temples expressed the kinship unity of agnates while rites before domestic shrines emphasized a more intimate connection between the living and the dead (Freedman 1958: 84; R. Watson 1985: 50). Missing from the south China pattern was the placement within a domestic setting of the representations of lineage unity and their accessibility to the lineage membership as a whole. In Yangmansa, worship of ancestral tablets and scrolls emphasized the lineage as a collectivity, but only insofar as it underscored the fixed genealogical basis of a network of agnatic ties.

Qingming

The only mobilization of the lineage as a group in a ritual context was during the Qingming (Clear and Bright) Festival, held early in April. Participation in the Qingming activities emphasized the associational domain of kinship, for it was not based in the first instance on particular genealogical ties between agnates but rather on the descent of all lineage members from a common ancestor. During the Qingming rituals, I was told, there was no special role even for the senior successor son of the lineage as a whole. "Networking" within a shared genealogically defined social sphere thus gave way to a communal display of solidarity whereby each member family would send a representative to participate in activities centered on the lineage graveyard that involved both feasting and graveside ritual. On Qingming the graves were rebuilt with fresh earth and tidied up, the intent being to "fix up the houses" (*xiuxiu fangzi*) of the deceased, who were held to be "at home" (*zai jia*) in the underworld. White paper streamers were placed on each grave to indicate that the dead still had descendants who worshiped them; incense was offered, ritual paper money burnt, and those participating prostrated themselves in front of the graves. The ritual activities of Qingming might be carried out by an individual family or on a group basis. Indeed, the basic grave rituals are still practiced in present-day Yangmansa, but only as an expression of lineal ties between near ancestors and their descendants. In the past, however, these rituals were placed in a communal setting when entire lineages were organized as Qingming associations (*Qingming hui*). The Qingming association represented the corporate aspect of lineage organization and terminologically was most clearly distinguished from the lineage itself. Thus when describing these associations my informants commonly would state that "our lineage [*jiazu*] had a Qingming association [*Qingming hui*]." The Qingming association transformed the lineage into a collectivity in which genealogical connections of line and generation gave way to membership based upon family units.

One villager described the relationship between the lineage and its Qingming association as follows:

On Qingming the lineage [*jiazu*] would act as a unit. Every lineage had a Qingming association [*Qingming hui*]. On Qingming, every lineage would have a meal together; one man from each family would come, and if there was no man then a woman could represent the family. If a lineage had collective property they would use its income to pay for the meal; if not, then individuals would each have to pay for the meal.

The implication that there could be a Qingming association without common property was confirmed by another man who noted how in the past his Ma lineage had a Qingming association. He added that "this association [*hui*] had no lineage property [*jiachan*, which literally means "family property"]; there was a person who went to each family to collect money. They would have lunch together on Qingming and then together go to the cemetery."

However, Yangmansa's lineages generally did have corporate property in the past, even if in some cases these did not suffice to subsidize Qingming ritual. These holdings were meager compared with the vast posessions of the more powerful lineages in southern China that were the subject of the previous chapter, where we saw how even in that part of China the far more numerous smaller lineages were much more modestly endowed. In Yangmansa, the common property of a lineage, as vested in its Qingming association, did provide a focus for group identity. Most such property was cemetery land. The prevalent pattern was that a plot purchased or contributed for use as a lineage cemetery would be large enough to accommodate later generations of deceased lineage members. While much of its land remained vacant of graves it would be rented out for cash, services, or both in order to subsidize the Qingming feast and ritual that represented the only occasion when the lineage would meet and act as a unit. Trees, held to represent longevity, were customarily planted in graveyards, where they came under lineage or village protection (Johnston 1910: 160–63, 167), such that resources in the form of timber, firewood, or even leaves could still be obtained from a graveyard that had already filled up, as was the case with most of Yangmansa's lineage cemeteries even well before the arrival of the Communists. The importance of such graveyard products in a north China countryside otherwise largely denuded of trees and other overgrowth should not be underestimated (Eberhard 1952: 115–16). The common arrangement was to require that the person given rights to whatever the cemetery might yield be responsible at least for providing the food for the lineage Qingming feast. Such a person, I was told, had to be "of the lineage" (*benzu*) and generally was "in poor economic circumstances." Sometimes the person given rights to the cemetery "was chosen after the lineage members had discussed the matter," while in others he was "selected by drawing lots."

Particular arrangements varied somewhat from one lineage to another, but in each case lineage holdings and access to them were within the framework of the Qingming association. In addition to their cemetery the Xu lineage's collective property included a "large water hole" (*da shuikeng*) in which there were reeds (*weizi*) and lotus roots (*ou*). These products would be sold to provide money for the Qingming feast, and also for the paper money, paper streamers, and other supplies required for the rituals. On the other hand, the right to collect leaves and small twigs for firewood from the "many trees" in the Xu graveyard would be rotated from one lineage family to another. "This would be on the basis of sets of brothers, with the oldest brother getting the right." This latter arrangement represented direct distribution of lineage resources to its membership, with each of these elder brothers presumably negotiating further distribution with his younger male siblings. The Guo were the only Yangmansa lineage to come to my attention whose holdings included ordinary farmland. Such land was the major form of lineage wealth in southern China; even elsewhere in the northern part of the country it was not uncommon for lineages to have small holdings (Huang 1985: 235–36).[11]

The comments of one member of the Guo lineage can be quoted to clarify the connections between Qingming associations, Qingming activities, and corporate holdings:

The Guo had a Qingming association; they had two meals together one or two days before Qingming. One [meal was] in the morning, after which they would carry baskets and take shovels to the graveyard. There would be earth inside the baskets, and they would use the shovels to place the earth on top of the graves and then fix them up; paper then would be placed on top of the graves and incense burnt. They then would return for another meal, lunch. If anything were left after the meal, they would divide it up among those participating. There was only one man from each family. At that time the Qingming association had a plot of land as collective property [jiachan]; they would sell the grain and use the income to purchase food for the Qingming association meal.

The identification of feasting as an association activity and collective holdings as association property points to the fact that relationships among agnates within the association context were different from those based upon the kinship principles dramatized during the lunar New Year. The collective ownership of association property and the family-based distribution of food contrasts with the emphasis on fixed genealogical position and senior-line succession so prominent on the first day of the lunar New Year and with respect to the distribution of ancestral tablets and scrolls. Since we have seen that in some cases agnates given access to the products of the lineage graveyard were held responsible for subsidizing the Qingming feasts, I would suggest that even these graveyards were owned not by the lineage as a genealogically arranged group of agnates, but rather by the Qingming association comprising member families having, in principle, equal rights to these holdings.

Expression of separate associational and fixed genealogical or "pure kinship" domains appears to have been commonly characteristic of north

China lineages. Thus Huang notes the connection between lineage property and the Qingming associations:

Typically, these small plots of lineage land were rented out, usually to one of the lineage's poorer members, and the rent was used to defray the expenses of the Qingming ceremony, when the members paid their respects to their ancestors. Usually, the prevailing rent was charged, which was paid either in cash to the heads of the lineage's Qingming association . . . or in the form of the paper money and incense the tenant was obliged to furnish for the Qingming rituals. . . . All the members of the more well-off and solidary lineages would gather for a meal at Qingming; the less well-off lineages limited participation in the meal to a few representatives. (Huang 1985: 235)

The Qingming associations represented an adjustment to the fact that kinship principles based upon generational and line differentiation were not compatible with property relationships grounded on the jural equality of families as units of ownership. This equality was expressed in the equal rights of brothers with respect to the family estate, and more generally was linked to the pronounced commodification of land and other valued goods so characteristic of late imperial Chinese culture (for more on this see chapter 8). Hereditary kinship discriminations were quite irreconcilable with such commodification, which provided a totally separate context for the emergence of economic and social differentiation. The quote from Huang includes reference to the heads of the Qingming associations and thus also points to another element of lineage social organization in its associational aspect. A Qingming association founded upon property rights was a corporation able to set its own rules and select leaders based upon criteria that could be quite different from the fixed genealogical frame of reference manifested in the New Year–based ancestral cult. In Yangmansa I was not able to learn much about the leadership or management of Qingming associations in pre-Communist times, but it is clear enough that in some cases wealthier men powerful in the local community also had similar positions of influence in their own lineage Qingming associations. Villagers spoke of some of Yangmansa's ward heads (*baozhang*) during the Japanese occupation as having sold Qingming association land belonging to their own lineages, based on falsified land deeds showing that the plots were their personal holdings. Such blatant embezzlement was hardly typical, but it does serve to highlight the fact that the Qingming associations might provide a context for the expression among lineage members of the unequal distribution of wealth and power in local society.

On the other hand, rotational arrangements might serve to distribute association leadership positions among a broader group of agnates. This appears to have been the case with some groups in Dingxian, according to a description that also confirms that there the associational aspect of lineage organization was closely linked to Qingming:

> For some of the large families [lineages] who had long been in [Dingxian] the maintenance of the family graveyard was a matter for the entire clan [lineage] and involved many related families and many people. . . . The families met at the home of the chairman and went together to the family graveyard to repair the graves and worship the ancestors with offerings, paper money, and incense.
>
> After the worship service the group often ate and drank together and discussed the repairing of tombs, the planting of trees, the leasing of the clan property, and any other clan problems. The chairman, collectors, business manager, and clerk were elected by the members. The chairman served for one year. . . . In some cases only the elders "of a suitable age" attended the "eating meeting." In others any one belonging to the clan was qualified to participate . . . but it was generally customary for no women or children to attend.
>
> The expenses for the care of the tombs and the "eating meeting" were met from the income from the clan property, or, if there was no property or the income was not sufficient to cover the expenses, by contributions from those who attended. (Gamble 1954: 392)

In another work, Gamble (1963: 239–52) clearly identifies the control of lineage property as being vested in a Qingming association. His example of a lineage in "Village H" to the southwest of Beijing is of special interest because it is one of the very few Hebei area lineages reported to have a full-fledged ancestral temple and relatively large landholdings. As noted earlier, Yangmansa lineage organization in its fixed genealogical aspect was given ritual expression by the transmission of scrolls and tablets through the senior line of successor sons, who, if wealthy enough, could build a family ancestral hall that would remain under the control of successor sons. A further move in the direction of ancestor worship elaboration would be the construction of a separate ancestral temple. The founder of the ancestral temple in Village H apparently followed this last procedure, for Gamble, basing his account on a lineage history written by the temple's founder in 1576, tells us that this man was a high official who, having "descended in a direct line from the oldest son of the founder . . . was entitled to hold the family's ancestral tablets. He built an ancestral hall to house the tablets and to honor his original ancestor" (p. 241).

Nevertheless, the lineage had acquired its landholdings (thirty-seven plots) over a long period, "usually by gift from wealthy members" (p. 249). These could hardly have been gifts to the senior line, and neither were they dedicated to more recent ancestors to provide the basis of corporate segmentation as in south China lineages. Such corporate holdings were thus quite incompatible with senior line succession, and it therefore is not surprising that control over the entire body of lineage property was organized within the Qingming associational framework: "[lineage] affairs and the [lineage] hall were looked after by the family's Ch'ing Ming [Qingming] Association." The association

consisted of fifteen family heads, chosen from the different branches of the [lineage] so that every branch had a voice in the [lineage] affairs. . . . The fifteen family heads were divided into five groups of three each. Each group, in rotation, took charge of the [lineage] affairs for one year and so served every five years. . . . The rotation of the groups meant that the [lineage] accounts would be scrutinized by each group as they took over responsibility for the coming year. (pp. 248–49)

Basing the rotation of association leadership responsibilities on lineage "branches" clearly proclaimed that each branch and its component families were equal as members of the corporate Qingming association, whereas in the fixed genealogical domain branching was the basis of ritual inequality.

The lineage described by Gamble comprised 69 families out of a total of 375 in Village H, which therefore was characterized by an agnatic heterogeneity we have seen to be common to north China communities. Single-lineage villages with ancestral temples could be found, however, and they seem to have been especially prevalent in the eastern coastal districts of Shandong. In this area, observed by Johnston, there are multilineage or mixed surname villages, but the "typical village" consists "of a group of families all bearing the same surname and all tracing their descent from a single ancestor . . . each family . . . sharing in the rights and responsibilities connected with the upkeep of the Ancestral Temple and its tablets, the family burial ground, and any land or property that may have been . . . set aside to provide for the expenses of religious ceremonies and sacrifices" (1910: 134–35). Yet in this part of Shandong lineage organization appears to have fallen well within the north Chinese pattern. There are both ancestral tablets and scrolls, and these "are not exposed, either in house or in temple, except on ceremonial occasions such as the first fifteen days of the first month of the year and the festival of the winter solstice" (Johnston 1910: 277). There is the circulation of agnates on the first day of the New Year (pp. 178–79), and graveyard worship by lineage members on Qingming (pp. 186–87, 255–56). Qingming associations are not identified as such by Johnston, but he does describe how the lineage cemeteries are managed "by the elders of the clan," and sometimes the different branches of the [lineage] are allowed to take turns in keeping the graveyard in proper order, in return for which services the caretakers are allowed to derive a little profit from a periodical grass-cutting and pruning of trees; sometimes, too, they are put in temporary and conditional possession of an area of arable land out of the proceeds of which they are expected not only to look after the graveyard but also to keep in repair the *chia miao* [*jiamiao*], or Family Temple. (p. 258)

While the associational emphasis with regard to both Qingming ritual and access to lineage grave sites and land is clear enough from Johnston's account, I am not able to determine from his text the extent to which genealogically based "networking" dominated ancestor worship during the New Year in this area of Shandong. Although Johnston makes several references to ancestral scrolls ("pedigree-scrolls"), I have found no clear descriptions of their being kept in homes. What does emerge from his account, as from Gamble's, is a connection between the presence of an ancestral temple and a movement toward a more associational form of ancestral ritual even during the lunar New Year period. Johnston gives evidence that the preferential holding of ancestral tablets by agnates in the senior line has given way to a focus on the lineage as a collectivity through the concentration of tablets in the ancestral temple: "The soul-tablets . . . of father, grandfather and great-grandfather are . . . preserved in every private house, while the tablets of the earlier ancestors are deposited in the family [ancestral] temples" (p. 277). Thus, on the first day of the New Year the "Ancestral Temple is also visited, and incense burned before the spirit-tablets and the pedigree-scrolls, which are unrolled only on solemn occasions" (p. 179). Johnston's account suggests that even during the New Year period networking among agnates occurs within a ritual context in which there is also emphasis on the lineage as a cohesive agnatic community. Temple worship, even if done separately by individual families, nevertheless contrasts with worship at the homes of a series of genealogically determined successor sons and therefore provides a focus that is separated from the network of agnatic kin. Again, the fact that both Gamble and Johnston note how care of ancestral halls was included among the duties of Qingming associations is further convincing evidence of the expansion of the associational aspect of lineage organization.

In north China the associational dimension of lineage organization was the context for the expression of asymmetrical segmentation, which is to be distinguished from the kind of lineage branching involved in the fixed genealogical domain. As we have seen, the latter form of segmentation simply differentiates senior and junior subdivisions within the lineage genealogical framework to form hierarchies of networks of interacting agnates. Such segmentation does not carry with it any recognition, at least at the ideological level, of the play of social, economic, or political factors external to pure genealogy. Asymmetrical segmentation, on the other hand, involves a focus on a selected genealogical link to both create and give special definition to a particular group within the larger lineage. In terms of the ideology of pure agnatic kinship, based exclusively on principles of senior line succession and generational ranking, the initiation of asymmetrical segmentation is an arbitrary act. In the context of Freedman's analysis of southeast China lineages, and as described in ethnographies of large lineages in Hong Kong's New Territories or in Guangdong,[12] asymmetrical segmentation involves the establishment of new corporate holdings or ancestral trusts that at a minimum subsidize the worship of a particular ancestor, who is, as it were, totally wrenched out of genealogical context. The most powerful expression of this mode of segmentation is the dedication to such an ancestor of a separate ancestral temple. The wealthier an individual or a lineage branch, the greater the inclination to assert and display higher social standing through the creation of a new agnatic corporation. Likewise, larger and richer lineages would tend to be characterized by greater internal economic and social differentiation, and therefore would boast more such corporations and temples (see chapter 5).

I have not come across evidence that would indicate the operation in north China of asymmetrical segmentation at a high enough pitch to result in the construction of more than one ancestral temple by members of a single lineage. Nevertheless, there can be no doubt that in some lineages agnatic subdivisions—although not marked by temples—were formed through this kind of segmentation. One interesting example, mentioned by both Duara (1988) and Huang (1985), is the Hao lineage in the southern Hebei village of Sibeichai.

The Hao lineage was . . . divided into five segments. The ceremonial identity of both the lineage and its segments was well marked, despite their poverty. The entire lineage behaved as one unit at New Year's. But during the other lineage ceremonies [Qingming and the Father and Sons Gathering], the western segment—the largest and the oldest—held its ceremony and banquet separately, while the rest performed their ceremony jointly. (Duara 1988: 93)

Thus among the Hao there was clear asymmetrical segmentation, whatever its economic basis, and this was manifested in what we have seen to be the associational domain of Qingming ritual.[13] At the same time, this lineage departed from the common pattern of New Year's ancestral ritual in that "all members would gather at the home of the senior member, when everyone *koutou*-ed before all their lineage seniors" (Huang 1985: 236). So even in the absence of an ancestral temple the Hao lineage had moved toward transforming their ancestor worship during this period into an assertion of lineage associational solidarity, a solidarity whose expression in the Qingming context had been compromised precisely by asymmetrical segmentation.[14] Yet this transformation appears not to have been complete, since the ritual was still held in the private home of an agnate whose special status lay in his genealogical position. There is no indication that there was incorporated into the New Year ritual lineage activity that clearly would dramatize it as an abstract collectivity, as distinct from the particular genealogical ties that defined for lineage members part of their social network.

Kinship Domains

The distinction within lineage ritual and ideology between fixed genealogical position on the one hand, and common descent on the other is tied to different aspects of lineage organization and more generally to different modes of interaction among agnates. What I have been calling the associational domain of lineage social organization is supported by the ideology of common descent from an apical ancestor, such that the status of all agnates is equal. This assertion of equality reinforced the powerful support given jural equivalence by the common rights of brothers to their family estate. This equality, either on the basis of families (or, more properly, male family heads) or of individuals (males) is with respect to kinship status only. In kinship terms, all families are equal actors within the lineage as well as within the larger society, and this kind of relationship can be dramatized by lineage feasts supported by lineage holdings or by direct contributions from the participants, or through various means of rotating responsibilities. While in north China the assertion of associational solidarity commonly involved lineages in which there was little social and economic differentiation among member families, such solidarity might also receive considerable ritual and ideological emphasis even in the very powerful and class-stratified lineages of southeastern China, as Rubie Watson (1985) has stressed. Associational solidarity within a lineage did not involve denial of genealogical relationships, but rather adjusted these relationships so that they reinforced an ideology of common descent. Thus within the associational domain of lineage organization the emphasis was on seniority, but only with reference to generation and absolute age within each generation. Both generational and chronological seniority, in the associational mode, are statuses purely relative to the life cycles of male agnates; in the fixed genealogical mode, the status distinction between senior and junior lines is permanent.

This ideology of equality as expressed in the associational domain of lineage organization did accord with the true circumstances of families in late imperial China, where each family unit was an independent actor whose success, survival, or demise was scarcely influenced by genealogical factors as such. Thus, this associational domain was quite compatible with the expression within the lineage framework of social differentiations as determined by economic, political, and other factors. In other words, within this domain kinship ties were mediated by the very elements that made late imperial China a society notable for stratification, commodification, reliance on contractual relationships, and institutionalized upward and downward mobility at all social levels (as described in chapter 1). The nature of relationships in this domain facilitated the outright creation of corporate lineages through the selection of focal ancestors, land purchases, and the initiation of contractual ties among the lineage founders, as has been repeatedly shown by anthropologists and social historians.[15] Such lineages, while bringing together certain agnates, might also exclude other men who were also agnates in terms of genealogical reckoning but were not involved in organizing the new group. Indeed, starting with Freedman's 1958 volume, almost the entire corpus of anthropological writings on the Chinese patrilineal descent group has been concerned with the implications for lineage organization of relationships based upon property, wealth, social standing, and political status.[16] It is therefore ironic that the fixed genealogical domain of lineage ideology, which in north China provides for the universalization of ritual inequality among agnates through the combination into one framework of distinctions based upon generation and senior line succession, in fact represents agnatic kinship unencumbered by real socioeconomic and political differentiations. By providing every agnate with a particular genealogically defined status it facilitates structured interaction that need not be mediated by factors external to those of pure genealogical reckoning. This fixed genealogical orientation does not as such define access to corporate holdings of any sort. Rather, it simply defines a formal kinship relationship between agnates.

In north China during late imperial times the strong ritual emphasis on the fixed genealogical domain of kinship appears to have been inversely correlated with the strength of corporate support accorded the associational domain, although far more evidence will have to be brought forward to confirm this suggestion. The lineages of north China in pre-Communist times, generally small, found in agnatically heterogeneous villages, and possessing only small common holdings, have been characterized as weak in comparison with those in the southern part of the country (Rawski 1986), although we have noted some important exceptions. Recent historical scholarship, however, has emphasized the continuing importance of lineages as components of village organization and government, and as constituting crucial social arenas for mutual assistance of many kinds (Duara 1988). Furthermore, "what is particularly noticeable is the ceremonial core defining the unity of the lineage" (Duara 1988: 100). From my reading of Duara and other sources I am not always able to determine the relationship between associational and fixed genealogical elements in the "ceremonial core," but it is nevertheless clear that ritual in the fixed genealogical domain could provide a sociologically significant lineage with powerful support irrespective of corporate endowment. In contemporary Yangmansa the strong sense of lineage affiliation continues to be given ritual support in the form of New Year's visiting among agnates that is guided by genealogical relationships even in the absence of ancestral tablets and scrolls. I am not implying that of itself "pure" kinship within the fixed genealogical domain was an independent force making for lineage solidarity. My point, rather, is that just as lineages could have sociological reality in the absence of significant corporate holdings, so could they also receive both ideological and ritual support under such circumstances.

The extent to which the distinction between two domains of lineage organization has applicability beyond north China must remain an open question, at least as far as I can see on the basis of my reading of the literature. In his 1958 volume Freedman identifies what he calls an "extended family" with the "domestic" mode of ancestor worship where families "had constantly to redefine themselves in relation to different ancestors" because "ancestral tablets descended by primogeniture until they were no more than about four generations from the man who maintained them," after which point they either were buried or transferred to an ancestral temple (pp. 46–47). Thus, "this primogenitory structure of the domestic cult was in contrast to the principle seen at work in higher segments by which benefits and responsibilities were circulated among components of a segment on the basis of equality" (p. 48).

Freedman does not allow for the extension beyond the "extended family" of the ritual superiority of the senior descent line so that as in north China, it forms an organizing focus for the lineage as a whole. In other contexts, according to Freedman, "the principle of seniority in line of descent was rarely manifested" (p. 67). Furthermore, kinship ties in the fixed genealogical domain play no part in his "A-to-Z" continuum of lineage organization, which we have seen in the preceding chapter to range from a small group of agnates without corporate holdings or significant internal economic differentiation at one extreme, to a large, wealthy lineage characterized by pronounced asymmetrical segmentation and conspicuous differences in wealth, political influence, and social standing among its membership at the other. At all points in this continuum lineage organization is firmly in the associational mode, such that where social ties are not mediated by property they are defined on the basis of generation and age only. In later publications, Freedman looks again at the matter of primogeniture, noting how it had "waned" or "decayed" in Chinese society (1966: 50, 53). Freedman surely is correct insofar as "primogeniture" is of significance for the transmission of property, and I have avoided use of the term because what is at stake in the north Chinese genealogical domain of lineage organization is simply stewardship in the senior line of the symbols and rituals of a lineage unity based upon ties of kinship set apart from property relationships. Indeed, it might be that senior line succession can be more readily distinguished as "pure" kinship precisely because of its incompatibility with dominant modes of property distribution in late imperial China.

Although not directly concerned with the contrasting patterns of lineage connection as I have described them, some criticisms of Freedman's approach do have a bearing on how this contrast relates to broader patterns of organization in Chinese society. Sangren, relying for the most part on Taiwan data, has argued that "Chinese lineage corporations," rather than resulting from the operation of "rules of descent and inheritance," are best understood in the larger context of Chinese organizational dynamics, because "the Chinese establish corporate groups very similar in form and function on bases other than kinship" (1984: 391; also see Cohen 1969b). Sangren's analysis squares with what I have called the associational domain, and there can be no doubt that in the north China context the Qingming associations rely on the same modes of organization as do groups not having agnatic kinship as the basis of membership, such as the territorial or religious organizations that were also known as "associations" (*hui, she*), and in many instances held corporate property (Duara 1988: 120–32; Huang 1985: 219–74; Smith 1970: 102–11). Families participate in all of these organizations on the basis of an equality that is incompatible with the ritual differentiations characteristic of the fixed genealogical domain. Likewise, relationships highlighted within this genealogical domain clearly do not play a role in organizations of the kind that Sangren wishes to identify.

If Sangren seeks to disentangle the organizational and kinship elements in Freedman's paradigm, Faure, writing in the first instance with regard to Hong Kong's New Territories, wants to add the important element of settlement rights to the bundle of attributes associated with lineage membership. In Faure's analysis, the "four dimensions" of the lineage include "the inheritance of the rights of settlement in the village"; the lineage as a "corporate body" or "collection of corporate bodies, that holds property"; the lineage "as an alliance across common surname groups"; and the lineage as representing "a claim to official status" (1986: 166). The first of these is to be historically distinguished from the rest, for the "lineage as a group tracing descent is a product of the rules of inheritance in the village, especially in so far as they concern settlement rights," while the lineage seen "through the functions of ornate ancestral halls—and the well-printed genealogies that went with them—is the product of an official culture" (p. 179). The relationship between membership in the lineage and in the village is confirmed in the case of north China. Although there is some disagreement regarding the extent to which north China villages were "corporate communities," such that acceptance of outsiders was restricted, research does confirm that vested in village membership were privileges of participation in social life and access to village collective resources, privileges that were inherited through patrilineal descent and, in some cases at least, validated by the presence of ancestors in the lineage graveyard (Duara 1988: 198–216; Huang 1985: 259–74). Because lineage membership confirmed village membership in north China, lineage solidarity can be seen as being supported by factors external to kinship ideology as such, even in the absence of lineage corporate holdings.

Nevertheless I do not see that Faure's contrast between "settlement rights" and the "official" lineage culture completely matches mine involving the fixed genealogical and the associational domains, for I have shown that the latter could be manifested in the absence of temples, especially in the form of Qingming associations. Yet I have also suggested that in providing itself with an ancestral temple a lineage would reorganize itself more fully on the basis of associational ties. These kinds of ties, as reflected in the organizational patterns emphasized by Sangren, or in the corporate lineages with official-style ancestral temples described by Faure, are notable for their potential involvement in broader territorial, political, and kinship relationships that might extend beyond the local community. They are thus very different from the fixed genealogical domain of lineage organization, which is supported by rituals presupposing close social familiarity and neighborliness, as during the New Year period. In this genealogical domain agnatic kinship is confirmed as a form of social intimacy, characterized by a high degree of ritual and nonritual interaction and cooperation, and thus is not readily adapted to large-scale lineage organization that monopolizes or transcends individual village communities. The fixed genealogical domain provides strong confirmation of settlement rights, and thus of membership in both lineage and village communities. In north China this is most readily apparent in the absence of large corporate lineage holdings; whether property-poor lineages in other parts of the country likewise were characterized by similar alternative domains of kinship organization is a question for future research.

A major concern of the "lineage paradigm" has been to show how corporate holdings affect lineage size, power, organization, and ritual. This paradigm sees corporate resources as at the core of the lineage, such that James Watson has proposed to define a lineage as "a *corporate group* which celebrates *ritual unity* and is based on *demonstrated descent* from a common ancestor" (1982: 594). Research has proven that property and other resources do indeed powerfully contribute to the configuration of a lineage's social structure, and in the preceding chapter I have suggested that lineage corporate holdings could importantly condition even social mobility and family organization. Yet I see no theoretical or comparative advantages to be derived from isolating out a "lineage" social formation based upon the combined presence of all three factors, such that other tight-knit groups of agnates are relegated to the rather vague category of "descent group."[17] There is no analytic advantage to be gained, for example, by considering one such group of agnates with a cemetery to be a lineage, yet another without a common graveyard but nevertheless united by the rituals of fixed genealogical kinship as something different. In this latter realm of lineage organization a meticulous demonstration of descent is the basis of ritual unity. In the associational domain, demonstrated descent means the demonstration of rights to corporate holdings that, in turn, give the group its definition. Rather than being concerned with what a lineage is and what it is not, it may be most useful at this stage of research—when the evidence for most of China is sparse indeed—to focus on a more complete elaboration of the dimensions of organized agnatic kinship in Chinese society.

CHAPTER SEVEN

Lineage Organization in East China

Eastern China, which according to G. William Skinner's analysis comprises the "Lower Yangzi macroregion" (1977d: 214–15; 1985: 273), was notable for the emergence of relatively small numbers of large property-endowed lineages "in a social landscape composed of residentially concentrated descent groups" (Hazelton 1986: 166). The large lineages had as their founders and among their subsequent leaders men of wealth or local prominence, as well as nationally prominent scholar-officials. The contrast between such lineages and more ordinary rural settlements was extreme, so much so that Fei Hsiao-tung (1946), who had in mind the Lower Yangzi region, was moved to make his famous observation that the lineage ("clan") was a "gentry" organization. The considerable later scholarship on Lower Yangzi lineages, almost entirely that of social historians, certainly has focused on the role of local and national elites in their creation and leadership—far more than it has been concerned with the details of lineage organization, distribution, and membership.[1] My own fieldwork in Shenjiashang from January to April 1990 confirms that there were mighty contrasts between lineages of the sort found there and those few in its vicinity that had ancestral halls, organized worship, elaborate genealogies, and corporate property. Even among the latter lineages a local distinction was made between those that were merely "big lineages" (*da zu*) and those that were "great lineages" (*wang zu*) and usually had as past or present members eminent degree holders or officials. Recent scholarship on the prominent lineages has tended to view them almost entirely as creations of the "official culture," to use David Faure's term (see chapter 6), and as far as the Lower Yangzi is concerned little has been said about the "popular culture" that may also have been involved. I will suggest that some elements in elite lineage organization were modifications or elaborations of those found in small lineages like those in Shenjiashang. Of course, popular beliefs and practices historically will have been importantly influenced by the elite, but I hope to show that by late imperial times the creation of elite lineages in east China was hardly occurring in a local cultural vacuum.

Shenjiashang is in Shanghai Municipality's Minhang District, incorporating what in 1990 had been Shanghai County. Prior to the Communist era Shenjiashang had been a farming community largely dependent on annual crops of rice and wheat; in recent decades it has been caught up in the expansion of the greater Shanghai urban area, such that during the period of my fieldwork only 29 of its approximately 650 residents were full-time agriculturists, and they grew nothing but vegetables for the urban market. Yet most residents are descendants of earlier villagers, and if nothing else their social orientation remains distinctly rural: social ties are dense and based upon agnatic, cognatic, and oath (or "fictive") kinship; villagers own their homes; there is a rich ceremonial life, as manifested in ancestor worship during the lunar New Year period and on occasions such as weddings, funerals, death anniversaries, and "raising the beam" (*shangliang*) of a new house; social relationships involve mutual assistance, as for house building, weddings, and funerals; and social relationships are also expressed in the constant reversal of host and guest roles during the banquets associated with almost all ritual occasions. Equally strong is the evidence of Shenjiashang's participation—especially as far as younger people are concerned—in the urbane popular culture of modern Shanghai, as can be seen in clothing style, new housing, forms of recreation, and romance and sex. But in view of the strong orientation to local society, and in terms of self-definition, Shenjiashang's native inhabitants are rural. For residents of the city proper they are *axiang*, a Shanghainese term for "yokel." As elsewhere in China, especially in rural areas, much of Shenjiashang's present-day ritual and ceremonial life represents a revival during the past decade of practices that had been repressed during the first thirty years or so of Communist rule, especially during the period of the Cultural Revolution (1966–76). The revival is far from total, however; much has been lost or modified with the passage of time or no longer seems relevant to contemporary circumstances. There has been a reappearance of much ritual behavior, in contrast to the continuing avoidance of ritual artifacts (such as ancestral tablets); while performance once completed leaves no evidence behind people may be reluctant to keep in their homes physical manifestations of beliefs and practices that officially are still held to be "feudal superstition." In recent years, however, even the physical evidence of popular religious practice has been reappearing in China on a wide scale. In any event, present-day revivals cannot be accepted at face value as representing pre-Communist practices, and for the purposes of researching the latter I have relied primarily on information provided by villagers who were already adults prior to 1949.

In turning to the local characteristics of patrilineal kinship and their relationship to lineage organization, I first note that corporate holdings that elsewhere in China provided an economic foundation for lineage ritual life and solidarity were nowhere in evidence in Shenjiashang, an absence more pronounced than even among the lineages in Yangmansa, described in the previous chapter. All persons asked agree that prior to the establishment of Communist rule Shenjiashang was one of the less affluent villages in its area. The earliest household register data show that in May 1953 the village had a population of 333 in 53 families. The registers also show that class labels (assigned during the 1950–51 land reform campaign) were distributed among family heads as follows: two hired hands (*gunong*); thirty-four poor peasants (*pinnong*); fifteen middle peasants (*zhongnong*); and two rich peasants (*funong*). There were no landlords (*dizhu*) in the village, while the two rich peasant families originally had been one family and had divided shortly after land reform. During my fieldwork, members of these same two families complained to me bitterly that the "bad class label" had been unjustly applied to them. They ought to have been classified as middle peasants, they said, for it was only shortly before the arrival of the Communists that they had obtained the additional fields from landlords who knew what was happening in north China—already under Communist control—and were desperate to sell at any price. Their story received ironic confirmation from other villagers, who pointed out that they had not been very smart. If the late purchases of the "rich peasant" family are discounted, tenanted land was owned entirely by outsiders, be they individual families or corporate groups of one kind or another.[2] Landholdings did not provide corporate support for lineage organization in Shenjiashang.

In the absence of such support, and given the relatively high rate of residential mobility that appears in pre-Communist times to have been especially common among poorer landless peasants, it is not surprising that Shenjiashang and other villages in the area were characterized by an

TABLE 7.1

Shenjiashang, Population and Families by Hamlet Residence and
Lineage Membership, May 1953

Hamlet[a] / Lineage[b]	Population	Families	Hamlet[a] / Lineage[b]	Population	Families
SHEN			WU		
Shen	97	14	Zhou	15	2
Zhang	50	8	He	11	1
Zhang	17	2	Chen	6	1
Yao	17	3	ZHU		
Lu	13	3	Zhu	13	3
Wang	6	1	Wang	10	1
Chen	5	1	JIANG		
Huang	5	1	Jiang	39	6
Dou	3	1	Zhang	12	2
Gu	3	1	Feng	6	1
			Huang	4	1

SOURCE: Household register data for May 1953.
  [a] The full name of the Shen hamlet is Shenjiashang, from which the larger village is named; the Wu, Zhu, and Jiang hamlets are Wujiashe, Zhujiazhai, and Jiangjiazhai. All of these place-names can be glossed as "Shen (Wu, Zhu, Jiang) Family Hamlet."
  [b] Figures for each lineage include women married virilocally, men married uxorilocally, and persons brought in by adoption. Separately listed lineages or families with the same surname trace their descent from different ancestors and had no ritual or social ties based upon agnatic kinship.

agnatic heterogeneity similar to that found in much of north China. Nevertheless, agnates who did remain in the village tended to cluster residentially. The village had been comprised of four hamlets separated by fields or canals; with the expansion of residential sites during the Communist era the hamlets have merged to become sections of the larger village settlement. Each hamlet was identified by a family name (still used in reference to the village neighborhoods). The present-day Shen, Jiang, and Zhu lineages still largely reside at the sites of the hamlets named after their ancestors, but even prior to the Communist period they had been joined by families with a variety of other surnames; the Wu family hamlet had seen the departure of the last person surnamed Wu well before the establishment of the People's Republic. Thus multi-surname settlement characterized both the village as a whole and its component hamlets. Table 7.1, based upon the earliest household register data, for May 1953, shows the distribution of Shenjiashang's population among its four hamlets and nineteen lineages or isolated families.

Shenjiashang's small lineages can be contrasted with those in southeastern China that are anthropologically famous; these latter were wealthy and some were large enough to comprise an entire village community or even several villages. There was also a marked contrast between Shenjiashang's lineages and a few nearby that were much larger. Agnatic kinship nevertheless was a powerful force in Shenjiashang's social life, and there was strong consciousness of common descent. As elsewhere in China, there were (and are) terms that describe a nested hierarchy of descent groups. The largest unit, which I gloss here as "lineage," was the *gen* (root). For example, one man referred to his Zhang lineage in Shenjiashang as "one *gen*" to distinguish it from another local Zhang lineage tracing its descent from a different ancestor. Likewise, in referring to the membership of a lineage there is the phrase "the people of a *gen*." At a lower level of genealogical reckoning is the *menkou*, a term for any agnatic subdivision of a *gen* focusing on a particular ancestor. In this context *"menkou"* can be translated as "branch" (literally, "those of a branch"). A *menkou* can be further subdivided into smaller segments called *fang*, the one term for "branch" in the local vocabulary of genealogical reckoning commonly reported from other parts of China and widely encountered in written genealogies.[3]

Conceptually, the genealogical terms do not have absolute referents but rather provide the means for expressing branching relative to larger units. As elsewhere in China, the genealogical orientation as such is fundamentally unbounded; any unit defined through descent from a common ancestor can be called a, *gen* or a *menkou*, for it is but a branch within a larger genealogical arrangement. In the final analysis, and in terms of cultural orientation, genealogical boundaries are framed by the totality of Chinese society, for they are defined only on the basis of sharing a remote founding ancestor as described by the origin myths of the different surnames or by the hall names or choronyms that locate the origin of particular surnames in the ancestral north China homeland of the Han Chinese. Thus there can be some variation in the terms used to designate groups of agnates. One man, for example, told me that everyone in Shenjiashang with his Shen surname (after which the village is named) comprised one *menkou*. I asked if this was the same as "one *gen*" and he said "yes." But when he and others were confronted with the written genealogies that I had compiled, they invariably identified the larger agnatic units inclusive to the village as a whole as *gen*, and the major branches of each of these as *menkou*.

Although the genealogical orientation as such does not provide boundaries for agnatic groups, we have considered in chapters 5 and 6 some of the factors that do give such groups definition. Among these, again, some of major significance elsewhere did not characterize lineage arrangements in Shenjiashang. In addition to the absence of corporate property, there were no ancestral temples or lineage cemeteries, and neither were there any rituals of ancestor worship that were organized above the family level in order to dramatize lineage solidarity. Furthermore, I see no evidence that lineage membership in Shenjiashang (unlike in north China) supported settlement rights in the village. Indeed, village solidarity in many ways received far more ritual emphasis than did lineage unity. Nevertheless, Shenjiashang's lineages were socially significant in the lives of their members. Because these lineages were expressions of a descent ideology receiving major ritual support within a domestic rather than lineagewide context, I turn first to domestic ancestor worship.

Shenjiashang fits into a broader Chinese pattern in that the focus of ancestor worship was on tablets (*shenzhupai*). Unlike those in north China but similar to those in south China and Sichuan, these tablets were kept in place throughout the year. A tablet in Shenjiashang was dedicated to an individual, not to a husband and wife together (as was often the case in north China) nor to a larger group of individually identified agnates (as sometimes happened in the south and in Sichuan). Inscribed on the right-hand side of a Shenjiashang tablet was the ancestor's year of birth; on the left, the year of death; and in the middle, his or her name. Because the tablets of particular persons were periodically removed there would also be in place a tablet dedicated to the unnamed earlier ancestors.

The tablets were kept in the main room or "guest room" (*ketang*) of a compound, which might be the residence of one family; with family division, the compound might continue to be shared by several families headed by brothers or even by third-generation agnates. Because housing was expensive relative to income, as were house sites, division resulted in the building of new stoves by each of the new family units and the distribution of residential quarters and other rooms among them. The *ketang* itself remained shared property and was now known as the "*zongketang*" (common guest room). The location of tablets in a residential compound's main room was common to much of China (for Taiwan see Cohen 1969a), but in this eastern part of the country their placement on a special platform was a local custom hitherto not described in the anthropological literature. Although it was called a *jiatang* (family hall), this was in fact a small platform placed high up on the wall facing the guest room's main door and attached to a roof beam (*liang*). (When this arrangement was first described to me I thought I might have misunderstood what was being said, for it seemed that the platform was placed too high for convenient access to the tablets. I was then assured that a ladder was needed to reach them.) Should a *jiatang* be in a shared *ketang* it might similarly be referred to as a "*zongjiatang.*"

Families would (and still do) worship their ancestors independently. If several closely related families shared a guest room and its tablets, each prepared on its own a separate offering of food, wine, and ritual paper money. In some cases each family would even use a separate offering table (usually an ordinary dining table, *baxianzhuo*). Most families, however, simply appear to have taken turns. In other words, ancestor worship was strictly lineal; it emphasized not the ties among agnatically related families, but rather the obligations of each family unit to its own ancestors. This lineality was also reflected in the disposition of tablets when a new residential compound with its own *ketang* and *jiatang* was finally built, usually after the passage of three or more generations. A person could transfer to the new *jiatang* the tablets of his direct ancestors, I was told, providing that these were not also the ancestors of those still living in the old compound. Thus, in the event that a man had left behind patrilineal uncles but no brothers or patrilineal nephews he could transfer his parent's tablets, but not those of his grandparents. In the far more likely circumstance that there were also brothers or nephews, all the tablets would have to be left in place. Under such conditions the usual procedure was to make new tablets for the parents and patrilineal grandparents and a new general tablet for all the ancestors. The disposition of tablets upon the setting up of a new *jiatang* highlights the fact that collateral patrilineal ties did not figure at all in domestic ancestor worship. In other words, that for a family worshiping in a *jiatang* shared for several generations there might be tablets of those who were not their lineal ancestors simply reflected the fact that the dead, like the living, might have to share a *jiatang*. Worship of tablets certainly expressed consciousness of descent, but it did not give ritual emphasis to agnatic ties among the living.

Even the focus on lineality was confined, for in those *jiatang* where the population of tablets continued to increase through the generations, the older ones were periodically removed and burnt. According to a member of the Shen lineage, the tablets were burnt after five generations, but other villagers reported they were so disposed of after "three or more generations" or "when the *jiatang* filled up." While it thus appears that tablets might be preserved for varying lengths of time it seems likely that a *jiatang* would contain few or no tablets of ancestors who had not been personally known by any of their living descendants. Because such ancestors were not ritually appealed to in the organization among the living of social relationships beyond family ties—as would be the case with ancestor worship that brought together larger groups of agnates into lineages or lineage segments—they could be forgotten as individuals and remembered only in the abstract, as contributing to the unending line of descent represented by the tablet dedicated to all earlier generations. The burning of a tablet thus represented the end of the last, ancestral phase of a person's social presence in the world of the living. It was that person's last rite of passage, carried out according to socially recognized procedures. It is not surprising, therefore, that the ceremony of tablet burning took place on Qingming and was held in the *ketang* under the supervision of a Taoist priest who would, I was told, "chant scriptures" (*nian jing*). Qingming is generally devoted to the care of the ancestral graves, and thus to the dead in the underworld. The burning of a tablet represented the complete transfer of the ancestor to that domain, perhaps to await anonymous reincarnation. Likewise, in this part of China Taoist priests far more than Buddhists were ritually involved in all aspects of the "cult of the dead."

In Shenjiashang and the surrounding region the extinction of ancestors through the burning of tablets in some cases went hand in hand with the preservation of their names in written genealogies (*jiapu*). As one person put it, "the names of the ancestors, and all the other information on the tablets, would have been written into the *jiapu* before the tablets would be burnt." The two practices are representative of the distinction between an ancestor or an ancestral soul still present among the living and an ancestor as symbolizing and validating for the living their ties of patrilineal kinship. In this area of China genealogies (*jiapu*) served as records and at least in some cases may have figured in ancestor worship or other rituals, perhaps as in north China (see chapter 6). A distinguished professor, now retired, told me he remembered how as a child in Suzhou he fetched a genealogy from the high platform where the tablets were kept; the genealogy was ordinarily placed there, for it was worshiped together with the tablets surrounding it. But as a book, or a set of them, the genealogy was worshiped for its representing agnatic lines of descent through the generations that went into making the living members of the lineage a collectivity in religious terms if nothing else: the lineage, if not a corporation, and not even a congregation periodically coming together for worship, at least maintained a record of shared ancestry. In contrast, tablets were worshiped as representing particular individual ancestors. Although I was told often enough in Shenjiashang that "before liberation most people kept genealogies," I was not able to fully determine how common they had been prior to the Communist era. It is of some interest that my firmest evidence for the keeping of genealogies comes from the Shen, the village's largest lineage. One of its members told me that his family had a *jiapu*, "which they burnt during a campaign [*yundong*] so as to avoid getting in trouble." The "campaign" probably was the Cultural Revolution during the mid-1960s, when there was widespread and near-total destruction of genealogies, tablets, and all other physical manifestations of traditional religion. Such turmoil hardly was new to the village, for a man from the Wang lineage recalled how his paternal grandmother told him that "they had a *jiapu* during Qing, but it was destroyed during the chaos [*luan*]. It might have been the Taipings, it might have been something else." According to people from the largest Zhang lineage, and from the Jiang, these groups did not keep genealogies.

The inconsistency of my evidence concerning the prevalence of *jiapu* may be related to the fact that succession to a lineage or branch genealogy was in the senior line, suggesting that by the time of my fieldwork there could not have been many people who still remembered what may have been only a very few such documents. All from Shenjiashang and nearby villages who did know about them agreed that the *jiapu* was invariably passed down to the eldest son, such that in a lineage there might be only one such text. Under such circumstances, the man holding the *jiapu* would be the representative of a senior descent line extending back to the eldest son of the lineage founder, an arrangement quite similar to the one we have seen to be prevalent in north China. Furthermore, the *jiapu* was open to all deceased lineage members, and thus was a genealogical record of the lineage as a collectivity. As the man who had kept the Shen *jiapu* put it, "all descendants were written into the *jiapu*, as long as collateral agnates reported the information to the man holding it." According to a man from a nearby village, there might be several *jiapu* in a larger lineage. Each would be a record of a lineage branch held by the man who was in its senior line of descent. Whatever the distribution of genealogies within a lineage, their compilation is evidence of continuing agnatic solidarity even in the absence of corporate holdings, lineage temples, or common worship by lineage members. So the "fixed genealogical mode" of agnatic kinship that was important in north China lineages (chapter 6) also had a role in Shenjiashang lineage arrangements.

Firmer and more immediately sociological evidence of lineage solidarity was the presence in all but Shenjiashang's smallest lineages of a "lineage elder," known as the *laozhangbei*. Under ordinary circumstances this person would be the oldest man of the lineage's senior generation; should the man with such genealogical qualifications be incapacitated for one reason or another, someone immediately junior to him might take his place. Thus "associational kinship" also appears to have had some significance as far as lineages in this village were concerned. The lineage elder can be viewed as playing a key role in the social relationships within his lineage. One man from the Jiang lineage spoke of the lineage elder as follows: "In the past there was a *laozhangbei* who would mediate quarrels between brothers or other family disputes. . . . In the past, the lineage was the important unit. And when they would discuss matters the *laozhangbei* was very important." The lineage elder's intervention in family affairs might extend to formally participating as a witness and mediator in family division, should there be strong disagreement among the brothers and other family members. Under ordinary circumstances, I was told, the father's brother and mother's brother were the kinsmen usually invited to help a family divide.

The way that another of the lineage elder's roles came to my attention perhaps illustrates some of the pitfalls involved in the ethnographic reconstruction of a social scene gone for four decades as of the time of my fieldwork. A member of the Zhang lineage first told me that he had never heard of the *laozhangbei*. Later, when our conversation had turned to a different subject, and without any prompting from me, he had this to say: "Before liberation there would be lots of buying and selling of a few *mou* of land here and there in this village [a *mou* is equivalent to about one-sixth of an acre]. Land sales didn't have to be registered in the township office; a contract was written and it was stamped by the ward head [*baozhang*] and by the *laozhangbei*." (Having in an appropriate context remembered one of the *laozhangbei*'s roles, the man I was speaking to was at first a bit startled by what he had just said, but then went on to give me the name of the last elder in his own lineage.) The lineage elder had to endorse the contract in the event that the seller was of his lineage, and by doing so he in effect involved the lineage as a whole in the transaction. As elsewhere in China, the participation of outside parties in a contract reinforced its integrity by expanding the network of social relationships that might be threatened should its terms be violated. In the case of Shenjiashang, the fact that the lineage elder had such a role is further evidence of the importance of lineage ties in social life.

Within the village, lineages were basic social units above the family level. Lineage members were (and still are) obligated to come to each other's assistance during events such as weddings and funerals, when help was needed to prepare for the rituals involved and for the banquets associated with them. The larger lineages, such as the Shen, Zhang, and Jiang, were in effect self-contained as far as mutual assistance among village families was concerned. In the smaller lineages, however, a family had to go beyond agnatic boundaries and appeal to neighbors as well, and all families would also request assistance from cognatic kin. The larger lineages might also express their solidarity in a more violent fashion, for I was told by several people that lineage feuds had been quite common.

Elsewhere in eastern China attributes of lineage unity were similar to those characterizing Shenjiashang's agnatic groups. Even in a rural community near Suzhou, where the largest lineage comprised only seven families, there was recognition of the lineage elder and of obligations linking lineage members:

The clans [i.e., lineages] in the surveyed area appear small and powerless. . . . Yet even such [lineages] retain some . . . consciousness. All . . . members readily identify the oldest member of the oldest generation as the [lineage] chief. . . . [Lineage] members co-own their buffaloes; they help each other during special occasions like weddings and funerals. . . . [Lineage] members act as witnesses when one of its members sells, purchases, or mortgages land. (Fukutake 1967: 87–88)

In Shenjiashang, another expression of the importance of the lineage as a social unit was the special position of the Shen in the village as a whole. When trying to identify elders of the various lineages, I was surprised to hear the Shen *laozhangbei* mentioned by several people who were not from the Shen lineage. I finally understood the relationship between the village and the Shen lineage elder after one man from one of the small Zhang lineages told me the following: "Before liberation there were only just over fifty families in this village. There was a person called *laozhangbei*, and he was recognized as such by the village as a whole. This man was Shen XXX, the grandfather of Shen YYY. . . . The *laozhangbei* was the *zhaizhang* [village head] of this village. The *zhaizhang* was the *laozhangbei*." The reason my Zhang informant, born in 1924, equated the Shen lineage elder with the village head seems clear enough. Mr. Zhang's grandfather had first moved to Shenjiashang, and had only one son, who in turn had three, including Mr. Zhang. For much of Mr. Zhang's life prior to the arrival of the Communists, his lineage consisted of no more than one family, so that there was hardly a context for the emergence of a distinct lineage identity. On the other hand, the fact that the same man headed both the village and its largest lineage gave him two equally well known titles; thus, for Mr. Zhang there was no other *laozhangbei* present in his local social environment. Later, I was informed by persons from nearby settlements that it was quite common for a village head to be from its largest lineage. Such a lineage would draw on its own strength and solidarity to assume a position of dominance within the village as a whole.

The village itself, although quite small, had considerable self-definition as a community. One man proclaimed with considerable pride that in pre-Communist times "this village was especially united [*tuanjie*], more than other villages." Indeed, Shenjiashang's lineages, at least the larger ones, derived much of their own solidarity precisely from their importance as units making up the local community. Perhaps because of its small size there was very little in the way of ritual or even physical expressions of solidarity and community interests in the village. There were neither village temples nor village festivals, which in much of China were characteristic expressions of village unity. Indeed, in Shenjiashang there was only one small shrine, with a god whose image was also small. The story behind the construction of this shrine is of some interest, because it may provide some understanding of the means the village employed to express its unity. According to one version of the story, the villagers originally "wanted to build it higher, to the height reached by a rocket they set off; but the rocket didn't go up very far and they made the shrine very short. Therefore the god [*pusa*] was unhappy and acted like a ghost [*gui*]; if it were to attach [*fu*] itself to you, you were doomed."

The god's anger may have been a reflection of the villagers' own dissatisfaction with the standing of their community within the region. In any event, it is clear enough that the major expression of village solidarity was Shenjiashang's annual participation and competition in the temple fair (*miaohui*), which also involved many nearby villages and was centered on a major temple in their common market town. This temple had a "temple sphere" (*miaojie*), which encompassed all the villages involved, and sponsorship of the temple fair rotated among them on an annual basis.[4] Only on the day of the temple fair was there a community banquet in Shenjiashang, with each family contributing money toward the cost. This banquet was a yearly event, linked to the temple fair, but not to the village's own turn at sponsoring it, for this occurred only once every several years. The banquet was of a kind other villages might associate with a festival focusing on their own temple. The connection between village solidarity and the temple fair certainly looms large in the memory of local residents. For example, when I asked one man about village leadership and village affairs in pre-Communist times, he replied as follows: "The various *laozhangbei* did not as such constitute a leadership group in village affairs. Rather, activists would organize the village's participation in the *miaohui*." In describing the *miaohui* procession, whose route took it to every participating village, another person noted how the unit representing Shenjiashang "was able to put up two or three dragons, and it was very rare for a village to be able to put up so many."

Perhaps the strongest expression of village unity during the day of the *miaohui* was a practice that also says much about the relationship between village and lineage solidarity. It was described to me as follows:

Men of the same generation would all change their personal names [*mingzi*] such that they included a common character. This was so that the village could express to the outside that it had great solidarity and influence. They would ask the ward head [*baozhang*], who was an educated man, to give them a new personal name, including a common generation name. This is why so many men here have the character *qi* in their *mingzi*. The saying here was *sanshiliu qi, qishi'er wen* (thirty-six *qi*, seventy-two *wen*). In fact, there were about thirty-six *qi*, but only fifty or so *wen*. There were not as many *wen*, but they used the numbers as an expression of village solidarity. . . . The *wen* name was given just before liberation, so many people don't use it [*bujiao*].

Many village men indeed have "*qi*" as the last character of their personal name. According to the household register data, which most likely do not tell the whole story, 25 out of 59 men born between 1907 and 1931 are so named; 24 of these men were among 37 born between 1907 and 1924. Among this total of 25 men there are nine surnames, including members of the Shen, Jiang, Yao, Lu, Zhou, Chen, and He lineages, two Zhang lineages, and two Wang lineages. Thus the village's major and smaller lineages are well represented. The registers also give "*wen*" as the first character in the personal names of 9 out of 44 men whose years of birth are between 1923 and 1937. These include members of the Shen, Jiang, Zhou, He, Wang, and two Zhang lineages, in all cases junior by generation or birth to members of the same lineage or family named with "*qi*." Both the "*qi*" and the "*wen*" groups included men of varying economic circumstances, insofar as these are indicated by the class labels assigned during the land reform campaign: Among the "*qi*" were two men labeled "rich peasants," six "middle," and 16 "poor." Of those named "*wen*," six were middle peasants and three poor. While it was and is common for people in a Chinese village not related agnatically to address each other as kin, I do not know of other cases where kinship usage was extended to include use of generation characters in a fashion usually restricted to agnates of a lineage or lineage branch.[5] I was unable to determine if there were other villages near Shenjiashang where there had been a similar custom. Although Shenjiashang's practice might be held to reflect an emphasis of village ties over those of the lineage, the expression of village solidarity in the idiom of agnatic kinship is in fact testimony to the latter's social and cultural importance. Dennerline provides an example of how in the Wuxi area a similar naming practice was used precisely in an agnatic context to genealogically unite the numerous and scattered descendants of a Song dynasty man named Hua Banzhou. He had fifteen grandsons with either "Tong" or "Qi" as the generation characters in their personal names, giving rise to as many major descent branches whose members (well over seven thousand males by the end of the nineteenth century) were collectively known as the "ten Tong" (*shitong*) and the "five Qi" (*wuqi*) (Dennerline 1979–80: 25).

In Shenjiashang, expressions of both agnatic and community solidarity were also to be found—quite unexpectedly, given prevalent anthropological understandings—in the context of uxorilocal marriage. The 1953 household registers record seven uxorilocal marriages, and in each case parents took in a son-in-law in the absence of sons of their own. Uxorilocal marriages under such circumstances are widely reported in China, as is the fact that usually some or all of the children resulting therefrom took their mother's surname. Furthermore, the incidence of such marriages seems to have been especially high in the Lower Yangzi region, as well as in some restricted areas of southeastern China. Cases of this kind of marriage, however, are also reported from other areas of the county, including north China, such that there cannot be any direct attribution of cultural difference to explain variations in frequency.[6] Insofar as men entering into such marriages agreed that some or all of their offspring would take the maternal surname they placed their own patrilineal descent line in a subordinate position or ignored it altogether, hence the common view in China that uxorilocal unions were undesirable arrangements forced upon certain men by their own poverty and isolation, or by economically unfavorable family circumstances (Pasternak 1985; J. Watson 1986: 284). The motives of families taking in a son-in-law might vary (Pasternak 1985), but a lack of sons was surely a common one and reinforced the negative reputation of this marriage procedure. Furthermore, in much of China uxorilocal marriage was productive of tensions involving the presence in one family of two succession lines whose interests had to be reconciled. For example, my first fieldwork in a south Taiwan village (Cohen 1976), confirmed and elaborated through subsequent work in that region, revealed that sons born of an uxorilocal union and given their father's surname had no rights to the family estate, unless such rights had been unambiguously spelled out in the original marriage contract. Their brothers who had taken the mother's surname, on the other hand, would share the estate equally among themselves (also see chapter 9). It is true that in east China a family's property might also become a bone of contention. Fukutake, for example, notes with reference to a village near Suzhou how occasionally in the context of uxorilocal marriage "some property is given to the [patrilineal] nephew who has the right of succession" (1967: 87). The point he is making is that such a nephew was not a member of the family party to uxorilocal marriage, but rather had residual inheritance rights on the basis of kinship that ordinarily could be exercised only in the event of his agnatic uncle's death, if the family headed by the latter lacked sons.

Such potential conflicts as noted by Fukutake aside, the fact remains that in Shenjiashang tensions were considerably reduced because uxorilocal marriage involved a man's total absorption both into his wife's family and into its lineage. A man marrying in unfailingly took his wife's surname, as did all of their children. He worshiped his wife's ancestors, upon his death his tablet joined theirs, and his name was recorded in the genealogy kept by the senior line descendant. Indeed, should this man in the senior line be without sons and have taken in a son-in-law through uxorilocal marriage, the latter would take over custody of the genealogy upon his father-in-law's death. A married-in son-in-law's full acceptance as a lineage member is also attested to by the circumstance that at one time Shenjiashang's largest lineage, the Shen, had as its elder (*laozhang-bei*) an uxorilocally married man who originally had a different surname. The characteristics of uxorilocal marriage as practiced in Shenjiashang were hardly restricted to this village, for persons from nearby settlements also uniformly identified these practices as being elements in a standard uxorilocal marriage arrangement.[7]

Given the importance of the Shen lineage elder in the village as a whole, it follows that uxorilocal marriage also meant absorption into the village community. Additional evidence to this effect is provided by the fact that uxorilocally married men were full participants in the naming rituals that proclaimed village solidarity. While two of the seven uxorilocally married men were born late in the nineteenth century, the remaining five had their years of birth recorded in the household register as falling between 1908 and 1931. Of these latter men, four had the character "*qi*" in their personal names.

Uxorilocal marriage involved a man's total surrender of his original agnatic identity, and in this respect it was identical to the adoption of a son from another lineage. Such adoptions did occur in the past, and they might involve adult men. In the late nineteenth century, for example, one elderly and childless couple, again in the Shen lineage, adopted two adult brothers, one a coppersmith and one a tailor, who changed their surnames and were incorporated into the Shen lineage. Both adoption and uxorilocal marriage appear to have been of considerable importance in the maintenance of lineage populations. On the basis of the household registers and the memory of informants I have reconstructed the Shen lineage genealogy so as to locate almost all present-day Shen within four large branches, each with a depth of four or five generations, although I have not been able to link these branches together. In any event, the survival of one branch was based on the adoptions just noted, and that of another on an uxorilocal marriage. My complete genealogy of the smaller Yao lineage reveals that its founder in Shenjiashang had no sons, but rather a daughter who married uxorilocally and also an adopted daughter who married in the same fashion, so that the lineage was able to produce third-generation families by bringing in from the outside one woman and two men in the second generation. Of the three Zhou lineage branches that I have reconstructed (but not fully linked), one owes its survival to an uxorilocal marriage. My genealogies of the remaining eight Shenjiashang lineages do not reveal additional early generation adoptions or uxorilocal marriages that might have played a pivotal role in lineage survival; the small Wang and He lineages do not appear to have resorted to such measures, and as far as the remaining lineages are concerned, I am unable to comment on early marriages or adoptions due to inadequate information on the first, second, or third generations. Nevertheless, the examples I have been able to provide certainly confirm that uxorilocal marriages and adoptions frequently enough were key to the survival of families and lineages.

I suggest that the ease with which adopted sons and uxorilocally married men were assimilated into community life at all levels was but one reflection of what might be characterized as the porous nature of local social organization in this village and in many others in east China. Given the marked absence of corporate holdings, common property did not serve to anchor lineages and provide them with resources that they might not easily be willing to share with outsiders. What was important in Shenjiashang's lineages was not the relationship between people and corporate wealth, but rather the fact that the social ties between lineage members were encumbered by particular obligations of mutual assistance, such that acceptance into a lineage of adopted sons or uxorilocally married men might actually be seen as a means of strengthening or at least reproducing its membership. However, if we accept James Watson's suggestion that "Intangible resources such as information, reputation, and job introductions can serve as the basis of corporate unity" (1986: 279), then even such lineages were corporate groups. Certainly, for ordinary rural Chinese social ties with agnates comprised an "intangible resource" of a most important kind.

Problems of reproduction aside, the generally small size of lineages reflected considerable population movement. The growth of Shenjiashang's older lineages was constrained by population outflow, while a consequence of migration into the village was the emergence of even smaller descent groups. The ethnographic evidence suggests that such agnatic heterogeneity was characteristic of much of east China (Fei 1939: 92–93; Fukutake 1967: 79–92; Huang 1990: 144–52). It is of some interest, therefore, that the Lower Yangzi region was in fact notable for its large and powerful lineages. If circumstances in the immediate area of Shenjiashang are any indication of the broader Lower Yangzi pattern, then these large lineages were scattered—few and far between—among the far more numerous smaller and agnatically mixed villages. Shenjiashang is in Huacao Township; according to information provided by local officials, the township covers an area of about twenty-one square kilometers, contains one larger town (Huacao Town), ninety-one "natural villages" (i.e., discrete settlement clusters), and as of 1989 had a population of about 23,000 in 5,130 households. Within this area there were only two major lineages prior to the Communist era. One lineage, of the Zhang surname, was spread across two villages and boasted two ancestral temples (*citang*). This Zhang lineage was founded by an official during the Ming dynasty, I was told, and "was famous all over Shanghai County for its many degree holders in Ming and Qing." The other large lineage, the Zhu, was in Huacao Town. Founded in Qing by an official who according to a present-day descendant "must at least have been a *juren* [holder of the second-highest degree]," the lineage continued to produce degree holders until the end of the nineteenth century. My informant insisted that the Zhu did not have an ancestral temple; rather, the lineage originally was formed by seven large residential compounds (*ting*), only one of which was not destroyed during the mid-nineteenth-century Taiping Rebellion. It was refurbished and survives today.

The fame of Huacao Township's two large lineages was eclipsed by that of the Hou lineage in the adjacent township of Zhudi. This lineage boasted holders of high degrees during the Ming, some of whom served in the imperial court or had important connections with it, while others later played a prominent role in resisting the Manchu invaders who established the Qing dynasty. These activities of members of the Hou lineage, well known locally, have been placed in social context and described by Dennerline (1981) in his account of the loyalists and their disastrous effort to defend the city of Jiading from Manchu conquest. Interestingly enough, this most prestigious lineage traces its origin to a man surnamed Yang adopted in early Ming (around 1400) by his mother's brother, who was a Hou (Dennerline 1981: 145). The failure of anti-Manchu resistance marked a low point in lineage fortunes, but I am told there was a revival during mid-Qing as the lineage continued to produce degree holders and maintain connections with the imperial court. In addition to its ancestral temple, the Hou lineage had "a large reception hall for important visitors," as well as a theater for "opera performances on special occasions." It is claimed locally (and perhaps apocryphally) that one such occasion was the visit of the eighteenth-century Qianlong emperor during his southern tour. In any event, the impressive Hou ancestral temple still survives and is testimony to the lineage's past prominence.[8]

Large lineages such as those of the Zhang, Zhu, and Hou appear to be worlds apart from the far more prevalent small agnatic groups like those in Shenjiashang. They were indeed clearly differentiated; one man living near Shenjiashang who is historically very well informed referred to the large lineages as "official" (*guanfang*), while those of ordinary people were "popular" (*minjian*). This gentleman was thus making a point quite similar to that of David Faure; we have already noted in chapter 6 how with reference in the first instance to southeastern China he distinguishes lineages embedded in rural social structure from those that are products of an "official culture." My informant's view, like Faure's, was that the "official" lineage involved not just wealth, social standing, and architecture, but also a characteristic pattern of organization different from that associated with "popular" lineages. Lineages of the official type thus did not represent the outcome of a developmental process whereby simpler and smaller agnatic groups such as those in Shenjiashang would gradually increase in size, complexity, and wealth. Rather, the creation and preservation of an official-style lineage were self-conscious undertakings on the part of "an elite core of activists" (Hazelton: 1986: 166) informed often enough by local examples, but also by a readily available textual model historically derived from the innovative construction of a lineage corporation in the Suzhou area during the eleventh century by the nationally famous scholar and statesman Fan Zhongyan (Twitchett 1959). The creation of such lineages in the Lower Yangzi area accelerated during later dynasties such that by the end of the imperial era they were well known and broadly if not densely distributed in this region. It seems reasonable to assume that linked to the spread of these lineages over the course of many centuries was diffusion of some of their characteristic features to smaller Shenjiashang-type lineages. Thus the keeping of genealogies in Shenjiashang and elsewhere may represent absorption by simpler lineages of procedures originally associated with the official model.

It is not surprising that comparison of Shenjiashang's descent groups with the three nearby official-style lineages also reveals major differences in organization. Most obvious is that in these latter lineages real leadership was in the hands of men who more generally were powerful in local society on the basis of their degree-holding status or wealth. Although it has long been established in the literature (i.e., as in Hu 1948: 26–30) that heightened social and economic differentiation within a lineage will have an impact on its organization, the emphasis has been on the shift away from kinship position in the determination of lineage leadership. However, the elite lineages near Shenjiashang also show that linked to the presence of men whose high standing was not derived in the first instance from their kinship position was a transformation of the role of agnatic kinship in defining leadership status. I have noted how in a Shenjiashang lineage the role of senior-line descent was restricted to custody of the genealogy, while it was the oldest surviving man in the senior generation who was the *laozhangbei*, or lineage elder. The coexistence of these two lineage positions shows how in the east China lineage context there was representation of the two modes of agnatic kinship discussed earlier with reference to north China (chapter 6). The fixed genealogical mode of kinship, focused on senior-line descent, is what defines the keeper of the genealogy In contrast, associational kinship, which denies the superiority, ritual or otherwise, of the senior descent line, proclaims kinship equality among descent lines such that special positions within the lineage group, as with the *laozhangbei*, can be defined on the basis of age, generation, or individual attribute.

When responding to my questions about the role of the *laozhangbei*, several people in Shenjiashang also used the more formal term "*zuzhang*," or "lineage head," but without fully equating the two. As one woman put it, "the *laozhangbei* was something like a *zuzhang*." It soon became clear to me that the term "lineage head" referred to a position within an official-style lineage, that this position was defined on the basis of membership in the senior descent line, and that it also involved—at least formally—custody of the lineage genealogy. A member of the large Zhu lineage in Huacao Town described the lineage head's position as follows: "The person in the lineage who had control over the genealogy was the *laozhangbei*. The genealogy passed down in the family [of the senior descent line]. Here the *laozhangbei* was called the *zuzhang*." In an official-style lineage—at least according to my informants—the two terms might be used interchangeably, but the important point is that they referred to a person whose position was defined according to criteria quite different from those applied in Shenjiashang's small lineages. After noting that "the *zuzhang* was known locally as the *laozhangbei*; he was in the senior line of succession," a man from the large Zhang lineage near Shenjiashang went on to insist that "the *zuzhang* would be in the senior line even if he was much younger than another man of the same generation but in a junior line." In these elite lineages seniority of descent in effect replaced seniority of generation as the significant genealogical determinant of lineage position. In other words, with reference to kinship-based position in the lineage, there is movement of the *laozhangbei* from the domain of associational kinship to that of the fixed genealogical mode.

This does not mean that in such elite lineages associational kinship was no longer significant. On the contrary, I suggest that elimination of generational standards with respect to a particular lineage position was linked to a broader deemphasis of genealogical status as a determinant of social standing in a lineage where the organization was in the hands of activists whose power was hardly based upon genealogical or generational criteria of any kind. Assignment of the *zuzhang* position only through senior line succession meant elimination from the associational domain of other kinship-based criteria in the determination of formal lineage leadership, thus giving full rein to employment of other standards. Degree holding, wealth, or other determinants of status based upon achievements or resources external to the genealogical framework were thus given ideological space for full expression. Another man from the Zhang lineage may have had such circumstances in mind when he stressed that one "must distinguish influential people in the lineage from the *zuzhang*. There can be only one *zuzhang* in a lineage. If he were very young, or a poor or uninfluential person, he might not have any real power." The socially impotent character of the *zuzhang*'s genealogically derived role was popularly recognized; if such a man was not influential in his own right he might be disparagingly referred to as a "living ancestral tablet" (*huo shenzhupai*), a man whose social worth was totally derived from his being the purely symbolic representation of the genealogical basis of lineage unity. The contrast between such a man and the real power holders in an important lineage was so striking as to impart to the phrase "living ancestral tablet" the more general meaning of "being useless." I was told that this phrase might be used, for example, by a woman to ridicule her husband or by a man to scold his son.

The historical literature on Lower Yangzi lineages certainly confirms the contrast in at least some elite lineages between a titular ritual head in the senior line of succession and a real leadership defined by criteria irrelevant to genealogical considerations. For this literature the often large and elaborate genealogies produced by such lineages form a major source; but in the sections of these genealogies dealing with lineage regulations the term *zuzhang* usually refers to the selected lineage chief, who may be but one of several designated lineage officials, while the ritual head is commonly known as the *zongzi*, which is the ancient term precisely for the "son in the senior line" (Beattie 1979: 115–16; Ebrey 1986; Hu 1948: 27–28; Liu 1959: 100–101). While employment of the term *zongzi* reflects an appeal to classical precedents in the construction of elite lineages, I am unable to say whether the inconsistency in the usage of *zuzhang* reflects microregional differences or colloquial as opposed to literary forms. Questions of terminology aside, the fact remains that in both ordinary and elite lineages seniority of descent line was given symbolic recognition; in both forms of lineage, furthermore, the role of the senior line successor was fundamentally passive. In a smaller lineage, where he was in charge of a genealogy in a context where the only other collective resource was formed by associational kinship, that is, by the social relationships of agnatic kinship, his position was eclipsed by a lineage leader defined on the basis of generational criteria that more generally provided a kinship structure for every lineage member. In an elite lineage characterized by significant corporate holdings and pronounced political and economic stratification, one in which the social relationships of agnatic kinship provided for some a framework for the expression of their greater power and influence, the expansion of his role to include titular and ritual lineage leadership really represented a reduction of the significance of fixed genealogical kinship position in lineage organization.

Although a contrast between Shenjiashang's small lineages and the few elite lineages in the immediate vicinity might suggest that there was a zero-sum relationship between employment of the generational criteria of associational kinship and the descent line criteria of the fixed genealogical mode in the use of kinship position to determine lineage leadership, evidence pertaining to other larger lineages in the Lower Yangzi area shows that a variety of combinations were possible. In Hu Hsien Chin's general survey of Chinese lineage organization, for example, arrangements in different Lower Yangzi lineages were as follows. One of her informants told her that in his lineage "the head . . . is the eldest of the oldest surviving generation, and his position is more nominal than real, although he heads the functionaries at the annual ancestral ritual" (Hu 1948: 122). According to a man from another lineage, the head "must be a member of the oldest generation living. He also has to be 'wise,' that is, capable of making decisions" (121). In a genealogy it is recorded that the

important affairs of the whole [lineage] are administered by the [son of the senior line]. . . . Should he be an upright man of no ability, he is to be assisted by the head of the [lineage]. . . . Elect the head of the [lineage]. The head of the [lineage] is the most respected man in the whole [lineage]. The choice is to be limited to the most respected [that is, earliest] generation, so that in the whole [lineage] there should be no one whose position is higher. Also, he need not belong to the eldest line and cannot be compared with the [son of the senior line]. . . . Only a man with an official rank and of ability . . . may receive the appointment" (126–27).

These examples, viewed in conjunction with the evidence from Shenjiashang and the large lineages nearby, suggest that, as in north China, both associational kinship and the fixed genealogical mode coexisted in lineage culture, but that these modes were differently expressed in relation to the dilemma posed by the conflict within a lineage structure between kinship solidarity and social and economic differentiation. Even in the most highly stratified lineages principles of agnatic kinship solidarity were appealed to at least with respect to the selection of a ritual leader on the basis of the fixed genealogical mode or simple generational seniority. In such lineages, therefore, the distinction between ritual leadership based upon generational or descent line seniority and real leadership based upon socioeconomic standing mirrored the distinction in family organization between the generational seniority of the family head (*jiazhang*) and the administrative responsibilities of the family manager (*dangjia*).[9] Furthermore, the fact that kinship-grounded positions of seniority might be figured on the basis of generation in some lineages, in terms of the senior descent line in others, or through a combination of both in yet others shows how even locally or nationally dominant lineages partook of precisely the same kinship culture that was involved in the formation of the small intimate lineages described in this chapter. It is perhaps ironic that because they share contradictory modes of agnatic kinship, both elite and smaller lineages can more readily be placed within a common cultural framework.

Addendum: Lineage Organization in West China

Although I do not include in this book details on my May–July 1990 fieldwork in Dadingqiao, in Sichuan's Meishan County, I want to briefly note how lineage arrangements there reflected the dispersed homestead settlement pattern characteristic of the Chengdu Plain (Skinner 1964–65), such that even with local concentrations of agnates there was considerable residential intermixing of different surnames. My own observations accord with the findings of Ruf (1998: 16–17, 51–56), based on his fieldwork in another area of Meishan County. The key unifying focus in this pattern of lineage organization was the *citang*, or ancestral hall. Such a hall was an independent structure, quite apart from the dispersed residential compounds. Typically such a compound, in addition to residential quarters and facilities, had a *tangwu*, or central hall with tablets inscribed with the names of recent ancestors. Compounds were home to a single family or multiple families. If the latter, the families would share a recent common ancestor and derive through family division from the family earlier settled there. In such a compound the *tangwu* was the site of domestic (family-based) ancestor worship and should be distinguished from the *citang*, which brought together patrilineal kin from families living in many different compounds and was structurally separate from all of them.

On the basis of associational kinship the *citang* united agnates as defined by common descent from the focal ancestor. Rather than being formed through contiguous territorial communities, lineage identity was articulated with reference to *citang* affiliation, such that people would say how such-and-such a surname belongs to a particular *citang*, or even how a particular person was from a certain *citang*. A *citang* was in the vicinity of much of its membership, but often a significant proportion lived farther away and sent family representatives to the *citang*, where they joined the others in major annual occasions of ancestor worship. So the full membership of a *citang* was defined as a congregation rather than as a local lineage community. There were hierarchies of *citang* sharing a genealogical frame and reflecting patterns of asymmetrical segmentation paralleling circumstances in southeastern China, as introduced by Freedman (1958), with the important difference that at every level the focus of membership was not the local community, or several such linked communities, but the *citang* congregation. At higher levels of segmentation *citang* tended to be found in rural market towns or, for some of the major *citang*, in the Meishan county seat.

The strong associational kinship orientation of *citang* was shown by their being connected in each instance to a Qingming association along lines quite reminiscent of north China (see chapter 6), whereby each member family was considered an equal shareholder. The wealthier Qingming associations owned land, income from which helped subsidize *citang* and Qingming association banquets and ritual activities. Smaller Qingming associations might lack corporate resources and in the absence of a *citang* be organized by agnates concentrated at a particular locale, yet affiliated with a *citang* at some distance removed. In effect, this was asymmetrical segmentation on the basis of Qingming association membership, which under traditional circumstances might eventually lead to the construction of a *citang* locally more convenient and genealogically more closely focused. "*Qingming hui*" was the term for both Qingming association and the Qingming feast that such an association would arrange for its membership together with ancestor worship. In addition to Qingming, the membership met for ancestor worship several more times during the year.

Although leadership arrangements varied from one *citang*-based Qingming association to another, importantly conditioned by size and by both private and corporate wealth, I found no evidence that leadership or even ritual roles and duties were assigned on the basis of the fixed genealogical mode. The latter received only peripheral expression in cases where segmentation was actually symmetrical, that is, where each of several *citang* took as its founding ancestor one of several brothers. The eldest brother defined the "senior" *citang*, where on occasions of banqueting and ancestor worship representatives from the "junior" *citang* would first come to pay their respects, with the "senior" representatives reciprocating only later. Otherwise, as far as I was able to determine, associational kinship was dominant.

Historical Anthropology

The Minong Community During Qing

CHAPTER EIGHT

Commodity Creation in Late Imperial China

China's late imperial period has been characterized by William Rowe as one of "intensified commercialization, monetization, and urbanization" (Rowe 1992: 1, n1). Commodification should be added as being of growing importance during this time, because while "commercialization" refers to the extent that the economy has gone beyond family self-sufficiency in the production and distribution of food and other necessary or desired goods, "commodification" relates more to economic culture itself. In the anthropological literature concern with what is termed commodification is expressed largely with reference to the introduction or expansion of the use of money, or to the movement from exchange to marketing arrangements in the circulation of valued goods or the employment of labor, with the stated or unstated assumption that such developments have an alienating, disruptive, or exploitative impact on labor and production arrangements.[1] Ironically, this view of commodification actually privileges the West, confirms its continuing global dominance, and represents non-Western cultures as hapless victims whose own—implicitly weaker—economies and cultures cannot but be totally reconfigured by the impact of such outside forces. This perspective denies the societies and cultures impacted any independent agency except resistance and response to the crushing economic, social, political, and ideological forces exerted upon them by the all-powerful West, forces variously characterized as capitalism, the "virus," colonialism, modernization, or various combinations thereof. This view, to mix different traditions of jargon, takes the underdog's independent agency to be a dependent variable. Such a Western-oriented view of commodification may to varying degrees be applicable in certain regional settings, but it nevertheless is badly in need of the comparative perspectives that could be provided by China and other East Asian societies; such views would incorporate, among other things, local, historically specific sources of modernity, especially as regards economic development. But for my present purposes I want only to take the small step of broadening the idea of commodification to include the cultural invention of things that can be bought and sold, such as rights to land or shares in corporations, and I want to show how during China's late imperial period such invention went on at a high pitch.

In this chapter I use data pertaining to what is now Meinong Township, an administrative subdivision of Gaoxiong [Kaohsiung] County, in southern Taiwan. I am concerned with Meinong when, like the rest of Taiwan, it was still part of the old Chinese empire under the Manchu Qing dynasty, the last of China's imperial lines. The Qing proclaimed their rule over mainland China in 1644 and the dynasty ended in 1912, but they controlled Taiwan from 1683 until ousted by Japan in 1895. In Meinong, settlement by Hakka-speaking Han Chinese did not begin until 1736. During Qing the region was known as Minong—the Japanese changed the name to Meinong in 1920—and since my concern here is with the pre-Japanese period it seems appropriate to use the older term. With a population (in 1895) of about ten thousand, Minong comprised—spatially and demographically—the larger part of a multivillage Hakka-speaking Han Chinese community; this local community itself was the northernmost "unit" of the Liudui or "Six Units" Confederation uniting the Hakka of southern Taiwan into a militia arrangement that also provided the framework for community organization. Data for this chapter (and for chapter 9) are drawn from documentary and field data gathered for a larger project whose goal is to describe and analyze from various perspectives Minong's economy, society, and culture as it was prior to the Japanese occupation, a project seeking to present a historical anthropology of Minong as a case study in late Qing community organization.[2] When Minong came under Japanese control its almost entirely Hakka-speaking population was composed of either the descendants of Han Chinese who had emigrated from the China mainland or, in a very few cases, immigrants themselves. In any event, economic culture in Minong was representative of that generally characteristic of the Han Chinese during late imperial times. In that culture commodification loomed large indeed, such that the creation of marketable commodities vastly outstripped the creation or definition of the products or other physical things, such as land, that this commodification involved. Land and the commodities associated with it will be my focus here, both because land was an obviously key resource in a primarily agrarian setting, and because it is to land that the data at my disposal concerning late imperial period commodification or, indeed, hypercommodification, primarily relate. One major data source is the cadastral survey carried out by the Japanese in 1902. Having overcome armed resistance and obtained Minong's surrender in November 1895, the Japanese had been in control of the area for a little more than six years. Yet the cadastral data do accurately depict the land-linked commodification of pre-Japanese times, for the purpose of the survey was precisely to set the stage for the imposition of Japanese land taxes and new ownership regulations. In other words, the survey was carried out so that the Japanese could start making changes in land relationships, which, subsequent to the survey, they indeed did.

Both the survey and other documents dating from the pre-Japanese Qing period, such as contracts and account books, that I was able to copy show that land-linked commodities well known in late imperial China were represented in Minong.[3] With respect to a particular plot of land, the three most important commodities were "redeemable sale" or *dian* rights, "small rent" or *xiaozu* rights, and "large rent" or *dazu* rights, with the latter two known under a variety of names in different areas of China, such as "surface" rights and "subsoil" rights. Redeemable sale involved payment giving the purchaser rights to land use until such time that the money was returned, with use rights then likewise returned. A "small rent" owner was obligated to make usually annual or biannual payments to the "large rent" holder, with the latter generally responsible for the land tax. With respect to all of these rights and, indeed, most commodities of any sort, families—as represented by their almost invariably male family heads—and not individuals were the units of ownership. Share-holding corporations could also own such rights, but under such circumstances the shares themselves would be family owned or, in some cases, owned by other corporations, as shall be shown. Later in this chapter we will also come across a few cases in which women owned commodities and property as individuals,[4] and so-called public entities such as village temples might own property on a non-share-holding basis, but it is clear enough that the vast majority of assets were family-owned. In terms of land rights, the simplest situation would be the case of a family having full ownership rights to a plot that they cultivated themselves, with no differentiation of "small rent" and "large rent" rights and without pledge of land through redeemable sale. At the other extreme, a plot of land might have a tenant as well as different owners of small rent, large rent, and redeemable sale rights, with the result that rights of one kind or another to this land would be distributed among four parties. In fact, both extremes and a variety of intermediate arrangements were all well represented in Minong, precisely because each kind of right was a marketable commodity.

These rights, which could be held with respect to farmland or land used for other purposes (such as house sites), said nothing regarding who actually worked the land or lived in the house: tenancy was common, with rent received by holders of redeemable sale rights or small rent rights, as the case might be. Unfortunately, tenancy information was not entered into the survey forms, although from the surveys it can be inferred that tenants constituted a considerable proportion of Minong's population. The 1902 cadastral survey classified all land into the nine categories of wet rice, dry field, building site, grave site, temple site, miscellaneous, mountain, pond, and undeveloped or wasteland. In economic terms the most important was wet rice land, followed by dry field. The 3,128 plots of wet rice land, having a total area of 1,733 *jia* (a Taiwan land unit equivalent to .97 hectares), amount to 43 percent of all 7,243 plots and 39 percent of Minong's total area of 4,379 *jia*. Dry field, with 2,345 plots covering 1,983 *jia*, amounted to 32 percent of all plots and 45 percent of all land. The 1,545 plots listed as building sites had a total area of 189 *jia*, or less than 0.5 percent of all land, but they accounted for 21 percent of all plots, as might be expected of residential land in an area where farming was dominant in the economy. Land in the other categories amounted to a little more than 10 percent of all land and need not be dealt with here.

People or other entities (such as associations or the state itself) were listed in the survey by name and with respect to the right they controlled: proprietor (*yezhu*), large rent owner (*dazu*), and owner of redeemable or *dian* rights (*dianzhu*). If a particular plot had a large rent owner, then the proprietor would be the small rent owner as far as local property relations were concerned. For each of these three rights yet other persons might be listed as managers;[5] this was always the case if an association rather than a person were listed as owner of a particular right. In all, the cadastral survey gives the names of 2,600 people with land rights of one sort or another in Minong, among whom Minong residents accounted for 2,387 people. These figures were obtained by manipulating the Japanese cadastral survey to eliminate first all associations and other entities that were not people and then multiple listing of the same individual as among those recorded as landowners, as having *dian* or redeemable purchase rights, as holders of larger rent rights, or as "managers" with respect to any of these rights. These were those having registered rights to land in Minong, although, as noted, in almost all cases they in fact were family heads, with the family as a corporation the unit of ownership.

Unsurprising but nevertheless notable is the near-total absence of women from the data sets; only 18 of 2,600 persons recorded are women, and four of these women were not resident in Minong. Fourteen of the 18 women are listed as managers of land owned by men outright or through redeemable purchase; one of these women is also listed as owner of a plot, while the remaining three women are listed as owners. A male manager is registered for the land listed under the name of one of these latter women. Some from among the other two women owners, or those listed as managers, were presumably widows whose sons, if any, were too young to be taken as family heads. But since available data from the household registers show that one or two of these women were owners whose husbands were alive at the time of the cadastral survey, there is also suggested the possibility that some land or rights thereto were held by women as their personal property, although the holdings so indicated were so few as also to suggest that more may have been registered in the names of their husbands. But the dominance of men was in any event overwhelming, thus confirming the male-headed corporate family as the key actor in the context of late imperial commodification.

Of the 2,387 owners of rights, 629, or 26 percent, were listed as having rights to building sites only, with such rights usually based upon their established residence as agnates in local compounds. Even though it is possible that some among these people owned or had rights to land outside the area covered by the available cadastral data, I take them largely to represent a landless population within which tenants were dominant. Some may have been short- or long-term field workers or engaged in one form of nonagricultural work or another. Others who were farmers were both shareholder members of and tenants in Minong's many corporate associations, given that these owned or held through redeemable sale about one-third of all Minong wet rice land. However, others among the landless were clearly tenants on holdings of the larger private Minong landlords, it being understood that a tenant might have more than one landlord and might also in some cases own land. Nevertheless, the 629 persons shown to own only building sites clearly indicate the presence of a rather large proportion of landless residents, fitting the circumstances of the concentration of land ownership in the hands of the associations and a minority of private family landowners. For example, the four largest private (that is, family) landowners owned or had purchased redeemable rights to 113 *jia* of wet rice and 99 *jia* of dry field, accounting for more than 15 percent of all wet rice land and about 5 percent of dry field; for the top fifty private landowners, or a little more than 2 percent of all persons represented, such control was over 346 *jia* of wet rice land, or more than 47 percent, and 421 *jia* of dry field, or about 21 percent. Thus while there was no extreme concentration of landlordism in the hands of one or two families, land rights were indeed concentrated at the higher reaches of the index as far as private family ownership was concerned; this, when combined with association ownership, accounted for most that was available.

However, these various rights hardly exhaust the inventory of land-related commodities available in Qing dynasty Minong. As already noted, there were also share-holding corporations. Most of these were dedicated either to an ancestor—in some cases genealogically close, and in others quite remote—of a group of agnates or to a particular deity or cultural hero, such as the goddess Mazu or even a figure such as Confucius. On the basis of Qing-period account books and the Japanese cadastral records I estimate at this stage of research that at a minimum there were more than 110 ancestral corporations and more than 70 other share-holding corporations in Minong. Assuming an average of 20 shares per corporation, 180 corporations would provide a total of 3,600 shares— again a minimum estimate—this with respect to a population of about ten thousand, and, obviously, a much smaller number of the family units in which most share ownership was vested.[6] Share ownership was widely distributed among local families, with many, especially the wealthier ones, having shares in several corporations. Likewise, I was told that a strategy of poorer farmers who could not afford to purchase land was to purchase shares giving them rights of cultivation as tenants. Membership in a corporation gave privileged access to corporate assets, as in the form of loans or first rights to rent corporate land, while some corporations also provided shareholders with periodic or annual dividends. Shares were commodities: the ancestral corporations restricted sales to other agnates, but owners could sell shares of other corporations to anyone in the community, or to a different corporation. Because the survey separately recorded land data from the six administrative villages into which the Japanese divided Minong, and because different corporations in different villages might have the same name (such as the very common earth god corporations), the survey data do not enable an accurate count. Nevertheless, the religious or other charter of a corporation usually can be identified from its name and on the basis of other information at my disposal.[7]

The survey does tell us about the relative representation of corporations with respect to the ownership of the various rights discussed so far. As already noted, wet rice and dry field taken together account for almost all farmland, with rights to the far more productive wet rice obviously being far more expensive. To simplify the discussion, I do not distinguish the various kinds of corporations noted above but place them all in one category: corporations owned "small rent" rights or full rights to 972 plots of wet rice or 25 percent of the total, amounting to 510 *jia*, or 29 percent, of all wet rice land; furthermore they owned redeemable sale rights to another 98 plots of wet rice having an area of 39 *jia*, thus giving them access to rental income from about 32 percent of all Minong wet rice land. At the same time, these corporations were making payments to the owners of "large rent" rights held with respect to 321 plots of their wet rice land, amounting to 174 *jia*, or 34 percent, of the total. The corporations owned "small rent" rights or full rights to only 184 out of 2,345 dry field plots, amounting to 152 *jia*, or 8 percent, of the total area of 1983 *jia*; they owned redeemable sale rights to another 41 plots totaling 44 *jia*, or a mere 2 percent, of all dry field land. That the corporations had rental income from only about 10 percent of dry field as opposed to almost one-third of all wet rice land was similar to the proportional distribution of ownership by land type among richer private landlords, as noted above, and reflects an investment strategy geared toward assuring returns that were greater and also steady rather than dependent on fluctuating rainfall.

It is of some interest that the cadastral records show each of two earth god associations as having purchased redeemable sale rights to land owned by two different ancestral associations, one purchase involving three plots, and the other one. With respect to the three plots of wet rice land owned by one of these associations, "large rent" rights were held by yet another party such that rights of one sort or another were held by two corporations, the owner of "large rent" rights and by whoever might actually be doing the farming. In a 1915 entry in the account book of yet another ancestral association, this corporation's assets—obtained well before the Japanese occupation—are recorded as including, in addition to land, shares in two Qingming or grave associations, these themselves being a variety of ancestral association; two shares in the Guansheng or God of the Military Association; one share in the Old Earth God Association; one share in the Quandou Village Lantern Association; one share in the Old Association of the God of Literature or civil bureaucracy; one share in the Lantern Festival Association; one share in the Association for Cemeteries for the Unworshiped Dead; one share in the Yongxing Bridge Association; one share in the Confucius Association; and one share in a local burial society. Although these different cases of corporations owning each other's shares hardly loom as dominant in the overall distribution of share ownership, they do illustrate how the corporation was a well-defined actor with respect to property and other commodity transactions. Indeed, they were so recognized by the Qing imperial state, as during the island-wide cadastral survey begun in 1885 (ten years before the Japanese conquest) by the then–Chinese governor Liu Mingquan and, later, as they were by the Japanese in their own cadastral survey.[8]

An association's shareholders generally met once a year, usually at the home of one shareholder who served as corporation manager, often under an arrangement whereby management was assigned to shareholders on a rotating basis. With all expenses paid for by corporation funds, key events at such meetings included worship of the corporation's charter deity or ancestor, a banquet, a report by the manager on corporation finances during the previous year, and entry of this report into the corporation's account book, of which two copies were usually kept, with two shareholders other than the manager making identical entries in each.[9] An account book was a rather thick volume with printed lines on each page, something like a notebook, and was commonly purchased and used by all sorts of enterprises and businesses. In such a book there usually was first written an introductory statement expressing the corporation's ideals and religious-ritual raison d'être, often followed by the texts to be recited as part of the ritual proceedings that took place during the annual shareholders meeting. The next few pages of the account book have the names of all founding shareholders; transfers of share ownership are indicated under the name of the particular share involved. In some account books there is also an itemization of land and ritual objects (such as tablets) possessed by the association, with landholdings sometimes described according to the historical sequence of purchases, including each plot's date of acquisition; the land transfer contracts for each plot are sometimes included (see chapter 9). The rest of the book is devoted to the annual entries, each taking up two or three pages; by the time a new account book had to be used the old one might contain a record of several decades of corporation finances. When a new account book was required, the introductory and religious texts and the list of original shareholders was copied in, so that in every account book a statement of the lofty religious and social ideals held to represent corporate aspirations prefaced the subsequent businesslike entries concerning membership changes and finances. This combination of texts mirrored the combination of ritual and business that characterized the annual meeting of the corporation. The distribution of corporate dividends may be illustrated by the following entry for December 17, 1886, from the account book of the Ritual Estate of the God of the Five Manifestations (Wuxian Sidian):[10]

> Guangxu reign period, twelfth year, eleventh month, twenty-second day. Accounting session of the Ritual Estate of the God of the Five Manifestations.
> Received: winter rent-grain from Zeng Xiuna, 55.000 piculs
> Paid out: large rent on our fields, 13.640 piculs
> Watchmen's grain on our fields, 1.364 piculs
> Total paid out: grain in the amount of 15.004 piculs
> After payments, sum remaining 40.000 piculs [exact amount should be 39.996]
> Paid out: for 14 [association] shares, [dividends] each at 2.5 piculs [for a total of 35 piculs]
> Balance: 5 piculs, equal to 3.6 dollars
> Today's banquet: 3.00 dollars
> Writing materials 0.20 [dollars]
> After disbursements left with 0.40 [dollars]
> Made into 14 shares equally divided for 0.029 dollars per share [these have a total value of exactly 0.406 dollars][11]

Throughout the Qing period new corporations were being formed, while those already present might be purchasing additional land. It is also probably the case that some corporations were also dissolved; although I have no direct evidence for this from Minong, Qing-period corporation dissolution contracts signed by all shareholders are known from other parts of Taiwan (see Appendix A). A corporation was formed when several people agreed to contribute money for the purchase of shares having a specified value, with the accumulated sum then used to acquire land. Obviously, such corporations could not be formed if land rights were not available as a freely marketable commodity, and if there were no place in local economic culture for the creation of the shares that became yet other commodities. For an ordinary farmer (that is, for him in his capacity as family head), among the possible advantages of association membership through purchase of shares was availability of loans from the association, or access to additional land for a sum far less than that required for purchase of "small rent" or full land rights. In some cases, I was told, a farmer too poor to purchase land might opt to acquire association shares as an affordable alternative. He would have to pay rent, to be sure, but he, like other shareholders, might also receive dividends. Also of no little significance was the opportunity provided by the annual meetings for rather intimate social interaction with shareholders who were members of the local elite, including degree-holders and the heads of wealthy families. For the latter, share holding was a relatively inexpensive form of investment; their families tended to own far more shares in more corporations than did ordinary people, such that share holding among the wealthy can be seen as but one dimension of their accumulation of diversified investment portfolios. Shares could be sold outright or transferred to another party through redeemable sale. That this transaction occurred frequently can be seen from the many transfers noted in the association account books, although these data await investigation. There is other evidence for the sale of shares, and elsewhere (Cohen 1993: 19, 22–23) I have shown through an analysis of two family division contracts how during the Qing dynasty a Minong man who was one of three brothers and a nephew involved in an 1863 family division received 4 out of the 21 shares in ten or eleven religious and ancestral corporations that the family then owned, while upon the division of his own family in 1898, the 13.5 shares that were then distributed among three brothers reflected the purchase of at least 9.5 new shares and the sale of at least two of the original four during the intervening twenty-five-year period. Of course, shares bought and then sold after 1863 but before 1898 would not be noted in either contract. As with the sale of land rights and other valuable commodities, share ownership transfers were on the basis of written contracts; although I have found none from Minong they were indeed written there, and examples of such contracts from other parts of Taiwan have survived (see Appendix B).

The overwhelming bulk of land-linked commodities were owned within the Minong community; with certain important exceptions to be noted below, the few outside parties involved were mainly from elsewhere in the larger south Taiwan Hakka settlement zone that was organized in the form of the Six Units (Liudui) militia confederation and in many ways constituted a higher-level territorial community, with Minong forming its northernmost extension and comprising most of the confederation's Right Unit (Youdui) (Cohen 1993; Pasternak 1972, 1983). That the creation and marketing of such land-related commodities, and many others, occurred almost entirely within the Minong community context is attested to, for example, by the fact that among the many Minong Qing-period contracts I have been able to copy or refer to only a small minority are so-called "red" contracts (hongqi)—those registered with the county government office (yamen).[12] Such localization hardly reflects a situation in which commodification is disruptive of local solidarities or is somehow subversive with respect to local society assumed to comprise a "moral economy."[13] There were indeed pronounced differences in wealth in Minong, and the area had its share of often violent internal conflict, while at the same time conflicts between the Minong Hakka and neighboring Hokkien-speaking Han Chinese or non-Han native communities were frequent and severe, but none of this is relevant to commodification as such, especially if commodification is assumed to be a socially and morally disruptive force in its own right. Such an assumption would be dead wrong in the context of late imperial Chinese economic culture, for precisely the opposite was true: in the marked absence of significant intervention by the state or by other outside forces with respect to the enforcement of most contractually defined economic links, it was community solidarity and the highly strategic significance of social ties within the Minong community that provided the environment within which commodification could flourish. Minong, like elsewhere in late imperial China, was a community in which a high degree of commodification was powerfully supported by an equally high propensity to resort to written contracts for transactions involving things of value, as I have noted. These overwhelmingly "white" contracts (baiqi),[14] or contracts not registered with the local county magistrate's office, were supported precisely by social relationships, using the time-honored Chinese device of involving a third-party middleman and other cosignatories, such that violation of a contract's stipulations would place into jeopardy a very large network of social ties of the kind vital to survival. This is not to say that the state was irrelevant. Certainly, aggrieved parties could sue in the magistrate's court and bring forward both red and white contracts as evidence. Although negative evidence is hardly conclusive, I have no record of anyone in Minong going to court during Qing, but in any event such actions were quite rare in relation to the number of contracts entered into in any region, indicating that recourse to the state in the protection of contractual agreements was powerfully subordinate to reliance on social ties.[15]

Kinship ties were among the most critical, but their importance did not take the form of a domination of relationships such that within the marketing domain the family's managerial autonomy—as represented by the family head—was compromised. In this context family members need to be clearly distinguished from kin outside the family. In Minong it was generally but not invariably the woman who moved from her natal family to her husband's, leading, of course, to the creation of kin ties between the two families if there had been none previously.[16] Likewise, upon family division married brothers underwent a massive change of status from being siblings within a unified family to being kin, each heading his own family. Kin beyond the family were reduced to ordinary actors in the commodity market, including that for human labor, at the same time that they were key participants in the family's long-term ritual, cooperative, and gift-exchange relationships, that is, participants in the "ceremonial sphere of the economy" (see chapter 1). Rather than there being conflict between the world of commodified relationships on the one hand, and that of enduring social ties on the other, there was mutual support precisely on the basis of clear differentiation. For example, in Minong, as in much of China, there was a distinction made between "labor exchange" and "help" relationships. The first, a simple contractual undertaking, could involve kin, neighbors, or anyone else deemed reliable, and it was a common procedure, especially during the busiest farm periods, such as planting or harvest. This labor swapping was supposed to involve equal contributions by all parties. If one party were to contribute less family labor than the others, they would have to hire workers to supply labor for the families to whom labor was due. Help relationships were quite different, even though they might involve the very same kin, among others: cooperation in matters such as house construction or repair and other tasks that could be performed according to a flexible schedule during the agricultural slack season was not precisely measured, with the result that help relationships were cooperative ties sustained over many years. Social ties, as among kin, neighbors, or local community members, framed feasting and gift exchange, as in the banquets provided to those attending and bringing cash gifts to weddings, funerals, and other family-sponsored events. Social ties might be strained or severed if a family expected on the basis of social links to be invited (always in the name of the family head) and was not, or, if invited, it did not attend (in the person of the family head or his representative). The weakening or destruction of social ties would have obvious negative consequences for a family's ability to negotiate the world of contracts and commodity transactions.

The contracts that were major instruments in both the creation and the transfer of commodities thus confronted kinship and other long-term supportive social relations in two major ways. In the first, close kin and sometimes other persons of local prominence were asked to serve as signatories to the contract. The middleman's participation as a signatory was crucial in any contract involving a transaction between two parties, for he would have preexisting social ties of one sort or another with each and serve as guarantor; he often was instrumental in putting a deal such as a land transfer together, and for this would be awarded a commission. In most cases another signatory was the amanuensis or scribe, who might be paid for his services but frequently enough was also kin to one of the contracting parties. In most contracts one or more witnesses also signed on, and these people were indeed tightly linked socially to the contract's executor, most often by kinship connections. Usually, only the seller, and not the recipient of the commodity, would be a signatory to contracts involving sales of one kind or another, such as the sale or redeemable sale of land, housing, or other items, or transactions in people, such as the adoption or sale of children (usually young daughters, but in some cases sons). The party receiving the commodity would also get the contract, which served as evidence that the property belonged to the family whose head had negotiated the purchase. The involvement of kin as signatories represented a positive use of kinship sentiments in that they could be recruited on the basis of generalized kinship obligations.

But, turning to the second major confrontation between contract and kinship, it was precisely these sentiments of kinship that had to be controlled in the negative sense of insulating commodity transactions from their potentially disturbing consequences. In part this was also achieved by having kin sign as witnesses. Since, as noted, the party selling or otherwise transferring the commodity was the contract's key signatory, it would be that party's kin who would acknowledge the transfer by signing on. In other words, they would indicate their acceptance of the removal of something of value from the domain over which they had claims of one sort or another based upon kinship, such as the inheritance rights of close agnates to property in the absence of male successors in the family. But the kinship circle from within which claims might be generated could hardly be totally covered by the recruitment of agnates and affines as signatories; "marked" kin, identified as noted above as through labor swapping or by reciprocal invitations to wedding and funeral banquets, could comprise a large group indeed, one that could scarcely be mobilized for the signing of every contract. And there was no way to prevent yet others from asserting kinship or some other kind of social connection so as to make a claim. While only the closest agnates would have inheritance rights to property where the family owning it had died out in the absence of male offspring, larger circles of kin might join in regretting the sale of a family's land or other assets to which they might otherwise have indirect access, as through the adoption of agnates or affines into that family. Therefore it is common to encounter in contracts standardized statements to the effect that agnatic kin especially are to keep away and mind their own business, and that the transaction is only between the two parties and no one else.

Examples of such statements can be seen in the following contract for the sale of a plot of land in Niupu, a small village in the larger Minong community:

The executor of this contract for the irrevocable sale of a parcel of land, Chen Jiayong of Niupu Village, obtained through succession from his paternal grandfather a plot of riverbank land that his grandfather had developed. Using local place names, the property is above [that is, to the east of] Niupu Village, on the southern edge of the river. Its boundaries extend eastward to the irrigation canal, westward to the plot belonging to Qiu Tinghai, southward to the bank of the river, and northward to the edge of the seller's field. The boundaries in all four directions have been inspected and clearly demarcated in the presence of the middleman. Now, because of family financial difficulties, the contractor desires to sell this land. After having first thoroughly inquired among his close kin of the same patrilineal branch, and with none able to make the purchase, he has availed himself of the introduction of a middleman, through which Liu Baozhi of Minong Lower Village has come forward to purchase this property. On this day, in the presence of the middleman, the three parties [buyer, seller, and middleman] have agreed on the basis of market value to the plot's sale at the price of nine large dollars.[17] In the presence of the middleman contract and cash are exchanged on the same day in full without any shortchanging and without such fraudulent practices as use of this property to set off debts or the multiple pledging of property to different parties. This plot of land was handed down to the seller by his own paternal grandfather, who developed it and established it as property. It has no connections with any of his uncles [generationally senior agnates] of other patrilineal descent branches. After sale the land is to be given over immediately and in person [by the previous owner] to the buyer, for him to manage and cultivate as his property. The seller's close agnatic kin of the same branch are not to dare dispute the sale, obstruct it, or make any trouble. As soon as the sale is done, the seller is to see to it that any complications are ended forever. Hereafter, the seller shall not dare to speak of redeeming the property or requesting gift-money [from the buyer]. This contract is entered into voluntarily by both parties, without any constraints. Because we fear that an oral agreement will be unreliable, we have drawn up this contract for the irrevocable sale of a parcel of land, and it is transferred [to the buyer] as certification.

On this day it is clearly noted that in the presence of the middleman there was received payment of nine dollars as per this contract. Noted.

Mediator/middleman: Lin Chuanshan
Witness and amanuensis: Matrilateral cousin, Song Qinchuan
Tongzhi reign period, fifth year, third month, sixth day [April 20, 1866]
Executor of contract for the irrevocable sale of a parcel of land: Chen Jiayong.

This is a relatively simple contractual transaction involving the transfer of an inexpensive plot of land. Nevertheless, it is of interest because it establishes that the parcel of land is a commodity unto itself in that there are no attached commodified rights in the form of "large rent," "small rent," pledges, or the like. As an "easy" contract it has as signatories only the buyer, the middleman, and one witness, who also is the necessary scribe. It concerns land created as property by the seller's grandfather, who developed it in the context of the ongoing settlement of the Minong region, with property creation, and therefore commodity creation, being a consequence of such development, in the absence of prior claims by other parties (at least as far as the Han Chinese were concerned). The contract is for an "unconditional sale" in that the seller waives all future claims. The statement that the seller "thoroughly inquired among his close agnatic kin of the same branch" before proceeding to arrange sale to a nonrelative is a standard boilerplate phrase commonly encountered in contracts (see chapter 9). Among such close agnates would be those with secondary inheritance rights to this property, effective only in the event that the owning family were unable to produce its own male successors through birth or adoption, or by skipping a generation and producing such a successor through uxorilocal marriage. Nevertheless, the first rights of refusal held by close agnates with respect to purchases and other transactions should not be taken as evidence that kinship sentiments and obligations formed a moral encumbrance interfering with the play of market forces in the circulation of commodities. On the contrary, the rights of refusal held by close agnates simply gave them the opportunity to make the purchase, but at no advantage with respect to price or other conditions. Thus these "first rights" represented precisely the adjustment of kinship ties to the leveled playing field of a commodified environment. That the phrase is so frequently encountered suggests that these agnates far more often than not were unable or unwilling to purchase, a circumstance hardly surprising given that within any region the effective market encompassed a population far greater than the number of people eligible to exercise first rights on the basis of close kinship ties. The first rights of agnates should not be confused with the control over land sales and other matters by strong and rich lineages, themselves owning much land, as discussed in chapter 4.

The following contract is introduced to show how property indeed obtained through secondary inheritance was nevertheless sold as a commodity, with the seller confronting and denying all potential claims of his close agnates:

The executor of this contract for the absolute sale of a house and house site is Liu Awen. In the past, paternal grandfather's brother Qingjie had handed down a three-room tiled house with earth foundation. Using local place names it is situated in Zhongyun Village, to the south facing north; to the east this plot extends to the base of the common wall shared with the house of Liu Denger; to the west it extends to the base of the common wall shared with my own central-room house [that is, the house with common room and ancestral hall, often forming the base of a larger compound]; to the south it extends to the bamboo fence at the edge of the well; to the north it extends to the eaves of Liu Denger's old house. The boundaries in all four directions have been inspected and clearly demarcated in the presence of the middleman. Now because of financial difficulties, and after having thoroughly inquired among my paternal uncles, every one of whom is unable to undertake purchase, I have relied on a middleman for an introduction to [honorific] elder brother Zhong Xigou, who has come forward to buy. On the same day through the middleman the three parties have agreed to a market price of 38 silver dollars exactly, and on that day money and contract have been straightforwardly exchanged, with no cheating or shortchanging during the proceedings. From the time of purchase this property is transferred to the buyer for him to control as his residence; the paternal uncles, paternal nephews, and brothers of the seller are not to raise objections or cause disturbances. This house site is a property originally bequeathed by [my father's] junior paternal uncle [father's father's younger brother] Qingjie and has no connection with my brothers or paternal uncles and nephews; the seller bears all responsibility. This contract is entered into voluntarily by both parties, without any constraints. Fearing that verbal agreement leaves no evidence, I have executed one copy of this contract for the absolute sale of the house and house site, which is given over [to the buyer] as certification.

On this day it is clearly noted that received in accordance with the specifications of this contract is the sum of 38 dollars. So noted.

It is also clearly noted that the flat surface in front of the main gate is an area of traffic and cannot be obstructed. So noted.

Also clearly noted is that the well water is drunk in common by the houses on both sides of the well. Clearly noted.

Also clearly noted is that after the sale of this house it cannot ever be expanded. So noted.

Middleman: Chen Lianfa
Witnesses: paternal uncle Liu Huilin
    older brother [father's brother's son] Liu Aming
[Contract written with] my own pen
Witness: Liu Asheng
Tongzhi, tenth year, sixth month, [blank] day [between July 18 and August 15, 1871]; Executor of contract for the absolute sale of a house and house site, Liu Awen.

Qingjie, the "paternal grandfather's brother," died without offspring, bringing to an end his agnatic line. As to the executor himself, Liu Awen, he has as witnesses Liu Hiulin, who is Liu Awen's father's youngest brother, and Liu Aming, the oldest son of yet another father's brother, already deceased at that time. Because the three other brothers of Liu Awen's father all died without offspring, Liu Awen and these two witnesses account for all surviving descent lines focusing on Awen's paternal grandfather. In other words, with these two witnesses signing on, agreement for the sale has been obtained from those close agnates who might have shared secondary rights of succession with respect to both Liu Qingjie and Liu Awen. Once again, although initially involved in a dense network of agnatic ties, the house and its building site are transformed by contract into a commodity, albeit one whose use is conditioned by additional contractual clauses. Under more complicated circumstances, the number of witnesses will be larger, in light of the fact noted above, that social relationships are the framework for the protection of contractual integrity. Such circumstances can be seen in the following contract for the five-year pledge of land in return for a redeemable cash payment:

Li Changhuaer, the executor of this contract of pledge, now owns as his portion through family division land obtained from his late paternal grandfather consisting of two wet rice plots, one the old site [purchased earlier] and one the newer site. Their position in terms of local place names is at the entrance to the Tanshui Stream outside of Jianshanliao Village. Their boundaries extend eastward to the wet rice plot of the Wen family ancestral estate, westward to Xingxiu's wet rice plot, southward to the wet rice plots of Li Faner and the Lin family, and northward to the foot of the mountain. These four boundaries have been clearly identified through personal investigation by the three parties, including the middleman. The land carries with it a native large rent of **four piculs of unhusked grain** [bold text overstamped with seal reading SEAL OF WULUO NATIVE SETTLEMENT LARGE RENT OWNER PAN WENYA]. At present, because of financial difficulties, I am willing to pledge through redeemable sale the fields to others. I first thoroughly inquired among my close agnatic kin of the same branch, and they all were unable to take the land in pledge. Through the introduction of a middleman, Lin Changshu has come forward to contract for these fields in pledge. In the presence of the middleman, the three parties have agreed on the basis of market value to pledge the land in return for two hundred dollars. Contract and cash are straightforwardly exchanged on the same day, without things like shortchanging and without such fraudulent practices as the multiple pledging of property. These fields truly are mine, obtained as property by succession to my paternal grandfather's land through [family] division. In the event that there is lack of clarity concerning previous ownership of this land, or arrears in large rent payments, none of these matters have anything to do with the party taking on the land as pledge. The party pledging out the land bears full responsibility for such things. Starting from the day the land is pledged out, the fields are to be turned over to the party contracting this land on pledge, for him to manage and collect rent as his own enterprise. The period of pledge starts from the winter of the *guisi* cyclical year [1833] and extends to the winter of the *wuxu* cyclical year [1838]. After five years, upon return of the purchase price, the land can be redeemed. This transaction is undertaken completely voluntarily by the two parties, without any compulsion. Today, because we desire evidence, we have written out this contract for the pledge of land, and it is transferred [to the party obtaining the land] as certification.

On this day it is clearly noted that there was received payment of two hundred foreign dollars [*foyin*] as per this contract of pledge; this sum was indeed received.

It is also clearly noted that these fields are irrigated by spring water from the Shuidi Spring; the flow of water must be from higher to lower levels.

It is also clearly noted that the middleman's signature fee of four dollars [his commission] will be repaid in full on the day that the fields are redeemed [the party pledging the land out now pays; he is reimbursed by the party taking the land when it is redeemed]

Middleman: Wen Fengchang
Witnesses: affine, Gu Guangchun
    father's elder brother's wife, Li née Liu
    father's elder brother, Yanlang
    father's elder brother, Qilang
    elder brother with adjacent field, Xingxiu
    elder brother, Xingzhu
    younger brother, Duanbo
    with adjacent field, Lin Zaiguan
Amanuensis: older brother, Huaxing

OWNER OF LARGE RENT RIGHTS:
[SEAL] SEAL OF WULUO NATIVE SETTLEMENT LARGE RENT
OWNER PAN WENYA [same seal as above].
Daoguang reign period, thirteenth year, being the *guisi* cyclical year, tenth
month, twenty-sixth day [December 7, 1833]
Executor of contract for the pledge of wet rice land: Li Changhuaer.

As in this contract, five-year periods were common for land pledges,
that is, for redeemable sales of land. The large number of people signing
on serves to protect Li Changhuaer in several ways. Since most are brothers or father's brothers, or, in one case, the widow of his father's
brother,[18] they are in the category of close agnates of the same branch
with first rights to purchase and share a strong interest in this land. As
close agnates they also have residual inheritance rights to the land in the
event that Li Changhuaer should leave behind no male descendant
through birth or adoption. Their signing the contract indicates that they
accept this loss of land to an outside party, for they were quite aware that
the loss might be permanent if the seller were unable to come up with redemption money.[19] Finally, because these were the very agnates involved
in the family division that gave this land to Li Changhuaer, their signatures confirm their agreement that this land does now belong to him (that
is, to the family of which he is head and representative). The older
brother and the other man identified as owners of "adjacent fields" sign
on as such because their land shares with the plot being transferred the irrigation setup mentioned in the contract; they acknowledge that in this
transfer of land there is a transfer of responsibility with respect to the coordination of irrigation arrangements. The large-scale involvement of kin
serves precisely to commodify this plot of land, for the final result is a
straightforward commodity transaction between two parties.

This contract also bears the seal of the holder of "large rent" rights, in
this instance the representative of a collective owner, the native settlement
of Wuluo, but more usually, as far as Minong was concerned, private
Han Chinese owners based in nearby towns such as Tainan or Aligang
(present-day Ligang, in Pingdong County). Given that they were due
rental payments from the holders of "small rent" rights, it is not surprising that the latter actively sought their endorsement of land transfers; it
was obviously in the interest of someone selling "small rent" rights that
the "large rent" owner be informed that "large rent" payments were now
due from another party. Likewise, it was in the interest of the "large rent"
owner to keep track of those from whom payments were due. The "large

rent" rights differed from the rest of the commodities discussed so far in that while they could be purchased throughout the Qing period, their creation was conditioned by circumstances particular to the years of Taiwan's colonization by the Han Chinese, during the late seventeenth and early eighteenth centuries. As has been well described in the literature, during this early period entrepreneurs who had obtained government land-grant patents and had taken up obligations to pay land taxes in some cases developed the land themselves and then let it out to ordinary tenants who would farm it. In other cases, however, those obtaining the land grants recruited settlers to undertake the land reclamation on their own, and in consideration of their investment of capital and labor these settlers received the permanent use rights known as "small rent," on the condition that they pay a stipulated "large rent." A variant of this process, as illustrated by the above contract, involved some of the non-Han native peoples of Taiwan, who likewise made available to Han settlers such rights with respect to land that the Qing government had recognized as belonging to the native communities (Shepherd 1993: 8–9). With "small rent" and "large rent" rights established, both were marketable commodities, but their creation appears largely to have ended together with the era of colonization.

The circumstances behind the creation of "large rent" rights explain why, as far as Minong was concerned, most were owned by outside families or corporate groups, while those owned by Minong residents or corporations appear to have been purchased at one time or another from these outside parties. Another kind of property where outside ownership loomed large was associated with the development of irrigation systems. Some canals were privately developed and owned; these canals themselves were commodities in that they could be sold, and they also represented investments whose return was in the form of water use fees paid by those farmers whose fields benefited from the irrigation. Unlike the land grants of the era of early colonization by Han Chinese, the development and expansion of irrigation systems in Minong continued throughout the Qing period. From the point of view of the farmers it was the water that formed the commodity. Water was yet another element in an already highly commodified environment, and certainly one no less "natural" than any of the others, as attested to by the fact that water fee obligations, like those pertaining to "large rent," could be noted in contracts of land sale or pledge. Although they were well known in Minong, I was unable to locate any surviving examples of such contracts, so for purposes of illustration I use a contract from the Fangliao region, to the south of Minong and east of the larger Hakka zone:

Yang Jilao is the executor of this contract of irrevocable transfer through sale. I and my partners Huang Xishi and Liu Duansheng jointly purchased two [adjacent] plots of wet rice land whose location in terms of local place names is by the northern dike of Dexing Village in Fangliao. The eastern, western, southern, and northern boundaries of this parcel, as well as the large rent fees and water fees, are clearly shown in the earlier [attached] contracts. Today, because I need money for other endeavors, I wish to sell what I ought to have as my share, as based upon division into three shares. I first thoroughly inquired among my close agnatic kin of the same branch and they were unwilling to take up my offer. Through the introduction of a middleman, Liu Duansheng has come forward to purchase my share. On this day, the three parties including the middleman have agreed on the basis of market value to a price of exactly 145 dollars. On this day through the middleman the money has been received in full, and the land has been transferred forthwith to the Liu family for them to manage as one [with their earlier share]. It is guaranteed that this land was purchased at the time by Yang Jilao and his partners and that this sale does not involve such matters as lack of clarity concerning previous ownership. In the event that there is lack of clarity or other irregularities, Yang Jilao bears full responsibility and these matters will be of no concern to the party purchasing the land. This transaction is undertaken completely voluntarily by the two parties, and neither intends to renege on it. Fearing that verbal agreement leaves no evidence I have executed one copy of this contract for irrevocable transfer through sale, attached to which are two earlier contracts, for a total of three documents, which are given over [to the buyer] for him to hold as certification.

On this day there was definitely received payment of 145 dollars as per this contract, this again being confirmation of payment in full.

Present as village manager [i.e., village head] and as amanuensis: Wu Er
Middlemen/witnesses: Huang Guangxing, Huang Tiansong
Qianlong, fifty-seventh year, fifth month, [blank] day [between June 19 and July 18, 1792].
Executor of contract for irrevocable transfer through sale: Yang Jilao.[20]

In addition to showing how water fee obligations, like those pertaining to large rent payments, were recognized as being attached obligations in the context of the sale of small rent rights, this contract also illustrates the connection between full formalization of a contract on the one hand, and full commodification on the other. Yang Jilao is selling his one-third share to one of the other two original partners, yet this presumably "in house" deal is given full contractual treatment, so to speak, including insertion of the standard clause concerning fulfillment of the obligation to give close agnates first rights of refusal, and participation of outside parties. First, the contract creates Yang's share as a commodity; then, through this contract the sale is brought fully into the public domain of commodified transactions as defined precisely by the kinship and other long-term social relationships that the contract must both acknowledge and resist.

Such relationships would have less immediate relevance for commodities such as irrigation systems or "large rent" rights, given that the usual circumstance was ownership by parties external to local communities. Thus the collection of large rent and water-use fees could hardly be supported by kinship and other ties within a socially intimate community framework. A common arrangement for the collection of large rent rights was for the owner to designate a local agent, known in southern Taiwan, including the Minong area, as a "manager" (*guanshi*); such managers were recognized by the state and they came to assume the duties of village head while remaining responsible for the collection of large rent payments in their communities. The state might also be directly involved in facilitating the collection of fees owed to parties with whom there were no community or kinship ties, as illustrated by the following proclamation by the Fengshan county magistrate, whose jurisdiction included the Minong area, and within it the villages of Zhongyun and Jingualiao:

Li, serving as expectant appointee for the Directly Administered Department, transferred to Fengshan County as acting magistrate, by imperial command praised and encouraged for his work, issues the following decree. Whereas on the eighth day of the third month of this year [April 13, 1894], Tao née Zhang, the wife of the late brigade commander-general, Provincial Military Commander Tao, petitioned through her family representative Tao Maoqi, who reported to me in her name stating:

"My late husband Tao Maosen formerly served as brigade-general of Xi'an Prefecture, Yan'an Prefecture, Suide Department, and Yulin Prefecture in Shaanxi Province [in north China]. Coming to Taiwan to offer his services, he was appointed as the forward coastal defense army commander concurrently responsible for pacification and land reclamation. Therefore, in areas of Fengshan County bordering the mountains he built irrigation canals and brought lands under cultivation; he also raised capital and built irrigation canals in Yanpu, Litoubiao, and Zhongyun, as well as a tile-roofed house in Jingualiao. All these canals irrigated lands of local people, which have become lands of happiness. Annual irrigation fees are paid by the people using the canals so as to provide in compensation a very modest profit. If there is need to repair the canals, the people who use them will assist with their labor. My late husband Maosen reported this clearly to the higher provincial authorities and undertook all proper procedures, as is on record. My husband died unexpectedly after achieving those successes, resulting in my family being reduced to poverty here, and we have wished to return to our home region for a long time. But we have had no way to raise funds for traveling expenses. So I have sold the irrigation canals at each site, connected through Yanpu, as well as the tile-roof house in their entirety to the Tan Family Agricultural Bureau [Tan Wusetang]. I received from them 800 dollars; I need this sum so as to escort my husband's coffin back to his native region for burial. I request that an edict be issued in order to let those people using water from the canals to irrigate their fields know that they should pay annually all of the irrigation fees and the management fees to the Tan Family Agricultural Bureau. Henceforth the canals and the house will have no connection with our Tao family."

Upon receipt [of this communication] I have found that these irrigation canals and the tile-roofed house were built by Brigade Commander-General Tao with his own funds, as is on file. Now that the properties have been sold and his coffin escorted home, all irrigation canals and the house are to be managed by the Tan Family Agricultural Bureau. It is therefore necessary to issue this proclamation:

It is proclaimed that we expect all farmers to know that if the irrigation canals in Yanpu, Litoubiao, and Zhongyun water their fields they must pay fees to the Tan Family Agricultural Bureau. If later this bureau rents the canals to other people, the farmers should also pay the fees accordingly, and must not fall into arrears so as to accumulate their own capital. If there are abuses such as being behind in fee payments or doing damage to the canals, as soon as these have been reported, without fail the offenders will be arrested and punished with no leniency. This will invigorate irrigation and secure respect for the proper payment of fees. The tile-roof house in Jingualiao also belongs to the Tan Family Agricultural Bureau and is under their management; it is their permanent property.

Each of these commands is to be tremblingly obeyed. Do not disobey! Special proclamation!

Guangxu, twentieth year, third month, fifteenth day [April 20, 1894].

Magistrate Li's proclamation is an effort to put the weight of the Chinese state behind the Tao family's sale of irrigation systems to the Tan Family Agricultural Bureau. Tan himself, who fully controlled his "agricultural bureau," had been brought from mainland China to Taiwan by Magistrate Li, for whom he had served in Fengshan County as a private secretary in charge of taxation and irrigation matters. Tan, who was not a native Hakka speaker, married a woman from Zhongyun, a major village in the Minong area, and moved there from the Fengshan county seat.[21] The proclamation refers to a house in Jingualiao, a smaller village in Minong; this building served as headquarters for the entire irrigation enterprise. It also mentions irrigation systems in Yanpu and Litoubiao, as well as in Zhongyun, with the first two being outside the Minong region, populated by Hokkien-speaking Han Chinese, and quite beyond the confines of the larger Hakka settlement zone. Thus what was indeed a contractual undertaking between Tao's widow and Tan's bureau could hardly be supported by a dense network of local ties. Least significant in this case was the fact that the two parties to the contract did not share local community roots, for both were indeed participants in a broader network of bureaucratic connections. It was more important that the distribution of these irrigation systems straddled several communities, with the obligations of individual farmers to pay water fees likewise appearing to have no support in terms of local social ties, but simply comprising the asset that had changed hands. In other words, the sale of the irrigation systems represented commodification at a level extending well beyond the local community. Commodification at such higher scales, as in the form of wide-ranging commercial ties that could cover large areas of the Qing empire, not to speak of Taiwan, involved contracts that could be supported by the ramified social ties of "functional" communities such as merchant guilds, and by the structure of the contracts themselves, as these might require, for example, that the two or more parties involved fulfill their obligations at exactly the same time (Brockman 1980). By reporting the transaction to Magistrate Li, Tao's widow satisfied the requirements of her contractual undertaking in yet another way: given that the irrigation systems formed an asset only to the extent that they yielded income in the form of farmer's water fees, hers was an appeal to the state to ensure that these payments continued.

State support of commodification was consistent with commodification's entrenched social support at the local level, as confirmed, among other ways, by pervasive reliance on written contracts. These contracts made an impression on the Japanese, for shortly after assuming control over Taiwan in 1895, the new colonial administrators began to survey local practices, an early result of which was a report presented by Okamatsu Santaro, who remarked as follows:

Where the power of the government is weak the people cannot hope for any security of property, and when their rights are not protected by the courts, it is natural that they should devise some means of self-protection. In Formosa [Taiwan] the custom of drawing up deeds [that is, contracts] for every kind of legal act was established. From the acquisition, loss, or transfer of property rights to a hundred other matters relating to personal affairs, even to marriage, adoption, succession, etc., special in[str]uments were in constant use. Such documents are possessed by the people throughout the island and a careful examination of them affords the best material for investigating Formosan usages. Upon such documents the present report is largely based. (Okamatsu 1902: 18)

It is not surprising that Okamatsu would seek to place the Japanese conquest within a progressive context by linking the propensity of the Taiwanese to engage in contractual transactions to the weakness, that is to the backwardness, of the Qing imperial regime. Of course, contracts as a symptom of backwardness flew in the face of many then-current theories of progress, summarized in Maine's famous statement that "the movement of progressive societies has hitherto been a movement *from Status to Contract*" (italics in original; Maine 1861: 141). But if this be progress, certainly it would have to have been denied by the Japanese conquerors of Taiwan, who could hardly have been expected to characterize their new colonial domination as being anything other than a boon to the local inhabitants. Okamatsu was not concerned as such with the larger issue of interpenetration of contracts and commodification—that is, with economic culture as a whole.

We have seen earlier (chapters 2 and 3) how in mainland China it was with respect to this economic culture that a new and decidedly negative perspective would soon emerge. Under the impact precisely of later versions of Euro-American theories of progress, with Marxism-Leninism prominently included, China's new post-imperial intellectual and political elites engaged in an interpretation of their own past that held that late imperial China's economy was "feudal," popular religion nothing but "feudal superstition," and "peasants" the principal upholders of all that was culturally backward about China. There was no room in this perspective for the entrepreneurial, managerially competent, commodity- and contract-engaged rural inhabitants. At the same time, some European and other foreign observers were remarking on rural culture and society with a sympathy made ironic by its contrast with the hostility of China's own elites. Surely it was this ongoing denigration of China's own past that prompted R. H. Tawney, in his famous survey of China's economy, to remark as follows:

[China] is not afflicted by the complicated iniquities of feudal land law; manorial estates worked by corvees, if they ever existed, have left few traces. . . . landlord and tenant are parties to a business contract, not members of different classes based on privilege and subordination. Hence, though questions of land tenure are in some regions acute, their character and setting are not those of Europe. (1932: 63)

In other cases foreigners might comment with hostility on what they perceived to be the economic and business sophistication of the Chinese in China's foreign-dominated "treaty ports," or of ordinary migrants from some of the poorest regions of rural China to southeast Asia and elsewhere, such immigrants being precisely the kinds of people China's elite would take to epitomize peasant backwardness. We have also seen how with the Communist victory in 1949, the image of traditional Chinese backwardness, earlier already dominant, became unchallenged. To this day the image is widely but certainly not universally accepted in elite political and intellectual circles, there being no readily apparent distinction in this respect among the current government's supporters, its opponents, or those who are neutral. Hence the almost bizarre contrasts between discussions of Chinese "economic sophistication" taking place outside China (for example, Freedman 1979a) and purported descriptions of Chinese "peasants" generated within China, of which the following, in the October 1992 issue of the prestigious *Politics and Law Tribune*, is quite typical:

As our rural society operated for thousands of years on a narrow, single-track natural economy, Chinese peasants have evolved enormous psychological momentum suited to it, so that a commodity economy is to them a novel idea to which they would like to adapt but do not know how. As sudden reform changes have put all old customs and new strange and conflicting ideas into a process of exchange and collision, they have naturally created a temporary imbalance in our peasant mentality. (Wei 1992: 33)

Observers of economic development during recent decades in Taiwan, Hong Kong, and indeed in mainland China might find such a characterization of the "mentality" of China's so-called peasants—and its supposed historical background—to be of little help in understanding the cultural sources of economic change in these regions. What might appear equally perplexing is the linking of "peasant" economic backwardness to "feudal superstitions," for what are held to be the latter have emerged from hiding with the greatest of vigor precisely where recent economic dynamism has been most pronounced. As an article titled "Severely Combat Feudal Superstitions Leading to the Commission of Crimes," in the February 1994 issue of *Outlook*, another important journal, put it, "According to the analysis of parties concerned, the resurgence of feudal superstitions in the 1990s started in the economically developed southeastern coastal regions" (Li 1994: 46).

Other than by linking popular religious beliefs to crime, the ongoing critique of "feudal superstition" seems unable to explain the strong association of popular religion with economic progress. However, we have seen the connection between religion and economic culture to be historically rooted. In Minong during Qing, the definition of the many shareholding corporations largely in religious terms hardly detracted from their economic significance in the context of wide-scale commodification, but rather provided further evidence that the instruments of commodification, as much as those of religion, were deeply entrenched elements of Minong's culture, and more generally of that of late imperial China as a whole. Such religious definition was but one aspect of the role of religion as the provider of a vocabulary for the expression of the overall arrangement of society. As elsewhere in China, religion highlighted the Minong community's organization, its history, and indeed its connections to the totality of Chinese society. Religion also reflected the community's conflicts with its neighbors. It was through religion that social arrangements received constant emphasis during the ceremonial year, when at different times various features of the social landscape were given ceremonial and ritual expression. Thus those currently so hostile to the popular religion they call "feudal superstition" might appear to be unaware of how it was generally the case in late imperial China, as in Minong, that just as one honored the gods and the ancestors through the creation of commodities, one honored commodities through the gods and the ancestors.

Appendix A: Share Sale Contract, Hsinchu (Xinzhu) Area, North Taiwan

Contract for the sale of ancestral association shares.

We, Lin Changtong and his [four] brothers, have received an allocation [of property] as bequeathed to us by our father, who in the past together with his patrilineal uncles and nephews contributed funds for the establishment of the Dayi Gong Ancestral Estate with 52.5 shares. We, [Lin] Changtong and his brothers, obtained four shares, with the land, cash [value], and names [of the shareholders] specified in the [association] account book. Today, because we are in need of funds, we are willing to sell our four ancestral association shares, including all property and income they entail. With [agnatically close] members of our [agnatic] branch unwilling to purchase [the shares] as offered through a middleman, we now through a middleman sell them to our junior agnates [literally, agnatic nephews] Shenduo and his brothers, who have come forward to purchase [them]. On this day, with the agreement of the three parties [sellers, purchasers, and middleman], and on the basis of their market value of 100 large dollars, the shares have been received in person [by the purchasers] in full settlement. [As recorded in the account book] the names of the owners of the four shares received by [Lin Chang]tong [and his brothers] today have been changed in conformity to this contract and [the shares] have been given to [Lin Shen]duo [and his brothers] as their permanent holdings. It is guaranteed that this property had belonged to [Lin Chang]tong and his brothers, that their branch agnates had no involvement with this [property], and that there has been no sale or redeemable sale [of this property] to other parties, or the like. If in the future such circumstances should arise [involving claims of other parties to the property], these will be forcefully dealt with by [Lin Chang]tong and his brothers and will be of no concern to the purchasers. This [contract] is entered into willingly by both parties, and neither will renege on it. Today, desiring proof [of this transaction], we have drawn up one copy of this contract for the sale of ancestral association shares, and it shall be kept as evidence.

Today it is affirmed that the sum of 100 large dollars has been received in full [by the sellers].

> Middleman: branch younger brother [Lin] Changtang
> Witnesses: branch older brothers [Lin] Changling
>> [Lin] Changse
>> [Lin Chang]man
>> [Lin Chang]dou
> Sellers of ancestral association shares: Lin Changtong
>> [Lin Chang]zuo
>> [Lin Chang]zu
> Daoguang, second year, tenth month [between October 14 and November 12, 1822].[22]

Appendix B: Contract for the Division of Ancestral Corporation, North Taiwan

We, the parties to this contract for the division of management, being Qingmeng, Qingqing, Shengfu, Shengkui, Shengshan, Shengchao, Qijian, and Qihui, have inherited the Gonghuangong estate for ancestor worship, which our ancestors established in the past in central Taiwan with contributions for the accumulation of a capital fund. The estate's share capital is divided into eight large portions, with each portion distributed equally into ten shares; there is an annual sacrifice on the twenty-second day of the eleventh [lunar] month to the ancestors on their death anniversary, and [after the expenses for the sacrifice] there remain additional funds [with respect to income from the estate] for interest [payments, to be distributed to shareholders]. Now because the descendants are numerous, it is difficult [for all of us] to be rewarded together [with feasting and interest distribution]; we members of this ancestral association have deliberated and have expressed willingness to individually sacrifice on the [ancestor's] death day. Therefore we have asked that our lineage elders be present and determine through the drawing of lots the distribution of the land and funds of the sacrificial estate of the Eleventh Ancestor as well as the assets of the estates(s) dedicated to earlier ancestors. On the death dates of our ancestors, each one of us individually will at the appointed time offer sacrifices. As to the equal distribution of the rental payments for the military lands [originally set aside for cultivation by local garrisons but later leased out by them], each household to which this responsibility rotates will make the payment in accordance with the amount due and shall not shirk its responsibility. As of the initiation of this division of management, with management [of the ancestral association's assets] based upon [the drawing of] lots, there does not remain [as association property] the slightest amount of land or money; each person will manage his own affairs, and from now on the descendants shall not squabble over trifles. Now, wishing to have proof [of this agreement], we have specially made three copies of this contract for the division of management; each [party] will keep one copy, which shall always serve as evidence.

[Four clauses omitted]

Daoguang, twenty-ninth year, eighth month [between November 17 and October 15, 1849]

[Signatories omitted].[23]

CHAPTER NINE

Writs of Passage in Late Imperial China

Contracts and the Documentation of Practical Understandings in Minong, Taiwan

> Contract, as the word is usually understood, is an initially voluntary agreement between two or more people to carry out certain obligations and gain certain rights, when these obligations are not part of any other relationship in which the contracting parties stand to one another. . . . Contract, thus, is a principle for creating a bond between two roles, with overtly stated obligations and rights—called a "consideration" by lawyers—being the determining characteristic.
>
> Paul Bohannan, *Social Anthropology*

There is growing scholarly recognition of the importance throughout Chinese society of documents that can be identified as contracts, and in the previous chapter we introduced several in considering Qing-period commodification. So it is timely to ask if the Western idea of "contract," no matter how broadly defined—such as above, for example—can be used to encompass every signed and witnessed written product of China's late imperial culture, when many basic arrangements of social life were fixed through the use of documents.[1] In other words, recourse to written understandings in "negotiating daily life" (Hansen 1995) led to a prodigious output of documents that precisely because of their importance reflected the contours of the society that produced them. Such practical documents of daily life might usefully be considered within the broader framework of the high valuation given writing and paper in Chinese culture, among other ways.

But with a focus on contracts there is the danger of imposing non-Chinese categories onto Chinese cultural formations, which are badly distorted thereby; these Chinese formations may be stripped of their own historical and cultural characteristics and transformed in accordance with alien cultural features. However, in the case of contracts we are dealing with an imposition rather different from others that may come readily to mind, because in the Western historical context the idea of contracts is precisely associated with that of progress, as we saw in chapter 8. So in moving beyond a narrow focus on documents that readily fall within a Western-derived category of contracts it should always be remembered how documents fitting into this category were numerous, formed a large portion of total documentary output, and were indeed of major significance in the lives of ordinary people. This point deserves emphasis because the role of Chinese contracts has been distorted in modern China, not so much by the way it has been described, but rather through construction of the particular context within which it has been disregarded.

Given the antitraditionalism of early-twentieth-century Chinese intellectuals—involving, as we have seen in earlier chapters, such notions as "feudalism" or the "backward peasant" immersed in the culture of the "natural village" and subsisting through participation in a "natural economy"—it is not surprising that contracts and other popular documents were ignored or their existence even denied.[2] This denial extended well beyond China's borders and was presumably encouraged by the ongoing development in the West of theories of progress involving contrasts such as those between "tradition" and "rationality."[3] As recently as the early 1980s (if not even later), some prominent American academic specialists on contemporary China believed that the "peasants" of that country had never had to deal with contracts until their exposure to the forces of "modernization" in recent decades.[4]

Such views were held in spite of the fact that much basic evidence for the importance in everyday life of signed and witnessed contracts and other such documents had long been available, including through the publication in the early twentieth century of compilations of Qing-period documents gathered in Taiwan by the Japanese during the first years of their occupation (when mainland China was still ruled by the Qing imperial house). Very early in the twentieth century there was published in Japan even an English version, entitled *Provisional Report on Investigations of Laws and Customs in the Island of Formosa* (Okamatsu 1902), which included in a lengthy appendix numerous examples in the original Chinese of documents of agreement covering a wide range of practical affairs among ordinary people. These and subsequent collections from various parts of late imperial China have certainly succeeded in establishing contracts as both common and important in society at large among both rich and poor—who might be involved in the same contract as buyer and seller or as landlord and tenant—and that contracts also loomed large even among those with holdings that were limited yet substantial enough to warrant preparing a family division agreement, for example. The country, including the countryside, was saturated with such documents, thus making the enduring denial by certain parties of their significance or indeed of their existence one of the more remarkable examples of the triumph of an ideology—or, better yet, of a fantasy focusing on "progress" and "modernization"—over facts that might call into question the assumption that all sources of modernity had to be from outside China, or at least remote from the culture of ordinary people.

The importance of contracts and similar documents in late imperial Chinese culture did begin to receive more confirmation in mid-twentieth-century scholarship,[5] but with the publication of additional compilations, consideration of the great variety of practical documents in China during Qing and earlier dynasties now involved other problems of interpretation. A major question was the extent to which variation reflects either regional differences or the complexity of local documentation activities. Obviously, to the degree that it is the latter, such variation also describes complexity in local economic and social relationships, especially as regards choices and arrangements made by individuals. While it is now clear that there are some regional differences in style and terminology, little has been done in the way of exploring the uses of contracts and other documents within particular community settings.[6]

Here I focus on such uses during Qing in the Minong local community, which included Minong Village and the other villages making up the Right Unit of the Six Units confederation. The Minong community was introduced in the previous chapter, where the concern was its late imperial economic culture, as characterized by pervasive commodification. Also introduced in that chapter were the texts of several contracts, introduced to illuminate some of the issues discussed there. For present purposes those texts can be reviewed in conjunction with the considerably larger number I present in this chapter, where I fix my attention on a much broader category of signed and witnessed statements put on paper to confirm and secure social and economic transactions and transformations. These Qing-period documents of declaration, all from Minong, were written for various purposes; they include but are hardly limited to "contracts." Documents of declaration follow the same basic format; each has an opening clause that titles the document and states its purpose, among which are contractual undertakings involving things and people and changes in the rights of the latter with respect to the former, but there can also be affirmations regarding property distribution or debt settlement, among others. I first introduce and discuss several documents illustrating how major local categories of written understandings include but also clearly go beyond what would be expected in a contract; I then turn to documents regarding distribution of property during family division, where again I show how contracts are not the only form of documentary confirmation. In this chapter I want to make the point that the comparative study of contracts requires not only analysis of local, culturally specific traditions and categories of documentation, but also consideration of how and the extent to which this documentation figures in social and cultural life. In particular, I want to show how in the documentation of changes in social or economic relationships written understandings readily identified as contracts might be resorted to in some instances, while in others the documentary outcome reflected changes wrought through clearly noncontractual means, with all documents sharing in common their function of legitimizing whatever such changes they might be associated with.

The twenty documents presented in this chapter range in date from 1797 to 1895, or from about sixty years after the first settlement of Minong by Hakka-speaking Han Chinese to just a few months before the arrival of Japanese soldiers.[7] During this century-long period there of course were major secular changes in Minong, as the area was brought under increasingly intensive agricultural development and as those born in Taiwan made up a steadily larger proportion of the population. Also during this time Minong increasingly achieved both self-definition and outside recognition as a region with its own customs, local products, and lore such that it made its own small contribution to the cosmopolitanism of late imperial China that was so much based on local differences and translocal appreciation of them. Nevertheless, all the documents retain the format characteristic of such writings throughout late imperial China. With eleven dating from the fifteen years immediately prior to the Japanese occupation, they do provide ample evidence of the complexities of local life in Minong within a relatively restricted time frame.

Sale agreements, especially those concerning land, were among the most important written documents of understanding, and most were clearly contractual. Following is a relatively simple example:

The executor of this contract for the irrevocable sale of dry field land, Liu Ayi, in the past obtained from his father through succession one parcel of land. Using local place names, it is situated in Zhongyun Village behind the Nantou River. Its boundaries extend eastward to Zhong Xunlang's dry field, and to Boggong Shuxia [Under the Earth God Tree]; westward to Zhong Yilang's dry field; southward to Zhang Liangna's dry field; and northward to Zhong Tianlang's dry field. The boundaries in all four directions have been inspected and clearly demarcated in the presence of the middleman. Now because my mother needs money and after having thoroughly inquired among those closest agnates who are my paternal uncles, each and every one of whom is unable to make the purchase, I have relied on a middleman for an introduction to my senior maternal cousin, Zhong Youhe, who is from this village and has come forward to contract purchase. On the same day, through the middleman, the three parties [buyer, seller, and middleman] have agreed on the basis of market value to a land sale price of twenty silver dollars exactly [valued in silver by weight at the ratio of] sixty-eight [ounces to one hundred dollars], and on that day money and contract have been straightforwardly exchanged, with no shortchanging and without such things as use of this property to set off debts. With this sale the land is to be given immediately to the buyer, for him to cultivate and manage as his property. Also, should original ownership rights be unclear, this is not something the buyer need be concerned with; it is the seller who is fully responsible. Hereafter, the seller is not to dare speak of redeeming the land or of gift-money. Upon sale, the seller will immediately settle any possible claims so as to end forever whatever complications there may have been. This transaction is entered into willingly by the two parties, without regrets and without compulsion. Because we fear that oral agreement is unreliable, we have drawn up one copy of this contract for the irrevocable sale of dry field land, which is transferred [to the buyer] as certification.

On this day it is clearly noted that as per this contract there was received payment of twenty silver dollars exactly [valued in silver by weight at the ratio of] sixty-eight [ounces to one hundred dollars].

Mediator/middleman: Li Jiexiang
Witness: Liu Yulin
Amanuensis: Li Jiexiang
Guangxu, nineteenth year, being the *guisi* cyclical year, twelfth month, [blank]
    day [between December 27, 1894, and January 25, 1895]
Executor of contract for the irrevocable sale of land, Liu Ayi.

This document exemplifies the standard format: first, it is identified as to its purpose, in this case a sale contract, and the executor is named. The land to be sold is identified in terms of location and boundaries, with the purchaser and price indicated. As elsewhere in Taiwan and areas of mainland China, especially during the later Qing period, the price is set in foreign silver ("large") dollars, usually Mexican-minted Spanish coins, but given its exchange value in terms of silver by weight: the ratio of sixty-eight Chinese ounces or "taels" (*liang*) to one hundred dollars was most common and in most Minong contracts simply indicated by writing the figure "68" (in business or accounting form) next to the price in dollars.[8] Identification of the purpose and executor, followed by the text of the document and the dated signatures of witnesses, the amanuensis, and executor are features of all documents of understanding, both contracts and documents in other categories. As in the above contract, it is common in such documents for the date not to include the day of the month, even though the Chinese character for "day" (*ri*) is written in, while the space which should indicate which day is left blank. In some cases the full date is given, and when it is not the avoidance is deliberate and reflects the power of horoscopic beliefs that define some days as inauspicious. Horoscopic judgments do differ, however, so that the problem is avoided simply by not indicating which day of the month it is. Another avoidance technique, most commonly used in the dated inscriptions carved on stone tablets, such as record contributions to temples or schools, is to fill in the blank space before "day" not with a number but with the character *ji*, meaning "auspicious."

All Minong written understandings share the use of standard phrases or boilerplate found in similar documents throughout late imperial China. Many of these phrases are encountered in Ming-period handbooks on documentary composition, or even in earlier Tang dynasty contracts.[9] Some phrases frequently encountered in both Minong contracts and those written elsewhere in the empire were stipulated by Qing legal regulations, at least insofar as transactions involving land were concerned. For example, "irrevocable sale" (*juemai*), as in this contract's opening clause, was a term mandated by the state if its courts were to recognize a contract as representing a full sale such that the seller lost all rights to make further claims or press for additional payments.[10] On the other hand, many documents also contain localisms pertaining to regions in Taiwan or involving Hakka vocabulary, as with the language used in some cases to describe a plot's location. Some documents use written characters that appear unique to Taiwan or to the Hakka in mainland China and Taiwan.[11] This combination of China-wide and locally specific usages very nicely reflects the dual status of these documents as local acts of legitimization, on the one hand, and as potential though very rarely used evidence for appeal to the state, on the other. This documentary duality in turn is but one reflection of how even a local community remotely located on the periphery of the empire was nevertheless connected to the imperial state in many ways (as through the examination system, for example) at the same time that it was configured by its own local history and self-constituted and self-regulating in almost all aspects of life.

In this particular document, buyer and seller are indicated by individual names, although it should be understood that each was acting as a family head (*jiazhang*). The buyer is family head, while the seller signs on with the explicit approval of his most probably widowed mother, under circumstances in which this woman may be de facto family head in the absence of her husband, but with representational authority in dealings outside the family kept in male hands, as usual, so that now her son (or eldest son) is the recognized family head as far as matters such as the sale of land are concerned. Thus the transaction represented the transfer of land from one family estate to another. As is well known, as far as most people were concerned, the family rather than the individual was the major property holder in late imperial China. Corporations could also be landowners, as in Minong, where we saw in chapter 8 that by the end of Qing about one-third of the best wet rice land was owned by associations, mainly those dedicated to the worship of gods or ancestors. A contract involving land purchase by one such group is as follows:

The executors of this contract for irrevocable sale of wet rice land are Lin Kuansheng, Lin Hesheng, and their paternal nephew Lin Fengchun, who in the past acquired through succession from their paternal grandfather a parcel of double-crop wet rice land. It is in the fourth portion of Shifenpu [The Ten-Portion Tract] Minong Village, and has an area of 3.808 *fen* [0.3808 *jia*].[12] Eastward it extends to Zhang Tianjin'er's wet rice land; westward to the wet rice land of Lin Ashou and Lin Xiuguan; southward to the irrigation channel; northward to the obliquely situated cart path. The boundaries in all four directions have been inspected and clearly demarcated in the presence of the middleman. Now, owing to financial difficulties, we desire to sell this parcel. After having first thoroughly made inquiries among our close agnates, none of whom were able to make the purchase, we have willingly relied upon a middleman, through whose introduction the Winter Solstice Association [Dongzhi Hui] of the Honorable [Ancestor Lin] Pingshi, represented by [Lin] Weilin, [Lin] Tianbao'er, [Lin] Bensheng, [Lin] Tiancai'san, and [Lin] Shengna has come forward to purchase this property. On this day, in the presence of the middleman, the three parties have agreed on the basis of market value to a price of 150 dollars. Cash and contract are openly exchanged on the same day without any shortchanging and without such things as use of this property to set off debts or the sale of other persons' property. After sale, the property is to be given over immediately to members of the Honorable Pingshi Ancestral Association for them to cultivate and manage as [the association's] property. Upon sale any problems must be immediately settled so as to forever put an end to whatever complications there may have been. The brothers, of whom Kuansheng is the oldest, must not dare to dispute this sale or cause trouble. If there are questions regarding previous ownership or unpaid grain rentals prior to this sale, these are not matters for which the buyer is responsible, and it is the seller who has to deal with them. For the two parties, this transaction is undertaken completely voluntarily and without any compulsion. Because we fear that oral agreement is unreliable, we have drawn up one copy of this contract for irrevocable sale, to which is attached one official title registration deed [zhangdan], for a total of two documents transferred [to the buyer] as certification.

Noted clearly that on this day in the presence of the middleman there was received payment of 150 dollars valued in silver by weight [at the ratio of] sixty-eight [ounces to one hundred dollars] as per the contract. Noted.

Also noted clearly is that neither the antecedent old contract nor the family division contract are attached; if [in the future] these are brought forward, they cannot serve as evidence [of ownership]. Noted.

Also noted clearly is that water from the Zhongzhenbi [Central Channel Reservoir] directly irrigates this field, flowing south. Noted.

Also noted clearly is that the middlemen's commission is four dollars fifty cents. Noted.

Middlemen: Bensheng
            Renlang
Witness: Younger brother Yousheng
            Paternal nephew Yunchun
Amanuensis: Longchun
Guangxu, sixteenth year, third month, [blank] day [between April 18 and May 18, 1890], executors of contract for irrevocable sale:
   Lin Kuansheng
   Hesheng
   Paternal nephew Fengchun.[13]

As was the common procedure, this contract specifies the irrigation circumstances of the field being sold, which included both the rights and obligations of the new owner with respect to irrigation coordination within the larger area. These rights and obligations, as well as those pertaining to other payment liabilities, were held to be attributes of the commodity itself. The contract also exemplifies in several ways the corporation as an independent economic entity separate from any individual member. First Lin Pingshi, the ancestral focus of the corporation making the purchase, is a key foundation ancestor of all persons with the surname Lin among the south Taiwan Hakka, for he is held by them to be the founder of the Lin surname in Guangdong, the mainland province from which the ancestors of most Minong Hakka had migrated. This corporation's membership originally derived from both of Minong's major Lin descent lines or hall names, irrespective of the fact that only one line has Pingshi as a direct ancestor.[14] In 1852, however, the corporation split into two, with each of the new corporate entities getting about half of the old corporation's property and with both still worshipping Pingshi, even though the separation was largely on the basis of hall name. Both before and after the split, the Lin worshipped Pingshi as the historical regional founder of the surname as such, and at yet an even higher genealogical level they were able to align themselves with respect to a common ancestor so as to come together as one congregation of agnates, although with division they formed two congregations. In this contract, which pertains to one of the derivative corporations, the representatives making the purchase, the sellers, the middlemen, the witnesses, and the amanuensis are all members of the same agnatic congregation, but the corporation as an economic property-owning agent is separate from the membership as a congregation or as individuals. Hence the standard disclaimer that close agnates were given first rights of refusal with respect to land purchase is perfectly true even though these agnates, like everyone else involved in this transaction, are members of the same congregation, for the first rights of agnates are in their capacities as family heads and not as members of a larger corporation. Likewise, the middleman Lin Bensheng also appears as a corporation representative; as an individual he gets a commission for being middleman, but as corporation representative he is but one of five members who as a group take title to the land. All these relationships are highlighted and confirmed by documentary validation. I know from local genealogies that Lin Bensheng shared a common paternal grandfather with the sellers Lin Kuansheng and Lin Hesheng and with the late father of the seller Lin Fengchun, although even these agnates that are genealogically very close are clearly demarcated as separate economic agents in the document.

That corporations in Minong were well-defined economic actors reflected circumstances generally common to late imperial China. Indeed, the family itself, the *jia*, was a corporate unit. Thus in China the common circumstance was that the individual was subsumed within larger economic and property-owning entities.[15] As far as the above contract is concerned, the fact that the two brothers and their paternal nephew are all signatories is symptomatic of the circumstance that they still are members of an undivided fraternal joint family, one in which the father has already died. In the absence of a father serving as family head on the basis of his senior generation authority, fraternal joint family dynamics suggest that every adult male potentially able to demand family division indicate his agreement to the sale so as to protect the purchaser from any claims that might later emerge in the course of family division disputes. The official registration deed (*zhangdan*) handed over with the contract was one of those issued for every plot of land resurveyed starting in 1886 (in Minong carried out in 1889) at the command of the Taiwan governor Liu Mingchuan. It goes to the new owner in keeping with the common and expected procedure whereby with the transfer by contract of land or housing, earlier contracts or other documentary evidence of property rights are transferred together with the new contract and the property itself. This procedure is in fact supported by the *zhangdan*, whose text specifies that it is to be transferred to the new owner in the event of land sale, thus indicating in this respect symmetry between state and local practice. However, in the above contract it is noted that the antecedent sales contract and a family division contract are not attached, such mention being yet another standard procedure when circumstances were appropriate. This latter clause in effect nullifies the potential use of such papers in the future for the purposes of contesting the transaction or the understanding dealt with in the later contract. In this particular case it is not clear why the documents were not transferred, but it was common enough for them to be kept in the event that only a portion of the land or other property whose possession they legitimized was disposed of. Such clauses giving explicit mention of documents either included with the contract or not included of course provide additional evidence of the importance of the documentary recording and reinforcement of transactions and understandings.

In the contract that follows there likewise is a clause noting how the earlier contracts have been retained by the parties involved. But I introduce this contract because it provides an example of exchange. Swapping was common and could involve exchanging one plot of land for another or, as in this case, different kinds of property. The contract is also of interest in that it involves transfer of property within the built-up portion of Zhongyun, one of Minong's major villages, hence the various stipulations concerning access to different paths and streets and the property status of bamboo and betel nut trees located on or near these paths:

The executor of this contract for exchange, the brothers, of whom Liu Binghua is the oldest, in the past purchased from Zhang Zhuna the southern section of a plot of vegetable land. It extends eastward to the base of Zhong Youhe's house;

westward to the bamboo fence of Dai Jinshui's vegetable garden; southward to the night watchman's path; and northward to the stone boundary of our building site. The boundaries in all four directions have been inspected and clearly demarcated in the presence of the middleman. Now we exchange this vegetable land for Zhong Youhe's one-room house and grain-drying area. After the exchange, the land is immediately given to Zhong Youhe to develop as he pleases. Available for ordinary passage of the three Zhong and Liu families will be the lower [i.e., western] section of the cart path up to the stone border of the large street. Henceforth we brothers, sons, and paternal nephews are not to dispute this or cause trouble. This transaction is entered into willingly by the two parties, without regrets. Because we fear that oral agreement is unreliable, we have drawn up one copy of this contract for exchange as certification.

It is clearly noted that there are three clusters of bamboo on the night watchman's path; the upper two clusters will be cut down, and the lower cluster will remain and be given to Binghua for his use. Noted.

Also clearly noted is that the betel nut tree below [i.e., to the west] still belongs to Binghua; if in the future this tree is destroyed, none of the three families should plant trees on that tiny piece of land. Noted.

Also clearly noted is that Zhong Youhe ought to be compensated nine dollars for the roof tiles on the house. Confirmed.

Also clearly noted is that the prior old contracts are to be retained by those making the exchange; in the future, those holding them cannot use them for certification. Noted.

Mediator/middleman: Li Yousheng
Witnesses: Zhong Xunlang, Xiao Caihua
Amanuensis: younger brother Fanghua
Guangxu, fifth year, being the *jimao* cyclical year, eleventh month, [blank] day [between December 13, 1879, and January 11, 1880]
Executor of contract for exchange, Liu Binghua.

Exchanges such as the one involved in this contract were to the benefit of both parties, and their common occurrence was especially powerful testimony to the lack of sentimental attachments to the land on the part of owners. Although it might be argued (quite erroneously) that land sales under financial duress occurred in spite of the emotional ties that people had to their land, the ease with which swaps could be arranged when both sides stood to gain requires that we view a sale resulting from financial need as just that. The much-heralded attachment of so-called peasants to their land is part of the larger fabrication of a tradition-bound "peasant mentality." There is no evidence of this mentality once the detailed facts of rural life in late imperial China are examined. It was obviously true that people forced to sell land were in bad shape, and indeed under ordinary circumstances a family selling land was held to be going down socially as well as economically. Likewise, the purchase of land was conspicuous evidence of a family's ascent, but all this simply testifies to the importance of land as a dependable source of subsistence and income in the rather insecure world of late imperial China. Rational rather than sentimental concerns made land desirable.[16] In this contract Liu Binghua signs for himself and his youngest of two brothers, who at the time could not have been older than eleven or twelve, as indicated by genealogical and household registration data. The second brother, who serves as amanuensis, had been adopted by Liu Binghua's paternal uncle; no longer a member of Binghua's family (*jia*), and thus not directly party to this transaction, the second brother was providing the kind of assistance commonly expected of close kin.

Swapping aside, another alternative to outright sale was *dian*—which can be variously rendered as pledge sale, redeemable sale, or conditional sale—whereby land or another commodity was turned over to the party advancing funds for that party to cultivate or otherwise put to use, with the understanding that upon the money's return the land or other commodity would also go back to its original owner. Given Taiwan's highly commodified late Qing economy, it is not surprising that *dian* rates for land mostly ranged from 70 to 90 percent of the price for outright purchase, with the figure being 80 percent in areas of south Taiwan (RTTC 1905: 104–5). That *dian* transfers fetched less of course reflected the fact that the land could be redeemed. Thus the prices represent the demands of sellers not willing to give up their rights completely and of buyers willing to invest at an attractive rate in commodities so defined. Most Minong *dian* agreements specified the duration of pledge, it being understood that the party holding the land would maintain control in the event that the other party did not return the money advanced when the pledge period ended. Minong *dian* contracts commonly were for five years, but the one that follows provides an example of how such pledge periods could be extended and in some cases renegotiated:

The executors of this contract for the redeemable sale of wet rice land, the brothers Liang Axiu and Liang Ayu, in the past obtained from their paternal grandfather as their due portion through family division a plot of single-crop wet rice land. Using local place names, it is one section of the lower row of plots in the second of the ten divisions of land outside Zhutoubei Village. Its boundaries extend eastward to the wet rice field of our father's elder brother Wenchang, westward to the edge of the irrigation canal, southward to the wet rice field of our father's elder brother Wenchang, northward to elder brother Chuanxing's wet rice field. The boundaries in all four directions have been inspected and clearly demarcated in the presence of the middleman. This field has a tax payment in unhusked rice of six *sheng* six *he* [0.0066 piculs]. It is irrigated by water from the Jingzailiao Canal. Now, owing to lack of funds, we are willing through redeemable sale to transfer this field to another party. Having thoroughly inquired among our close agnates, none of whom were able to take the land through redeemable sale, we have availed ourselves of the introduction of a middleman, through whom Wang Tianding of Minong Village has come forward to contract for these fields in conditional purchase. On this day, in the presence of the middleman, the three parties have agreed on the basis of market value to pledge the land for the price of thirty silver dollars. Cash and contract are straightforwardly exchanged on the same day in the presence of the middleman, without such fraudulent practices as use of this property to set off debts, or the prior guarantee of redeemable sale to another party. Starting from the day the land is pledged out, it must be personally turned over to the party contracting this land on pledge purchase, for him to cultivate and manage as his own enterprise. The close agnates of the party pledging out the land are not to dispute this or make trouble and disturbances. The period of redeemable sale lease is five years, starting from the eleventh month of the *gengchen* cyclical year [1880] and extending to the eleventh month of the *yiyou* cyclical year [1885]. At the expiration of this period, upon return of the purchase price the land will be redeemed. If the land is not redeemed, the party holding it in pledge will continue to control it in accordance with this contract. Neither party is to be obstinate concerning this transaction, for it is undertaken voluntarily by the two parties, without any compulsion. Today, because we fear that verbal agreement is not reliable, we have drawn up one copy of this contract for the redeemable sale of wet rice land, which is transferred [to the party obtaining the land] as certification.

On this day it is clearly noted that in the presence of the middleman there was truly received the price for land transferred through redeemable sale in the sum of thirty silver dollars. Noted.

It is also clearly noted that if in the village there are local taxes these will be dealt with according to village regulations.

Middleman: Li Haiying
Witness: Father's younger brother Wenchang
Amanuensis: older brother, Chuanxing
Guangxu, sixth year, eleventh month, [blank] day [between December 2 and December 30, 1880]
Executor of contract for the pledge of wet rice land: Liang Axiu, Liang Ayu.

Above the signatures of the original text was a later addition to the document as follows:

Done during the fifteenth year of Guangxu, *jichou* cyclical year, third month [between March 31 and April 29, 1889]: taking into account previously accumulated interest and principal on the loan of four dollars, amounting in all to seven dollars, together with an increase in the redeemable sale price of wet rice land in the amount of three dollars, gives a total of ten silver dollars.

Also, it is clearly noted that truly received as an increase to the price for land given as pledge was the sum of ten silver dollars. Noted.

> Executor of contract for an increase to the price for redeemable sale of wet rice land: Liang Axiu
> Amanuensis: Chuanxing.

The above amendment to the contract is dated four years after the original term for redemption had expired. This amendment maintains the transfer through an additional payment of ten dollars, strongly suggesting that this extra sum was agreed to after the party who originally pledged out the land had threatened to redeem it. That part of this additional payment is defined as a loan's principal and interest and only three dollars as an addition to the redeemable sale price itself means that seven of the ten dollars need not be returned in order to recover the land. As with outright purchases, corporations could also acquire land through *dian* contracts, given that they were fully constituted as entities unto themselves. In the redeemable sale contract that follows, the land is conveyed for payment involving grain as well as money. In fact, the land is transferred by the party who had originally obtained it through redeemable sale, this being but an example of the fluid credit market within this late Qing commodified economic culture, one in which Minong fully participated.

Liu Jingzhao, the executor of this contract for the transfer of land acquired through redeemable sale, in the past through conditional purchase acquired for cultivation a tract of wet rice land. In terms of local place names, it is at Shanzaibei [Behind the Hill], and it comprises a number of fields of varying sizes. Its boundaries extend eastward to the mountain, westward to the mountain, southward to Huang Rupo's field, and northward to the small gully. The boundaries in all four directions have been clearly demarcated. Also included is a row of wet rice fields extending across the high land at Fenjiwo [Manure Basket Hollow] and bounded from north to south by the mountain. At present, because of financial difficulties, I am willing to transfer redeemable sale rights over these fields to others. Through the introduction of a middleman, members of the Zhong Mashi [Zhong née Ma] Ancestral Estate, Zhong Zhengrong, [Zhong] Jingxiang, [Zhong] Jinwen, Zhong Kaichang, [Zhong] Yuhui, and [Zhong] Lianxing have come forward to take these fields through redeemable sale. Today, through the middleman, the three parties have agreed on the basis of current market value to transfer the land through redeemable sale in return for 101 foreign silver dollars [*foyin*] and forty piculs of husked rice.[17] On this day, in the presence of the middleman, cash and grain are straightforwardly exchanged for the contract, without there being things like prior use of this property to set off debts. After the land's redeemable sale, it is to be immediately turned over to the party purchasing it for that party to cultivate and manage as its enterprise. This land truly is property obtained by me through redeemable sale. It is not land already transferred to another party through redeemable sale, and neither have there been such fraudulent practices as multiple transfers of the same land. In the event that previous ownership of this land is unclear, or that there are arrears in large rent payments, none of these matters have anything to do with the party taking on the land through redeemable sale. The party transferring out the land bears full responsibility for such things. Because we fear that verbal agreement is not reliable, we have set out one copy of this contract for the redeemable sale of land, to which is attached one antecedent redeemable sale contract as well as a red contract, for a total of three documents transferred [to the party obtaining the land] as certification.

On this day it is clearly noted that there were received funds for the redeemable sale of land to the amount of 101 silver dollars as well as forty piculs of husked rice. Noted.

Also, this tract has an area of three *fen* and large rent payments and local taxes of 3.07 piculs [three *dan* seven *sheng*]. Noted.

Also noted, if the money and grain are returned before the end of the time limit, the contract will be returned; also, the day of redemption must be during the tenth lunar month. Noted.

Also noted that today the signature money amounting to one dollar is paid by the land's original owner, Zhang Gengxi; later it shall be returned to him on the day the land is redeemed. Noted.

> Mediator/witness: Zhang Yongkong
> Witness: Zhang Yongyuan, Gengxi
> Witness: son, Liu Qiulin
> Amanuensis: son, Liu Nanlin
> Daoguang, eighteenth year, tenth month, eighth day [November 24, 1838], executor of contract for the transfer of land acquired through redeemable sale, Liu Jingzhao.[18]

The "large rent" or *dazu* payments noted in this contract relate to the fact, discussed in chapter 8, that with respect to one plot of land small rent and large rent rights were separate commodities that could be bought and sold independently of each other. In this contract, as in the example given earlier, the corporation obtaining land has as its focus an ancestor, but in this interesting case the ancestor is a woman, Zhong née Ma, on the basis that centuries before it was the eldest of her seven sons who remained to tend and worship at her grave and thereby become the ancestral founder of the Zhong surname in the Fujian-Guangdong Hakka areas, while his six younger brothers went their separate ways. This example also differs from the earlier one in that a man with the Liu surname is transferring land through redeemable sale to a Zhong ancestral corporation. That in this case there is no common membership in one agnatic congregation simply reinforces the earlier point that when there is such common membership among the parties to land transfer this does not change the fundamentally commodified framework within which it takes place. This contract does not specify the original agreed-upon holding period, for this presumably is detailed in the "antecedent redeemable sale contract" transferred together with the land and the above document. Also transferred was the "red contract," the original contract of sale. It is referred to as "red" because it was registered with the local yamen (government office), in this case that of Fengshan County, unlike the large majority of Minong land sale contracts, which were "white," that is, unregistered, and thus totally legitimated and supported by local understandings and local acceptance of signed agreements as binding statements of economic and social transactions. One role of witnesses to a signed document of understanding was to place on record their assent to and support of whatever changes the understanding might entail, including those that might directly concern them. In this case the involvement of two of the witnesses is clear enough; one is the son and sole successor of Liu Jingzhao, the man transferring the land out, and another is Zhang Gengxi, the original owner. The two other witnesses with the Zhang surname are probably his close agnates. Note that another son of Liu Jingzhao serves as amanuensis; as in the previous contract, this son had already been adopted out to one of his father's brothers.

Surprisingly few contracts pertain to rental arrangements as compared to sale or redeemable sale, at least as far as the Minong documents that have come to my attention are concerned. Simple tenancy, whereby the tenant cultivator had neither "small rent" nor "large rent" rights to the land he and his family worked as part of their farm, was hardly uncommon. Tenancy obviously followed from the high proportion of land owned by corporations, but there were also some larger private landlord families in Qing-period Minong. Since tenancy, whether based on oral or written agreement, did not create additional rights to land that could be commodified along lines similar to "large rent" and "small rent," it may be that even written tenancy contracts were more readily disposed of once the tenancy relationship had terminated. In any event, the two rental contracts that I did find hardly pertain to simple tenancy. The first, in fact, is of interest because it involved the creation of "small rent" rights:

I, the executor of this tenancy contract, am Wang Tianyun of the Talou Native Settlement. Using local place names, my own tract of wet rice and garden land is situated within Zhongyun Zhuangtou [Zhongyun Village's Front Neighborhood]. Its boundaries extend eastward to the cart path; westward to elder brother Zhanmei's three plots of wet rice land; southward to elder brother Tingyu's wet rice land; and northward to Yuandong['s land]. The four boundaries of this tract are clearly marked. Another tract of wet rice land consists of four plots. Its boundaries extend eastward to the dry field; westward to the cart path; southward to Diandi's wet rice land; and northward to elder brother Erfan's wet rice land. The four boundaries of this tract are clearly marked. Now I am willing to accept the tenant Zhong Chuanyang as cultivator [of all these holdings]. Should there be any uncertainties regarding ownership of this land, I, Wang Tianyu, will do all in my power to deal with them, for they are not the cultivator's responsibility. For the two parties this transaction is undertaken totally voluntarily and without regrets. Today we desire to have evidence of it and have drawn up this tenancy contract, which is transferred [to the tenant] as certification.

Also clearly noted, in the event of a flood [sentence incomplete in original document].

Also clearly noted is that in addition to the tenant borrowing two locally made foreign-style silver dollars [tu foyin][19] and cultivating the land during a three-year period, the tenant is willing to pay rent in husked rice of one picul according to standard measure [gong(ping) dou]. When paid in full [during this three-year period], this [contract] will be reconfirmed.

Amanuensis: Liu Xiangyuan

Jiaqing, eighteenth year, tenth month, [blank] day [between October 24 and November 22, 1813], executor of this tenancy contract, Wang Tianyun.

The earliest of a series of surviving rental receipts for this plot of land, each for one picul as per the contract, are dated Jiaqing 22, 23, and 25 (1817, 1818, 1820). In the first two, payment received is recorded as for "rent" (dianzu), but in the third there already is transition to payment described as for "large rent" (dazu), meaning that Zhong Chuanyang's "small rent" ownership of this land was confirmed (and maintained by him and his descendants). In this particular contract, the creation of small rent ownership rights is not associated with the development of the land, since the fields given over to Zhong Chuanyang are described as already prepared for cultivation, and it is unclear who the earlier tillers were. But it is also noted that the land belongs to a member of the Talou Native Settlement, such that either direct cultivation or short-term temporary tenancy arrangements would not necessarily be attractive alternatives insofar as land placed within a Hakka-speaking Han Chinese community was concerned. For Zhong Chuanyang, proof of the contract rests in the fact that together with the land he gets the document, with the absence of any witnesses other than the amanuensis, highlighting how social relationships play little if any role in protecting the contractual ties between Zhong and someone from the Talou Native Settlement, about ten miles to the south of Minong. Rather, as noted in chapter 8, holders of "large rent" rights typically relied on locally posted agents, or "managers" (*guanshi*) for rental collection, even if in this case it is not clear where Zhong Chuanyang delivered his rental grain. The contract provides a three-year period after which reconfirmation means permanent small rent rights, with later surviving receipts, although not a complete series, showing payments until 1854.[20] Subsequent developments are unclear, but by 1902, when the Japanese surveyed land now listed in the name of Chuanyang's grandson, the large rent rights had been transferred to another party, presumably through sale.

The other instance of a rental contract seems at first to be a straightforward tenancy agreement, one not involving the creation or allocation of permanent small rent rights. However, the document that follows shows the creativity of the contract as an instrument of transfer, for closer inspection reveals how the rental arrangement is in fact something else:

A contract for tenancy and security money drawn up by Xu Zuolin and his son [Xu] Shan'er. Presently we have a parcel of two-harvest wet rice land that in the past was allocated to us by our [Xu] Ancestral Estate [for us to rent from the estate]. Using local place names, within [the area of] Minong Village [known as] Zhongzhenxia [By the Main Canal], in [the section of land called] Bafenzai [The Eight Plots], there is one plot on the eastern side of the upper row of fields situated crosswise on the surface of the large irrigation channel's [supporting banks]; directly adjacent on the lower row of fields there are two plots, for a total of three plots. This parcel extends eastward to the wet rice field Wang Piguo [rents from the] Five-Grain Ritual Trust [an association dedicated to Shennong, the God of Agriculture]; westward to the high embankment on the surface of the irrigation channel; southward to my paternal grandson Asheng's wet rice field; and northward to my son Awu's wet rice field. The borders on the four sides have been marked out and are clearly indicated. Now because we need money we are willing to rent this land out to a party who will provide a security payment. We have called upon our kin Chen Quanlin, who has come forward and agreed to farm this land, which has an annual large rent of one picul [*dan*]. Today it has been agreed that for this land the total rental grain for the two annual harvests will be 6.10 piculs [six *dan*, one *dou*]; subtracting the one-picul large rent grain, there is rental grain of 5.10 piculs [five *dan*, one *dou*]. Today there has been personally received from the party undertaking to farm the land security money to the sum of seventeen dollars. The annual per dollar interest on this money is three *dou* of grain, for a total of 5.10 piculs [five *dan*, one *dou*] of rental grain.

Once this land has been rented out, it will be given to the tenant who will be in full charge of cultivation and management. The lessee may not dispute the agreement or stir up trouble. The period of rental extends from the winter of the *wuchen* cyclical year [1868] to the winter of the *guiyou* cyclical year [1873]. After the five-year period, if the lessor wishes to resume cultivation he must return the security money.

This contract is entered into voluntarily by both parties, with neither acting under any constraints. Now, wanting to have proof, we have made one copy of this contract for cultivation rental and security money, which will be transferred [to the lessee] as certification.

On this day it is clearly noted that there was received security money to the sum of seventeen dollars.

It is also clearly noted that if in the village there are local taxes, these will be dealt with according to village regulations.

Witnesses: Shansan, Shanwu
Amanuensis: younger brother Shi'er
Tongzhi, seventh year, eleventh month, [blank] day [December 14, 1868, to January 12, 1869], executors of contract for tenancy and security money Xu Zuolin, [his son] Shan'er.

First, it can be noted that there is no middleman in this contract, with all of the stock phrases adjusted to exclude mention of one. Since Shan'er, Shansan, and Shanwu mean "Shan Two," "Shan Three," and "Shan Five," these would all be Xu Zuolin's sons, according to customary local naming practices. One son serves as coexecutor and the other two as witnesses, with Xu Zuolin's younger brother being the amanuensis. Thus outsiders beyond the kinship range of very closely related agnates are completely excluded as signatories. The impression that this deal is being kept quite private, even by local standards, is also supported by the fact that the interest on the security money, when converted into grain, turns out to be exactly the same as the specified rent, once the large rent payment has been subtracted. In other words, Xu Zuolin and his son receive no rental payment from the "tenant" Chen Quanlin, who is also their kin, at the same time that Chen takes on the obligation to pay the one-picul large rent to the holder of large rent rights. Thus while this document designates the seventeen dollars changing hands as "security money," a common enough payment in true rental contracts, this money functions precisely as it would if it were involved in a redeemable sale or *dian* contract, even though it is phrased as a rental agreement. Indeed, the clauses concerning the five-year rental period, with right of redemption, read quite like an aboveboard *dian* contract. Perhaps key to the particularities of this contract is that it concerns a parcel of land owned not by the contract's executor but rather by his ancestral association, from which he himself rents the land. The pledging of land under such circumstances was hardly unknown in the Minong region, as attested to by the fact that it is roundly condemned and forbidden in the written regulations of many associations, including those dedicated to gods as well as to ancestors. Indeed, it will be seen that the last document that I translate and discuss in this chapter very much concerns the pledging of ancestral estate holdings. Perhaps phrasing the contract as a rental agreement was thought to render less blatant the conditional alienation of ancestral land that an explicit *dian* agreement would proclaim. In any event, by not invoking redeemable sale, Xu Zuolin and his son continued to assume responsibility for whatever rent was owed their ancestral association; presumably, they felt that the cost of rent was more than offset by the seventeen dollars they now had for their own use.

Land is also involved in the document that follows, but as a contract it is more an affirmation and clarification of an earlier contractual relationship than the creation of a new one. If additional confirmation of the importance of documentation in local economic culture is needed, it is provided by this example that shows how written evidence provided a legitimating "tag" for major transactions:

The joint executors of this contract, Song Longbo and Chen Bigui, together expended capital amounting to 149 dollars and jointly purchased from Huang Changguan a tract of land west of the cow path in Niupu Village, Minong, having an area as measured by the proprietor [large rent holder] of five *fen*, two *li*, two *hao*, five *xi*, six *hu* [0.52256 *jia*]; also land amounting to one *jia*, seven *fen*, eight *li*, eight *hao*, eight *xi* [1.7888 *jia*]. Now, because the three documents making up the text of the contract and the attached antecedent contracts cannot readily be separated, they are given to Song Longbo for him to temporarily retain, but in the future he must not take these properties to be his own and engage in abuses. In light of this situation, it is only proper that the amount of large rent to be paid by each party as well as the area of land each has acquired be clearly written on a document. Song Longbo has paid out capital of ninety-four silver dollars and gets land whose location in the four directions is eastward to the cow path, westward to the Ye family field, southward to the irrigation canal, northward to [two characters missing]; this share of the land is one *jia*, five *fen*, two *li*, eight *hao*, nine *xi*, six *hu* [1.52896 *jia*]; it has an annual large rent payment in unhusked grain of seven *dan*, eight *dou*, one *sheng*, three *he* [7.813 piculs]. Chen Bigui has paid out capital of fifty-four dollars and gets land whose location in the four directions is eastward to the cow path, westward to his own land, southward to the stream, northward to the irrigation channel. This contract is entered into voluntarily by both parties, with neither acting under coercion or having regrets. Fearing that verbal agreement lacks proof, we specially have drawn up two copies of this contract; each of us will hold one as certification.

Chen Bigui gets land with an area of seven *fen*, eight *li*, two *hao*, four *xi* [0.7824 *jia*], with an annual large rent payment in unhusked grain of four *dan* [4.00 piculs]; again this is certified.

Amanuensis: Jiang Yaoxiang
Middleman: Zhou Lunguan
Jiaqing, second year, second month, [blank] day [between February 27 and
    March 27, 1797]. Parties to the contract: Song Longbo, Chen Bigui
Witness: section head [*jiatou*] Liao Hua.

The different figures mentioned in this document are quite consistent: Song and Chen bear 64 percent and 36 percent, respectively, of the land's purchase cost, there being the same proportionate distribution with respect to the area assigned each and to their large rent payment obligations.[21] The purpose of this document is to reconcile the shared (albeit unequally) rights to property created by a joint purchase with the standard procedure whereby the sales contract and antecedent contracts are turned over to the purchaser together with the land. Since there was no way for Song and Chen to physically share custody of these documents, the documentary record or "paper trail" had to be extended so that each party had acceptable evidence of their jointly held rights. In this contract the witness identified as "section head" was probably the local representative of the "proprietor" (*yezhu*) or holder of "large rent" (*dazu*) rights. It was in the interest of all parties that responsibility for payment of the large rent payment that came with the land be clearly specified.

Moving further away from contracts as such, there follows a document that might be characterized as an affidavit, although in basic format it is as one with the other documents introduced here so far. Like these latter, it is also local, civil, and linked to economic transactions:

I, Liu Shouqian, am the executor of this statement of receipt of payment in full. The circumstances are that because my junior agnate Liu Yuegui from Nanzixian needed cash to set up a sugar mill, he requested that I approach the Fucheng Merchants Guild [Fucheng Hang][22] and obtain a loan from them. On the thirteenth day, fourth month of the *renwu* cyclical year [May 29, 1882], at the home of Song Laikai in Minong Lower Village, lineage younger brother Wangxing was present to contract for the purchase of a plot of dry land [from Liu Yuegui]. I, Shouqian, invited elder brother Zhong Atian to attend as a witness, with Yuegui's debt in the sum of fifty dollars to be taken from Wangxing's payment [to Yuegui] and turned over to Atian, who was to go to the Fucheng Merchants Guild and settle younger brother Yuegui's account. But until now Atian has yet to settle it [because Wangxing never gave him the money]. In the fifth month of the *jiashen* cyclical year [May 25 to June 22, 1884], younger brother Wangxing sold the land to elder brother Song Shousi. The money for which I had been pressing Wangxing has been personally paid in full by elder brother Shousi [who accordingly subtracted fifty dollars from his payment to Liu Wangxing]. This complex situation should be clarified by writing it down. If in the future elder brother Zhong Atian should come to demand payment from Wangxing, the funds truly have already been repaid by me, Shouqian, in settlement of the account at the Fucheng Merchants Guild, and I, Shouqian, am the one who is responsible; Wangxing has nothing to do with this matter. Fearing that verbal understanding is not reliable, I have drawn up this statement of receipt of payment for transfer [to Liu Wangxing] as certification.

> Witnesses: Huang Zideng
> Song Shousi
> Guangxu reign period, being the cyclical year *jiashen*, fifth month, [blank] day [between May 25 and June 22, 1884], executor of this statement of receipt of payment in full, Liu Shouqian.

This document is meant for Liu Wangxing's use in the event that he is confronted by Zhong Atian. The absence of an amanuensis, and the inclusion in the statement of language drawn from colloquial spoken Hakka, indicate that it was composed in a setting less formal than those in which the other texts I use in this chapter were penned. In this somewhat more vernacular environment, the prevalence of "older brother" and "younger brother" as honorific expressions reflects how all parties mentioned in the document were on familiar terms with and socially and economically roughly equal to the person drawing it up. Otherwise, it is in the same style as those documents in witness of transactions seen earlier, for each attests to some kind of change in relationships between people or between people and other resources. The initiation of a contract involves such an alteration of relations, but just as there are transformations achieved by means other than contractual agreement, so are there the appropriate documents.

The signed and witnessed documentation of transformations extended well into the domain of social relations as such. Marriage certainly represented a contract between the two families concerned, but unlike other kinds of contracts, marriage in its ideal and preferred form involving virilocal residence and patrilineal descent was given strong religious affirmation by being defined horoscopically as a product of the cosmic order and ethically as an expression of filial dedication to the continuity of the descent line. In this preferred form of marriage there was a powerful emphasis on religious and ritualized public validation confirming the agreement; the ritual sequence involved the transfer of the bride, her worship of her husband's ancestors, and many other steps that need not be mentioned here. Suffice it to note that this strong ritualization naturalized, as it were, many dimensions of the marriage agreement, including details such as the understanding that boys born from the union remain members of their parents' family, as do daughters until they marry out. These details are not spelled out in documentary form, but rather incorporated into the symbolic, ritual, and religious statements of the wedding ceremony itself. Likewise, nitty-gritty marriage details regarding betrothal payments and dowry were arranged through the go-between and not put into writing, for treating such matters as an ordinary transaction would rob them of what the marriage rituals proclaimed was their cosmically preordained character. It is true that documents mainly devoted to horoscopic and other forms of cosmic-religious elaboration were incorporated into the marriage rituals as ceremonialized statements transferred between the families of bride and groom. But these documents were themselves highly ritualized in content, in physical form, and even in the type of paper used.[23]

The contrast between such documentation of the preferred form of virilocal marriage and that concerned with the practical events and transactions of the kind we have been considering so far is marked, with all the latter documents sharing the structure already noted and a format whereby the contents are largely or entirely businesslike, with at most some minor formulaic appeals to the successful outcome of the undertaking. It is of interest, therefore, that agreements concerning marriages deviating from the ideal are in the same documentary format and receive precisely the same contractual elaboration of detail as do the transformations we have already considered. Uxorilocal marriage, common as it might have been in certain areas and under certain conditions, was quite disparaged ideologically, with the husband who moved into his wife's natal home often the subject of ridicule by his neighbors new and old. All marriages diverging from the intertwined ideal virilocal/patrilineal complex had to be negotiated with respect to every step involved because the reasons for such divergence varied from case to case. Also, and much more important, they had to be negotiated because for marriage deviating from the ideal there can be no ritualization such that details of the undertaking not arranged by quiet negotiation through the go-between could be taken for granted or stated ceremonially and symbolically. Ritualization means, among other things, idealization, which is just what is absent in the deviant marriage forms, for these marriages were expressed as adjustments of one sort or another resulting from varying degrees of grim necessity. Uxorilocal marriage contracts illustrate how substitutions for the ideal form of marriage result in settlements that, just like the written understandings discussed earlier in this chapter, differ from each other because each involves a negotiation process put in motion when the particular interests of the parties to a marriage cannot be satisfied on the basis of the assumptions and expectations expressed and confirmed through the prestiged marriage ritual.

The expected and probably most common form of uxorilocal marriage contract involved a man moving into another couple's home to marry their daughter under circumstances in which such a move reflected the poverty of the son-in-law's natal family and the fact that his new bride had no brothers (or none that were marriageable), with his presence in the household thus providing male labor for the family farm and the possibility of male offspring for his father-in-law's descent line. Following are a pair of such contracts, one signed by the man marrying in as a son-in-law and the other by his parents-in-law, who have arranged this uxorilocal marriage. In these contracts the distribution of the sons resulting from this marriage is specified, as is the ultimate disposition of the family estate. Identical text in the two contracts is given in bold type in the first, and is eliminated from the second:

Good Fortune
The executor of this contract for marrying in is the son-in-law Li Ading. Seeking to marry, through the go-between Liao Awu he has married in and wed the Wu family member with the milk name [*ruming*] Adui.[24] Husband and wife will live in harmony and grow old together. After marrying in **he shall support and wait upon his parents-in-law while they are alive and see to their burial after they have passed away. In the future, when [Li A]ding and his wife have children, their oldest son goes to the Li family succession line. Should there be second, third, fourth, fifth, or sixth sons, they will transfer one to the Wu family succession line. If there is only one son born, he will be the successor in both descent lines.** As to [Li A]ding's other sons, when these brothers later grow up, marry, and are no longer able to live in unison, **each couple will then found their own family and grow old together, with numerous sons and grandsons, and with multitudes of descendants spreading in all directions.** This contract is to attest that the two surnames have come together through [the groom's] marriage in, and each will keep one copy as certification.

On this day it is clearly noted that if in the future father-in-law and mother-in-law have not passed away, but husband and wife nevertheless depart, then there must be received [from Li Ading] **a betrothal gift of fifty silver dollars for [Wu A]dui. Noted.**

It is also clearly noted that if in the future the brothers cannot live together, then farm tools, cattle, and household effects and equipment are to be divided equally between the Wu and Li surnames. Noted.

Go-between: Liao Awu
Witnesses:
    Paternal grandfather's younger brother, Fan'er
    Senior generation agnate, Kunsheng
    Affine, Chen Asheng
    Affine, Xu Laofan
    Mother's mother's brother, Guo A'er
Amanuensis: Senior generation agnate, Kunsheng
Great Qing dynasty, Guangxu, twenty-first year, fourth month, twenty-first day [May 15, 1895], executor of contract for marrying in as son-in-law, Li Ading
The two surnames are [horoscopically] matched for marriage. (RTKC 2.2: 71–72)

Good Fortune
The executors of this contract for marrying in a son-in-law are Wu Shunxing and his wife née Cai. Presently we have a daughter with the milk name Adui, who is seventeen years old. From ancient times it has been the practice that when a girl grows up she is married out. But because we have had no sons we husband and wife have discussed the matter and through the go-between Liao Awu we have married in Li Ading as our son-in-law. He keeps to his own affairs and is an admirably honest man. He will diligently look after his father-in-law and mother-in-law; [omitted text same as above]. This is to attest that the two surnames are pleased with this agreement. We have executed this contract for marrying in a son-in-law in two copies, with each party keeping one copy as certification.
    [omitted text same as above]

Go-between: Liao Awu
Witnesses:
    Mother's brother, Guo A'er
    Mother's brother, Zhu Xiurong
    Affine, Chen Runde
    Younger brother, Wangxing
    Younger brother, Luxing
    Younger brother, Fuxing
Amanuensis: Father's older brother['s son], Wanxing
The two surnames are [horoscopically] matched for marriage.
Great Qing dynasty, Guangxu twenty-first year, fourth month, twenty-first day [May 15, 1895], executors of contract for marrying in a son-in-law, Wu Shunxing, his wife née Cai. (RTKC 2.2: 73)

Although the key stipulations of both contracts are identical, each is executed in two copies, for each represents the assent of key kinship clusters of both sides to the uxorilocal marriage. These clusters are linked by

Guo A'er, whose kinship ties in both directions presumably facilitated the contacts leading to the marriage agreement, although the formal go-between is Liao Awu, who also signs on to both contracts. Among witnesses to the contract executed by Li Ading are only two relatively remote agnates, one also serving as amanuensis, with the absence of brothers or paternal uncles strongly suggesting Ading's isolation from a larger family context, precisely a circumstance commonly associated with poverty and, therefore, with recourse to uxorilocal marriage. In any event, the witnesses that do sign on, as in other contracts, commit themselves to backing up the agreement and stepping in in the event that Li Ading somehow fails to live up to its stipulations. The same applies to those witnessing for Wu Shunxing and his wife, but among these witnesses close agnates are strongly represented, as would be expected with reference to a marriage that brings in a nonagnate male whose sons to varying degrees will succeed to the Wu family estate that otherwise might have gone to a close agnate in the absence of direct male descendants. Thus these witnesses also sign on to indicate their approval of an arrangement that might be held to be against their own best interests.

In the above contracts, Li Ading, the man marrying in, undertakes to support his wife's parents and then see to their proper burial; it is clear that such support is to be rendered in a context where he himself is supported through his working their family farm and whatever other productive assets might be part of family holdings. But his absorption into the family economy is coupled with only limited rights to the family estate, for the contract stipulates that of his sons one must take his wife's surname and that subsequent family division will be equal between the two surnames, such that if there are more than two sons the division in fact will be quite unequal, with those brothers surnamed Li, no matter how many, having to divide among themselves their joint one-half share of those family assets noted in the contract. It is hardly insignificant that land is nowhere mentioned in these documents, for what is not mentioned is thereby excluded; should there be land, and the family did indeed have land when these contracts were written, succession to it will be confined to the Wu descent line, with the Li only getting a portion of the farm buildings, furnishings, tools, and animals.[25] These contracts thus anticipate and indeed encourage early family division in the generation after Li Ading. But the contracts also reinforce Li's agreement to stay with his wife's parents by requiring that he pay out fifty dollars as "betrothal money" in the event that he and his wife leave while her parents are still alive. Betrothal money is incorporated into the ritualized exchanges of marriage in its preferred form, but negotiated orally within a well-understood customary range and, ideally, should be matched or exceeded in value by what the bride brings as dowry, because its ultimate use is to contribute to the endowment of the married couple. But under the circumstances fixed by the uxorilocal marriage contracts, betrothal money becomes compensation for labor lost; ironically, it is less bride-price than groom-price. Such groom-price also figures in the contract that follows, but here right of payment is asserted by both parties to the agreement, with the party taking in the man identified as a widow and her daughter:

The executor of this contract for bringing in a son-in-law is Xiao née Liu of Longdu Village. Circumstances are that I gave birth to a daughter named Axiang who is now twenty-one years old and ready for marriage. Now, through a go-between, Xu Tianfu'er of Minong Village is called in [to be her husband]. On this day, acting through the go-between, the three parties have come to an agreement. Because Tianfu'er's family is poor they are unable to provide betrothal money, so it is agreed that if this daughter gives birth to three or four sons, no matter it be the eldest or second son, the Xiao family as it sees fit can choose one to be in the Xiao family line of succession. In the event that there is only one son he will be in both the Xu and Xiao lines of succession. Through the go-between it is also agreed that after Tianfu'er is called in as a husband, he and his wife have to take care of Xiao née Liu until the end of her days, and only then are they permitted to go back [to his natal home]. If they want to go back two or three years after he has married in, he has to prepare betrothal money in the amount of sixty-four silver dollars, and only then can they go back to his family. The two parties come to this agreement voluntarily and without regrets. After he is called in as a husband, my daughter is joined with Tianfu'er as husband and wife. Let them grow old together; let their descendants be numerous, let them multiply and spread. Now because I desire evidence, I have drawn up this contract in one copy, which will serve as permanent certification.

On this day it is clearly noted that subsequent to his having married in, should Tianfu'er provide the sum of betrothal money, he and his wife can return to the Xu family; Xiao née Liu is not to obstruct this. Noted.

Go-between: Zeng Meizhi
Witnesses:
    Father's older brother, Niao'er
    Father's older brother, Jinxiang
    Father's younger brother, Erxiang
    Father's younger brother, Sanna
    Father's younger brother, Zengxiang
    Older brother, Xiao Agu
    Older brother, Xiao Axi
    Xu Zenglong
    Xu Wanglun

Amanuensis: Xiao Asi

Guangxu, sixteenth year, twelfth month, thirtieth day [February 8, 1891], executor of contract for bringing in a son-in-law, Xiao née Liu. (RTKC 2.2: 59–60)

This contract shares with other uxorilocal marriage agreements conditions pertaining to the distribution of surnames among male offspring and the requirement that betrothal money be paid should the man move back with his wife to his natal home. However, it is one of the few contracts of any kind where the sole executor is a woman, owing to the circumstance that in this particular family there simply was no man to serve as family head or representative to the outside world. As we have seen, a man signs the contract even should his widowed mother still be in the family. Women often cosign with their husbands contracts involving uxorilocal marriage, and they almost always join their husbands as signatories to agreements involving the adoption out of their children. Widowed women commonly appear as witnesses to land sale contracts for which their sons are the executors, given that such sales reduce the holdings of a family that even after division remains collectively obligated to support aged parents. Although this is a subject clearly deserving its own extended treatment, it can be noted here that women appear as active parties—witnesses or executors—in contracts where the transactions impact upon their rights, as defined by the ethics of filiality, to have descendants and to be supported by them. Likewise, it is common in family division contracts that implementation of filial duties such as care of parents be negotiated among those sharing the obligations, with the duties themselves taken as givens. All of this of course relates to the fact that in the commodified and contract-oriented world of late imperial China the major social and economic unit was the family and not the individual, not rugged individualism but rather rugged familism, as reflected in the documents we are considering here and in other areas of life.[26]

In such a social context, dominated by male-headed families, a woman with a daughter or daughters and without a husband or sons might feel especially vulnerable. Yet in the particular case we are considering, a phalanx of her deceased husband's closest agnatic kin sign on as witnesses: her husband's father's two older brothers and three younger brothers together with her husband's two older brothers, these being precisely the kinds of relatives who, with secondary inheritance rights to his estate, might otherwise most resent bringing in a man from the outside to produce successors for the deceased husband's line. Here they support her, perhaps to the extent that the man marrying in felt it to be in his interest to insist that it be specified in the contract that it is also his right to leave upon payment of betrothal money. But the full display of agnatic support also suggests that these relatives would do their best to ensure that if the husband left he would pay up and either leave behind or later return the one son taking the mother's surname.

The following two contracts also involve uxorilocal marriages, but each incorporates additional conditions, such that the two taken together further confirm how under the rubric of such marriage there is created a kind of open space for negotiating and arranging a variety of possible outcomes. In the contract that follows, there is resort to uxorilocal marriage so as to find a replacement for a deceased husband:

The executor of this contract for bringing in a husband who will raise the children is Zhang Qingxisan of Youzailin Village. Now in consideration that previously my younger brother Zhang Geng'er married [a woman] surnamed Zhong, who gave birth to one boy and one girl, that he then unfortunately passed away, and that the family was short of money, there was no choice but to use a go-between to call in Li Axi's paternal nephew Li Wangquan to be [Zhong's] husband. After he is called in as a husband, he is to raise the son to adulthood; all sons and daughters born after he is called in are to be in the Li family line of succession. This contract is entered into voluntarily by both parties; fearing that verbal understanding is unreliable, I execute this contract for bringing in a husband who will raise the children, which shall be kept as certification.

> Go-between: Zhong Shuanglang
> Witness: Zhang Adeng
> Amanuensis: He Asheng
> Guangxu, eighteenth year, being the *renzhen* cyclical year, tenth month, thirteenth day [December 1, 1892], executor of contract for bringing in a husband who will raise the children, Zhang Qingxisan. (RTKC 2.2: 133)

In this contract the marrying-in husband undertakes to raise the children of his wife and her deceased first husband and is allowed to maintain within his own descent line all children born from his own marriage; that is, they will take his surname. The husband gets some security of family membership under circumstances in which his membership in the family headed by his paternal uncle, or perhaps his own physical circumstances, were sufficiently adverse for one reason or another to prevent his marriage in the preferred way. What is missing from the contract is any mention of his rights, or the rights of his own children, to the Zhang family estate, in all likelihood meaning, again, that such rights were not granted and that children bearing his surname would have no share of that estate, which, therefore, would be succeeded to by the son of the first, deceased, husband. Given that arrangement of an uxorilocal marriage contract meant opening the entire procedure to negotiation, the following document illustrates how a nominal uxorilocal marriage was deliberately invoked so as to place the fate of those sons resulting from it within the domain of contractual understanding.

> The executor of this contract for bringing in a husband is Fu Qianyi, forty years old. In consideration that I have a second daughter whose milk name is Daidi, and that she is twenty-one years old and adult, I am now willing to entrust to the go-between Fu Aman the arrangement of her marriage by bringing in as her husband Li Hongquan, the younger brother of Li Gangu, our relative living in this village. Following a period of twelve days after he has married in, he will take her back to the Li home. Let them be husband and wife and grow old together. On this day, acting through the middleman, the three sides have agreed on a betrothal gift of forty silver dollars, and on the same day, in the presence of the go-between, contract and money have been straightforwardly exchanged. If later there is a son, he will go to the Li family's line of succession. The second son goes to the Fu family's line of succession, and after raising him [at the Li family] for seven years he will be brought back to the Fu family. In the event of ineffective *fengshui* [bad fortune], no matter be it the third, fourth, or fifth son, one must go back to the Fu family. In the event that there is only one son, he will be in both families' lines of succession, and each family will act in good faith. The two parties enter into this agreement voluntarily, without regrets, and without doubt that in the future there will be numerous descendants. Fearing that verbal agreement lacks proof, we have drawn up two copies of this contract for bringing in a husband, with each of the two surnames [families] keeping one copy. Also with [the copy for the Li family] is a horoscopic record [*gengzi*] in one copy [for them] to hold as certification.
>
> Go-betweens: Fu Aman, younger brother Qiansan
> Witnesses: patrilineal junior uncle Yunde, Gu Weifan
> Amanuensis: Fu Zhaorong
> Guangxu, thirteenth year, twelfth month, [blank] day [between January 13 and February 11, 1888], executor of contract for bringing in a husband: Fu Qianyi
> The two surnames are united through marriage. (RTKC 2.1: 344–45)

This contract opens with the executor, Fu Qianyi, asserting his age to indicate that at forty years (*sui*) time is pressing for him to arrange for a male successor. The practical issue is the time needed for the latter to grow to adulthood in order to supplement and then replace Fu Qianyi's contribution to the family, most likely centered on the family farm. The religious and ethical issue is the requirement that the family patrilineal descent line be maintained. At this point Fu Qianyi presumably considered himself still vigorous enough to handle family work continuing into the near future, with the result that the agreement allows his son-in-law

Li Hongquan to return to his natal family following an initial uxorilocal move and a twelve-day stay with his father-in-law. This brief conjugal residence was deemed sufficient to establish the marriage as deviant from the ideal and therefore susceptible to the kind of negotiated claim on future offspring as a condition of the marriage, which the preferred marriage form, by its ritual and religious expectations, powerfully denies. Yet in this particular contract the uxorilocal phase is carefully constructed so as to minimally but strategically interfere with the standard expectations of the favored type of marriage. The groom with his bride do finally reside virilocally, so that there would appear to be no question that all but one of their future sons would stay with their patrilineal family and be involved in its expected succession arrangements.

Yet for Fu Qianyi getting one of those sons is so important that the possibility of "ineffective *fengshui*," a tactful but clear reference to early death, is dealt with in a grim but practical way by stipulating that his son-in-law and daughter first raise the son for seven years before turning him over to his maternal grandfather. The stipulations concerning "ineffective *fengshui*," the son's seven years with his parents, and Fu's right to a son, be it the third, fourth, or so on, together give Fu claim to a son even if only one is born or survives to adulthood. As in the other uxorilocal marriage contracts we have seen, there is a stipulation of a sum of betrothal money to be paid by the groom's side. In this contract payment is in fact made, because bride and groom do leave her father's family, whereas in the other contracts payment is stipulated only as a future obligation in the event of their departure. In spite of such powerful assertion of contractual privilege as connected with uxorilocality, in this marriage the contract stipulates reversion to the approved virilocal family arrangement, with bride and groom entering the family headed by the groom's older brother. But the evidence provided by the contract can take us only so far and says nothing about matters such as dowry. In any event, the restored virilocality may be linked to the fact that there is appeal to cosmic sanctions beyond contractual support, although such appeal is minimal in comparison to what is found in the desired form of marriage. As in prestigious marriage, the bride's side hands over to the groom's the *gengzi*, a document indicating the matching horoscopes of bride and groom, but this contract records the act of transfer in its own businesslike text, which ends with the perfunctory appeal to cosmically harmonious marriage, as in the first uxorilocal marriage discussed here.

Contracting for the transfer of children or other people for a price was not confined to uxorilocal marriage arrangements in Minong or else-where. Taking late imperial China as a whole, it is well known that men, women, and children could be sold (Watson 1980). With human beings as commodities it is not surprising that the sale of people should be placed in precisely the same documentary and contractual contexts as the sale of other goods or rights. In Minong such sale through contracts char-acterized not only the acquisition from strangers of infant or young boys for the purpose of adoption, but even adoption arrangements tradition-ally resorted to on the basis of kinship ties. One such contract is as fol-lows:

The executors of this contract for carrying on the line of succession are older brother Sendie and his wife née Zhong. We have three sons. Considering that full younger brother Chengdie is of the same flesh and blood, we willingly transfer our third son, named Dekeng, to younger brother's line of succession on the same day that there is proffered [by Chengdie] fourteen silver dollars as milk money [*ruziyin*]. After the transfer to his line the child is given over to be raised by younger brother. Let this child grow up and take a wife. We wish him numerous offspring, multitudes of descendants spreading in all directions, and a posterity forever enjoying good fortune. Fearing that verbal agreement lacks proof, we have drawn up one copy of this contract for carrying on the line of succession, which is transferred [to Chengdie] as certification.

Clearly noted is receipt of fourteen silver dollars as milk money.

Witnesses:
  Mother, née Huang
  Junior paternal uncle, Guansheng
  Younger brothers Fudie, Baodie
  Affinal kin, Zhong Pengdie, Zhong Xiudie
Amanuensis: Younger brother, Qindie
Xianfeng, eleventh year, eleventh month, [blank] day [between November 28 and December 12, 1856], executors of contract for carrying on the line of succession, older brother Sendie, his wife née Zhong. (RTKC 2.2: 204)

This contract fixes a particular instance of what in an earlier work I referred to as "agnatic adoption," as distinct from "affinal adoption," or adoption of a married-out daughter's son, and adoption through pur-chase. I noted that between parties to the first two kinds of adoption there were ongoing social ties, in contrast to their absence in cases of adoption by purchase (Cohen 1976: 30–31). But it is now clear from doc-uments such as the one above that all three kinds of adoption were in-volved in the commodified world of contractual transactions, where prices and other obligations are specified in writing, although the evi-dence does not warrant assumption that every case of adoption was handled in this fashion.[27] In the above example, whatever the degree of closeness of the brother-brother tie, one adopted the other's son through cash payment. Such payment and contractual transfer has to mean that at that time each brother already headed his own family, for they would not be tolerated if both brothers still were living in an undivided joint family context. Although the payment, called "milk money," may suggest that it is compensation for having nursed the child, it is in fact simply descriptive of a particular kind of purchase. Obviously, the adoption out of a son was a serious business for his parents, not least in the world of late imperial China, where sons were highly valued and their survival problematic given high rates of infant mortality. So, in spite of the money received, it is likely that with three sons, their father and mother were willing to adopt one out only in consideration of the father's younger brother's plight, it being further understood that their son would now succeed to this younger brother's estate and in all likelihood continue to live in close proximity to his biological parents. Irrespective of monetary considerations, there was strong moral support and encouragement for this form of adoption, commonly known as *guofang* or *guoji* in many parts of China, since it meant one brother's facilitating the continuation of another's descent line by giving him a son who was also expected to take care of his new parents during their old age.[28] Two examples of this kind of adoption were encountered earlier in this chapter, with an adopted out son serving in each case as the amanuensis for a contract executed by his father.

A rather different term was used to convey both the fact and the social implications of adopting sons out to parties who in kinship terms were either remote or total strangers. The *mingling*, an insect whose offspring were believed to be carried away by wasps, who then raised them as their own kind, inspired the term "*minglingzi*," a son adopted from strangers. As might be expected, such adoptions commonly reflected the economic desperation of the family giving up the child; for the family buying the child the problem usually was demographic. It might also be expected that such adoptions, unencumbered by prior social ties or obligations between the giving and receiving parties, might be most fully commodified and businesslike. Such at least is indicated by the following contract, even though the family adopting the child out was economically better off than most:

I, paternal nephew Shouqian, execute this contract for adopting out a son. I have heard that a nation's prosperity through the generations is affected by how its monarchs govern, and that each enters into the inheritance of his ancestors; such is recorded in the *Book of Odes*. Yet as the *mingling* has young ones and the wasp carries them off [to nurture as its own], so the ancients had this caring act [of adoption], handed down from earliest times. Now I proceed in consideration of the following. Last year, the *wuyin* cyclical year, on the fifteenth day of the eleventh month, at the *chen* hour [December 8, 1878, between 7 A.M. and 9 A.M.], my wife, neé Zhong gave birth to our sixth son, truly a very bright child. But before he was one month old, his mother fell ill and died. So I thought to myself, with this child without a mother, who could I rely on to be disposed to rear him and endure the consequent hardship? Therefore, after consulting with my [older] sons, I expressed my willingness to adopt out this, my sixth son. On this account, after having first thoroughly made inquiries among my older and younger brothers, my paternal nephews, and other close agnates, none of whom were able to contract for adoption, I then relied on a middleman through whose introduction adoption will be undertaken by Shuangchun, the eldest son of our agnatic kin, senior uncle Furan of Zhongyun Village. On this day, in the presence of the middleman, the three parties have deliberated and accordingly [the party undertaking adoption] has prepared suckling money [*rubuyin*] to the sum of thirty foreign dollars [valued in silver by weight at the ratio of] sixty-eight [ounces to one hundred dollars]. Cash and contract are openly exchanged this day, without any shortchanging and without fraudulent practices such as use of property to set off debts. Upon my entering into this contract, my youngest son, who is in his second age-year [*sui* (children were considered one age-year at birth, two with the lunar New Year; at the time of this contract he was no older than two and a half months)], originally named Ayin, but now renamed Liande, is given over to Shuangchun as his son for him to rear to adulthood. Let this son continue the ancestral line and go on to enhance the family reputation, bring glory to the family abode, and have people sing praise of his numerous sons and grandsons and of his multitude of descendants spreading in all directions. These will all be the descendants of Shuangchun and will have no connection with Shouqian, his younger brothers, patrilineal uncles and nephews, or other close kin. This contract is entered into voluntarily by both parties, with neither having regrets. Fearing verbal agreement lacks proof, I have drawn up one copy of this contract for adopting out a son, and it is transferred [to the adopting party] as permanent certification.

On this day it is clearly noted that as per this contract there was truly received payment of suckling money in the sum of thirty foreign dollars exactly [valued in silver by weight at the ratio of] sixty-eight [ounces to one hundred dollars]. Noted.

Middleman: Li Junyi
Amanuensis: Chen Fengxiang
Witnesses:
    Eldest son, Xinglong
    Uterine younger brothers, Shouan, Shouren, Shouding, Shouxin
Guangxu, fifth year, being the *jimao* cyclical year, first month, [blank] day [between January 22 and February 20, 1879], executor of contract for adopting out a son: paternal nephew Shouqian. (RTKC 2.2: 207–8)

With Shouqian's four younger brothers and his eldest son signing on as witnesses, the core of close agnates confirm the adoption out of one member of their group and thus endorse the severance of ties as proclaimed in the body of the contract. In 1902, about twenty-two years after this contract was signed, the Japanese, now in control of Taiwan, carried out the cadastral survey discussed in chapter 8. According to their investigation, Liu Shouqian, still the head of his family, owned 5.57 *jia* dry field, 1.52 *jia* of "undeveloped" land, and another 1.88 *jia* dry field as his share of jointly owned land, if equally divided among all owners. These data confirm that Liu Shouqian was well off by local standards then, but not nearly as wealthy as Liu Shuangchun (or his family), listed as owning 2.76 *jia* of far more expensive and productive wet rice land as well as 6.92 *jia* dry field.[29] Of course, these Japanese data say nothing about economic circumstances in 1879, but at least as far as Liu Shouqian is concerned, his being signatory to the 1884 "statement of receipt of payment in full," a document introduced earlier in this chapter, shows that even by that time he already had some financial clout and interacted closely with wealthy Minong families. In any event, it is clear enough that financial distress as such was not a factor in this particular case of *mingling* adoption, even though distress of another kind is given some attention in the contract itself. Nevertheless, given the use of boilerplate commonly found, for example, in land transfer agreements, the focus of the contract on the adoption as a commodified transaction is obvious, in spite of the fact that kinship terms are used so as to create nominal agnatic ties on the basis that both parties are surnamed Liu. So, while it is true that both parties were members of one agnatic congregation, along lines described earlier, this contract stands as further evidence that such common membership hardly precluded them from acting as totally independent agents of their own interests. However, their agnatic link did play some role, in that adoption to a family with the same surname precluded future problems connected with the prohibition against same-surname marriage, something taken quite seriously in Minong. As with the "milk money" mentioned in the first adoption contract, "suckling money" here describes more the transaction than any notion of compensation.

With very few exceptions, family division was the fate of any family in which two or more sons survived to marry and to the point that they could later claim their shares of the family estate. The same overlap we have already observed between contractual and other forms of written understanding within one documentary tradition applies just as well to family division arrangements. Recently Wakefield has dealt with family division in a broad survey spanning Taiwan and several China mainland provinces. He distinguishes two basic categories of division-related documents: *fendan*, or documents of immediate family division, and *yizhu*, or documents similar to Western wills in which a future distribution of property among sons is detailed in advance by their father or, in some cases, through joint signature of father and mother, with the principle that brothers have equal rights to the family estate reflected in all documents of family division (Wakefield 1998: 58). Although based on his multiprovincial survey, his findings are rather close to what I found earlier. In my 1976 book, on the basis of documents borrowed and copied during the course of 1964–65 fieldwork in only one small hamlet of sixty-eight families within Meinong Township, I note the distinction revealed between family division as "a contractual undertaking," on the one hand, and the distribution or hoped-for distribution of property through the writing of "a true will," on the other, with seven of the eight documents discussed being of the contractual type, while one was my example of a will. I noted that as a whole the documents "offer concrete evidence of the strength of customary practices of family division" (Cohen 1976: 211, 215). Of the eight documents given in an appendix in full or partial translation (pp. 243–53), one dated from 1939, the rest from between 1953 and 1965. Yet in format, content, and legitimization through use of witnesses, go-betweens, scribes, and the like, these documents were clearly derivative of those written during the late imperial era and, like the latter, were products of procedures deeply rooted in local social relationships and in shared understandings regarding the definition of property rights and succession to such rights.

If in regard to family division there was such variation within a community as small as the one where I did my first fieldwork, it is hardly surprising to find it in the larger but still interconnected society of Qing-period Minong. From among the documents at my disposal I now turn to three involving family division but otherwise differing from each other in important respects, as discussed below. I begin with one clearly contractual, with brothers the signatories to what is plainly the confirmation of a negotiated agreement between them. Family division documented in this way might occur before or after the death of one or both parents, with division during the lifetimes of both parents quite common. Written statements of the brother-brother family division contract variety were probably the most common of all division-related documents in late imperial China (Wakefield 1998: 44–52). The following is one of the simpler Minong documents in this category:

The parties to this contract for the establishment of separate dwelling and eating arrangements, the two brothers, Liang Xiangchang and Liang Wenchang, are Anding Line Liang surname descendants.[30] Each is married and has sons. Now, because our dwelling is small and the number of people living in it is growing, family affairs have become complex and each party will separately seek his livelihood. Today, as passed down from father and mother, all fields, dwellings, household items, farm animals, furnishings, and debts are equally divided, and we have invited agnates and affines here so as to settle the division through the drawing of lots. Each party will manage his own affairs, and there are to be no mutual recriminations. Let each strive to renew the family's fame, with the real hope that in the future the family attains wealth, repute, and splendor. Let them seek these goals prudently.

Item: There is a tile house with front and rear main halls [each with three rooms, and joined on each end by] two side halls [each with one room,] comprising a total of eight rooms [i.e., a compound surrounding a courtyard]; also to the rear there is a one-room structure and also a latrine for a total of nine rooms. Noted.

Item: The main [center] rooms of the two halls and the open area between them [i.e., the courtyard], and also the area on the right [eastern] side of the front hall not divided into rooms are for common use. Noted.

Item: The room on the western side of the front hall goes with the room on the western side of the rear hall and with the eastern side hall. Noted.

Item: The room on the eastern side of the rear hall goes with the one-room structure to the rear, with the western hall and with the latrine behind the house. Noted.

Item: There is a holding of two shares of ancestral land, reserved to support annual worship; this will be cultivated and managed by the brothers. Noted.

Item: To the west of the compound there is a one-room tile house, a plot of garden land, waste land in an area the size of two rooms, and one water buffalo pond, all of which are held through redeemable sale [thus liable for recovery at some point] and cannot be assigned, so temporarily both branches will jointly manage them. All debts to private parties in cash and grain, and debts to deity associations, are to be equally borne by both parties.

Item: It is clearly noted that Wenchang obtains through division by drawing lots the room on the western side of the front hall and the room on the western side of the rear hall together with the eastern side hall. Noted.

Item: It is clearly noted that Xiangchang obtains through division by drawing lots the room on the eastern side of the rear hall and, behind the house, the one-room extension, the one-room latrine, as well as the western hall. Noted.

Amanuensis: Father's older brother Zhaochang
Witnesses: Father's younger brother Chongyi
    Mother's brother Zeng Duanxiu
    Matrilineal cousin Zeng Jinan
Xianfeng, sixth year, eighth month, [blank] day [between August 30 and
    September 28, 1856], executors of division contract, Xiangchang and
    Wenchang.

In this contract, written after their parent's death, the brothers agree to
what is an equal division of their previously common compound into
quarters for what are now two separate residential units, with areas of
the compound still set aside for common use. Most of this agreement in
fact concerns this compound, thus identifying the contract as the product
of a dividing family of modest means, or of one even closer to poverty. It
does not appear that the brothers farmed land owned as family property.
Reference to a share of ancestral land, and to debts to god associations,
indicates that the land they farmed was owned by corporate share-based
associations taking as their focus the worship of particular gods or different ancestors. Since, as described in chapter 8, such associations controlled more than one-third of Minong's wet rice land, their holdings in
fact supported a large tenant or part-tenant population, including the
Liang brothers. Presumably these lands are not mentioned in the contract
because the brothers held no permanent rights to them, with the result
that any understanding as to which brother would cultivate which plot
would in any event be only for the duration of their tenancy contract.
Land and other property indicated in the document as held through redeemable purchase could not be divided insofar as it might have to be returned if the previous owner did pay up for redemption. Limited as the
holdings of the Liang brothers were, the fact that their residential and
economic separation into two families was backed up by contractual documentation provides yet more evidence of the importance of written,
signed, and witnessed understandings in the everyday lives of ordinary
people.

It might be thought that because of the modest economic circumstances of the parties to the division very little was at stake, so that the
outside participants signing on as amanuensis or witnesses were limited
to only a small group of close kin, representing minimal required participation of nonfamily members. To invite even fewer participants from beyond the family might call into question the very legitimacy of a contract
needing for its enforceability the social support provided by outsiders.

They serve not only as witnesses and scribe, but also as mediators or even more forceful participants in the process whereby family holdings are identified, divided into shares, and then distributed among the parties holding rights to them. These nonfamily participants, similar to people serving in similar capacities in other kinds of contracts or agreements, can also be called upon later to resolve differences should these emerge. In fact, in neither family division contracts nor other documents does there appear to be a simple correlation between the economic assets involved and the number of outsiders brought into the proceedings.

In this document all but one of the nonfamily members signing on to the contract are brothers of the father or mother, these relations being the key kin usually appealed to during family division by dint of their social intimacy and their genealogically equivalent ties with all their nephews who are parties to the division. And the only person among these outsider participants who is not a father's or a mother's brother is the son of a mother's brother. In other words, the important social and economic transition involved in an act of family division in this instance received external assistance and legitimization only from a limited number of closest kin, representing those families with which the family undergoing division has the most intimate ties. The mobilization of such a small social network often reflects a relatively unproblematic division process, for if brothers or other parties to family division are unable to come to an agreement, more outsiders, especially those locally prominent, will be asked to help hammer out an accord. If the economic stakes are relatively small, it does not necessarily follow that division will be a smoother undertaking. Almost by definition, whatever the assets may be, they do represent what the contending parties have as joint holdings, which include most if not all of what they own. In this particular instance, division can be seen to involve a straightforward equal division of the family compound among the two brothers, with other assets remaining under their joint control, at least for the time being. Family division contracts, like the one above, for which the signatories are all brothers, state perhaps most explicitly the equality of the participants insofar as each enters into the negotiations with a preexisting claim to an equal share of the family estate. In all the contracts we have been considering, however, the social equality of the parties involved is at least implicitly acknowledged in that the contracts are freely made, and the text of each contract, as we have seen, gives the reason for the action undertaken by the contract's executor. This is true even if it is frequently the case that in contracts involving land transfers and the like the sale of land is due to the increasing poverty of one party and the growing wealth of another. In the documents of understanding that follow, however, relations of superordination and subordination do enter into the picture.

The following division agreement, still contractual, insofar as the agreement of brothers is clearly stated, also involves what appears to be a strong dose of paternal authority:

I, Liu Zhaolang, am the executor of this contract for division through drawing lots and distribution of property. I have three sons; the eldest is Liu Daidie, the second Liu Fudie, and the third Liu Guidie. I venture to say that I have established a material foundation of wet rice fields, dry fields, and house sites whose benefits can be shared. Today, [it is distributed as follows] in concurrence with those close agnates and brothers invited to banquet and to deliberate the division among my sons and grandsons of flourishing agricultural and commercial endeavors for them to cultivate and manage for ever as their own enterprises. At Nantou River, Dashuxia [Under the Great Tree], there is a tract of two-crop wet rice land consisting of five fields, obtained through redeemable sale [*dian*]; this goes to the estate for ancestor worship. Also, at Hebei [River's Far Bank], on the eastern side of Jiadong Shuxia, there is one dry field that cost ninety dollars; it extends eastward to Liu Fan'er's dry field, westward to Liu Aquan's dry field, southward to the edge of the cart path, and northward to Liu Along's dry field; this field is clearly demarcated and goes to the second branch [i.e., the second brother] as its estate. Also, there is the one dry field at Baisanlin, which cost one hundred dollars; it extends eastward to Liu Guanna's dry field, westward to Liu Fulang's dry field, southward to the embankment, and northward to the cart path; this field is clearly demarcated and goes to the third branch as its estate. Also, in Jingualiao Village Rear there is one plot of dry field, which cost fifty dollars; it extends eastward to the cart path; westward to the Zhang family dry field; southward to the Liu family ancestral estate; and northward to the irrigation canal; this field is clearly demarcated and goes to the senior branch as its estate. Also, in Jingualiao Village Front there is a building site sold to the Zhong family for eight silver dollars, which sum is to be equally divided among the three branches. Also, when the three brothers have divided they should conduct themselves properly, with each attending to his own allotment received through division, so there will be no doubt that in generation after generation sons and grandsons will prosper, forever hand down a patrimony, and multiply. The three branches voluntarily and without regrets today draw up in three copies this contract for family division through the drawing of lots and the distribution of property, which are kept [one by each branch] as certification.

Agreed: At Nantou River, Dashuxia, there is a tract of two-crop wet rice land, consisting of five fields, obtained through redeemable sale; this goes to the estate for ancestor worship. Clearly noted.

Agreed: At River's Far Bank, on the eastern side of Jiadong Shuxia, there is one dry field; it goes to the second branch as its estate. Clearly noted. It cost ninety silver dollars.

Agreed: There is one dry field at River's Far Bank, Baisanlin; it goes to the third branch as its estate. Clearly noted. It cost one hundred silver dollars.

Agreed: In Jingualiao Village Rear there is one plot of dry field; it goes to the senior branch as its estate. Clearly noted. It cost fifty silver dollars.

Agreed: In Jingualiao Village Front there is a building site sold to the Zhong family for eight silver dollars, which sum is to be equally divided among the three branches. Clearly noted.

Witnesses:
  Paternal uncles [father's younger brothers] Panna, Jiali, Dengna
  Older brothers Shouqian, Kuidie
Amanuensis: Paternal nephew Yuanlin
Guangxu, eleventh year, eleventh month, twelfth day [December 17, 1885],
  executor of contract for family division through the drawing of lots and the
  distribution of property, Liu Zhaolang
Eldest son Liu Daidie, second son Liu Fudie, third son Liu Guidie.

Although each of the documents presented and discussed so far reflects the commodification that so importantly infused social and economic life in late imperial times, the above division contract is a particularly force-ful expression, in that every plot of land mentioned is given its purchase price, as is also the case in the document that follows, and in that there is noted a sum of money available for distribution. Insofar as this document has Liu Zhaolang assigning property among his three sons, it would ap-pear to be edging toward the will category; the document is styled a "contract for division through drawing lots and distribution," with the term "distribution" (fenbo) often associated in division documents with a decisive act by a parent or other senior, as we shall see. Furthermore, the first portion of the document reads as if it is the father who is de-scribing and allocating land and other family property, and concludes with his urging his sons to behave properly and so forth. But if the fa-ther's action makes this division agreement seem similar to a Western-style will, the context of Chinese family property arrangements renders it rather different. The father is not at all bequeathing his property to his sons, because in the first instance the property does not belong to him but instead constitutes the holdings of the family estate; rather, the document says that he is taking the initiative and overseeing a family division process that might otherwise at some point involve negotiation among his three sons themselves. Thus this document also differs from a will in that it is a contract for immediate division and reads as such in its final portion, which repeats details already given, but now in the context of an agreement among the three sons. The sons together with their father are signatories, and there can be little doubt that the integrated family is at this point separated into three smaller units. According to available Japanese household registration data, at least two of Liu Zhaolang's three sons were married and with children prior to family division. Thus his family had attained a level of complexity requiring close coordination, cooperation and mutual trust among adult family members, all hardly compatible with the penning of a division contract, which therefore would be tightly associated with the act of division itself.

In this division far more property is at stake than in the previous case; yet with six men from outside the family signing on, the involvement of witnesses and the scribe seems not much larger, albeit that they are all agnates. It would appear from the document that the eldest son's share is rather less than that awarded his two younger brothers, but this first son may have obtained benefits not explicitly noted in the document; for example, the agreement sets aside ancestral land without specifying who is to cultivate it. Given that parental support is nowhere mentioned, it may be that ancestral land income was also meant for the senior generation while they (or he) were still alive. In any event, the authoritarian slant of this document may reflect a decision-making process in which the father's power obviated the necessity for active intervention on the part of the outsiders invited to participate.

In the following document, also in the *fenbo* (distribution) category, the contractual element has given way to one party's straightforward assignment of family assets:

I, elder brother Dafeng, draw up this directive for the distribution of property. I affirm that of the six brothers born to our parents I am the oldest. With a poor family and elderly parents, I had no choice but to come to Taiwan in the twenty-first year of Qianlong [1756]. At first I experienced great hardship in establishing the family estate. I was responsible for our affairs and behavior, and I had to cope with our suffering. I managed our business for more than fifty years but was unable to build up any great enterprises. Alas, such was destiny. Now this year I am eighty years old, and the time of my departure is not distant. Considering that the holdings developed in Taiwan are in my name, and remembering how we are brothers by birth, I fear that if we do not now uniformly divide our uncultivated, garden, and paddy fields, and our houses, in the future there will be conflicts and incidents stirred up among the paternal uncles and nephews. Therefore, on this the first day of the eleventh month of the year Jiaqing 11 [December 10, 1806], I have invited lineage and affinal relatives here to banquet and to see to the uniform distribution of the uncultivated and wet rice fields and buildings obtained in

Taiwan and itemized as follows: In the twenty-second year of Qianlong [1757] there were purchased from our paternal nephew Gongyuan and his brothers two sugar mill shares,[31] dry fields, sheds, household items, and cattle for the price of 1,200 dollars; in the thirty-sixth year [1771] there was purchased from our relative Wu Jiu'an one large wet rice field as well as a house site for the price of 360 dollars; in the fifty-sixth year [1791] there was purchased a large tract of dry field at Weilishui Jingualiao for the price of 260 dollars; in the fourth year of Jiaqing [1799] there were purchased two portions of dry land at Xiabeitou from the party surnamed Zhan for the price of 60 dollars and constructed there a large building complex with two main halls and two side halls to their left and right, a gate tower, cattle pen, storage bins, all covering an area extending to the bamboo barricade by [the village's] south gate. Today I divide these dry fields, wet rice fields, and buildings into ten large shares for distribution. [Liu Da]feng's [my] portion is two shares, for sustenance while alive and to pay funeral expenses upon death; younger brother [Liu Da]lun's portion is two shares; younger brother [Liu Da]fu's portion is one share; younger brother [Liu Da]kang's portion is one share; the younger brothers [Liu Da]wei and [Liu Da]an jointly have as their portion one share; [my sons,] the four brothers, [the oldest being] Jingyuan, jointly have as their portion two shares, and one share is for our [deceased] parents to serve as their sacrificial land.

I think it's fine if we divide our holdings equally into ten shares; however, if we were to divide them into ten portions for cultivation, then none could form a viable estate; so it is necessary that one person be responsible for renting and farming the land. Therefore it is agreed that for the large portion of wet rice land extending from south to north behind the house there will be in addition to the large rent payment an annual payment of small rent to the amount of sixty piculs [of rice] going to the person who rents the sugarcane fields. The payment will be used to cover expenses for replacing cattle; maintenance of the house, farm buildings and equipment; repair of the sugar mill; common basic necessities; and the sugar mill tax. Each year the person cultivating the sugarcane fields, in addition to paying the large rent and all other expenses, will pay out annual sugar field rent to the real amount of three hundred dollars to be divided equally per share among the holders of the ten shares. But at present we still owe the money we borrowed last year, amounting to more than nine hundred dollars. Therefore, there will be no distribution of rental for the years *bingyin, dingmao,* and *wuchen* [1806, 1807, and 1808] in order to pay up last year's loan. Starting from the winter of *jisi* [1809], irrespective of the sugarcane crop being good or bad or of the price for sugar being expensive or cheap, the annual payment will be the real amount of three hundred large dollars as paid to the ten shareholders on the basis of equal per-share distribution. The rent cannot be reduced; if the amount due is not paid in full, the sugarcane and wet rice fields will be given over for rent by another party, and this transfer must not be resisted. In regards to someone among the holders of the ten shares wanting to transfer his share through redeemable sale, today it is agreed that irrespective of the amount received for the sale, the annual interest on each dollar will be 15.2 cents. If someone wants to sell a share, the holders of the other nine shares should make ready purchase money to the sum of 250 dollars to buy back this share and manage the enterprise on the basis of nine shares. Redeemable sale or sale to outside parties is forbidden, and this rule shall be permanent.

In regards to the share due elder brother's wife, her annual receipts of rental grain, grassland grain, and rotating credit club funds have been turned over for common use since the fifty-sixth year of Qianlong [1791], with the total amount coming to more than one thousand dollars. Therefore it is fair that elder brother's wife be given control over our purchase of the one-half share of Zhongyun Village land rented by Zhang Zhensheng and his brothers.

After paying up past cash and grain debts, there can be no opposition to payments for land included among the ten shareholders' property in the village against which taxes are levied per area and borne equally half-and-half by landlord and tenant. There are annual payments of owner's large rent, the Zhongyun-wei grassland grain aboriginal's rent [fanzu], and the Jingualiao taxes; these must be paid in full the year they are due by the party whose turn it is to rent the estate; this duty cannot be disclaimed.

Today, wanting to have verification, this distribution agreement is executed in five copies, with each party keeping one copy as proof.

This is to clearly list [holdings and obligations]:
The large block of uncultivated land, area 2.12 jia.
One parcel of wet rice land behind the house, area 2.18 jia.
Second section uncultivated land, Xiabeitou, 0.80 jia.
Jingualiao taxes, 5.922 piculs.
Ancestral Hall Association wet rice land, 0.6 jia.
Zhongyunwei annual grassland payment, 2.0 piculs.
Also, rent to Wang Fusheng, 10 piculs.
Shengmu Association river bank grassland, 1.45 jia, small rent 12 piculs.

Witnesses:
Agnates
Qingjie, Zirong, Mengjin, Sunyuan, Liangxian, Tingfu, Guanyan, Sunhuan, Sunguang
Affines
Xiao Yuexin, Zeng Fengyao, Lin Changming, Xu Rongchun, Jiang Zongde, Li Jibo
Executor of directive for the distribution of property: Older brother Dafeng.
Jiaqing, eleventh year, eleventh month, first day [December 10, 1806].

The key phrase in this document is fenbo; unlike its use in the preceding contract, "distribution" here is not modified by any contractual agreement by the parties concerned. Rather this document expresses Liu Dafeng's determination as to the distribution of a family estate, which, he states, was built up through his efforts and under his management and is held in his name. Liu Dafeng is said to have first come to Taiwan with his father to seek out new opportunities; later they returned to the mainland, and then Liu Dafeng and his brothers sailed for Taiwan once again. They established themselves in Minong's Zhongyun region during the early phase of its settlement, said to have begun in 1748; arriving seven years later, it took them only a year to make their first purchase of land, as recorded above. The document attests to the importance of commercial sugar production even during this early period within, as noted previously, a larger context of thoroughgoing commodification, also confirmed with particular force in this document. In addition to the various rents and payments it mentions, it also describes how Liu Dafeng promulgates the transformation of his family estate into a share-based organization. By assigning shares to particular individuals he attests to their status as property holders and therefore as the heads of separate families, it being understood, again, that men as individuals do not own property but rather control family property. This is thus a document of family division, and the tension between shared ownership on the one hand and separate families on the other is confronted head on. The total division of family resources is rejected in favor of separation through the creation of shares, with cultivation of corporate assets placed in the hands of a tenant whose rental payments for the sugar plantation will be divided among shareholders on a per-share basis. Although not stated explicitly, the wording of this document suggests that the tenant would be one of the shareholders, perhaps Dafeng himself, now as head of the smaller family including his sons, but not his brothers.

If this document is an instrument of family division, several apparent anomalies remain to be considered. First, note that Liu Dafeng gets two shares and his four sons collectively receive two shares. Liu Dafeng's shares are specified as being for his [and his wife's] support while alive and then for burial expenses, such terminology being usually employed in family division contracts where brothers dividing among themselves the family estate leave some land or other assets as set-asides for their parents. Here, however, there is seemingly a structural distortion in that Liu Dafeng defines his shares as set-asides, thus reducing the value of all other shares, not only those going to his sons but also those assigned his own younger brothers, thus clearly infringing on their equal rights to the estate. The imbalance I have just noted holds up precisely because this is a document reflecting Liu Dafeng's single-handed disposition of shares; by describing his two shares as set-asides for himself and his wife, he removes them from the body of assets available for distribution among the eligible parties at the same time that he removes himself as such a party, thereby facilitating the definition of his own sons as the active party whose rights to shares are equivalent to those held by their father's brothers. In so doing, and in the absence of any considerations concerning the use of the two shares after he and his wife have died, Liu Dafeng in effect has defined them either as an ancestral estate dedicated to him and his wife or as shares that could only be held in common by his sons. Likewise, through a rarely encountered appeal to the rights of women to their own property, Liu Dafeng claims for his wife some rental land owned by the larger family, thereby removing this land from the larger corporate holding to which rights are held on the basis of the ten shares. It is indeed the case that women's private property was recognized as a category separate from family property and that there could be property set aside during the course of family division, and the claims made by Liu Dafeng are voiced precisely in the language used to define new property relationships.[32] But in the present case it would appear that the invocation of these claims by Liu Dafeng served to facilitate his or his son's continuing control over a far larger portion of family assets than equal division among him and his brothers would have allowed.

This document fits readily into the category and typology of written understandings common in late imperial China. But we have moved a considerable distance from the sphere of contracts. Liu Dafeng stands alone as instigator; others appear in the text as recipients of shares, but hardly as active participants in the process of deciding who gets what. Even though mention of "agreement" is made in passing, the overriding emphasis is the authoritarian allocation of shares by Liu Dafeng himself, as confirmed by the fact that among all parties designated as recipients of shares he is the only person who signs as executor of this deed of distribution. Thus the division of the estate into ten shares is given as Liu Dafeng's individual decision; the distribution of these shares between the six brothers is decidedly unequal; assigning one share to the ancestral estate of his father, Liu Huasheng, Liu Dafeng gets two in his own name and two in the name of his sons, as noted above; his brother Liu Dalun is also allotted two shares, but the other four either get one share or one-half share each. It is not surprising that under these circumstances the number of witnesses is far larger than in the other documents. There are fully fifteen of them, such that the nine agnates and six affines who have signed on represent large-scale social consent to a procedure seemingly in far less than total accord with local norms of property succession. Given that property relations are sanctioned and indeed protected by the social relationships in which they are embedded, Liu Dafeng was able to mobilize a large group of kin who through their signatures and concomitant support in effect normalized and legitimized the particular arrangement he had crafted.

But from the document that follows it appears that Liu Dafeng's word was not followed by succeeding generations, such that a readjustment was attempted by means of what was indeed a contract, written thirty-six years later:

This contract is made by the people of the six great branches [*fang*] [of the Liu lineage], being Jingzhao, Jingyang, Haidong, Huaidong, Rundong, the paternal nephews Lianglin, Changlin, Senlin, Jielin, Tianlin, Nanlin, Shenlin, Qiulin, Zhulin, and the paternal grandnephew Lüyuan.

In former years father Dafeng and paternal uncles Dafu, Dawei, Dakang, Dalun, and Daan came to Taiwan. They lived a hard life in Zhongyun Village and later gained holdings and lands. They lived there peacefully and the family began to grow big. However, they never went back to the China mainland and were concerned that no one was there to take care of the family graves. So the brothers consulted with each other about this matter and decided to pay paternal uncle Dakang to go to the mainland to take care of the graves and worship the ancestors.

The holdings built up by the brothers had already been distributed equally according to the old contract. Each brother took care of his own share and cultivated the land. In regards to the field by the front of the compound and the field behind the house on the bank of the Beiwei River, they were allocated as permanent ancestral fields for the worship of the honorable Huasheng [father of Dafeng and his brothers].

Later, we paternal uncles and nephews through redeemable sale disposed of the three sections of land by the Zhongdu Beiwei irrigation canal; we still retained one parcel in front of the main gate [of the compound] and two plots behind the house, and each of these was divided up for cultivation and has yet to be given over to the ancestral estate. Although setting up the ancestral estate was a beautiful thing to do it has so far been only an empty gesture. So in the fall of the *renyin* cyclical year [1842], people from the six branches met to discuss this matter and decided that the land belonging to the sacrificial estate must be returned by each family so as to maintain the estate as the source of funds for ancestral sacrifices. In the future nobody will be allowed to resume cultivation of this land on his own. This land should be rented out by the entire group and the receipts should come to the entire group. Those who are among the descendants of the honorable Huasheng are not permitted to rent this land for cultivation; other tenants should be recruited. Except for what is sent back to the mainland to meet expenses for Qingming and other festivals, all rental grain should be stored, whatever the amount. The group will meet for discussion and choose someone who is well off and propertied to store the grain and use it for generating interest. As time goes on, the amount of grain will steadily increase; not only will this provide funds for the sacrificial rites, but it will also magnify the fame of our ancestor.

If only we descendants will work together as one, avoid distrusting one another and provoking strife, and refrain from benefiting oneself and abandoning the ancestors. If we can keep to this path, why can it not be that both in Taiwan and on the mainland we will achieve renown, thrive, and forever enjoy happiness?

Concerned that verbal agreement leaves nothing for verification, we have therefore executed this contract in six identically written copies, with each branch keeping one copy as evidence.

Agreed: Whoever wants to cultivate this sacrificial land, be they agnates [zuqi] or anybody else, must pay forty piculs of rental grain in two equal installments, one each season.

Agreed: When surplus interest becomes available, it should be used to recover for the ancestral estate the land in front of the Beiwei Zhongdu irrigation canal that was given out through redeemable sale last year.

Agreed: Whatever was pledged out [dianchu] or pawned out [dangchu] in the past by common agreement will revert to the ancestral estate upon redemption. So agreed.

Agreed: The descendants are not allowed to take out new loans from the interest or rental grains that are accumulated each year. So agreed.

Agreed: If the interest from this ancestral estate becomes quite considerable, it can never be divided up to take back to the mainland and start enterprises there. The interest will always be kept in the ancestral estate of the honorable Huasheng. So agreed.

Agreed: The common holdings that were not distributed last year go to the ancestral estate to be rented out. So agreed.

Witnesses:
Elder brother Mengri
Paternal nephew Kedong
Paternal nephew Junfang
Paternal nephew Fulin
Maternal cousin Xu Cenglian
Daoguang, twenty-second year, renyin cycle year, fifth month, [blank] day [between June 9 and July 7, 1842], executors of the contract of the six great branches:
Liu Huaidong, Haidong, Jingzhao, Jingyang, Rundong
Paternal nephews Yulin, Qiulin, Nanlin, Jielin, Senlin, Changlin, Zhulin, Shenlin, Tianlin
Paternal grandnephew Lüyuan.

On the face of it there would appear to be a rather vast discontinuity between the older and later documents. The most important difference is that in the first practically all family assets are maintained intact as a corporate entity in which the various parties own shares, including one share set aside as the ancestral trust for Liu Huasheng. In the second document there is no mention of such a corporate entity but rather of the distribution of family property such that the brothers separately cultivated their shares. In fact, these two documents describe the starting and end points of a process whereby the original ancestral trust was blended into the larger corporate holding. Although somewhat different terms are used to describe the locations of various plots, major portions of what had been the corporate entity created by Liu Dafeng are now described as land specifically belonging to the ancestral trust, even though in Liu Dafeng's document this ancestral trust is simply designated as being the owner of one out of ten shares. It is clear from the second document that in the first the apparently hypothetical discussion of the procedure to be followed if one shareholder wished to sell out was in reality the format decided to provide Liu Dakeng funds for his return to the China mainland. Thus, again, what the second document takes as use of resources from the ancestral trust is in the first held to be the purchase of one share such that the corporation would now consist of nine shareholders.

That the corporation—or a large part of its holdings—should later appear to be redefined as the ancestral trust is hardly surprising in the environment of late Qing Minong, where corporations whose memberships were made up entirely of close agnates commonly had ancestor worship as a religious focus and might provide dividends on a share-holding basis. In other words, in the absence of a previously established nonancestral religious focus, it was hard to be an agnatic corporation without ancestor worship, especially if the corporation in part was already dedicated to such worship. Put another way, in spite of Liu Dafeng's expressed desire that the land remain intact, it is clear that the land was indeed divided, although I cannot determine if this was along lines reflecting the proportional distribution of shares in the original document. Whether this division was on the basis of yet another written understanding dating from some time between the two made available to me I have no way of knowing, and it would appear that the Liu descendants who allowed me to copy the two documents also have no knowledge of any others. But from the second document it is apparent that if allowance was made for a separate ancestral trust it was demarcated from a proportion of total holdings far larger than that equivalent to merely one share out of ten. Whatever the story's full details, it seems clear that because Liu Dafeng's plan for family division was simply on the basis of shares to an undivided estate, this estate's distribution between family holdings and an intact ancestral corporation could more readily be negotiated once more. It would be ironic if such negotiation had been made easier by the fact that Liu

Dafeng was the only person signing the original document, for the absence of a contract between parties may have facilitated renegotiation by the descendants as they saw fit. Then, on the basis of the established designation of more land as property of the ancestral corporation, the groundwork was laid for the contract that once again committed the descendants of Liu Huasheng to reunite as a corporate lineage with well-defined holdings.

Among the fifteen signatories to the contract are the sons, patrilineal grandsons, and one patrilineal great-grandson of Liu Dafeng and those of his brothers who remained in Taiwan. I have not been able to identify several of the signatories, however, and given that six branches are mentioned, thus giving representation to the descendants of all six brothers, and also given the document's appeal for amity between the mainland and Taiwan descendants, and that one of its provisions explicitly prohibits use of corporation funds for investments in the mainland, there is strongly suggested the possibility that included were sons of Dakang, who had come from mainland China and later went back. In the end, it would appear that those of his brothers benefiting least from Liu Dafeng's original distribution of shares continued to be severely disadvantaged, for after the passage of at most three generations, the lines of Da'an, Dafu, and Dawei were terminated, leaving only those of Dafeng and Dalun to survive into the twentieth century on Taiwan. In addition to the Liu Huasheng ancestral corporation that continued to unite the descendants of the two brothers, at some point there was also created one dedicated to the worship of Liu Dafeng, and both exist to this day.

The descendants reendowing the Liu Huasheng ancestral corporation signed on to a contract that included some regulations as to how this corporation was to conduct its affairs and deploy its funds. This contract thus serves as both an agreement and an organizational charter. A similarly creative but usually far more complex use of this documentary format was also behind the numerous other corporations founded in Minong and elsewhere during Qing. Many focused on ancestors, with some formed by close agnates for the worship of a near ancestor, often Taiwan-born or the first to settle on the island. Some—such as the Lin and Zhong ancestral associations encountered earlier purchasing land or obtaining it through redeemable sale—took as their object of worship far more remote ancestors, bringing together in Minong persons of the same surname whose origins traced back to different mainland China settlements. Other corporations took gods as their objects of religious devotion or were dedicated to the maintenance of bridges, ferry services, and the like. Since, as noted, these corporations came to own about one-third of the best wet rice fields in Minong, their impact on economic and social life in the region was considerable.[33] Thus, while most of the documents we have encountered in this chapter relate to transactions and transformations at the level of the family and its members, the creative potential of such documents of understanding could be expressed with respect to much larger groupings. Through these documents there could be supported major social realignments within a larger community context. Such documents, then, were significant instruments of social life; they were products especially of those economic and social activities where management and choice loomed large. In this sense, a focus on such documents provides an important corrective to an unfortunately still-prevalent perspective on late imperial Chinese local culture and society, especially that of the countryside, which emphasizes ritualization, custom, and habit at the expense of agency, rationality, and competence.

Whether contractual or another type of document, each document of understanding proclaims that a transformation has occurred and specifies its nature. In some cases the document also serves as a guide to the new procedures and relationships it describes, as we have seen, and in all cases it is meant to serve as evidence in the event that parties who regret the transformation might seek to contest or nullify it. In other words, such a document commits all signatories, be they executors, witnesses, or others, to whatever obligations and transformations are detailed by the text. Such a document also serves to protect these transformations from interference by outsiders precisely by describing them as fait accompli and by setting up a social protective shield composed of all parties who have signed on in one capacity or another. These documents, then, are far more social than they are legal insofar as they are basic instrumentalities in the regulation of social, economic, and even religious affairs in daily life.[34] They are protected by the social connections they invoke in the persons of those signing on. Yet, because they are material evidence, they can indeed be made available to state institutions, such as during lawsuits, about which much has been written as far as late imperial China as a whole is concerned, although I have no record of any involvement on the part of Minong people in such activities.[35] Thus in the context of a "weak" state presence extending no further down than the yamen of the county magistrate, these documents function as double-edged swords in protecting the transformations they record. Rooted in social relationships, they are generally protected by them, but if need be they can be brought to the attention of state authority by parties who feel that there is no other way. However, because contracts and other documentations of transformation were basic instruments in social life, their use was common even in regulating and confirming blatantly illegal transactions, such that they might also serve as evidence of criminal wrongdoing if brought to a magistrate's attention (Osborne 2004: 156). In the final analysis, contracts and other documents of practical understanding were products of late imperial culture as such; they were not linked to particular institutions, but rather were among the basic means used by people to deal with the world in which they lived.

REFERENCE MATTER

Notes

Introduction

1. The Han or ethnic Chinese both during Qing and at present make up more than 90 percent of China's population. According to nineteenth-century Western perceptions of China's sociopolitical and physical geography, the Qing empire consisted of "China Proper" (the historical agrarian China of the Han Chinese), Mongolia, Manchuria, Chinese Turkestan (now Chinese central Asia), and Tibet. The Han Chinese were, of course, concentrated in China Proper. In reading an earlier version of this introduction, a well-known U.S. specialist on China criticized my use of the term "Han," asserting that it was a product of the late-nineteenth-century movement to overthrow the Qing and set up a republic; it was "an invention of Sun Zhongshan [Sun Yat-sen] to focus anti-Manchu activism." In fact, during the Qing period the distinction between Han and other ethnicities within the borders of the empire permeated local understandings where relevant, as in inner or borderland frontier regions where the Han interacted with various other peoples. There was also the fundamental distinction that the Manchu rulers themselves made between Han and Manchu, as in the system of dual Manchu-Han headship of important government agencies and in many other respects. To make recognition of Han and other Chinese ethnicities solely the product of developments during modern times is one example of ignoring the content, complexities, and legacy of late imperial culture and their influence in Chinese culture today. On Chinese ethnicities and their transformation into "nationalities" in the People's Republic, see Harrell 2001b for a recent treatment. The notion of Han ethnicity does not preclude lower levels of ethnic differentiation among the Han themselves as with Hakka, Cantonese, Shanghainese, and so forth.

2. In China it is not uncommon for a region's inhabitants to claim a shared ancestral place of origin, or a series of such places. See, for example, Szonyi 2002: 26–27 for the Fuzhou area, where Gushi County in Henan Province is the claimed ancestral homeland. During recent years the revival of interest in ancestral and genealogical matters has led not only to the reconstruction of ancestral halls and the publication of genealogies, but even to the reemergence of national

surname associations. In 1995, during an earlier visit to Meixian, in Guangdong Province, I was taken to the home of a local scholar who was in communication with a national surname association (focused on his surname) based across the country in the northern province of Shaanxi.

3. For an anthropologist's analysis of factors leading to the construction of the Hakka common ancestral hall, see Shi 2000.

4. "Traditionalism" as used here should not be confused with the same term employed to describe the ideology of reactionary antimodernity movements in Europe, especially during the early twentieth century. On these, see Sedgwick 2004.

5. In 1964–65 my fieldwork in the south Taiwan village of Yanliao, in Meinong Township, Gaoxiong [Kaohsiung] County, was over a period of eighteen months. In 1970–71, a year's fieldwork conducted jointly with Professor Burton Pasternak was focused on Meinong Township as a whole. Fieldwork in Hebei Province, Xincheng County, Yangmansa Village took up two months in 1986 and two in 1987. In 1990 I first spent about three months in Shenjiashang, a village in Huacao Township, Shanghai County (now incorporated into Minhang District in the city of Shanghai); from there I went to Sichuan Province, where I spent about another three months in Dadingqiao, a village in Meishan County.

6. See, e.g., Fei 1939; Freedman 1958, 1966; Fried 1953; Hsu 1948; Lin 1947; Osgood 1963; Skinner 1964–65; M. Yang 1945. Sociologists such as Sidney Gamble and C. K. Yang were also active contributors to China ethnographic research during this period.

7. For recent overviews of this research in Hong Kong, see Watson and Watson 2004; for Taiwan, see Hsu and Lin 1999 and Hsu and Huang 1999 (especially Harrell's article).

8. See, for example, Ma 1999; He 2000; Huang 1999; Wang 1995.

9. Harrell 2001a focuses mainly on trends in China anthropology as they pertain to the work of non-Chinese researchers.

Chapter One

1. See Naquin and Rawski 1987; and Richard J. Smith 1994 for excellent general surveys of Chinese culture and society during Qing.

2. All page-number references in the text are to the 1970 reprint of Smith's *Village Life in China*, for which this introduction was originally written.

3. There is by now a large body of literature on local organization in late imperial China. C. K. Yang's classic study (1944) describes hierarchies of market towns and marketing arrangements in a county in Shandong, the province that Arthur Smith deals with in his book. But the works of G. William Skinner have provided a framework for the study of Chinese local and regional organization and set standards of analysis, starting with his 1964–65 articles on marketing in rural China. Then, in his own contributions to a book on the late imperial city that he also edited (Skinner 1977a–d), and in Skinner 1976 and 1985, he expanded his scope to include urban-based regional systems up to the level of the several "macroregions" into which China as a whole was divided. Kuhn's study

(1970) of militia mobilization during late Qing helped firm up the understanding that levels or hierarchies of local, that is, spatial, community arrangements reflected organizational tendencies inherent in Chinese culture, as distinct from the economic functions of marketing systems. Groves 1969 is an early but still outstanding analysis of how one particular instance of mobilization involved preexisting social hierarchies of community and market organization.

4. The best studies of social mobility during late imperial times remain Chang 1955, 1962; Ho 1962; and March 1961. These largely focus on mobility into, out of, and within the degree-holding classes.

5. Rawski 1979 is still the best source of information on overall literacy rates in China during Qing. Given local variations and differences along a continuum ranging from full literacy, including mastery of the classical texts, at one extreme to recognition of "only a few hundred characters" at the other, she concludes that 30 to 45 percent of men but only 2 to 10 percent of women were literate during late Qing (1979: 140).

6. Tenancy contracts were responsive to market conditions. Rental auctions, during which the farmer bidding the highest rent obtained tenancy rights, often through an oral one-year contract, were associated with a demand for land far greater than what was available. At the other extreme, where land was plentiful but cultivators scarce, written contracts gave tenants permanent cultivation rights on the basis of use fees incorporated into the contract's text (on the latter, see chapter 9).

7. Present-day China has seen the massive comeback of rotating credit clubs and other credit arrangements with roots in late imperial culture; all of these are making a contribution of major significance to China's current very rapid economic development. See Tsai 2002 for an original and comprehensive analysis, largely based on fieldwork.

8. My brief discussion of the ceremonial sphere of the economy in this essay, originally published in 1970, anticipated by many years the discovery (or rediscovery) of this domain of Chinese life by anthropologists doing fieldwork in the 1980s and 1990s. See especially the ethnographic works by Mayfair Yang (1994) and Yunxiang Yan (1996).

9. This discussion of the Chinese family can be referred to in conjunction with the consideration of Chinese family arrangements in north China found below in chapter 4. Also see Cohen 1976.

Chapter Two

1. As any decent dictionary will note, Mandarin the language derives from "mandarin," meaning "government official," via Portuguese. An interesting account of Mandarin as the common speech of Qing officialdom, and of the extent of its dissemination even in the city of Canton (now Guangzhou) during the first half of the nineteenth century, is provided in Meadows 1847: 13–58.

2. See the articles in Johnson, Nathan, and Rawski 1985.

3. See Watson 1985, 1988a.

4. See the essays in Liu 1990.

5. Rawski 1988.

6. See, for example, Watson 1988a; Wolf 1989.

7. Skinner 1964–65.

8. The classic English-language treatment of this subject is Levy 1967. Important recent works having a bearing on footbinding include Mann 1997 and Ko 1994, 2001, but these mainly focus on footbinding in the elite cultural context. Gates 1999, 2001 deal with footbinding in society at large and stress how it could be compatible with women's economic productivity in a commodified family context.

9. On this subject, see Skinner 1977c.

10. For example, many of the non-Han groups regarded as "raw savages" during the Qing had already taken to wearing Han-style clothing.

11. Hsu 1948. Another important earlier study is Fitzgerald 1941. David Wu 1990, 1991 discusses the Bai with reference to the issue of ethnicity in modern China.

12. The Manchus imposed their hairstyle on all Chinese men shortly after their conquest of the country. See Kuhn 1990: 53–59.

13. For one interpretation of the implications of the "bureaucratic model" in Chinese popular religion, see Ahern 1981. A view of this model as shaping popular religion is provided by Wolf 1974. On ritual and visual standardization, see J. Watson 1985. To embrace the "bureaucratic model" with excessive enthusiasm is to invite criticism that this model hardly accounts for the totality of Chinese popular religion. Such criticism is the uniting theme in Shahar and Weller 1996. But rather than seeing or denying the "bureaucratic model" as the defining factor in Chinese popular religion, it is more useful to place those elements of Chinese religion reflecting this model within the larger array of beliefs, rituals, and images comprising this religion as a whole. What needs emphasis is that Chinese popular religion frames and represents local social and political arrangements, some involved with the "bureaucratic model" but others going far beyond it. The important issue is not the state's monopolization of religion, for it is impressive enough that the "bureaucratic model" is based on evidence of the imperial establishment's widespread penetration of local religion and culture.

The general issue of Chinese popular religion's representation of social arrangements is taken up at length by Sangren in an analysis of "the productive force or power of ideological alienation," which he takes to "invert the relations between producer and product" (Sangren 2000: 1–2), such products importantly including representations in the domain of Chinese popular religion. Somewhat surprisingly he refers to this line of analysis as "Marxian" and makes no mention of Ludwig Feuerbach, whose analysis of religion, especially Christianity, appears to accord far more closely with Sangren's. Feuerbach saw religion "as an alienated form of human emotion" where the "relation between subject and object was reversed . . . it no longer appeared that Man created God, but that God created man" (Jones 2002: 105). Marx famously repudiated Feuerbach's theory of alienation precisely because of its involvement with religious ideas and critiques (Jones 2002: 141), so that from the point of view of Marx's later classical writings, Sangren's approach might very well be considered anti-Marxist. But Sangren's analysis of course accords with the more general approach of China anthropology, which sees much of popular religion's content as in one way or another projecting or reflecting basic social and psychosocial patterns.

14. On the contrasts between "heterodoxy" and the dominant form of popular religion, see Cohen 1988, Liu and Shek, eds., 2004.

15. Translated in Ramsey 1989: 3.

16. See Hung 1985: 158–60, and Duara 1991. The small number of folklorists who are the subject of Hung's book might be held to represent a countercurrent during the May Fourth era of antitraditionalism. While sharing the pronounced anti-Confucianism of other Chinese intellectuals, they held that the gap between the masses and China's modern elite had to be bridged. Key to this effort was the recording, publication, and analysis of folk literature, which they saw as a form of traditional creativity suppressed by the old Confucian elite. Among the folklorists there was an even smaller group who viewed popular religion with sympathy and emphasized its importance for people in the countryside. Nevertheless, they also shared the view that these beliefs were superstitions that would have to be eliminated as China developed. For them as for other Chinese intellectuals, popular traditions were to have no role in the construction of a new nationalism.

17. The force of nationalism in present-day Chinese culture, absent other elaborated cultural unifiers, continues to receive notice, as in Nicholas D. Kristof's op-ed column in the *New York Times*, December 20, 2003. Kristof writes how he is troubled by the "growing nationalism that the government has cultivated among young people," concluding that "the Chinese government has been pushing nationalist buttons in an effort to create a new national glue to hold the country together as ideology dissolves." Kristof here presumably refers to Maoism as the dissolving ideology, but my point is that the "national glue" that has yet to be replaced is late imperial culture.

18. See Hobsbawm 1990. Although China does not figure importantly in Hobsbawm's analysis, its traditional culture matches all his criteria for the "popular proto-nationalism" that elsewhere contributed to the construction of modern nation-state ideologies.

19. There are separate national religious associations for Buddhists, Muslims, Taoists, Protestants and Roman Catholics.

20. The destruction or conversion of village temples toward the end of the Qing dynasty as decreed by the government is described in Duara 1988: 148–55.

21. On the religious revival see, for example, Jing 1996; Lozada 2001; Pas 1989. Most recently, the official attitude regarding the much-reviled popular religion has been showing signs of change.

For example, in Chinese government circles, increasingly replacing the hostile designation of this religion as "feudal superstition" is the far friendlier phrase "popular beliefs." Yet, notwithstanding this apparent change in attitude, and the large-scale reemergence of religious activities since the early 1980s, the Chinese state is still quite capable of attacking religious organizations it deems undesirable, a major case in point being the Falun Gong movement. Even campaigns against elements of popular religion are still launched, as with the movement during 1995 and 1996 to rid Beijing's restaurants of images of the God of Wealth (McCarthy 2004).

22. For a discussion of Mazu as a case illustrating the Taiwan government's present policy of actively embracing and interpreting elements of popular religion, see Sangren 1988.

Chapter Three

1. On the emergence of a new popular culture and its transnational dimensions, see Davis 1999; Watson 1997.

2. Hayford 1990: 113. For more on the transformation of farmers into peasants, see p. 62. Hayford's discussion in this book and in some later, unpublished writings is the stimulation for my own consideration of the role of the "peasant" in modern Chinese culture.

3. James Yen is the subject of Hayford 1990, and Liang Shu-ming's life and works are considered in Alitto 1979. Representative works of the social scientists include Fei 1939; Lin 1947; C. K. Yang 1959; Martin M. C. Yang 1945.

4. On such elite views, see Nathan 1985.

5. See P. Cohen 1992: 82–113.

6. The significance of such terms will be evident from perusal of the partial but comprehensive listing provided in Li Yu-ning 1971: 70–107. A much larger listing of new terms taken into modern Chinese, including words from Japanese as well as from other languages, is in Liu 1996: 265–374.

7. In Hayford 1990, but especially in Hayford 1992.

8. Thus the term *nongmin* is nowhere to be found even in the second and final edition (Giles 1912) of what for its time had been the definitive Chinese-English dictionary. This large volume, representative of late-nineteenth-century Mandarin, glosses as "labourers; agriculturalists" the terms *nongfu, nongding, nongjia, nongren, zhuanghu,* and *zhuangjiahan.* Most of these terms, and several not in the Giles work, are glossed as "farmer" in Mathews 1931. Mathews glosses *zhuangjiahan* and *zhuanghu* as "farmers; peasants" and the term *minfu* (which I have not found in Giles) as "coolies; peasants." *Nongmin* does make its appearance in his dictionary, in the totally Japanese-derived phrase *nongmin xiehui,* glossed as "Peasants Union." Mathews's dictionary superseded Giles's product, and a slightly revised 1944 edition is still widely used today. Cortenay H. Fenn's dictionary, first published in 1926, likewise has long served as a source of basic vocabulary; in its fifth and last edition with major revisions (Peking: 1940) there is still no entry for *nongmin,* with terms such as those listed by Giles and Mathews being glossed as "farmer," "farm laborers," or "husbandman." As far as I have seen, *nongmin,* glossed as "peasant" or sometimes as "peasant; farmer" is a standard entry in all Chinese-English dictionaries of the modern language published during recent decades in China, Taiwan, Hong Kong, and elsewhere. According to several knowledgeable Chinese with whom I have consulted, the most common "prepeasant" term for "farmer" probably was *nongfu.*

9. For a classic study of the European transformation, see Weber 1976.

10. Mote 1977: 102–3.

11. On this, also see the other essays in Skinner, ed., 1977.

12. For good descriptions of land reform campaigns, see C. K. Yang 1959, which is based on fieldwork observations, and Friedman, Pickowicz, and Selden 1991, which describes the process as reconstructed on the basis of later long-term fieldwork and interviews. See Kraus 1981 for a general discussion of the role of class in China during the Maoist era.

13. Chan, Madsen, and Unger 1992: 283.

14. For a comprehensive discussion of the origins and social implications of the distinction between peasants and workers or urban residents, see Potter and Potter 1990: 296–312. Recent years of rapid economic growth in the coastal regions, the spread of private or privately managed firms, and the continual shrinkage of state-owned enterprises have encouraged the appearance of a vast, overwhelmingly peasant-registered "floating population" seeking work in the cities. See Zhang Li 2001.

15. On the use of these terms, see Liu 1992: 293–316.

16. Household registers in the Hebei village where I did fieldwork carried the notation "peasant changed to nonpeasant" (*nongmin zhuan feinongmin*).

17. In the entire village, with a population of about 650, there were only 29 people (28 of them women) whose major employment was agriculture. They were all vegetable farmers working on what was left of village land. However, because they were assigned their own plots by the village-run vegetable farm, with their income based upon individual output, they were assisted during the busiest phases of work by other family members, whether they were "workers" or "peasants."

18. For classic studies in this tradition, see Wolf 1966; also Shanin 1971.

19. Hill 1986: 9.

20. For discussions of this controversy, and evaluations of some of the major writings involved, see Feuerwerker 1990; Myers 1991; Huang 1991; Wong 1992. Some additional relevant works include Brandt 1989; Faure 1989a; Huang 1985, 1990, 2001; T. Rawski 1989. Walker 1999 is another recent participant in this controversy. Without ever explicitly telling us what a peasant is, she considers that as originally published, my article, which is now this chapter, takes peasants to be farmers because "in both practice and attitude they had become petty capitalist entrepreneurs" (257, n7). All this ignores the key elements of social and cultural commonality, especially as in family organization, including the diversification of family economic activities, even though her book makes such diversification between agriculture and other sources of income key to her approach to rural society. It is hardly my point that they are "petty capitalist"—terms that never appear in my discussion—but rather that they are Han Chinese.

21. On the development of the economic culture approach, see M. Cohen 1992. For more on contracts, corporations, and credit in Chinese economic culture, see chapters 8 and 9, below. Also see Chen and Myers 1976, 1978; Freedman 1979a; E. Rawski 1989; Sangren 1984.

22. For discussions of family diversification strategies and consequences in both late imperial China and in more modern contexts, see Cohen 1976, 1992.

23. See Fei et al. 1986.

24. On the "floating population" and its interconnections with family arrangements, see Zhang Li 2001.

25. For discussions of such attitudes among both power-holding and opposition intellectual and political elites in China, see Young 1992 and Perry 1992.

Chapter Four

1. The field research involved two-month stays in Yangmansa during 1986 (October, November) and 1987 (March, April), plus an additional five days there during the intervening lunar New Year period.

2. Population and household figures are as of April 1, 1987. Those for all of present-day Yangmansa (including Jumansa) are based for the most part on the household registers kept by the village government, which do not necessarily reflect actual family residential arrangements. My only correction to these records has been addition of family members resident in the village but registered elsewhere, usually as a consequence of salaried employment in a "unit," which changes their status from "peasant" (nongmin) to "nonpeasant" (feinongmin) or "worker" (gongren). In urbanized areas of China, another possible status change would be from "peasant" to "urban resident" (jumin). For more on the development of the "peasant" category in contemporary China, and its cultural and political implications, see chapter 3, above.

The figures for old Yangmansa also reflect the same modified household registration data. In fact, my own survey reveals that there were 272 economic households when figured on the basis of residence and commensality, but even this finding says far too little about actual family arrangements, as I will show in this chapter.

3. See below for more on women's property (sifangqian in standard Mandarin).

4. Implementation of this policy began in 1980. During my 1986–87 fieldwork there had not yet been a major impact on family organization as such, even though recent births did reflect the one-child (or, in some cases, two-child) policy of the government.

5. See Yan 1996 for a description of these procedures in rural northeastern China. Contribution ledgers compiled as guests arrive and present gifts of cash are characteristic of weddings, funerals, or other family-sponsored events in Japan, Korea, and Vietnam, as well as in China. Such prevalence throughout China-influenced East Asia suggests that this pattern of gift giving and accounting has a long history.

6. "State grain" refers to grain purchased at prices subsidized by the government. Such grain was available to people with urban or worker household registrations. Those with "peasant" household registrations were expected to use grain they themselves grew, and if this did not suffice, their only recourse would be to purchase grain in the "free market," at prices higher than state grain.

7. During my 1990 fieldwork in the village of Dadingqiao, Meishan County, Sichuan, the local party secretary explained to me in some detail how fangchan, or conjugal unit property, was assembled and defined through marriage and how

it was not liable to claims by other *jia* members during family division, exactly as I was told earlier in Taiwan and in Hebei.

8. Although based upon my field research in Yangmansa, this brief summary of the place within the larger family economy of women's personal holdings (*sifangqian* in standard Mandarin) applies just as well to the other villages where I have done fieldwork: in Taiwan, near Shanghai, and in Sichuan. For Taiwan, I have provided a detailed description and analysis of women's private property (Cohen 1976: 178–91), including references to the subject in earlier literature dealing with mainland China. But it was only later that Serruys (1947: 33–34) came to my attention; quoting from a report by E. Wauters, he provides an especially important description of women's property of particular relevance to Yangmansa, for it concerns the old Jehol (Rehe) Province, portions of which are now part of northern Hebei. The following extracts are of sufficient significance to warrant my adding them here:

> *T'i-hsi* [*tixi*], also *t'i-ch'i* [*tiqi*], mostly consists of money that is invested but also it may consist of land, beasts, such as chickens, sheep, goats, pigs, cows, etc. The *t'i-hsi* has its origin from the money that the bride has got from her own family, or money that she has earned and saved before or after marriage, or sometimes from the money that her husband has had to give her at marriage. The reason for the *t'i-hsi* and its income together with the money she gets from the family, is said to help the wife in caring for the clothing and other special expenses made inside her own family branch, and also to be wealthier and have easy means of life when later on the family wants to separate. This way the *t'i-hsi-ch'ien* [*tixiqian* or "*tixi* money"] does many services and has a good side.
>
> *T'i-hsi-ch'ien* however also has its bad side, because it often happens that money or objects are stolen or kept back in order to form a *t'i-hsi* or to increase it, f.i., by cheating in buying and selling anything, or keeping back the wages earned outside, stealing of grain etc. in detriment of the head of the family. It also happens that the community-affairs are neglected by different branches of the family, or that the different branches lack cooperation and are too much occupied with increasing their own *t'i-hsi* part. This way it may happen that every branch is busy growing wealthier, while the family is becoming poorer and poorer, so that debts have to be divided among themselves in order to be paid. The *t'i-hsi-ch'ien* also gives many occasions for jealousy and disunion within the different branches of the family. It is the reason for separation of the branches [i.e., family division].

Given its close association with other elements in Han Chinese property relationships, it is not surprising that women's property has deep historical roots, as does its use as a conduit for the deflection of family funds. Schurmann 1956: 511 mentions how during Southern Song a commentator on family matters noted that "family members often sought to aggrandize their private holdings through a variety of subterfuges, such as claiming it as the wealth of the wife (the traditional foreign element in the Chinese family), thus withdrawing it from the category of things to be equally divided among the heirs."

9. Although it has been reported (C. K. Yang 1959) that the marriage code did lead to agitation for divorce in rural China, especially on the part of recently married women, there appear to have been few such cases in Yangmansa. Nevertheless, local cadres did take part in a national campaign to discourage what was feared might turn into a massive wave of marital separations. Villagers reported that these cadres "began propaganda work in 1952–53; that was when the divorce cases began," and that "they tried to mediate; if this didn't work, they granted the divorce. Not many people wanted to divorce." My own survey of old Yangmansa did not reveal a single case of divorce during the 1950s. Out of a total of seven divorces, one (involving the only pre-Communist uxorilocal marriage) took place before 1949, while the earliest of the others dated from 1964. It is quite possible that the survey may have missed some cases from this early period, and there may have yet been others in the part of the village that was not covered. Nevertheless, it is clear enough that if there were divorces, there could not have been very many.

The absence of divorce in the 1950s is not surprising given that marriage continued to involve the transfer of a woman from one family corporation to another, in a social and economic environment in which membership in such a corporation remained essential for survival. Where could a divorced woman go if her natal family refused to take her back, as would generally be the case? Traditional alternatives such as nunneries or brothels had always been most unpleasant prospects, and under the Communists many of these alternatives to family life had been eliminated, as had others such as servitude or concubinage in wealthy homes. Yet other arrangements substituting for marriage, such as religious retreats or vegetarian associations organized by women, were given even greater negative evaluation than they had received in the past, and the Communists—especially during this early period of their rule—offered precious few alternatives in rural China as a whole for the many women who might otherwise have been candidates for divorce.

10. Data concerning women marrying out are too sparse to be of use, and since this category would include a small number of women marrying into urban areas, it may be that the total proportion of women involved in "free love" marriages is somewhat higher than my figures indicate. There can be no doubt, however, that "free love" marriages were quite uncommon even at the time of my fieldwork. As of 1987, there was no indication that the trend was toward a proportional increase in this form of marriage: only five of the fourteen "free love" marriages took place after 1982, out of a total of sixty-two marriages, with no relevant information concerning seven of these. Indeed, except for two such marriages in 1979, and two in 1984, each of the remaining "free love" marriages for which I have information occurred during a year when it was the only marriage of its kind.

11. The terms *xiaodengji* and *dadengji* literally mean "small registration" and "large registration," perhaps reflecting the Communist-era importance of bureaucratic involvement in marriage, as represented by registration at the township government office. *Xiaoding* and *dading* precisely mean "small betrothal" and "large betrothal."

12. This custom was known as *xiangkan*, or "mutual visiting." See, for example, Takeda 1935: 4–7. During such visits neither of the prospective spouses would accompany their parents and other family members, but when one party reached the other's home they would want to see the young person who might become bride or groom.

13. See Gamble 1943.

14. The value of the labor of individual family members, as well as that of the family as a corporation, would also be conditioned by political factors such as class designation; "poor peasants" and "lower-middle" peasants were in an especially favorable position, while "landlords" and "rich peasants" could suffer many forms of discrimination and might be the targets of public abuse during various state-sponsored campaigns. Furthermore, villagers in leadership positions or with greater political influence in the production teams and brigades or in the commune as a whole might enjoy certain advantages, as when, for example, they partook of feasts prepared to entertain outside cadres from the county or higher government and party levels. Other than the finding that "landlord" and "rich peasant" families found it more difficult to obtain spouses for their children, I do not have the data that would reveal the impact of such political assets and liabilities on marriage patterns and the associated economic transactions.

15. That this form of betrothal payment emerged during the collective era in many areas of China is confirmed by my later fieldwork findings in villages in Sichuan and near Shanghai. For more on betrothal payments in Guangdong, see Siu 1993.

16. The link between *caili* and poverty has been reported in the literature concerning other areas of north China. According to Yang Derui's description of practices in Beijing during the early 1920s, for example, "destitute families do not send dowry; on the contrary, they may even demand several yuan's worth of *caili*" (1973: 145).

17. For more on the relationship between weddings and the assertion of a woman's right to private property, see Cohen 1976: 178–90.

18. Huang 1985: 258 describes similar distinctions with respect to wedding banquets in a Hebei village north of Beijing.

19. In Chinese the term for this clothing is "*Zhongshan zhuang*," or "Zhongshan-style clothing," referring to the uniforms popularized by Sun Zhongshan (Sun Yat-sen) as revolutionary attire for members of his party or for other activists in the construction of the new China he envisioned. Having spent considerable time in Japan, he based the style on uniforms worn by middle school students in that country.

20. See Yan 2003 for more discussion of the emergence and current dominance of conjugalism, based upon field research in a village in Liaoning Province, in northeastern China.

21. See Cohen 1976 for a detailed discussion of woman's private property as representing the assets of the conjugal unit within a complex family and the merging of this property with that acquired by her husband at the time of family division. This merging is what the husband expects, but it is also true that sometimes a woman will secretly keep some of her private holdings.

22. For a discussion comparing actual changes in Chinese family organization with the changes anticipated by modernization theory, see Davis and Harrell 1993.

23. For more on this practice, see Ocko 1991.

24. That is, a childless couple or isolated individual previously supported by the collective and now by the village government.

25. On *danguo* (*tan kuo*) in pre-Communist times, see Shiga (1979: 136–38), who uses the terms "*danguo*" and "*lingguo*" (*ling kuo*) to describe a situation completely parallel to that found in present-day Yangmansa, with the important exception that he links such arrangements to a son's being expelled from the family by his father:

> The life led by such an ejected son is known by such terms as *ling kuo* [*lingguo*] (to live apart) and *tan kuo* [*danguo*] (to live alone).
>
> Division of a household (*fen chia*) [*fenjia*] is an act severing the legal relationship of "common living, common budget" and has nothing to do with the externally visible separation of dwellings; *ling kuo* is a word referring to a situation in which the externally visible features of daily life such as lodging, meals, and the like are maintained separately, while the legal relationship remains as it was. (p. 136)

Because *danguo* is now an accepted and increasingly common arrangement, no longer associated with "ejection," the question arises as to whether its being linked to expulsion in earlier times reflected the fact that residential and economic separation prior to family division then required parental approval and justification. In other words, I am suggesting the possibility that *danguo* as a breach of family solidarity might have been rationalized as ejection so as to publicly uphold the father's authority even if such separation of son from father prior to family division had been agreed to by all parties concerned.

26. See Skinner 1997 for use of these terms with reference to the Chinese case and more generally in the context of his development of a "family systems" approach in anthropological demography, such that the terms either refer to family forms (as developmental stages) or characterize particular family systems.

27. See Yan 2003 on privacy as a component of contemporary changes in family relations, based on fieldwork in Liaoning.

28. See Cohen 1976; for more recent research on this point, see Harrell and Pullum 1995 and Liu 1995.

29. This plot originally belonged to a childless *wubaohu* ("five-guarantee household") and reverted to the team when they died.

30. Such "temporary employment" consists of full-time and often long-term jobs, but without the health, retirement, and other benefits otherwise associated with nonfarming urban employment.

31. See Selden 1993: 150–51 for a discussion of the emergence of similar "bimodal" patterns of family development in another Hebei village following decollectivization.

Chapter Five

1. Freedman's elaboration of variations in lineage arrangements, developed in his two major studies on the subject (1958, 1966), goes considerably beyond the A-to-Z model. His interests in lineage organization, development, and distribution have been taken up in recent years mainly by social historians. The papers in Ebrey and Watson 1986 provide a selection and refer back to much of the earlier work. See also Chow 1994; two especially important and comprehensive works relating particularly to southeastern China are Szonyi 2002 and Zheng 2001. Anthropologists in China retain a keen interest in lineage organization, as, for example, in He 2002; Ma 1999; and Xie and Fang 1999.

Chapter Six

1. For another dimension of kinship in north China, see Judd 1989 on the ties in rural Shandong between married women and their natal families. More recently, Yan 1996 and 2003 and Liu 2000 briefly consider patrilineal kinship and elements of lineage organization in north China villages, largely with respect to contemporary society, with Liu noting that the Shaanxi village where he did his fieldwork "fits into Cohen's general picture quite well" (2000: 193, n7), his reference being to the original version of this chapter.

2. The fixed genealogical mode of kinship bears a formal resemblance to the *zongfa* system of preimperial antiquity. Unlike the *zongfa*, however, the genealogical mode was not associated with succession to significant political position. See Ebrey 1986 on the *zongfa* and efforts to revive it during the imperial period.

3. Same-surname marriage between members of different lineages has been acceptable since at least late imperial times in Yangmansa and, it would appear, in much of north China. Intralineage marriages are taboo. Same-surname marriage outside of the lineage was also accepted even during the late imperial period in the villages in Sichuan and near Shanghai where I carried out field studies in 1990. This distribution suggests that the strict ban on such marriages, as widely reported for southeastern mainland China and for Taiwan, was in fact characteristic of these areas of the old empire. So in spite of common belief to the contrary, total avoidance of same surname marriage was not a trait of the Han Chinese in general.

4. The matter of asymmetrical segmentation is far more complex than my brief characterization here indicates. For a comprehensive discussion of this and related issues, see R. Watson 1985, especially chapter 2.

5. Chen 1984 criticizes the anthropological analysis of family and lineage organization for its failure to clearly distinguish the genealogical orientation, basic to Chinese patrilineal kinship, from segmentation linked to property-owning groups. Chen's discussion relates to the associational mode of agnatic kinship.

6. This woman, in fact, did not have a personal name, and she would be recorded only by her husband's surname followed by her natal surname and the suffix *shi* (which in this context can be glossed "*née*"). Wives' names were also

indicated in this fashion on ancestral tablets and scrolls and, traditionally, even in speech. For the "namelessness" of Chinese women, see R. Watson 1986.

7. This was still the case during the period of my fieldwork in Yangmansa, when the arrival of the mother's brother for his sister's funeral was dreaded by members of the family into which she had married and by their close agnatic kin. For evidence from southeastern China on the mother's brother's role during her funeral, see Freedman 1966: 58–59.

8. Illustrations of north Chinese tablets and scrolls can be found in Johnston 1910: plates facing pages 264, 278, 280. Ancestral scrolls are shown in the "Long Bow" (Zhangzhuang) films of a village in southern Shanxi, including *All Under Heaven: Life in a Chinese Village* (1985), *To Taste a Hundred Herbs: Gods, Ancestors and Medicine in a Chinese Village* (1986), and *First Moon: Celebration of the Chinese New Year* (1988). All are from New Day Films. Such scrolls were also observed in some but not all households by Dr. Laurel Bossen during her 1989 fieldwork in a north Henan village. Thus at least this element in the north China pattern of lineage organization is documented for areas in Shanxi, Hebei, Henan, and Shandong. Ancestral scrolls are also hung and worshiped in northeastern China, as illustrated in Yan 2003, in one of the photographs between pp. 111 and 112.

9. Dr. Laurel Bossen informs me that ancestral scrolls were kept on display until the fifteenth day of the New Year in the Henan village where she did her fieldwork. This was also the practice in eastern Shandong (Johnston 1910: 277).

10. Such steamed delicacies, stuffed with pork and vegetables, continue to this day to be the major luxury dish of the New Year festival in north China.

11. Huang 1985 and Duara 1988, using data gathered by Japanese field workers, discuss lineage organization in the context of their more general social histories of rural north China. It will be clear that in writing this chapter I have benefited considerably from both books.

12. I.e., Baker 1968; Potter 1968; Potter and Potter 1990; Siu 1989; J. Watson 1975b; R. Watson 1985; Xie and Fang 1999.

13. For some north China lineages the Father and Sons Gathering or Day of the Cold Feast was another occasion for joint worship and feasting (Duara 1988: 93). Factors behind variations in the ritual calendars followed by lineages in north China remain to be explored, especially as these pertain to the relationship between the associational and fixed genealogical modes of lineage organization.

14. Both Duara 1988: 98 and Huang 1985: 236 mention that the several lineages in Houxiazhai, a village in western Shandong near the border with Hebei, organized graveyard ritual and lineage feasting on the New Year rather than on Qingming. It is not clear, however, as to whether at that time there was also the form of ancestor worship more commonly seen in north China during the New Year period.

15. Cohen 1969a and Pasternak 1969, 1972 deal with the creation of lineages in southern Taiwan. For a study of the formation of a lineage in what is now Hong Kong's New Territories, see R. Watson 1985, who also discusses earlier work on this subject. Faure 1986, 1989b is concerned with the historical establishment of Guangdong-style lineages.

16. See chapter 5; also see Potter 1970 for an important early statement on the connections between such factors and lineage organization. General surveys of the literature on the southeastern Chinese lineage are in J. Watson 1982 and 1986.

17. The distinction between "lineage" and "descent group" dominates the volume edited by Ebrey and Watson 1986.

Chapter Seven

1. Important historical studies of elite lineages in the Lower Yangzi area include Beattie 1979, Cole 1986, Davis 1986, Dennerline 1979–80, 1981, 1986, Elman 1990, Hazelton 1986, Hymes 1986, Twitchett 1959, Zurndorfer 1990.

2. In this area of China subsoil rights and surface rights to land were separate commodities that could be independently sold, rented, or mortgaged. The owner of surface rights had to pay rent to the possessor of the subsoil; full ownership required that both subsoil and surface rights be in the same hands (Jiangsu 1934: 40–42; Fei 1939: 177–94; Huang 1990: 156–58). In Shenjiashang outside ownership was largely with respect to subsoil rights, the sale of which often was a matter of little significance for a village family owning the surface. Unlike the situation in the village described by Huang, however, transactions involving surface rights were not at all uncommon; the difference may be related to the relatively greater residential mobility in Shenjiashang, perhaps encouraged by its proximity to Shanghai. Corporate holdings, as by larger lineages or other groups, for the most part appear to have consisted of subsoil rights. Likewise, ownership of subsoil rights seems to have been the major consideration in the assignment of class labels during the land reform campaigns initiated by the Communists.

3. Shenjiashang accords with the broader Chinese pattern in that the family as such (*jia*) is not a unit involved in genealogical reckoning. The family is a unit in terms of property, work, the pooling of income, and commensality, such that a family's members are commonly referred to as "those eating from one stove." Thus the term *fenzao* ("division of the stove") is used interchangeably with *fenjia* ("family division") to refer to family partition. Furthermore, insofar as the family as such has a religious focus, it is provided by the Stove God (Zaojun). With family division (*fenjia*) there is no change in the genealogical ties between brothers, for they obviously continue to share the same ancestors, but each new family will have its own stove and Stove God.

4. Such temple fairs, well documented for many areas of China, were both economic and religious events. For a recent and comprehensive discussion, see Feuchtwang 2001.

5. On the use of generational names in a lineage context, see J. Watson 1986: 287–88. R. Watson 1986 more generally discusses Chinese naming practices.

6. For more on uxorilocal marriage and its distribution, see Wolf and Huang 1980. See also Wolf 1989 for an example of a culturalist explanation of uxorilocal marriage taking frequency to represent distribution and cultural variation.

7. A report translated and quoted by Wolf and Huang (1980: 12) suggests that in east China there may have been a rather broad distribution of uxorilocal

marriages of the kind found in Shenjiashang: in an area east of Nanjing, people "who have no male children usually bring in a son-in-law to act as their son. On entering the family the son-in-law changes his name, and a contract is written so there will be proof. If the wife's father has a son or an agnatic nephew, he gives him some property to avoid disputes. Other than this, he need only pay a fee to the ancestral hall to have his son-in-law entered in the clan genealogy and accorded the rights of a successor."

8. The now rather dilapidated temple is no longer in use, but it is maintained by the government because of its architectural importance.

9. See chapter 4 for discussion of the roles of the family head and family manager.

Chapter Eight

1. For some discussions along these lines, see Appadurai 1986; Parry and Bloch 1989.

2. For more on the Hakka in Minong and in the larger Six Units organization, see Cohen 1976, 1993, 1999; Pasternak 1972, 1983.

3. Many of the documentary sources concerning Minong during the Qing era, including the land survey data and copies of contracts, account books, and genealogies, were obtained in 1971–72, as was some additional information from historically well-informed residents, all in the context of fieldwork carried out jointly with Professor Burton Pasternak (see Pasternak 1983). Several additional contracts and other documents were acquired later, some as recently as 2002, and a few more still were discovered through examination of published collections. Unless otherwise noted, all Qing-period documentary materials introduced or translated in this chapter are drawn from photocopies; the original documents are held by families in Meinong Township who kindly gave us permission to copy and use them. Permission to copy that portion of the cadastral survey data covering what is now Meinong Township was granted in 1971.

4. See chapter 4 and Cohen 1976 for discussions of women's property.

5. The cadastral survey did depart from Qing categories of land ownership and other rights through its requirement that for every plot of land owned by a corporation a "manager" be identified; likewise, in the absence of documented family succession, as through a family division agreement, ownership might still be listed in the name of a deceased party, with his son, widow, or another party cultivating the land listed as "manager." As far as corporations were concerned, every "manager" was indeed a shareholder, but in some cases he was also the tenant on that plot of corporate land, while in others he was at the time of the survey the designated manager of the corporation as a whole; but even this position might be held on a rotating basis. My ongoing analysis of these records simply treats the "manager" designation as a signal for the need to determine the underlying relationship.

6. As noted, the cadastral survey lists 2,387 persons resident in Minong as owners of land rights of one kind or another. This figure must closely approximate the total number of family units, given that in the vast majority of cases

each person listed in the cadastral survey is a family head. However, while a very few of those listed were women owning rights to land as their private property, some of the men listed were in fact deceased, and some completely landless families might not have appeared even as sharing ownership in residential compounds. Precise figures as to family numbers and composition must await completion of an ongoing analysis of the Japanese-period household registers. In the registers, first compiled about four years after the cadastral survey, the number given as the household address is the same as the plot number for residential land given in that survey. The two bodies of data are thus totally compatible and in fact cross-index each other. When the job is done we should have moved very close to knowing exactly who was where in Minong just prior to the arrival of the Japanese.

7. Such other information includes genealogies giving names of ancestors that match names listed as owners, thereby showing them to be ancestral corporations. Most important is the identification of corporation charters by informants during fieldwork in Meinong Township at different times between 1964 and 2002.

8. Both the Liu Mingquan and the Japanese surveys simply listed by name an association as owner, when appropriate. Liu Mingquan's surveyors issued a *zhangdan*, or "certificate of measurement," for each plot of land, and I have copies of association *zhangdan* with the association listed as owner. Liu's survey was implemented in Minong in 1889.

9. An annual or periodic meeting including worship, a banquet, and a manager's report was the common arrangement among many different kinds of associations during Qing. For urban occupational associations ("guilds"), see, for example, Morse 1909. Such a widespread pattern, over large areas of China and firmly entrenched in city and countryside alike, represents yet another example of the many rural-urban cultural continuities in culture and society during late imperial times, continuities later ignored, denied, or forgotten with the postimperial construction by China's own intellectual and political elites of that country's traditional "backwardness."

10. For more on this god, see Cedzich 1995.

11. The picul (*dan* in Chinese) is equivalent in weight to about 133 pounds. During the nineteenth century, prior to the 1895 Japanese occupation, money in Taiwan for larger purchases was usually in the form of foreign silver coins, mainly Spanish silver "dollars" minted for the most part in Mexico or in South American territories under Spanish control. Smaller purchases would use Chinese state-minted copper "cash," usually at the rate of between 1,000 and 1,300 cash per dollar. The common use of Spanish dollars in Taiwan and elsewhere in the Chinese empire reflected the centuries-long importation of foreign silver and silver coinage. In contracts from Minong and elsewhere in Taiwan, as well as from mainland China, these imported silver coins were commonly referred to as "dollars" (*yuan*), "large dollars" (*da yuan*), "Buddha silver" (*foyin*), or "Buddha-head silver" (*fotouyin*). The latter two appellations were consequent upon the fact that Spanish coins commonly featuring profiled heads of monarchs such as Carolus III, Carolus IV, or Ferdinand VII were taken to portray the head of the

Buddha. In Taiwan and in some mainland China districts the value of foreign dollars was calculated on the basis of their weight in Chinese ounces or "taels" (*liang*). That the Chinese designated these coins as *yuan* or dollars did not reflect their monetary value, but rather their serving as units for the convenient reckoning of weight in silver. In fact, these coins were minted with the inscribed value of eight reales ("8R"), equal to a Spanish ounce, hence in English they were commonly referred to as "pieces of eight." So within the Chinese economic and cultural environments these coins were tranformed into dollars and the images they bore into Chinese icons; they were further transformed as they were stamped with "chops" by the various money changers through whose hands they passed. See Clark 1896: 76–77, 127–28, 136–37; Kaohsiung 2002. For more on this, see chapter 9.

12. I have copies of nineteen Minong Qing-period contracts concerning the outright sale of land or house sites, transactions with the potential to involve red contracts. Yet only one document is a red contract; two more red contracts are referred to in other contracts as attachments. In the account book of an ancestral association there is reference to the purchase of yet another two plots of land, with both transactions registered at the county seat and therefore confirmed by red contracts. See chapter 9 for more on contracts and related documents in Minong during Qing.

13. See Scott 1976.

14. The distinction between "red" and "white" contracts concerns contracts related to transfers of rights pertaining to land, including house sites; it also applies to some forms of contracted bondage, which were supposed to be registered with the district's yamen. For more on this, see chapter 9.

15. As one of his duties, a Qing-period county magistrate had to hold court and serve as judge periodically during the week. On the magistrate's court, see Allee 1994.

16. Only a minority of marriages were uxorilocal, and they commonly involved a man who married into his wife's home because he had no family, or had come from one so poor as to yield little significant payoff in the form of important affinal ties. Likewise "little daughter-in-law marriages," also often associated with much weaker links between affines, were rare compared with other areas of Taiwan. For more on this, see Pasternak 1983.

17. "Large dollars" are foreign dollars; see note 11.

18. For this contract I have rendered as "Li née Liu" the woman's signature *Li Liu shi*, which might be translated literally as "the woman Liu, now of the Li family." Her signature follows the format generally used for the few female contract signatories and used in many other contexts where women are named. Unlike men, women were usually named without being given personal names, a circumstance considered in some detail by R. Watson 1986.

19. In an 1840 contract not included in this chapter Li Changhuaer does indeed give up all rights to the land in exchange for additional funds.

20. Original contract published in RTKC 1910–11, vol. 1, section 3: 428–29.

21. Information concerning Tan was provided me by his grandson, who also

gave me access to an original copy of Magistrate Li's proclamation, which he kindly allowed me to transcribe.

22. Original Chinese text provided by Professor Chuang Ying-chang, Institute of Ethnology, Academia Sinica, Nankang, Taipei, Taiwan.

23. Original Chinese text in Chuang 1985: 216.

Chapter 9

1. Valerie Hansen (1995: 10), in her book on Chinese contracts, defines these in particular as "written agreements between two or more parties to buy, sell, rent, or borrow a given commodity." Although this definition is based squarely on Chinese documents, it would exclude those that, while not agreements, can be placed together with these in particular spheres of document production, as I show later in this chapter.

2. See chapters 2 and 3.

3. Mid-twentieth-century anthropological theory also placed the "peasant" economy as intermediate between "primitive" and "modern" economic relationships. Jack Potter, in dealing with the impact of economic development on rural Chinese villagers in Hong Kong's New Territories, asserts how in this process, pace Maine, "status gives way to contract" (1968: 3).

4. Two such widely known specialists, separately and on different occasions, stated these views in my presence, and I have been reliably informed about others with similar notions. In one of the cases I witnessed, the immediate context was a discussion of the then recent onset of decollectivization, under the procedure of "contracting production down to the household" and involving the use of simple written contracts between the household head and the collective. The scholar concerned opined that "the peasants never had to do that before," and that in signing these contracts they were exposed to the modernizing forces unleashed during this new era of reform. Factually the remark was nonsense, and it may be suggested that appeal to contracts at that time reflected precisely the deep familiarity with such documents within society at large. For example, family division contracts and uxorilocal marriage contracts, among others, continued to be written and of importance throughout the collective era and well into postcollective times, at least through my different periods of fieldwork in China, up to 1990. On this, see chapter 6 and M. Cohen 1992.

5. On the widespread use of contracts in late imperial society, see Cohen 1969b; Fu-mei Chang Chen and Ramon Myers 1976, 1978. Chen and Myers provide, en passant, a good introduction to Japanese surveys and documentary collections. Prasenjit Duara (1988: 181), in his study of north China during the late Qing and Republican periods, gives some discussion to "the contracts into which Chinese villagers entered with great frequency." The best full monographic treatment so far is Hansen 1995, even though it considers the history and use of contracts only through the end of the Yuan dynasty, that is, just prior to the onset of Ming-Qing, the period usually taken to be late imperial. Qing and Republican-era law and contractual uses are well covered in Zelin et al. 2004, which also includes the original version of this chapter.

6. Some major collections of Qing-period or earlier documents pertaining to particular locales have been published but await analysis. See, for example, Chen 1997; Lin 1990; and Zhang 1988.

7. Unless otherwise indicated, all documents presented in this chapter are translations of original documents borrowed, copied, and then returned to their private owners. The twenty that I introduce here (and another 3 in chapter 8) are drawn from and are representative of a larger collection of fifty-three (as of early 2004) Qing-period documents from Minong already translated and examined. Nineteen concern the outright sale of land or house sites; the other thirty-four relate to pledge sale, family division, or loans, or to transactions in people, such as uxorilocal marriage contracts or contracts for the sale-adoption of children. Such analyzed Qing-era documents amount to about one half of those from the Minong region I have so far located and copied.

8. Although commonly the value was sixty-eight Chinese ounces for one hundred dollars, I have seen contracts and account books where the value for one hundred dollars is given at seventy-two or seventy-six ounces. A sales contract from the Mei County (Meixian) area, in mainland China's northern Guangdong Hakka heartland, rather than directly indicating the ratio of sixty-eight ounces to one hundred foreign dollars, states that the price of a plot of land is "172 dollars, weighing a total of 116.96 ounces," which is equal to .68 ounces to the dollar. This contract was acquired in Mei County; it is dated Daoguang 13/12/17 (January 26, 1834). In a land-sale contract from Zhenping County (now Jiaoling), dated Guangxu 24/04/08 (May 27, 1898), the ratio is presented as in the Minong, Taiwan, contracts, except that it is sixty-five ounces to one hundred dollars, but the equivalent in Chinese ounces is also given, as follows: "thirty silver dollars [valued in silver by weight at the ratio of] sixty-five [ounces to one hundred dollars] weighing a total of 19.5 ounces exactly." The large majority of Hakka immigrants settling Minong came from Zhenping, suggesting historical links in contract style.

9. See Yang 1988: 43–90 for a survey of the standardized forms and content of land transaction documents throughout China during the Ming and Qing periods. On enduring phrases already appearing in ninth- and tenth-century Dunhuang contracts, see Hansen 1995: 6, 47.

10. See Chen 1997: 86–88. Mark Allee 1994: 56 describes a case in northern Taiwan where, in spite of an "irrevocable sale" clause, additional payments were made under threat of court action, but the circumstances behind this outcome are not clear.

11. *Pu*, a character apparently confined to Taiwan meaning rent, is common to Hakka and Minan documents, while a modified form of the character for *dian*, to pledge, is used in the Hakka Meixian region of Guangdong, on the mainland, and in the south Taiwan Hakka areas. See the character glossary under *pu*, rent, and *dian*, pledge (Hakka variant). There even appears to be differential usage of certain boilerplates between contracts from regions of Hakka and Hokkien settlement.

12. The Taiwan *jia* is equivalent to .97 hectares.

13. From *Taiwan shi tianye yanjiu tongxun* (Newsletter of Taiwan history

field research), no. 14, March 1990, in which issue a photograph of this contract appears on the front cover.

14. According to one local genealogical manuscript, Lin Pingshi settled in Dabu County, Guangdong, at the end of Song; this genealogy gives Minong's two major Lin lines or hall names a common ancestor who, on Lin Pingshi's side, precedes him by sixteen generations. A hall name (*tanghao*) is the basic agnatic identifier in that it asserts common ancestry, usually, as in this case, by identifying the supposed north China homeland of that surname's founding ancestor. Associated with some surnames are more than one *tanghao*, in which case common ancestry is expressed with respect to a particular *tanghao* but sometimes also in the context of written genealogical explanations of how the surname has more than one *tanghao*, each having as focus a particular ancestor, with these various ancestors themselves related at even higher and temporally more remote genealogical levels. A case would be the Lin surname in Minong.

15. See chapter 8, above, for more on individual and corporate ownership in Minong.

16. That the rural Chinese regarded land as a potentially disposable resource was a point made quite some time ago by Bernard Gallin (1964). However, there continues to be a contrasting view, focusing on what are taken to be the particularities of the "peasant" condition in late imperial China, as in Huang 2001, who contrasts Western market rationality with the supposed sentimentality of China's "peasants" who adhere to their own differentiating "ethos." Such an approach comes perilously close to the notion of "peasant backwardness," as described in chapter 3.

17. On *foyin*, "Buddha silver," and *fotouyin*, "Buddha-head silver," see chapter 8, note 11.

18. This contract was obtained from the account book of the Zhong Mashi Ancestral Estate. Ancestral and other land-owning corporate associations commonly copied into their account books the texts of contracts accumulated as land was purchased. In some cases also recorded in the account book was the name of the association member responsible for keeping the original contract document. As noted earlier, these associations owned about one third of the wet rice land in Minong. I gloss as "large rent and local taxes" the phrase *dazu xinlao*; *dazu* is large rent, with *xinlao* literally being the "exertions" of the village managers or *guanshi*; as noted in chapter 8, the *guanshi* generally had the functions of village headmen but were also, and originally, in charge of collecting large rent payments on behalf of absentee holders of large rent rights. Records of *xinlao* payments can commonly be encountered in account books of Minong associations but are only rarely noted in contracts.

19. *Tu* means local; for *foyin*, see chapter 8, note 11.

20. In all, twenty receipts survive for annual rent payments during the forty-year period 1814–54. Although the contract stipulated a three-year period prior to reconfirmation, it can be seen from the receipts that there were at least five years prior to the transition from *dianzu* to *dazu*.

21. The precise calculations are as follows:

0.52256 + 1.7888 = 2.31136 total area of land purchased
1.52896 + 0.7824 = 2.31136 total area of the two shares of land
1.52896 / 2.31136 = .661498 percentage of land owned by Song
0.7824 / 2.31136 = .338502 percentage of land owned by Chen
.630 (94/148 = .635) percentage of cost paid by Song
.362 (54/148 = .364) percentage of cost paid by Chen
Song's *dazu* rent 7.813 piculs + Chen's *dazu* rent 4 piculs = total *dazu* 11.813
.661389 Song's portion of *dazu*
.338610 Chen's portion of *dazu*

22. In the context of southern Taiwan's Qing-period sugar production, the various *hang* were organizations of guild merchants whose payments in advance to farmers for their subsequent sugar crop were in the form of interest-bearing loans. In this document there is no mention of any obligation to supply the Fucheng Hang with sugar, but in any event the point of the document was to assert that the loan was settled. On the *hang* of southern Taiwan, see Daniels 1996: 120–27.

23. See Maurice Freedman's (1979b) classic analysis of Chinese wedding ritual; for Taiwan Hakka weddings, see Liao 1967. Hong 2002: 38 notes how in "formal marriages" it "usually was not necessary to execute a marriage contract." In such marriages it was common, however, for the bride's family to send with her dowry an itemized list of the dowry's contents; this was not a contract, for it simply confirmed what had been sent to the groom's side.

24. A "milk name," or child's pet name, was given to girls and boys shortly after birth. But boys when grown would be given adult names, while grown women remained "nameless" except for the appellation of their infancy. For more on this, see R. Watson 1986.

25. Japanese troops landed on Taiwan not long after this contract was written, and Minong surrendered to these forces about six months later, in November 1895. In 1902 the new Japanese colonial authorities carried out a cadastral survey of Minong, according to which Wu Shunxing owned a large 1.88 *jia* plot of dry field. These survey data also reveal that Wu owned this land before Li Ading entered the household in 1895.

That succession rights for sons keeping their uxorilocally married father's surname had to be explicitly noted in the marriage contract was already made clear to me during my first fieldwork in Meinong Township during 1964–65. Then it was still the customary arrangement, based on procedures well established during Qing and maintained during the period of Japanese rule, with several examples being pointed out to me of Qing-period families in which sons with the wrong surname had been left out in the cold.

26. On women's inheritance and succession rights to the family estate during imperial and postimperial times, see Bernhardt 1999, which focuses on relevant state law and legal practice.

27. In Minong during Qing there were cases of boys being kidnapped by men wanting sons, hardly a contractual undertaking (Cohen 1976: 30).

28. *Guofang* and *guoji* can both be translated as "to transfer from one ag-

natic branch line to another." *Guofang* is the term commonly used in spoken Hakka (at least in Meinong), while *guoji* is used in documents such as this contract. These Minong practices can be compared with *guoji* procedures in north China, as discussed in chapter 4.

29. Using the cadastral survey, entered into a computerized database, a preliminary ranking of all listed owners resident in Minong has been developed. It is based upon a combination of area and quality of land owned as well as the different kinds of rights to land that were owned. In this list Liu Shuangchun is seventh richest in all of Minong and Liu Shouqian is eighty-forth, this out of a total 2,151 persons ranked. Although the list is subject to further modification, there can be no doubt that as of 1902 both were well off by local standards.

30. Anding is the Liang surname "hall name" (*tanghao*). For more on hall names, see note 14 above.

31. In Taiwan, as in areas of mainland China, sugar mills commonly were jointly owned and managed by the direct producers. Rights to use a mill so owned were distributed on the basis of share ownership, such that a share gave its owner rights to crush a specified quantity of sugarcane. Sugarcane growers wanting to increase production had to buy more shares. As this document demonstrates, sugar mill shares, like shares in other corporations, were commodities. Although Liu Dafeng purchased these two shares in 1757, it is clear from what follows in the document that at some later point he and his family came to own a sugar mill outright. On sugar mill shareholding, see Daniels 1996: 120–21.

32. In a book titled *Women and Property in China* (Bernhardt 1999), there is no mention of women's private property (*sifangqian*) as a recognized (in practice and in ritual) category of property distinct from family property (*jiachan*) and from the property of the conjugal unit (*fangchan*). On *sifangqian*, see chapter 4, note 8, above and Cohen 1976. On set-asides, see Wakefield 1998.

33. On associations in Minong and more generally among the south Taiwan Hakka, see chapter 8 and Cohen 1993, 1999; Pasternak 1972.

34. As in contracts and other written agreements with the gods or with the dead. See Hansen 1995 for early examples.

35. See Allee 1994 on law and litigation on Taiwan during Qing. Although I know of no instance when a contract or other witnessed document deriving from Minong was used in yamen litigation, this obviously is not to deny the possibility. In fact, on the basis of the Fengshan magistrate's periodic involvement in various Minong affairs, it is likely that such documents would have come to his attention at one point or another. Indeed, Liu Mingquan's land survey, which began in 1886, included Minong, as we have seen, and contracts of land transfer or family division documents were probably shown to officials as evidence of ownership.

Bibliography

Ahern, Emily Martin. *Chinese Ritual and Politics*. Cambridge: Cambridge University Press, 1981.

Alitto, Guy S. *The Last Confucian: Liang Shu-Ming and the Chinese Dilemma of Modernity*. Berkeley: University of California Press, 1979.

Allee, Mark A. *Law and Local Society in Late Imperial China: Northern Taiwan in the Nineteenth Century*. Stanford, Calif.: Stanford University Press, 1994.

Appadurai, Arjun, ed. *The Social Life of Things: Commodities in Cultural Perspective*. Cambridge: Cambridge University Press, 1986.

Baker, Hugh D. R. *A Chinese Lineage Village: Sheung Shui*. Stanford, Calif.: Stanford University Press, 1968.

———. *Chinese Family and Kinship*. New York: Columbia University Press, 1979.

Beattie, Hilary J. *Land and Lineage in China: A Study of T'ung-Ch'eng County, Anhwei, in the Ming and Ch'ing Dynasties*. Cambridge: Cambridge University Press, 1979.

Bernhardt, Kathryn. *Women and Property in China, 960–1949*. Stanford, Calif.: Stanford University Press, 1999.

Bestor, Theodore C. *Neighborhood Tokyo*. Stanford, Calif.: Stanford University Press, 1989.

Bohannan, Paul. *Social Anthropology*. New York: Holt, Rinehart and Winston, 1963.

Brandt, Loren. *Commercialization and Agricultural Development: Central and Eastern China, 1870–1937*. Cambridge: Cambridge University Press, 1989.

Brockman, Rosser H. "Commercial Contract Law in Late Nineteenth-Century Taiwan." In *Essays on China's Legal Tradition*, edited by Jerome Alan Cohen, R. Randle Edwards, and Fu-mei Chang Chen, 76–136. Princeton, N.J.: Princeton University Press, 1980.

Cedzich, Ursula-Angelika. "The Cult of the Wu-t'ung/Wu-Hsien in History and Fiction: The Religious Roots of *Journey to the South*." In *Ritual and Scripture in Chinese Popular Religion*, edited by David Johnson. Berkeley, Calif.: Chinese Popular Culture Project, 1995.

Chan, Anita, Richard Madsen, and Jonathan Unger. *Chen Village Under Mao and Deng.* Berkeley: University of California Press, 1992.

Chang, Chung-li. *The Chinese Gentry: Studies on Their Role in Nineteenth-Century Chinese Society.* Seattle: University of Washington Press, 1955.

———. *The Income of the Chinese Gentry.* Seattle: University of Washington Press, 1962.

Chen, Chi-nan. "Fang and Chia-Tsu: The Chinese Kinship System in Rural Taiwan." Ph.D. diss., Yale University, 1984.

Chen Chiu-kun. *Taiwan Gushuqi (1717–1906) (Archaic Land Documents of Taiwan [1717–1906]).* Taipei: Rainbow Sign Publishing Co., 1997.

Chen, Fu-mei Chang, and Ramon H. Myers. "Customary Law and the Economic Growth of China During the Ch'ing Period." Part 1. *Ch'ing-Shih Wen-T'i* 3, no. 5 (Nov. 1976): 1–32.

———. "Customary Law and the Economic Growth of China During the Ch'ing Period." Part 2. *Ch'ing-Shih Wen-T'i* 3, no. 10 (Dec. 1978): 4–27.

Chow, Kai-wing. *The Rise of Confucian Ritualism in Late Imperial China: Ethics, Classics, and Lineage Discourse.* Stanford, Calif.: Stanford University Press, 1994.

Chuang, Ying-chang. "The Formation and Characteristics of Taiwanese Lineage Organization." In *Proceedings of the Conference on Modernization and Chinese Culture,* edited by Chiao Chien, 207–20. Hong Kong: Chinese University of Hong Kong, 1985.

Clark, John D. *Formosa.* Shanghai: Shanghai Mercury, 1896.

Cohen, Myron L. "Agnatic Kinship in South Taiwan." *Ethnology* 8, no. 2 (1969a): 167–82.

———. "The Role of Contract in Traditional Chinese Social Organization." In *Ethnology.* Vol. 2 of *Proceedings, VIIIth International Congress of Anthropological and Ethnological Sciences, 1968, Tokyo and Kyoto,* 130–32. Tokyo: Science Council of Japan, 1969b.

———. "Developmental Process in the Chinese Domestic Group." In *Family and Kinship in Chinese Society,* edited by Maurice Freedman, 21–36. Stanford, Calif.: Stanford University Press, 1970a.

———. "Introduction." In *Village Life in China,* by Arthur H. Smith. Boston: Little, Brown, and Co., 1970b.

———. *House United, House Divided: The Chinese Family in Taiwan.* New York: Columbia University Press, 1976.

———. "Lineage Development and the Family in China." 2d rev. ed., 1992. In *The Chinese Family and Its Ritual Behavior,* edited by Jih-chang Hsieh and Ying-chang Chuang, 210–20. Taipei: Institute of Ethnology, Academia Sinica, 1985.

———. "Souls and Salvation: Conflicting Themes in Chinese Popular Religion." In *Death Ritual in Late Imperial and Modern China,* edited by James L. Watson and Evelyn S. Rawski, 180–202. Berkeley: University of California Press, 1988.

———. "Lineage Organization in North China." *Journal of Asian Studies* 49, no. 3 (Aug. 1990): 509–34.

———. "Family Management and Family Division in Contemporary Rural China." *China Quarterly* 130 (June 1992): 357–78.

———. "Shared Beliefs: Corporations, Community and Religion Among the South Taiwan Hakka During Ch'ing." *Late Imperial China* 14, no. 1 (June 1993): 1–33.

———. "Being Chinese: The Peripheralization of Traditional Identity." (Rev. and expanded version of 1991 article originally published in *Dædalus*, vol. 120, no. 2). In *The Living Tree: The Changing Meaning of Being Chinese Today*, edited by Tu Wei-ming, 88–108. Stanford, Calif.: Stanford University Press, 1994a.

———. "Cultural and Political Inventions in Modern China: The Case of the Chinese 'Peasant.'" (Reprinted from *Dædalus*, vol. 122, no. 2 [Spring 1993]). In *China in Transformation*, edited by Tu Wei-ming, 151–70. Cambridge, Mass.: Harvard University Press, 1994b.

———. "Lineage Organization in East China." In *Proceedings of the International Conference on Anthropology and the Museum*, edited by Tsong-yuan Lin, 9–35. Taipei: Taiwan Museum, 1995.

———. "North China Rural Families: Changes During the Communist Era." *Études Chinoises* 17, no. 1–2 (1998): 60–154.

———. "Minong's Corporations: Religion, Economy and Local Culture in 18th and 19th Century Taiwan." In *Anthropological Studies in Taiwan: Empirical Research*, edited by Hsu Cheng-kuang and Lin Mei-Rong, 223–91. Nankang, Taipei: Academia Sinica, Institute of Ethnology, 1999.

———. "Commodity Creation in Late Imperial China: Corporations, Shares, and Contracts in One Rural Community." In *Locating Capitalism in Time and Space: Global Restructuring, Politics, and Identity*, edited by David L. Nugent. Stanford, Calif.: Stanford University Press, 2002.

———. "Writs of Passage in Late Imperial China: Contracts and the Documentation of Practical Understandings in Minong, Taiwan." In *Contract and Economic Culture in China*, edited by Madeleine Zelin, Jonathan Ocko, and Robert Gardella, 37–93. Stanford, Calif.: Stanford University Press, 2004.

Cohen, Paul A. "The Contested Path: The Boxers as History and Myth." *Journal of Asian Studies* 51, no. 1 (Feb. 1992): 82–113.

Cole, James H. *Shaohsing: Competition and Cooperation in Nineteenth-Century China*. Tucson: University of Arizona Press, 1986.

Constable, Nicole, ed. *Guest People: Hakka Identity in China and Abroad*. Seattle: University of Washington Press, 1996.

Daniels, Christian. "Agro-Industries: Sugarcane Technology." In *Biology and Biological Technology. Part 3: Agro-Industries and Forestry, Science and Civilization in China*, vol. 6, no. 3, Christian Daniels and Nicholas K. Menzies. Cambridge: Cambridge University Press, 1996.

Davis, Deborah, ed. *The Consumer Revolution in Urban China*. Berkeley: University of California Press, 1999.

Davis, Deborah, and Stevan Harrell. "Introduction: The Impact of Post-Mao Reforms on Family Life." In *Chinese Families in the Post-Mao Era*, edited by Deborah Davis and Stevan Harrell, 1–22. Berkeley: University of California Press, 1993.

Davis, Richard L. "Political Success and the Growth of Descent Groups: The Shih of Ming-Chou During the Sung." In *Kinship Organization in Late Imperial*

China, 1000–1940, edited by Patricia B. Ebrey and James L. Watson, 62–95. Berkeley: University of California Press, 1986.

Dennerline, Jerry. "The New Hua Charitable Estate and Local-Level Leadership in Wuxi County at the End of the Qing." Edited by Tang Tsou. In *Select Papers from the Center for Far Eastern Studies*, vol. 4, 19–70. Chicago: University of Chicago, 1979–80.

———. *The Chia-Ting Loyalists: Confucian Leadership and Social Change in Seventeenth-Century China*. New Haven, Conn.: Yale University Press, 1981.

———. "Marriage, Adoption, and Charity in the Development of Lineages in Wu-Hsi from Sung to Ch'ing." In *Kinship Organization in Late Imperial China, 1000–1940*, edited by Patricia B. Ebrey and James L. Watson, 170–209. Berkeley: University of California Press, 1986.

Duara, Prasenjit. *Culture, Power, and the State: Rural North China, 1900–1942*. Stanford, Calif.: Stanford University Press, 1988.

———. "Knowledge and Power in the Discourse of Modernity: The Campaigns Against Popular Religion in Early Twentieth-Century China." *Journal of Asian Studies* 50, no. 1 (Feb. 1991): 67–83.

Eberhard, Wolfram. *Chinese Festivals*. New York: Henry Schuman, 1952.

Ebrey, Patricia Buckley. "The Early Stages in the Development of Descent Group Organization." In *Kinship Organization in Late Imperial China, 1000–1940*, edited by Patricia B. Ebrey and James L. Watson, 16–61. Berkeley: University of California Press, 1986.

Ebrey, Patricia Buckley, and James L. Watson, eds. *Kinship Organization in Late Imperial China, 1000–1940*. Berkeley: University of California Press, 1986.

Elman, Benjamin A. *Classicism, Politics, and Kinship: The Ch'ang-Chou School of New Text Confucianism in Late Imperial China*. Berkeley: University of California Press, 1990.

Faure, David. *The Structure of Chinese Rural Society: Lineage and Village in the Eastern New Territories, Hong Kong*. Hong Kong: Oxford University Press, 1986.

———. *The Rural Economy of Pre-Liberation China: Trade Increase and Peasant Livelihood in Jiangsu and Guangdong, 1870 to 1937*. Hong Kong: Oxford University Press, 1989a.

———. "The Lineage as a Cultural Invention." *Modern China* 15, no. 1 (Jan. 1989b): 4–36.

Fei Hsiao-tung [Fei Xiaotong]. *Peasant Life in China: A Field Study of Country Life in the Yangtze Valley*. London: Routledge & Kegan Paul, 1939.

———. "Peasantry and Gentry: An Interpretation of Chinese Social Structure and Its Changes." *American Journal of Sociology* 52, no. 1 (July 1946): 1–17.

Fei Hsiao-tung [Fei Xiaotong] et al. *Small Towns in China: Functions, Problems, and Prospects*. Beijing: New World Press, 1986.

Fenn, Cortenay H. *The Five Thousand Dictionary. Revised American Edition Based on Fifth Peking Edition [1940]*. Cambridge, Mass.: Harvard University Press, 1942.

Feuchtwang, Stephan. *Popular Religion in China: The Imperial Metaphor*. Richmond, Surrey (England): Curzon, 2001.

Feuerwerker, Albert. "An Old Question Revisited: Was the Glass Half-Full or Half-Empty for China's Agriculture Before 1949?" *Peasant Studies* 17, no. 3 (Spring, 1990): 207–216.

Fitzgerald, Charles Patrick. *The Tower of Five Glories: A Study of the Min Chia of Ta Li, Yunnan.* London: Cresset Press, 1941.

Freedman, Maurice. *Lineage Organization in Southeastern China.* London School of Economics Monographs on Social Anthropology, vol. 18. London: Athlone Press, 1958.

———. *Chinese Lineage and Society: Fukien and Kwangtung.* London School of Economics Monographs on Social Anthropology, vol. 27. London: Athlone Press, 1966.

———. "The Handling of Money: A Note on the Background to the Economic Sophistication of Overseas Chinese." In *The Study of Chinese Society: Essays by Maurice Freedman,* edited by G. William Skinner, 22–26. Stanford, Calif.: Stanford University Press, 1979a.

———. "Rites and Duties, or Chinese Marriage." In *The Study of Chinese Society: Essays by Maurice Freedman,* edited by G. William Skinner, 255–72. Stanford, Calif.: Stanford University Press, 1979b.

Fried, Morton H. *Fabric of Chinese Society: A Study of the Social Life of a Chinese County Seat.* New York: Praeger, 1953.

Friedman, Edward, Paul G. Pickowicz, and Mark Selden, with Kay Ann Johnson. *Chinese Village, Socialist State.* New Haven, Conn.: Yale University Press, 1991.

Fukutake, Tadashi. *Asian Rural Society: China, India, Japan.* Seattle: University of Washington Press, 1967.

Gallin, Bernard. "Chinese Peasant Values Towards the Land." In *Symposium on Community Studies in Anthropology,* edited by Viola E. Garfield and Ernestine Friedl, 64–71. Proceedings of the 1963 Annual Spring Meeting of the American Ethnological Society. Seattle: American Ethnological Society, 1964.

Gamble, Sidney D. "The Disappearance of Foot-Binding in Tinghsien." *American Journal of Sociology* 49, no. 2 (Sept. 1943): 181–83.

———. *Ting Hsien: A North China Rural Community.* New York: Institute of Pacific Relations, 1954.

———. *North China Villages: Social, Political, and Economic Activities Before 1933.* Berkeley: University of California Press, 1963.

Gates, Hill. "Chinese Modernity in Taiwan: The View from the Bound Foot." In *Anthropological Studies in Taiwan: Empirical Research,* edited by Hsu Cheng-kuang and Lin Mei-rong, 291–318. Nankang, Taipei: Academia Sinica, Institute of Ethnology, 1999.

———. "Footloose in Fujian: Economic Correlates of Footbinding." *Comparative Studies in Society and History* 43, no. 1 (2001): 130–48.

Giles, Herbert A. *A Chinese-English Dictionary.* 2d ed. Shanghai: Kelly & Walsh, Ltd., 1912.

Goody, Jack. *The Oriental, the Ancient, and the Primitive: Systems of Marriage and the Family in the Pre-Industrial Societies of Eurasia.* Cambridge: Cambridge University Press, 1990.

Groves, Robert C. "Militia, Market, and Lineage: Chinese Resistance to the Occupation of Hong Kong's New Territories in 1899." *Journal of the Hong Kong Branch of the Royal Asiatic Society* 9 (1969): 31–64.

Hansen, Valerie. *Negotiating Daily Life in Traditional China: How Ordinary People Used Contracts, 600–1400.* New Haven, Conn.: Yale University Press, 1995.

Harrell, Stevan, ed. *Chinese Historical Microdemography.* Berkeley: University of California Press, 1995.

———. "Lessons from the Golden Age of 'China' Ethnography." In *Anthropological Studies in Taiwan: Retrospect and Prospect*, edited by Hsu Cheng-kuang and Huang Ying-kuei, 211–40. Nankang, Taipei: Academia Sinica, Institute of Ethnology, 1999.

———. "The Anthropology of Reform and the Reform of Anthropology: Anthropological Narratives of Recovery and Progress in China." *Annual Review of Anthropology* 30 (2001a): 139-61.

———. *Ways of Being Ethnic in Southwest China.* Seattle: University of Washington Press, 2001b.

Harrell, Stevan, and Thomas W. Pullum. "Marriage, Mortality, and the Developmental Cycle in Three Xiaoshan Lineages." In *Chinese Historical Microdemography*, edited by Stevan Harrell, 141–62. Berkeley: University of California Press, 1995.

Hayford, Charles W. *To the People: James Yen and Village China.* New York: Columbia University Press, 1990.

———. "The Storm over the Peasant: Rhetoric and Representation in Modern China." Paper presented at the 44th annual meeting of the Association for Asian Studies, Washington, D.C., 1992.

Hazelton, Keith. "Patrilines and the Development of Localized Lineages: The Wu of Hsiu-Ning City, Hui-Chou, to 1528." In *Kinship Organization in Late Imperial China, 1000–1940*, edited by Patricia B. Ebrey and James L. Watson, 137–69. Berkeley: University of California Press, 1986.

He Guoqiang. *Weiwuli de Zhongzu Shehui* (Lineage society in wei wu). Nanning: Guangxi Minzu chubanshe, 2002.

Hill, Polly. *Development Economics on Trial: The Anthropological Case for the Prosecution.* Cambridge: Cambridge University Press, 1986.

Ho, Ping-ti. *The Ladder of Success in Imperial China: Aspects of Social Mobility, 1368–1911.* New York: Columbia University Press, 1962.

Hobsbawm, Eric J. *Nations and Nationalism Since 1780: Programme, Myth, Reality.* Cambridge: Cambridge University Press, 1990.

Hong Liwan. *Taiwan shehui shenghuo wenshu juanji* (An annotated collection of contracts related to social life in Taiwan). Taipei: Academia Sinica, Institute of Taiwan History.

Hsiao Kung-chuan. *Rural China: Imperial Control in the Nineteenth Century.* Seattle: University of Washington Press, 1960.

Hsu Cheng-kuang and Huang Ying-kuei, eds. *Anthropological Studies in Taiwan: Retrospect and Prospect.* Nankang, Taipei: Academia Sinica, Institute of Ethnology, 1999.

Hsu Cheng-kuang and Lin Mei-Rong, eds. *Anthropological Studies in Taiwan:*

Empirical Research. Nankang, Taipei: Academia Sinica, Institute of Ethnology, 1999.

Hsu, Francis L. K. *Under the Ancestors' Shadow: Chinese Culture and Personality*. New York: Columbia University Press, 1948.

Hu, Hsien Chin. *The Common Descent Group in China and Its Functions*. Viking Fund Publications in Anthropology, vol. 10. New York, 1948.

Huang, Philip C. C. *The Peasant Economy and Social Change in North China*. Stanford, Calif.: Stanford University Press, 1985.

————. *The Peasant Family and Rural Development in the Yangzi Delta, 1350–1988*. Stanford, Calif.: Stanford University Press, 1990.

————. "A Reply to Ramon Myers." *Journal of Asian Studies* 50, no. 3 (Aug. 1991): 629–33.

————. *Code, Custom and Legal Practice in China: The Qing and the Republic Compared*. Stanford, Calif.: Stanford University Press, 2001.

Huang Shuping, ed. *Guangdong Zuchun Yu Shechu Wenhua Yanjiu* (Research on Guangdong regional ethnicity). Guangzhou: Guangdong gaodeng jiaoyu chubanshe, 1999.

Hung, Chang-tai. *Going to the People: Chinese Intellectuals and Folk Literature, 1918–1937*. Cambridge, Mass.: Council on East Asian Studies, Harvard University, 1985.

Hymes, Robert P. "Marriage, Descent Groups, and the Localist Strategy in Sung and Yuan Fu-Chou." In *Kinship Organization in Late Imperial China, 1000–1940*, edited by Patricia B. Ebrey and James L. Watson, 95–136. Berkeley: University of California Press, 1986.

Jiangsu. *Jiangsu Sheng Nongcun Diaocha* (Rural survey of Jiangsu province). Edited by Xingzheng yuan nongcun fuxing weiyuanhui. Shanghai: Shangwu, 1934.

Jing, Jun. *The Temple of Memory: History, Power and Morality in a Chinese Village*. Stanford, Calif.: Stanford University Press, 1996.

Johnson, David, Andrew J. Nathan, and Evelyn S. Rawski, eds. *Popular Culture in Late Imperial China*. Berkeley: University of California Press, 1985.

Johnston, Reginald Fleming. *Lion and Dragon in Northern China*. London: John Murray, 1910.

Jones, Gareth Stedman. "Introduction." In *The Communist Manifesto*, by Karl Marx and Friedrich Engels, 3–187. London: Penguin, 2002.

Judd, Ellen R. "*Niangjia*: Chinese Women and Their Natal Families." *Journal of Asian Studies* 48, no. 3 (1989): 525–44.

Kaohsiung. "Taiwan Guqian Yu Gushu de Duihua" (A dialogue between ancient coins and archaic land deeds in Taiwan). Exhibit brochure, Kaohsiung Museum of History, 2002.

Ko, Dorothy. *Teachers of the Inner Chambers: Women and Culture in Seventeenth-Century China*. Stanford, Calif.: Stanford University Press, 1994.

————. *Every Step a Lotus: Shoes for Bound Feet*. Berkeley: University of California Press, 2001.

Kraus, Richard Curt. *Class Conflict in Chinese Socialism*. New York: Columbia University Press, 1981.

Kuhn, Philip A. *Rebellion and Its Enemies in Late Imperial China: Militarization and Social Structure, 1796–1864*. Cambridge, Mass.: Harvard University Press, 1970.

———. *Soulstealers: The Chinese Sorcery Scare of 1768*. Cambridge, Mass.: Harvard University Press, 1990.

Levy, Howard S. *Chinese Footbinding: The History of a Curious Erotic Custom.* New York: Bell Publishing Company, 1967.

Li Guodong. "Severely Combat Feudal Superstitions Leading to the Commission of Crimes." (Excerpted in JPRS-CAR–94–025, April 19, 1994, pp. 58–59). *Liaowang* (Outlook) 6 (Feb. 1994): 45–46.

Li, Yu-ning. *The Introduction of Socialism into China*. New York: Columbia University Press, 1971.

Liao Su-chu. "A Study of the Matrimonial Ceremony of the Hakkas of Taiwan" (Taiwan kejia hunyin lisu zhi yanjiu). *Taiwan Wen Shian* 18, no. 1 (Mar. 1967): 19–87.

Lin Meirong. *Caodunzhen Xiangtu Shehuishi Ziliao* (Historical materials for the local history of Caodun [Tsaotun] township). Panchiao, Taipei: Taiwan Folkways (Taiwan fengwu), 1990.

Lin Yueh-hwa [Lin Yuehua]. *The Golden Wing: A Sociological Study of Chinese Familism*. New York: Oxford University Press, 1947.

Liu, Hui-chen Wang. *The Traditional Chinese Clan Rules*. Monographs of the Association for Asian Studies, no. 7. Locust Valley, New York: J. J. Augustin, 1959.

Liu, Kwang-Ching, ed. *Orthodoxy in Late Imperial China*. Berkeley: University of California Press, 1990.

Liu, Kwang-Ching and Richard Shek, eds. *Heterodoxy in Late Imperial China*. Honolulu: University of Hawaii Press, 2004.

Liu, Lydia H. *Translingual Practice: Literature, National Culture, and Translated Modernity—China, 1900–1937*. Stanford, Calif.: Stanford University Press, 1996.

Liu Ts'ui-jung. "Demographic Constraint and Family Structure in Traditional Chinese Lineages, ca. 1200–1900." In *Chinese Historical Microdemography*, edited by Stevan Harrell, 121–40. Berkeley: University of California Press, 1995.

Liu, Xin. *In One's Own Shadow: An Ethnographic Account of the Conditions of Post-Reform China*. Berkeley: University of California Press, 2000.

Liu, Yia-ling. "Reform from Below: The Private Economy and Local Politics in the Rural Industrialization of Wenzhou." *China Quarterly* 130 (June 1992): 293–316.

Lozada, Eriberto. *God Aboveground: Catholic Church, Postsocialist State, and Transnational Process in a Chinese Village*. Stanford, Calif.: Stanford University Press, 2001.

Luo Zhufeng, ed. *Religion Under Socialism in China*. Translated by Donald E. MacInnis and Zheng Xi'an. Armonk, N.Y.: M. E. Sharpe, 1991.

Ma Guoqing. *Jia Yu Zhongguo Shehui Jiegou* (Chinese *jia* and social structure). Beijing: Wenwu chubanshe, 1999.

Ma Zhisu. *Zhongguo de hunsu*. (China's marriage customs). Taipei: Jingshi Shuju, 1981.

MacInnis, Donald. *Religious Policy and Practice in Communist China*. New York: Macmillan, 1972.

Maine, Henry Sumner. *Ancient Law: Its Connection with the Early History of Society and Its Relation to Modern Ideas*. London: J. Murray, 1861.

Mann, Susan. *Precious Records: Women in China's Long Eighteenth Century*. Stanford, Calif.: Stanford University Press, 1997.

March, Robert M. *The Mandarins: The Circulation of Elites in China*. New York: Free Press, 1961.

Mathews, Robert Henry. *Chinese-English Dictionary, Compiled for the China Inland Mission*. Shanghai: China Inland Mission and Presbyterian Mission Press, 1931.

———. *Chinese-English Dictionary, Revised American Edition*. Cambridge, Mass.: Harvard University Press, 1944.

McCarthy, Susan. "Gods of Wealth, Temples of Prosperity: Party-State Participation in the Minority Cultural Revival." *China: An International Journal* 2, no.1 (March 2004): 28–52.

Meadows, Thomas Taylor. *Desultory Notes on the Government and People of China, and on the Chinese Language: Illustrated with a Sketch of the Province of Kwang-Tung, Shewing Its Division into Departments and Districts*. London: W. H. Allen and Co., 1847.

Miller, Eric T. "Filial Daughters, Filial Sons: Comparisons from Rural North China." In *Filial Piety: Practice and Discourse in Contemporary East Asia*, edited by Charlotte Ikels, 34–52. Stanford, Calif.: Stanford University Press, 2004

Morse, Hosea Ballou. *The Gilds of China, with an Account of the Gild Merchant or Co-Hong of Canton*. London: Longmans, Green and Co., 1909.

Mote, Frederick W. "The Transformation of Nanking, 1350–1400." In *The City in Late Imperial China*, edited by G. William Skinner, 101–53. Stanford, Calif.: Stanford University Press, 1977.

Myers, Ramon H. "How Did the Modern Chinese Economy Develop?—A Review Article." *Journal of Asian Studies* 50, no. 3 (Aug. 1991): 604–28.

Naquin, Susan, and Evelyn S. Rawski. *Chinese Society in the Eighteenth Century*. New Haven, Conn.: Yale University Press, 1987.

Nathan, Andrew J. *Chinese Democracy*. New York: Alfred A. Knopf, 1985.

Ocko, Jonathan. "Women, Property, and Law in the People's Republic of China." In *Marriage and Inequality in Chinese Society*, edited by Rubie S. Watson and Patricia Buckley Ebrey, 286–312. Berkeley: University of California Press, 1991.

Okamatsu Santaro, comp. *Provisional Report on Investigations of Laws and Customs in the Island of Formosa. Compiled by Order of the Governor-General of Formosa*. Kobe: Kobe Herald, 1902.

Osborne, Anne. "Property, Taxes, and State Protection of Rights." In *Contract and Property in Early Modern China*, edited by Madeleine Zelin, Jonathan K. Ocko, and Robert Gardella, 121–58. Stanford, Calif.: Stanford University Press, 2004.

Osgood, Cornelius. *Village Life in Old China: A Community Study of Kao Yao, Yünnan*. New York: Ronald Press, 1963.

Parish, William L., and Martin King Whyte. *Village and Family in Contemporary China*. Chicago: University of Chicago Press, 1978.

Parry, Jonathan, and Maurice Bloch, eds. *Money and the Morality of Exchange*. Cambridge: Cambridge University Press, 1989.

Pas, Julian F., ed. *The Turning of the Tide: Religion in China Today*. Hong Kong: Oxford University Press, 1989.

Pasternak, Burton. "The Role of the Frontier in Chinese Lineage Development." *Journal of Asian Studies* 28, no. 3 (May 1969): 551–61.

———. *Kinship and Community in Two Chinese Villages*. Stanford, Calif.: Stanford University Press, 1972.

———. *Guests in the Dragon: Social Demography of a Chinese District, 1895–1946*. New York: Columbia University Press, 1983.

———. "On the Causes and Demographic Consequences of Uxorilocal Marriage in China." In *Family and Population in East Asian History*, edited by Susan B. Hanley and Arthur P. Wolf, 309–36. Stanford, Calif.: Stanford University Press, 1985.

Perry, Elizabeth J. "Casting a Chinese 'Democracy' Movement: The Roles of Students, Workers, and Entrepreneurs." In *Popular Protest and Political Culture in Modern China: Learning from 1989*, edited by Jeffry N. Wasserstrom and Elizabeth J. Perry, 146–64. Boulder, Colo.: Westview Press, 1992.

Potter, Jack M. *Capitalism and the Chinese Peasant: Social and Economic Change in a Hong Kong Village*. Berkeley: University of California Press, 1968.

———. "Land and Lineage in Traditional China." In *Family and Kinship in Chinese Society*, edited by Maurice Freedman, 121–38. Stanford, Calif.: Stanford University Press, 1970.

Potter, Sulamith Heins, and Jack M. Potter. *China's Peasants: The Anthropology of a Revolution*. Cambridge: Cambridge University Press, 1990.

Ramsey, S. Robert. *The Languages of China*. 2d rev. ed. Princeton, N.J.: Princeton University Press, 1989.

Rawski, Evelyn S. *Education and Popular Literacy in Ch'ing China*. Ann Arbor: University of Michigan Press, 1979.

———. "The Ma Landlords of Yang-Chia-Kou in Late Ch'ing and Republican China." In *Kinship Organization in Late Imperial China, 1000–1940*, edited by Patricia B. Ebrey and James L. Watson, 245–73. Berkeley: University of California Press, 1986.

———. "The Imperial Way of Death: Ming and Ch'ing Emperors and Death Ritual." In *Death Ritual in Late Imperial and Modern China*, edited by James L. Watson and Evelyn S. Rawski, 228–53. Berkeley: University of California Press, 1988.

———. "Property Rights in Land in Ching China." In *Proceedings of the Second International Conference on Sinology, Section on Ming, Ching and Modern History*, 357–81. Taipei: Academia Sinica, 1989.

Rawski, Thomas G. *Economic Growth in Prewar China*. Berkeley: University of California Press, 1989.

Rowe, William T. "Women and the Family in Mid-Qing Social Thought: The Case of Chen Hongmou." *Late Imperial China* 13, no. 2 (Dec. 1992): 1–41.

RTKC (Rinji Taiwan Kyūkan Chōsakai), comp. *Dai Ichi-bu Chosa Dai 3-Kai Hokokusho Taiwan Shiho Furoku Sankosho, Compiled by Rinji Taiwan Kyūkan Chōsakai* (First investigation, third report, private law of Taiwan, supplementary reference materials, compiled by the Temporary Commission for the Survey of Traditional Customs in Taiwan). 3 vols. in 7 sections. Tokyo: Rinji Taiwan Kyūkan Chōsakai, 1910–11.

RTTC (Rinji Taiwan Tochi Chōsakyoku). *Taiwan Tochi Kanko Ippan, Vol. 3.* (Temporary Office for the Investigation of Taiwan Land Tenure, overview of Taiwan land usage customs). Taihoku (Taipei): Rinji Taiwan Tochi Chōsakyoku, 1905.

Ruf, Gregory A. *Cadres and Kin: Making a Socialist Village in West China, 1921–1991.* Stanford, Calif.: Stanford University Press, 1998.

Sangren, P. Steven. "Traditional Chinese Corporations: Beyond Kinship." *Journal of Asian Studies* 43, no. 3 (May 1984): 391–415.

———. "History and the Rhetoric of Legitimacy: The Ma Tsu Cult of Taiwan." *Comparative Studies in Society and History* 30, no. 4 (Oct. 1988): 674–97.

———. *Chinese Sociologics: An Anthropological Account of the Role of Alienation in Social Reproduction.* London School of Economics Monographs on Social Anthropology. London: Athlone Press, 2000.

Schurmann, Franz. "Traditional Property Concepts in China." *Far Eastern Quarterly* 15, no. 4 (Aug. 1956): 507–16.

Scott, James C. *The Moral Economy of the Peasant: Rebellion and Subsistence in Southeast Asia.* New Haven, Conn.: Yale University Press, 1976.

Sedgwick, Mark J. *Against the Modern World: Traditionalism and the Secret Intellectual History of the Twentieth Century.* New York: Oxford University Press, 2004.

Selden, Mark. "Family Strategies and Structures in Rural North China." In *Chinese Families in the Post-Mao Era*, edited by Deborah Davis and Stevan Harrell, 139–64. Berkeley: University of California Press, 1993.

Serruys, Paul. "Folklore Contributions in Sino-Mongolica: Notes on Customs, Legends, Proverbs and Riddles of the Province of Jehol." *Folklore Studies* 6, no. 2 (1947): 1–128.

Shahar, Meir, and Robert P. Weller, eds. *Unruly Gods: Divinity and Society in China.* Honolulu: University of Hawaii Press, 1996.

Shanin, Teadore, ed. *Peasants and Peasant Societies.* Rev. and expanded ed., Oxford: Basil Blackwell, 1987. Harmondsworth, England: Penguin, 1971.

Shepherd, John Robert. *Statecraft and Political Economy on the Taiwan Frontier, 1600–1800.* Stanford, Calif.: Stanford University Press, 1993.

Shi Yilong. "Ninghua Shibi Kejia Gongci de Jiangou Yu Xiangzheng Yiyi" (The construction and symbolic significance of the Hakka common ancestral hall in Shibi, Ninghua). In *Shibi Yu Kejia* (Shibi and the Hakka), edited by Liu Shanqun and Zhang Siting, 145–53. Beijing: Zhongguo huaqiao chubanshe, 2000.

Shiga Shūzō. "Family Property and the Law of Inheritance in Traditional China." In *Chinese Family Law and Social Change in Historical and Comparative Perspective*, edited by David C. Buxbaum, 109–50. Seattle: University of Washington Press, 1979.

Siu, Helen F. *Agents and Victims in South China: Accomplices in Rural Revolution.* New Haven, Conn.: Yale University Press, 1989.

———. "Reconstituting Dowry and Brideprice in South China." In *Chinese Families in the Post-Mao Era,* edited by Deborah Davis and Stevan Harrell, 165–88. Berkeley: University of California Press, 1993.

Skinner, G. William. "Marketing and Social Structure in Rural China," parts I, II and III. *Journal of Asian Studies* 24, no. 1–3 (1964–65): 3–43, 195–228, 363–99.

———. "Mobility Strategies in Late Imperial China: A Regional Systems Analysis." In *Economic Systems.* Vol. 1 of *Regional Analysis,* edited by Carol A. Smith, 327–64. New York: Academic Press, 1976.

———. "Introduction: Urban and Rural in Chinese Society." In *The City in Late Imperial China,* edited by G. William Skinner, 253–74. Stanford, Calif.: Stanford University Press, 1977a.

———. "Introduction: Urban Development in Imperial China." In *The City in Late Imperial China,* edited by G. William Skinner, 3–31. Stanford, Calif.: Stanford University Press, 1977b.

———. "Introduction: Urban Social Structure in Ch'ing China." In *The City in Late Imperial China,* edited by G. William Skinner, 521–54. Stanford, Calif.: Stanford University Press, 1977c.

———. "Regional Urbanization in Nineteenth-Century China." In *The City in Late Imperial China,* edited by G. William Skinner, 211–52. Stanford, Calif.: Stanford University Press, 1977d.

———. "*Presidential Address:* The Structure of Chinese History." *Journal of Asian Studies* 45, no. 2 (Feb. 1985): 271–92.

———. "Family Systems and Demographic Processes." In *Anthropological Demography: Toward a New Synthesis,* edited by David I. Kertzer and Thomas E. Fricke, 53–114. Chicago: University of Chicago Press, 1997.

Smith, Arthur H. *Village Life in China.* New York: Fleming H. Revell, 1899. Reprinted 1970, Boston: Little, Brown & Co., with a new introduction by Myron L. Cohen.

Smith, Richard J. *China's Cultural Heritage: The Qing Dynasty, 1644–1912.* 2d ed. Boulder, Colo.: Westview Press, 1994.

Spencer, Robert F., and S. A. Barrett. "Notes on a Bachelor House in the South China Area." *American Anthropologist* 50, no. 3 (1948): 463–78.

Strauch, Judith. "Community and Kinship in Southeastern China: The View from the Multilineage Villages of Hong Kong." *Journal of Asian Studies* 43, no. 1 (1983): 21–50.

Szonyi, Michael. *Practicing Kinship: Lineage and Descent in Late Imperial China.* Stanford, Calif.: Stanford University Press, 2002.

Takeda Suyama. *Han Man lisu.* (Han and Manchu ceremonies). Dalian, Manchuria: Jin Feng Tang Shudian, 1935.

Tawney, Richard Henry. *Land and Labour in China.* London: George Allen and Unwin, 1932.

Topley, Marjorie. "Marriage Resistance in Rural Kwangtung." In *Women in Chi-*

nese Society, edited by Margery Wolf and Roxanne Witke, 67–88. Stanford, Calif.: Stanford University Press, 1975.

Tsai, Kellee S. *Back-Alley Banking: Private Entrepreneurs in China*. Ithaca, N.Y.: Cornell University Press, 2002.

Twitchett, Denis C. "The Fan Clan's Charitable Estate, 1050–1760." In *Confucianism in Action*, edited by David S. Nivison and Arthur F. Wright. Stanford, Calif.: Stanford University Press, 1959.

Wakefield, David Ray. *'Fenjia': Household Division in Qing and Republican China*. Honolulu: University of Hawaii Press, 1998.

Walker, Kathy Le Mons. *Chinese Modernity and the Peasant Past: Semicolonialism in the Northern Yangzi Delta*. Stanford, Calif.: Stanford University Press, 1999.

Wang, Mingming. "Place, Administration, and Territorial Cults in Late Imperial China: A Case Study from South Fujian." *Late Imperial China* 16, no. 1 (1995): 33–78.

Watson, James L. "Agnates and Outsiders: Adoption in a Chinese Lineage." *Man*, n.s., 10 (1975a): 293–306.

———. *Emigration and the Chinese Lineage: The Mans in Hong Kong and London*. Berkeley: University of California Press, 1975b.

———. "Chattel Slavery in Chinese Peasant Society: A Comparative Analysis." *Ethnology* 15, no. 4 (1976): 361–75.

———. "Hereditary Tenancy and Corporate Landlordism in Traditional China: A Case Study." *Modern Asian Studies* 11, no. 2 (1977): 161–82.

———. "Transactions in People: The Chinese Market in Slaves, Servants, and Heirs." In *Asian and African Systems of Slavery*, edited by James L. Watson, 223–50. Berkeley: University of California Press, 1980.

———. "Chinese Kinship Reconsidered: Anthropological Perspectives on Historical Research." *China Quarterly* 92 (1982): 589–622.

———. "Standardizing the Gods: The Promotion of T'ien Hou ('Empress of Heaven') Along the South China Coast, 960–1960." In *Popular Culture in Late Imperial China*, edited by David Johnson, Andrew J. Nathan, and Evelyn S. Rawski, 292–324. Berkeley: University of California Press, 1985.

———. "Anthropological Overview: The Development of Chinese Descent Groups." In *Kinship Organization in Late Imperial China, 1000–1940*, edited by Patricia B. Ebrey and James L. Watson, 274–89. Berkeley: University of California Press, 1986.

———. "The Structure of Chinese Funerary Rites: Elementary Forms, Ritual Sequence, and the Primacy of Performance." In *Death Ritual in Late Imperial and Modern China*, edited by James L. Watson and Evelyn S. Rawski, 3–19. Berkeley: University of California Press, 1988a.

Watson, James L., and Rubie S. Watson. *Village Life in Hong Kong: Politics, Gender, and Ritual in the New Territories*. Hong Kong: Chinese University Press, 2004.

Watson, Rubie S. "Class Differences and Affinal Relations in South China." *Man*, n.s., 16, no. 4 (1981): 593–615.

————. *Inequality Among Brothers: Class and Kinship in South China*. New York: Cambridge University Press, 1985.

————. "The Named and the Nameless: Gender and Person in Chinese Society." *American Ethnologist* 13, no. 4 (1986): 619–31.

————. "Corporate Property and Local Leadership in the Pearl River Delta, 1898–1941." In *Chinese Local Elites and Patterns of Dominance*, edited by Joseph W. Esherick and Mary Backus Rankin, 239–60. Berkeley: University of California Press, 1990.

Weber, Eugen. *Peasants into Frenchmen: The Modernization of Rural France, 1870–1914*. Stanford, Calif.: Stanford University Press, 1976.

Wei Pingxiong. "An Analysis of China's Current Rural Crime Problem." (Excerpted in JPRS-CAR-92-004, January 25, 1993, pp. 50–56). *Zhengfa Luntan* (Politics and law tribune) 47 (Oct. 1992): 29–36.

Wolf, Arthur P. "Gods, Ghosts, and Ancestors." In *Religion and Ritual in Chinese Society*, edited by Arthur P. Wolf, 131–83. Stanford, Calif.: Stanford University Press, 1974.

————. "Introduction: The Study of Chinese Society on Taiwan." In *The Chinese Family and Its Ritual Behavior*, edited by Hsieh Jih-chang and Chuang Ying-chang, 3–18. Taipei: Institute of Ethnology, Academia Sinica, 1985.

————. "The Origins and Explanation of Variation in the Chinese Kinship System." In *Anthropological Studies of the Taiwan Area: Accomplishments and Prospects*, edited by Kwang-chih Chang, Kuang-chou Li, Arthur P. Wolf, and Alexander Chien-chung Yin, 241–60. Taipei: Department of Anthropology, National Taiwan University, 1989.

————. "Marriage Among the Min-Nan: An Open Letter to Li Yih-Yuan on the Occasion of His Retiring." *Bulletin of the Institute of Ethnology, Academia Sinica*, no. 89 (part 2) (2000): 1–16.

Wolf, Arthur P., and Chieh-shan Huang. *Marriage and Adoption in China, 1845–1945*. Stanford, Calif.: Stanford University Press, 1980.

Wolf, Eric R. *Peasants*. Englewood Cliffs, N.J.: Prentice-Hall, 1966.

Wong, R. Bin. "Chinese Economic History and Development: A Note on the Myers-Huang Exchange." *Journal of Asian Studies* 51, no. 3 (Aug. 1992): 600–611.

Wu, David Y. H. *The Chinese in Papua New Guinea: 1880–1980*. Hong Kong: Chinese University Press, 1982.

————. "Chinese Minority Policy and the Meaning of Minority Culture: The Example of Bai in Yunnan, China." *Human Organization* 49, no. 1 (Spring 1990): 1–14.

————. "The construction of Chinese and non-Chinese identities." *Daedalus* 120, no.2 (Spring 1991): 159–79.

Xie Jian and Fang Xuejia. *Weibuju de Weilongwu* (The unconquerable weilongwu). Dalin, Jiayi, Taiwan: Hua'nan Daxue, 1999.

Yan, Yunxiang. *The Flow of Gifts: Reciprocity and Social Networks in a Chinese Village*. Stanford, Calif.: Stanford University Press, 1996.

————. *Private Life Under Socialism: Love, Intimacy, and Family Change in a Chinese Village, 1949–1999*. Stanford, Calif.: Stanford University Press, 2003.

Yang, C. K. *A North China Local Market Economy: A Summary of a Study of Periodic Markets in Chowping, Shantung.* New York: Institute of Pacific Relations, 1944.

————. *A Chinese Village in Early Communist Transition.* Cambridge, Mass.: MIT Press, 1959.

Yang Derui. "Beijing de jiushi jiehun" (Old-style marriage in Beijing). In *Hunyin geyao yu hunsu* (Wedding songs and customs of China), by Bai Qiming et al., 141–52. Taipei: Chinese Association for Folklore, 1973 [1924].

Yang Guozhen. *Ming-Qing Tudi Qiyue Wenshu Yanjiu.* (Research on land contracts during Ming and Qing). Beijing: Renmin chubanshe, 1988.

Yang, Martin M. C. *A Chinese Village: Taitou, Shantung Province.* New York: Columbia University Press, 1945.

Yang, Mayfair Mei-hui. *Gifts, Favors, and Banquets: The Art of Social Relationships in China.* Ithaca, N.Y.: Cornell University Press, 1994.

Young, Ernest P. "Imagining the Ancien Régime in the Deng Era." In *Popular Protest and Political Culture in Modern China: Learning from 1989,* edited by Jeffry N. Wasserstrom and Elizabeth J. Perry, 14–27. Boulder, Colo.: Westview Press, 1992.

Zelin, Madeleine, Jonathan K. Ocko, and Robert Gardella, eds. *Contract and Property in Early Modern China.* Stanford, Calif.: Stanford University Press, 2004.

Zhang, Li. *Strangers in the City: Reconfigurations of Space, Power, and Social Networks Within China's Floating Population.* Stanford, Calif.: Stanford University Press, 2001.

Zhang Yanxian, ed. *Taiwan Guwen Shuji Santian Yuci Zang* (Collection of antique documents of Taiwan from the collection of Mida Yuji). Taipei: Nantian, 1988.

Zheng Zhenman. *Family Lineage Organization and Social Change in Ming and Qing Fujian.* Translated by Michael Szonyi. Honolulu: University of Hawaii Press, 2001.

Zurndorfer, Harriet. *Change and Continuity in Chinese Local History: The Development of Hui-Chou Prefecture, 800 to 1800.* Leiden, Netherlands: E. J. Brill, 1990.

Character List

axiang 阿鄉
ba ta gei pinle 把他給聘了
baxianzhuo 八仙桌
bazi 八字
bai 拜
bai tiandi 拜天地
bainian 拜年
baiqi 白契
baisan 拜三
banshi 辦事
banzhuozi jiahuo 半桌子家伙
baochan dao hu 包產到戶
baogar 包幹兒
baoyang 抱養
baozhang 保長
benzu 本族
bubanshi 不辦事
bubaogar 不包幹兒
buchu damen 不出大門
bujiao 不叫
buxing 不行
caili 彩禮, 財禮
chabuduo 差不多
changgong 長工
chenggar 秤桿兒
chenghuang miao 城隍廟
chi dinghun fan 吃訂婚飯
chi guojia de liangshi 吃國家的糧食
chuyi 初一
citang 祠堂
culiang 粗糧

cuizhuang 催妝
cun 村
cunzhang 村長
da dengji 大登記
da guanhua 大官話
da shuikeng 大水坑
dading 大定
dama 大媽
dayuan 大圓
dazu 大租
daibiren 代筆人
dan 石
danguo 單過
danwei 單位
dangchu 當出
dangfushuji 黨副書記
dangjia 當家
dizhu 地主
dian 典
dian (Hakka) 陝
dianchu 典出
dianzu 典主
dou 斗
duangong 短工
fanzu 番租
fang 房
fangchan 房產
feinongmin 非農民
fen 分
fenbo 分撥
fendan 分單

fenjia 分家

fenjiadan 分家單

fenqing 分清

fenqingchu 分清楚

fenzao 分灶

fengjian 封建

fengshui 風水

fotouyin 佛頭銀

foyin 佛銀

fu 附

funong 富農

fuqiang 富強

fuye 副業

gaitou 蓋頭

gen 根

gengtie 庚帖

gengzi 庚字

gongci 公祠

gongkai 公開

gongpingdou 公平斗

gongren 工人

gongyuan 公元

gunong 雇農

guxiang 故鄉

guanfang 官方

guanhua 官話

guanshi 管事

guijie 鬼節

guofang 過房

guoji 過繼

guoli 過禮

guotie 過帖

hanyi 寒衣

hanyizhi 寒衣紙

hang 行

hao 毫

he 合

hongqi 紅契

hu 忽

hukou 戶口

huxiang jianjianmiar 互相見見面兒

huzhu 戶主

huan shoujuar 換手絹兒

huanqin 換親

hui 會

huimen 回門

huo shenzhupai 活神主牌

ji 吉

jigongber 計工本兒

jigongyuan 計工員

jia (unit of land) 甲

jia (family) 家

jiachan 家產

jiali 家裏

jiamiao 家廟

jiapu 家譜

jiatang 家堂

jiatou 甲頭

jiazhang 家長

jiazu 家族

jian 間

jianmian 見面

jianmin 賤民

jiaozi (palanquin) 轎子

jie xifu 接媳婦

jie zuzong 接祖宗

jiefu 姐夫

jiehun 結婚

jin 斤

jiujiu 舅舅

jumin 居民

juren 舉人

juemai 絕賣

ketang 客堂

ke tou 磕頭

keyi 可以

lao zuzong 老祖宗

laozhangbei 老長輩

li (land measurement) 厘

li (ritual/propriety) 禮

liang (ounce) 兩

liang (roof beam) 梁

liangjia huanqin 兩家換親, lianghuan 兩換

linshigong 臨時工

ling jiehunzheng 領結婚證

lingguo 另過

Liudui 六堆

lüxing jiehun 旅行結婚

luan 亂

mai yikuai bu liangtou fu 買一塊布兩頭服

mantou 饅頭
meiren 媒人
meirenpo 媒人婆
men dang hu dui 門當戶對
menkou 門口
miaohui 廟會
miaojie 廟界
minfu 民夫
minjian 民間
minzhengban 民政辦
mingling 螟蛉
minglingzi 螟蛉子
mingzi 名字
mou 畝
nainai 奶奶
ni kan ta zemeyang 你看他怎麼樣
nianhua 年畫
nian jing 念經
nongcun 農村
nongding 農丁
nongfu 農夫
nongjia 農家
nongmin 農民
nongmin xiehui 農民協會
nongmin zhuan jumin 農民轉居民
nongren 農人
ou 藕
pai 派
pailou 牌樓
pang xueqin 旁血親
peili 賠禮
penjing 盆景
pinli 聘禮
pinnong 貧農
popo 婆婆
pu 賻
pusa 菩薩
qi 岐
qinqi 親戚
qing shen 請神
qingchu 清楚
qingming 清明
qingming hui 清明會
qiuhun 求婚
ri 日
rubuyin 乳哺銀

ruming 乳名
ruziyin 乳資銀
sanjia huanqin, sanhuan 三家換親,
　三換
sanshiliu qi, qishi'er wen
　三十六岐, 七十二文
shang dianxin gong 上點心供
shang hong gong 上紅供
shang jiaozi gong 上餃子供
shangbai 上拜
shangliang 上梁
shao xiang 燒香
sheyuan 社員
shenshen 嬸嬸
shenzhupai 神主牌
shenzi 嬸子
sher 嬸兒
sheng 升
shi 氏
shitong 十通
shubai xiongdi 叔伯兄弟
shushu 叔叔
shuangxi 雙喜, 囍
si damer 四大門兒
sifangqian 私房錢
song zuzong 送祖宗
sui 歲
tai buhaoting 太不好聽
tanhua 談話
tanghao 堂號
tangwu 堂屋
tichu fang'an 提出方案
tiqi 體己
tixi 體息
tixiqian 體息錢
ting 廳
tongbei de ren 同輩的人
tongyangxi 同養媳
tu 土
tubu 土布
tudi 土地
tuanjie 團結
wangzu 望族
weizi 葦子
wen 文
wubaohu 五保戶

wufu　五服
wuqi　五奇
Wuxian Sidian　五顯祀典
xi　系
xiliang　細糧
xiachuanzi　下傳子
xian　縣
xiang　鄉
xiangkan　相看
xiao　孝
xiao dengji　小登記
xiao guanhua　小官話
xiaoding　小定
xiaozu　小租
xinfang　新房
xinlao　辛勞
xiuxiu fangzi　修修房子
yamen　衙門
yezhu　業主
yijia　姨家
yiyi　姨姨
yizhu　遺囑
yizhuozi jiahuo　一桌子家伙
yinghun　應婚
Youdui　右堆
yuan　圓
yundong　運動
zahuopu　雜貨舖
zaliang　雜糧
zai jia　在家
Zaojun　灶君

zerentian　責任田
zha you　榨油
zhaijidi　宅基地
zhaizhang　宅長
zhangdan　丈單
zhangmen laoda　長門老大
zhengren　証人
zhi　支
zhi xueqin　至血親
zhongbaoren　中保人
zhongnong　中農
zhongren　中人
Zhongshan zhuang　中山裝
zhongzhengren　中証人
zhuanghan　莊漢
zhuanghu　莊戶
zhuangjiahan　莊稼漢
zhuangyuan　狀元
ziliudi　自留地
zongfa　宗法
zongjiao　宗教
zongjiatang　總家堂
zongketang　總客堂
zongzi　宗子
zufen　祖墳
zupai　祖牌
zupu　祖譜
zushu　族叔
zuxia　祖匣
zuxiantang　祖先堂
zuzhang　族長

Index

In this index an "f" after a number indicates a separate reference on the next page, and an "ff" indicates separate references on the next two pages. A continuous discussion over two or more pages is indicated by a span of page numbers, e.g., "57–59."